THE DISAPPEARANCE OF
LYNDSEY BARRATT

THE

DISAPPEARANCE
OF
LYNDSEY BARRATT

A Psychological Thriller

John Wilson

WILLIAM MORROW AND COMPANY, INC.
NEW YORK

Library of Congress Cataloging-in-Publication Data

Wilson, John, 1937–
    The disappearance of Lyndsey Barratt : a psychological thriller / John Wilson.
        p.   cm.
    ISBN 0-688-15280-5
    I. Title.
    PR6073.I46785F58 1998
    823'.914—DC21   97-26861
                                                                                CIP

Printed in the United States of America

First U.S. Edition

1 2 3 4 5 6 7 8 9 10

BOOK DESIGN BY GIORGETTA BELL MCREE

www.williammorrow.com

*To my wife, Herta; my daughters, Holly and Jemma;
and my sister, Shelagh*

Prologue

POOLE HARBOUR

Poole Harbour: August

HE STOPPED IN TO THE BLUE ANCHOR FOR HIS USUAL Friday pint of beer before making his way to the mooring. The pub was full of weekend sailors, breathing cigarette smoke and bonhomie into the warm evening air. At the bar, he nodded hello to the retired couple who moored their Westerly next to his Contessa. Jack Holton saw him and called a greeting in his deep bass voice.

"What'll you have, Alan?"

"Just ordered a pint, thanks all the same."

"Well, come and join us, why don't you?"

Holton was surrounded by friends at the long table by the window. He had skippered the overall winner in the 1996 Trade Winds Race. A good sailor.

Alan paid for his drink and squeezed into the small space between Holton and a large girl with a weather-beaten face.

"This is Hannah, and that's Helen, and that's Eileen. You know the lads." More nods. "Alan's known as the old man of the sea. The solo sailor. The solitary yachtsman. Always off on one-man jaunts, for some nefarious reason."

The nefarious reason was that his stultifying five-year marriage, recently terminated by the High Court on the spurious grounds of his mental cruelty to the cowlike Anthea, had made him appreciate the advantages of his own company, and the thirty-six-foot *Tiger Shark* was his haven. Women, he had decided like many a man before him, were more bloody trouble than they were worth.

Hannah ignored him. Helen smiled brightly and asked about his boat.

"A thirty-six-foot Contessa? Gosh!" Her smile widened as she projected total personality at the lucky owner. Any young guy who could afford to run a thirty-six-foot Contessa was okay by Helen.

A sailing groupie.

Eileen, the kind of girl he called "sort of," glanced at him briefly and said hello before carrying on her conversation with the thin man who owned the chandler's shop. She was sort of attractive, sort of nondescript. Sort of nice eyes.

Helen pumped information at him, making clear that she was available in more ways than one. The utterly compatible seafaring companion. She had grown up on boats. She could cook on a gimballed butane hob and clean out the heads, set sails and navigate by the stars, provided one of them was a satellite—well, a girl had her limits.

The deluge rolled over him, and once or twice Eileen looked over and gave a small, sympathetic smile. She had startlingly green eyes and deep auburn hair.

He told Helen for the fourth or fifth time that he wasn't planning on crewing his boat for the weekend.

"That's a pity," Holton roared. "Eileen here's looking for a chance to take some pictures of life at sea, aren't you, my darling? She got me last week, poor thing. I already told her, what she really needs is a good-looking young bastard like yourself. What d'you say, old son?"

Even if he wanted to take her, which he didn't, he could hardly say yes, not with the gushing Helen sitting there. On the other hand, what a glorious opportunity to shut the bitch up.

"What kind of pictures?"

"I take background and establishing shots for a video agency."

"I wouldn't want you getting in the way."

"Not a problem," Holton interrupted. "She knows her way around a foredeck, does Eileen."

"Excuse me!" Helen left the table and marched to the ladies' room, face red with indignation.

"I don't think I should," Eileen said. "You were obviously planning another solo trip."

"That's okay, but it's an overnighter. I've got all the basic provisions. If you have any weird fads, you'll have to sort them out yourself."

"I've already got my supplies for the weekend."

"Okay. I'll be casting off at nine-thirty. If you're at the slipway by the naval storage depot at nine, you've got yourself a sail."

He couldn't believe his luck. Despite the summer heat, the wind was holding, the tides were running to his advantage, and the sea temperature was slightly above the August norm. He had two clear days of sailing to enjoy before returning to work. And his surprise companion was already making life easier on board the *Tiger Shark*. She held the tiller confidently as they motored around Brownsea Island against the breeze. Auburn hair tied back, caught by the wind. Sun visor. Safety harness strapped under life jacket. Didn't believe in taking unnecessary chances, she said. So he was wearing his harness too, preparing the jib as they passed the ferry and made for the open sea. He was pleased to see that she was also tidy. All halyards were tucked neatly into jammers, and loose ropes were neatly coiled in spirals on the deck. Very meticulous, even to the point of wiping the stainless steel fittings. When the wind caught the sails she cut the engine at exactly the right time. He reckoned he'd made a good decision, taking her.

It was ten A.M., and the wind and tides were set to take them to the Needles in time for lunch. Binnel Bay should do nicely; then he'd catch the light easterly wind and the ebb tide to sweep past Swanage to Kimmeridge, Hobarrow or maybe Lulworth. And here was a chance to use his new spinnaker for the first time, not an easy task for a solo yachtsman. Piece of cake with a crew.

When the sails were set she asked if she could film him at the tiller, and he began to feel rather flattered by the attention. They passed the Needles just before noon, and during a leisurely lunch she told him her videos were placed in libraries and used as backgrounds for documentary programs and movies. From the sound of it she made a good living. He'd have to sign a standard model release form, of course. Not a problem, he told her.

The wind veered and lightened, and he decided to set off for the night anchorage. By five o'clock the wind had dropped completely, and they were still southeast of Swanage, so he switched to the diesel engine and headed for Chapman's Pool to the west of St. Aldhelm's Head. It was a popular place, and they had to anchor at the end of a line of other yachts, one of which was Jack Holton's *Clochemerle*.

She had not lied about bringing her own provisions. Krug, Premier Cuvée. Two bottles, chilled in the fridge, along with caviar and wafer biscuits. Just the thing on a hot, sticky evening. She let him open the first bottle, watching with the slight smile that bowed her lips so nicely. Not a hint of flirtatiousness, but her direct gaze was beginning to excite him. He wondered how she would react to an overture. As he was sipping his champagne she picked up the video camera and began filming him again, so he raised his glass to the lens. Then, somehow, they were kissing, the camera whirring on a shelf above the echo sounder.

She pulled back.

"I'm sorry. I didn't mean that to happen, really I didn't," she said.

He'd read somewhere that kissing was the human animal's way of assessing sexual compatibility. Something to do with pheromones. Lips tasting like honey. He thought it was a load of crap, but the touch of her lips on his made his senses reel. He could still feel the pressure of her breasts on his chest. Damp with sweat.

He put down the glass and reached for her, but she stepped back.

"Can't we find somewhere a little less crowded?"

The boat next to them was blasting out heavy rock. Pretty distracting. If she wanted quiet, quiet she would have.

"There's a place farther west that no one goes to at this time of day. It's a tidal bay that the nudists use, but it's not a good anchorage, even in a light wind."

They sipped champagne as the cliffs slipped past, she leaning gently into him, nuzzling his arm and neck. Occasionally she reached down and squeezed his penis and said "Ah!" with a funny little catch in her voice that made him more and more excited.

The sea was calm and still when the anchor hit the water again. Ten feet of chain and forty feet of rope under limestone cliffs turned red by the setting sun. She took more shots as he made sure the anchor was holding and swung around the mast to return to the cockpit.

"Let's do it up here," she said. "It's too hot below. And I must have a smoke. I can't do it if I don't have a smoke."

He hadn't smoked since school.

"Shit. I haven't got the makings. Shit."

"That's all right. I've got everything we need. You just lie back and relax."

She went below and came back with her waterproof kit bag. He watched excitedly as she fished around and brought out a small leather case. He hadn't had sex for weeks. No, by Christ, it was months. That's what a fucking divorce does for you.

The joint she rolled was as big as a firecracker. It tasted like heaven. He held it in until his lungs were bursting.

"Oh shit. Oh shit, that's good."

He unclipped his safety harness, but she put her hand out and stopped him.

"No, don't. It turns me on. Let me make it tighter."

She pulled hers tighter too, until her breasts were jutting at him. He sucked at the joint again and handed it to her. She was feeling his prick again. He hadn't had an erection like this since, since . . . shit, what did it matter? All he could think about was her hand moving softly up and down, and her tongue wetting her lips as she eased his shorts down and he arched his back, and then this wet, wet mouth clamped down over him like a bloody sword-swallower, and he was grabbing her tits. . . .

She stopped abruptly.

"I can't do it if you touch me."

The drug was clouding every sense but one. Had he heard her correctly?

"What?"

"I told you. I can't do it if you touch me."

"I've got to touch you. Jesus Christ." He giggled. "You're extremely touchable."

"No," she insisted. "I need you to lie there quietly. It's much better for me—and for you. I can make it last and last that way."

"Jesus," he said. "What are we going to do?"

"You must promise to keep still."

"No way, no way . . ." God, he needed it.

"I'll have to tie you up, then." She reached out for one of the coiled ropes and looped it round his right wrist. "Naughty Alan must keep still when I suck him." She held the joint to his mouth and then tied his other hand, then his legs. "There. Now we can suck and suck, and naughty Alan can't touch us. Mmmmmmmmm."

She was right. It was better. His entire being focused on the inside of her mouth. How could anyone do that? How could anyone make him feel like this? He began pushing into her, and she quickly slid away, squeezing his prick hard, so that the orgasm stayed where it was.

"Holy shit. Holy shit, don't stop, please . . ."

"I told you it was better this way, didn't I?"

"Oh yes, yes." His voice was a rasping whisper.

"Shall I do more? You want me to do more?"

He tried to move his arms, to catch hold of her, but she laughed and used the winches to pull his limbs farther apart.

"Christ," he said. "Do it to me. Do it to me."

"Really?" she teased. "You want me to do it to you?"

A moan. "Yes, yes, yes."

She rummaged in the kit bag again, but he couldn't see what she took out. Christ, not a vibrator! All he wanted, needed, was her mouth working on him again. But she was straddling his body with her back to him, pushing her arse into his face, using her fingers to keep him erect, to keep the orgasm growing inside him.

When she felt it coming again she stood up, her arms high above her head, and he heard her say, "Naughty Alan," and then there was this movement, this *Swoosh!* And a glint of steel in the moonlight.

The partygoers back at Chapman's Pool came out on deck to listen, to argue, calling from one boat to another. It was some kind of animal in a trap. It was sea gulls screaming over a fish carcass. It was a whale mating. But it was all over in a minute, so they went back to their rock music and their beer and broiling their steaks.

Eileen threw the little ax out to sea and clipped Alan's safety line to the stays before rolling his body over the side and attaching a second, broken, safety line to the stays. She detached all the bloodstained ropes from their fittings and threw them overboard. Thirty minutes later, she had hosed the deck, scrubbed everything with bleach and hosed down again. After she'd turned the hose on herself, she packed the video camera and her other belongings into the water-proof kit bag. Then she replaced the ropes with spares from the sail locker. She started the engine and eased the boat forward so she could pull up the anchor and coil the rope neatly on deck. As she made her way back to the cockpit, she polished all the fittings she had touched. Then she put the engine into neutral and dragged Alan around to the stern. By lying on the transom and shining a flashlight, she was able to loop his safety line around the propeller shaft without going into the water.

Moments later, Eileen was swimming strongly to the shore with her kit bag, and *Tiger Shark* was heading out to sea, towing its owner behind, the propeller occasionally snagging the safety line and slowly reeling the body toward the rotating blades.

Part I

HOPE GREEN

Chapter 1

PHILIP WARNER, PRINCIPAL OF THE HERSHAL ACADEMY OF Theater and the Performing Arts, wiped his domed brow with a large red handkerchief and watched contentedly as his students filled the rows of chairs in the auditorium and their parents eased along the narrow aisles into the balcony seats. Awards Day was always held in June on the last day of the summer term, a Friday. On this the most important day in the college calendar, it was pleasing to see so many ex-students in attendance, too. A sign of appreciation for everything the college had done to prepare them for their careers in the world of entertainment.

He looked down at Lyndsey Barratt, sitting in the third row. Lyndsey had passed her final examinations with Exemplary Honors, only the third student to have done so in his fifteen years at the college. The other two graduates had done brilliantly in film and television, but while Lyndsey also excelled in those areas, her first love was theater. She soaked up information on the history of drama, production techniques, and the various schools of acting. And on stage she created a depth in her roles out of all proportion to her age and experience. She took Greek tragedies, Shakespearean comedies, Chekhov dramas, and fringe productions in her stride. She was a joy to work with, and Warner realized that he would miss her presence in his classes very much. Yet there was little in her appearance to suggest that Lyndsey was anything out of the ordinary. Good figure, bordering on the thin side, with one of those faces you could miss in a crowd. Nothing special to look at. At least, that's the first impression. But her Ophelia, her Lady Macbeth! She could set you on fire with passion, make the hair on your neck prickle with fright, exhaust you with despondency, or elate you with triumphant achievement. A truly great acting talent, if only it could be nurtured into maturity. Warner sighed. The entertainment world was not renowned for its nurturing qualities, and although Lyndsey had talent he worried that she might lack the drive, the staying power, to turn that talent into a successful career.

As the time for the ceremony approached, Lyndsey kept looking toward the back of the hall to see if her family had arrived. Warner had not met the sister, but Lyndsey must be keen that she would be able to attend at least this one important college function. Her mother was disabled, and arrangements had been made to provide space for her motorized wheelchair. Nice woman, Warner thought. Quietly proud of her daughter. He wasn't too sure about the father, though. Busy executive-type. Quite good-looking, in a Kenneth Branagh way. A bit pompous and a little too fond of his wine, if his behavior at last year's student play was anything to go on. It was the first and only time that Mr. Barratt had attended a college function, and Warner had not been very impressed. Still, it was not for him to judge.

Three minutes to go, and the sounds and movements in the hall began to change subtly as people settled in their seats, only to unsettle themselves as latecomers squeezed past.

His thoughts were interrupted as his secretary hissed and waved at him from the wings. There was always a last-minute hitch. What was it this time?

"Lyndsey Barratt's father just called," she whispered. "He's been delayed at work, and there's no time to arrange a cab for Mrs. Barratt. They won't be able to make it."

"What about her sister?"

"He didn't mention her sister, just that he and Mrs. Barratt couldn't come."

"Thank you, Mrs. Bellamy," he said. "And would you ask Mr. Mannersley to open a few more windows before we all melt away."

Lyndsey watched as Warner made his way off the stage and beckoned to her. Although her expression was blank, he had the impression she knew exactly what he was going to say.

"Your father's been on the phone," he said. "There's been a delay of some kind at work, so I'm afraid your parents won't be able to come. I'm very sorry, Lyndsey. Perhaps your sister will make it in time."

Her eyes clouded for a moment, took on that "other dimension" that Warner had often noticed when she was working on a particularly challenging role.

"That's all right, Mr. Warner," she said. "Thank you for letting me know."

He looked for tears, found none, but they were there all the same.

"We'll make sure the photographer takes some really good pictures of you," he said. "Something for your mother to be proud of." He meant to say family, but it didn't come out that way.

"Yes," she said. "That'll be nice."

Her friends looked up curiously as she went back to her seat.

"What did Hamlet want?" Jenny Freeman whispered. They called him Hamlet because he smoked panatela cigars, not because of any acting ability.

"My parents can't come," she said.

"Oh God, Lyndsey, that's awful. Why can't they?"

She shrugged. "Something at Dad's work, apparently. It doesn't matter."

But it did matter. Very much. She had done it all for her parents. And her sister Linda, of course. A kind of tribute to them. If only . . . But Lyndsey had long ago promised herself not to spend time going down that road. Her family couldn't make it to her graduation, and that was that. But still, it hurt. She sat patiently as the program of events unfolded. Mr. Warner introduced the guest speaker, a senior executive from Geisner Entertainment Corporation, who explained how opportunities in new interactive media outlets were arising for talented young performers, despite the appearance of so many computer-generated actors such as Morph and Arnold Schwarzenegger. This brought a dutiful titter from the audience, but even the youngest students were under no illusions. Apart from megastars, performers were still not paid very much. They clapped politely when she finished, reserving their genuine applause for the seniors who were graduating today. Everyone appreciated what an effort their fellow students had made to stick it out through the three years, and everyone recognized who was the least and who was the most talented. So when Mr. Warner reached the end of his list, they all knew that he had left the best until last.

"And now, ladies and gentlemen, we come to our final presentation. Every once in a while, a student arrives at the Hershal Academy who brings a very special quality to the college, and I know that not a single student or guest will begrudge this distinction being conferred on Lyndsey Barratt. During her time with us, Lyndsey has excelled in every aspect of college life. In her studies, in her performances, and in her final examinations she has achieved standards that one feels cannot adequately be described, even by the highest award that we are able to give, the award of Exemplary Honors." Mr. Warner paused and shuffled his notes. "On this, surely the happiest day of her young life, I trust Lyndsey will not mind if I offer my respects to her family, who unfortunately have been unable to attend today. I now call upon our guest to make the presentation."

Lyndsey made her way onto the stage.

"Well done," Mr. Warner whispered as he shook her hand.

There was a crescendo of clapping and cheering, as the audience stood to applaud the new graduate. The photographer tiptoed up the steps and hovered while Lyndsey was presented with her parchment.

"If you could just stand behind the two ladies, Mr. Warner," he said in a lilting Welsh accent, waving his hand like a conductor. They shuffled into position while he took several shots. "Thanks very much. And if I could take one or two of, er, Lyndsey on her own." Everyone stood back, and the photographer positioned Lyndsey against the backdrop and took more shots before handing her his card. "Give me a call if you want to order some prints for yourself," he told her. "I can run off a couple, no charge." She was quite a looker, if you could imagine her with makeup, he thought. And you never know your luck.

As the photographer packed away his equipment and the guest of honor took her leave, Philip Warner rubbed his hands with satisfaction. Another Awards Day to add to the collection. Another positive report to prepare for the college trustees. He looked warmly at Mrs. Bellamy as she shooshed members of his staff from the hall so she could tidy things up before the cleaners moved in.

"It seems your worries about Friday the thirteenth were groundless, Mrs. Bellamy," he called. "Everything went swimmingly, thank the Lord, and thanks to your usual magnificent organization."

Mrs. Bellamy sniffed. She had taken every commonsense precaution a body could take, including bringing her rabbit's foot and her lucky shamrock, but the day was by no means over yet.

As the college doors closed behind her for the last time, Lyndsey's friends crowded around, congratulating her, promising to keep in touch, waving as their parents started car engines. What a pity her family had missed all this fun. Still, she'd got her diploma, and with Exemplary Honors: That was the main thing, Lyndsey thought as she picked up her bag and walked down the college drive to the road.

Getting home was not normally much of a problem. A fifteen-minute walk to the station, a twenty-minute train ride, and a fifteen-minute walk to her house. In practice, it all depended on how long she had to wait for a train. It was easy traveling at the beginning and end of a working day, but college always finished early on the last day of term, and trains ran every two hours during off-peak periods.

Jenny Freeman's father slowed his car as he drew level.

"Can we give you a lift anywhere, Lyndsey?"

She smiled and shook her head. He'd probably have driven her home, but she knew that Jenny was in a hurry to show her new diploma to her brother and sister, and on a warm and sunny day like this walking was no hardship.

"No thanks, Mr. Freeman," she said. "I'd be taking you out of your way. I'll be fine on the train."

She waved as the car accelerated. Anyway, the walk would give her time to think about things. She had so looked forward to driving back with her folks. Her mum would be so pleased for her. And she knew her dad would be too, even though he might not seem to care. Her mum had always encouraged her, right from the start. Nothing effusive, like some of the other mums. God, they could go on about their daughters. How talented they were. How accomplished. Always putting them in auditions they weren't ready for. Lining up agents who were totally unsuitable. But her mum never went in for that kind of thing. She knew where Lyndsey wanted to go, and quietly helped her to get there. Even now, when she was in so much distress, she always wanted what was best for Lyndsey, without making a fuss.

Lyndsey remembered the days before MS, when they'd gone on holidays together, battling their way through airport departure lounges, with Dad snarling and laughing alternatively at the delays

and the lines and the battles for a cart. He used to be so funny. And
they always made lots of friends, wherever they were. Singapore,
Malta, Portugal, Bermuda—they had friends all over the place. Used
to have friends, that is, before Mum started to get funny twinges in
her arms and legs and Dad became so withdrawn. It's funny how
people react to that kind of thing. She remembered the day she arrived home to find her dad waiting for her at the front door. Mum
had been going to the hospital more and more, passing off the visits
as women's problems. And Lyndsey had believed her. How stupid
can you be? She'd looked at her dad and saw he was crying. But
when she asked him what was wrong he couldn't speak. Just stood
there, tears trickling down his cheeks and snot running from his nose.
So she ran inside, and her mum was sitting in a kitchen chair looking
all little and frail.

"Sit down, darling," Mum had said. "There's something I have to
tell you."

And so Lyndsey found out about multiple sclerosis. By the time
her mum had finished telling her, she was crying as well, and she
hugged her mum and ran to her dad and hugged him too. She had
never loved them as much as she did then. Now, even though her
dad had changed, she still loved him, because she knew why he had
changed. If she hated anyone or anything, it was herself, because she
still felt as she had felt before they told her about her sister, and before
her mum became ill, and she couldn't help feeling that it was dreadfully wrong to feel that way. Unchanged. Untouched.

When she arrived at the station the ticket office was closed and no
one was on duty, as usual. Four million unemployed, and they had
staff shortages. It didn't make sense. The only other person on the
platform was the young photographer, who was standing with his
bags where the back of the train would stop. She moved away from
him, toward the other end of the platform and sat in the sun, touching
her briefcase every now and again as if to reassure herself that the
diploma was still safely inside, ready to show her mum. And her dad.

Chapter 2

PORGY WESTON, CAPTAIN OF WINSTANTON SCHOOL'S A team, looked around the cricket field at the deployment of his team. Tiger Ramshir was squatting behind the wicket, gloved hands resting easily on the grass as he waited for Porgy's next delivery. Bloody good wicketkeeper, Tiger. Plucked them out of the air, no matter how fast you sent them down. Moved just like a tiger, but that wasn't why they'd given him the name. His eminent Sri Lankan family was always getting shot up by the Tamil Tigers, a guerrilla group, and they all thought it was a hoot to call him Tiger. Good old Tiger! Christ help the batsman who tried to sneak one between Tiger and the slips. That's where Weston had put Oak Elmwood, Thumper Hodgkins, and Nig Odonga today, in the slips, crouching, plucking at their trousers, swaying from side to side, on their toes, ready to pounce. He'd put his vice-captain, Shackers, at silly mid-off, close to the batsman. Big Pee was at square leg. Pain, Nezzer, Timmo, and H were spaced on the boundary. Between every ball, they moved a few steps to one side or the other. It was a field designed to intimidate, and it would have given the shits to a county team, never mind Betherbridge Bloody Grammar School.

When Smoky Haddock appointed him captain, the bastard had simply said, "Winstanton expects only one thing from her cricket captains, Weston. Success." And Weston had drawn himself to attention as if they were on parade in the Combined Cadet Corps.

"Yes, sir." And that was it. That was the agreement. That was the contract. That was the obligation. Anyway, he didn't want to get on the wrong side of Smoky. There were rumors that the stocky little sod had been in the SAS before taking his appointment at Winstanton. Porgy Weston could handle himself all right. Crack shot with the .303 rifles they still used on weekend training exercises. A sure hand at unarmed combat. Member of the boxing team, and all that. But the first week Smoky arrived, he got into the ring with Ginger Baker, the school boxing champion, and made him look like Donald Duck. Then he took the rest of the team on, one by one, and knocked each of them to the canvas in less than a round. No one said a thing about it afterward. It was a secret between Smoky and the boxing team. But the point was well made, and if Smoky whispered jump, you jumped as if someone had rammed an Exocet up your arse. Besides, the last thing Weston needed his father to see on his sports report were those scrawled letters LOVI. Smoky's second teaching subject was Latin and LOVI was his little joke: *Labor omnia vincit improbus*, "Never-ending work conquers all things." Weston's old man had a temper that made the Incredible Hulk seem like a peace worker. One LOVI, and poof would go the Porsche he'd been promised for when he left Winstanton to join the old man's construction company.

So when he took over the captaincy, he was determined that each member of the team should be absolutely committed to the business of winning. He dropped several of the A team squad to the B team. They were good players, but they lacked commitment to the game and commitment to Weston. He replaced them with his friends from the Combined Cadet Corps whose lesser skill as individual players was more than compensated for by an understanding of what teamwork was all about. It was all about sticking together, working hard, and playing even harder. It was all about getting pissed together. Smoking Tiger's skag after lights-out. And groining. That had been a real stroke of genius. He'd got the idea from a phrase someone used in explaining some of the characters in *Julius Caesar*. "Bound together by common bonds of guilt." That's how groining worked, and there were several girls in the surrounding towns and villages who knew it to their cost.

Porgy was aware of Smoky Haddock watching him from his umpire's position at square leg. At the bowling crease, the old fart from Betherbridge was stooped over the stumps, trying to get him with another no-ball. The batsman was Betherbridge's captain, who'd lasted right through the innings and had made a fifty. Weston had bowled every ball in his book at the bastard and been smacked for a few fours. On the credit side, there had been several mis-hits and two "Howzat?" calls for LBW that the Betherbridge umpire had unashamedly rejected. Weston's lively bowling had slowed the batsman down, but even so the sod was still knocking off the singles, and now they needed only fifteen runs to win. Bloody dangerous. Despite this, Weston was feeling good about his next ball. It was nothing that Weston could put into words, but he knew it was there. An instinct.

Weston attracted the attention of his men in the slips and moved them out toward the offside boundary; then he sent Big Pee over to join them. He motioned Shackers at silly mid-off to stand closer to the wicket. He took a couple of steps and stopped. Weston motioned him on until Shackers was standing only ten feet from the batsman. The Betherbridge umpire turned to look at him questioningly, but before the stupid shit could say anything Weston began his run-up. He felt the power, the rhythm of his steps, the harmony of his effort, the arm preparing to send the ball hurtling down the wicket, straight at the middle wicket . . . but as he reached the bowling crease he stamped his foot down a fraction early, eased the speed of delivery and changed the direction ever so slightly to the off stump.

The result was to present the batsman with an irresistible chance to hit a six from a full toss, but he had to come off the crease to do it. Risky. But the delivery was slower than usual. There was plenty of time to step into position and give it everything he had. He moved forward, bat raised for the stroke, but Shackers was standing almost near enough to touch, staring at him with a look of pure contempt, and instead of driving it low and hard he sent the ball high over Shackers's head. It soared into the air on a trajectory that would bring it down near Odonga.

"Yours, Nig," Weston roared without even looking.

Nig moved a few steps, one hand held out nonchalantly, and the ball dropped into it.

"Howzat?" Weston said sarcastically to the Betherbridge umpire.

The teacher glared at him and lifted a finger, but the batsman was already walking back to the pavilion to sympathetic applause from the home spectators. Weston's team hurtled toward their captain, caps flying in the air, cheering and beginning their victory chant.

"Win! Win! Winstanton!"

"Remarkable team you have this year," the Betherbridge head-master said to Smoky Haddock as the players returned to the pavilion.

"Well motivated, Headmaster," Haddock said noncommittally. "Good teamwork." He turned to find George Weston and Nig Odonga waiting for him.

"Nig hurt his finger in the catch, sir. He may have broken it. I wondered if you could take him back to Winstanton in your car."

Haddock looked at the swollen finger. "Hurt, does it?"

"Yes, sir."

"Serves you right. Next time you take a catch like that you'll play the rest of the game with your other hand strapped behind your back. See how you like that. When you get to school, report to Matron. Weston, I'm putting you in charge of the others for the journey back."

"It's all right, Nig," Weston said as the sports master strode off to the parking lot. "Tiger's had a packet from his uncle. Couple of puffs, and you won't know you've even got a bloody finger."

Haddock was well pleased with the result of the match, but it was not his way to show emotion. He had chosen the right captain in George Weston. The lad had all the right qualities to make it in the army. Entry to Sandhurst, and possibly the regiment itself. It wasn't just leadership or his capability in field exercises and with weapons: He was incapable of accepting defeat. Above all, he was ruthless, a bully without a whiff of the bully's cowardice. He'd lead from the front or push from behind. He was always in the thick of the action. Ideal 22nd Regiment material. The only problem that Haddock could see was Weston's father, John, owner of Weston Construction. The man wanted George in the firm. The father's-footsteps syn-drome. And the father was a bigger bully than the son.

Chapter 3

LYNDSEY SAT WAITING FOR ALMOST HALF AN HOUR BEFORE she heard the train rumbling toward the station. As it slowed down, she automatically scanned the coaches to find one that had several people in it. The first was empty. The second had one passenger. Safer to travel with lots of people. Every schoolgirl had that message drummed into her by parents and teachers. Bad things didn't happen often, but best to be on the safe side. Two years ago a young secretary coming home early from work had been attacked on this very line. Sales of personal attack alarms had skyrocketed. Lyndsey and her friends had carried them for weeks, until the novelty wore off. So when she saw the schoolboys in smart striped blazers and white open-necked shirts, she walked along with the slowing train until she could get into their compartment. In fact, she heard them before she saw them. They were traveling with the windows open and seemed to be enjoying themselves after playing cricket, if the long sports bags were anything to go by. They were all at the far end of the car and didn't appear to notice her, so she settled into a seat and took out her book. She always read on the train. This one was a critique of the Edinburgh Festival, comparing its influence on new playwrights with off-Broadway theaters. One thing both venues had in common was that they attracted many talented people who were angry about something. Lyndsey could identify with that. She was angry that her parents had not come to the awards ceremony.

But that anger was overwhelmed by the greater anger she felt about her mother's disease.

There had been plays about crippling illness, of course. But most of them were written for television, and television simply could not convey the appalling horror of even the simplest aspect of life in an electric wheelchair, when fingers were so weak that they could hardly operate the controls. Lyndsey wondered if anyone had tried to write such a play for theater, and then she wondered if anyone should. Theater was, above all, a place of entertainment. But it was legitimate to entertain and inform at the same time, wasn't it?

She was pondering this when Tiger Ramshir leaned over the seat in front and smiled at her.

"Hello," he said. "I was wondering if you'd like one of these."

He had a nice face. Bright, friendly eyes. She thought he might be from India.

"No, thank you," she said politely. "I don't smoke, and I think you'll see this is a no-smoking compartment."

Tiger looked back at his friends and called, "I say, you fellows, this young lady says we're in a no-smoking compartment."

For some reason she could not understand, his remark caused a great deal of merriment. Somebody shouted, "Groin," and every-body laughed.

"Seriously," Tiger said to her. "It's very good. The best. My uncle has it brought here from Colombo in his diplomatic bag, and my cousin steals some for my friends and I. Go on. Have a smoke." He held a joint toward her.

She shook her head, smiled at him, and returned pointedly to her book. One of his friends walked down the aisle to join him, banging the windows shut on the way. She could smell the drug now, the same pungent, bittersweet aroma that hung in the air around some of the other students at the college. They had often tried to persuade her to smoke, but it didn't appeal. They were always persistent when they were high, wanting everyone to share their enjoyment. She found it very distasteful.

"Having a problem, Tiger?" the second schoolboy asked.

"Not a bit of it, Timmo, old chap. The young lady seems to prefer reading, that's all."

Before Lyndsey realized what he was doing, the second boy had pulled the book out of her hands.

"*Edinburgh and Off-Broadway,*" he read loudly. "An analysis by Hubert D'Arcy. The property of Lyndsey Barratt . . . What d'you make of that, skipper?"

A third boy joined them, big, with confident eyes and a flushed face.

"Very groinworthy," he said, looking hard at Lyndsey.

"Not her. I meant the book," the second boy said.

"Will you please give me back my book?" she asked angrily.

The first boy lit the joint and blew a cloud of smoke at Lyndsey. It made her cough. He passed it to the other two.

"Just give me my book and leave me alone, will you!" Lyndsey said.

"We're only trying to be friendly," the second boy said. "Aren't we, Porgy?"

The train began to slow as it approached the next station. Without a word, some of the other boys went and stood by the doors. An elderly woman tried to get into the compartment, but they held the door closed. She went off to another car, tutting. Lyndsey fought an impulse to call out. She was being so stupid. She should be able to handle this. The train began to move.

"You know why we call him Porgy?" one of the others called. " 'Cause his name's George."

They set up a chant.

"Georgy porgy pudding and pie, kissed the girls and made them cry. . . . Go on, Porgy, make her cry."

Someone shouted, "Groin!" again, and the others echoed him.

"I really think she should enjoy a smoke with us, skipper," the first boy said. "My cousin went to such a lot of trouble."

Another boy joined them and held the joint close to Lyndsey's mouth. She shook her head violently.

"Go on, Nig," Porgy said. "Give her a drag."

When Nig Odonga tried to push the cigarette into her mouth, she snapped forward and bit his finger hard. She was very angry, but his scream of pain turned her anger into something else.

"Shit, shit, shit!" he shouted. "My bloody fucking finger. Look what the bitch has done!"

Porgy picked the joint off the floor and blew the end thoughtfully. Then he grabbed the back of Lyndsey's head and forced her forward.

"Which end will it be, then? Your choice."

One of the boys said, "Steady on, Porgy."

"Don't worry, Timmo. She knows which end is which, don't you, Lyndsey?

It was fear now, although she didn't realize it at first. It started with a very cold feeling in the pit of her stomach that spread along her bones as if someone was pushing icicles into her marrow. As the glow came nearer her lips, it began to burn her skin, and the smoke made her eyes water. Hands were creeping up her arms and legs as she tried to struggle. "Please," she said. "Please don't do this to me." Fingers pinched her nose shut, and when she opened her mouth to breathe Porgy Weston jammed the joint in and held it there until she had taken several drags. She began to retch, and they left her alone for a few minutes, watching, and chanting, "Groin! Groin! Groin!"

Another station came and went. And then Porgy eased his trousers down and waved his penis at her. Someone grabbed her arms, and someone else pulled her head back.

She heard one of the boys say, "Maybe we should leave her alone, Porgy. We'll be at Winstanton soon."

And the big lad said, "Well, we'll just have to be quick, won't we?" The drug was making her laugh and cry at the same time, as Porgy forced himself into her mouth and began pumping away, making her head bang against the back of the seat. She couldn't bite him because she couldn't breathe. His sperm made her choke, and she could barely see what they were doing through the haze of smoke that surrounded her, bodies lining up, shouts of "Groin! Groin!," laying her down, turning her over, and over, and over, pushing another joint into her mouth, pressing themselves into her body, forcing her buttocks apart, chanting, "Go on, Shackers, up the arse, up the arse. Shackleton, up her bum! Shackleton, up her bum!," pain ripping into her vagina, as someone started slapping her face, punching, and voices shouting, "Come on, Timmo, don't be a namby-pamby. Get it out, and get it up! Get it out, and get it up!"

A railway cleaner found Lyndsey, seconds after the almost empty train arrived at the Hope Green terminus. She thought it was a bundle of rags that someone had stuffed under a seat, until she tried to pick it up. Lyndsey's body was covered in bruises and white stains. She was barely breathing. The cleaner crossed herself, staggered out of the railway car, and began shrieking. The young photographer lugging his cases along the platform dropped them and rushed toward her. She pointed into the car.

"In there, in there. She needs help . . ."

He went inside and stared down at Lyndsey. Her face was so badly cut and bruised that he didn't recognize her. One hand went into his jacket pocket and emerged with a point-and-shoot Nikon. As other people began to hurry toward the coach, he quickly took shots of Lyndsey from different angles, then moved down the car, taking more shots of the interior. He noticed several articles on the luggage racks: a couple of striped blazers, some school ties hanging down, and a cricket bag with the owner's name and address in a leather tag. He scribbled some notes and took close-ups. He'd almost finished two rolls of film when a guard appeared.

"What's going on, mate?"

The photographer pointed down the car and heard the guard say, "Sweet Jesus!" before his voice was drowned out by a siren. The photographer put away his Nikon and collected his bags. If the story hit the news, he had some pix to back it up. Maybe he'd even earn some extra money.

As he left the car at one end, two green-clad paramedics were going in at the other. Women, short hair, decidedly dykey, he thought. He wondered if he should stay around to see if anything else happened worth a shot, but decided against it. He had several rolls of film to develop from his day's commissions, and the later he left the processing the fewer prints would be ordered by his clients. He was particularly keen to see how the shots of that student had come out. The local news sheet might use one: "Honors girl heads for show business. Following a proud tradition."

The paramedics checked Lyndsey for life-threatening injuries, talking to her gently while they worked. A young police officer came into the coach as they were taking her blood pressure.

"Where's the corpse, then?" he asked cheerfully.

The paramedics ignored him. He took his helmet off and peered over their shoulders.

"Phew. It'll be a long time before I'd want to get my leg over that."

One of them stared at him. "Why don't you shut the fuck up and let us get on with our jobs, you . . ."

Her colleague interrupted. "Don't bother with that arsehole. See if you can make her more comfortable while I clean her up a bit."

"Here!" the policeman said. "SOCO will need all that for evidence."

"We're using swabs, peabrain," she told him. "Why don't you make yourself useful. Go jump in front of a train."

The policeman stepped down onto the platform and told the gathering crowd of onlookers to stand back. A tall man in a sports jacket accompanied by a uniformed WPC pushed his way though and flashed his badge.

"DI Illiffe, British Transport Police," he said. "What's going on, Officer?"

"Well, sir, this . . . er . . . as a matter of fact I've only just got here myself."

"What we've got here, Detective Inspector," the first paramedic said flatly out of the coach door, "is a young woman in her late teens or early twenties who has been beaten up and raped in just about every orifice you could get your dick into."

Illiffe thought it would be prudent not to react to the aggression in her voice. The WPC's radio hissed at her.

"SOCO's here, Inspector," she told him. "And Region wants to know if we need backup."

"Not for the moment," Illiffe said. "Keep them informed. Tell them one of their constables is on the job." He turned to the police officer. "Find out if anyone saw anything, and keep those people away from this compartment. I don't want a damn thing touched inside or out, okay? Not one damn thing." He went into the carriage. "What's the prognosis?"

"Difficult to say at this stage," the first paramedic said without looking up. "She's been pretty badly beaten up, but none of the individual injuries seem serious. Christ knows what X ray'll find."

The Scene of Crime officer stuck his head into the car.

"Afternoon, Frank. Long way from Tavistock Place, aren't you?"

"Good to see you, Lionel. Been on a recruitment drive in the Midlands. We were on the way back when the call came through."

"What've we got, then?"

"We've got a major crime," Illiffe said. "Young girl's been seriously and indecently assaulted, probably raped."

"How is she?" The SOCO asked the paramedics.

"In shock," the second paramedic said tersely. "She's not said anything yet, but her condition seems stable."

"Okay for me to carry on?"

"Don't see why not. We'll be moving her out of here in a minute."

The SOCO gazed at Lyndsey's ripped clothing and at her briefcase with the contents scattered around it. Torn pages from a book about the theater. And a diploma. He craned his head to read it.

The Hershal Academy

In the final examination under the auspices of the
International Commission for Theatre and the Performing
Arts we hereby certify that

Lyndsey Barratt

having attended courses of study and completed the
examination syllabus approved by the Commission has been
awarded

Exemplary Honours.

[signed] Philip Warner LAHN (Principal)

There was a damp white stain in the middle of the parchment. The SOCO held it to his nose, grimaced, then began putting everything into plastic bags. The first paramedic handed him several packets, each with a note attached in careful handwriting.

"Thought you'd find these useful," she said. "We had to clear her ears, her nasal passages, and her throat. They'll do the rest at the hospital."

"See if our colleague has come up with any witnesses, and you better get a statement from the cleaner," DI Illiffe told his WPC.

"Right." She paused. "Do I need to get back to HQ today, guv? I'd like to stay with this."

"What have you got on?" he asked.

"Nothing that the others can't handle."

"Check it out with the duty sergeant, and if it's okay with him it's okay with me. Then when you've got a moment, book us into a hotel."

"Thanks, guv," she said. "How many nights?"

He looked down at Lyndsey. He needed a statement from her, and the hospital would need her permission to carry out high and low vaginal and anal examinations. Until that was done, an investigation into the crime of rape could not officially start.

"One night should do it."

Chapter 4

PAM BARRATT SAT BY THE OPEN FRONT-ROOM WINDOW IN her wheelchair, trying to catch a breeze to relieve the heat, trying not to feel disappointed about Lyndsey's awards ceremony. She knew Harry had chickened out. He just couldn't handle being seen with her in public. It had nothing to do with embarrassment. It was simply that he was liable to start crying. Not the sobbing kind, just tears rolling down his face, right in the middle of saying something. It wouldn't even sound in his voice. Most people didn't notice, unless they were close. Then they'd say something like, "Got something in your eye?" He couldn't bear it, and neither could she. So they hardly ever went out. But today was special. They'd agreed that going to Lyndsey's ceremony was more important than anything else, and Harry had promised. He'd just pop into work, sort a few things out, then be back in time to load the wheelchair into the Space Wagon, and off to the college. Only something came up at the last minute, as it always did, and she had missed her daughter's graduation ceremony. Still, Lyndsey would be home soon. Any minute. In fact, Pam had expected her home some time ago. Maybe she had stayed to chat with her friends. After all, they might not be seeing each other for a long time. Or ever again. They'd probably met in the student bar to have a last get-together.

A movement caught her eye, and she saw a police car move slowly into the road, a uniformed woman driver peering at the house numbers. It stopped in front of her house, and the driver and a tall man in his mid-thirties wearing a dark suit got out and walked up her pathway. The bell rang, but she couldn't move her arms to operate the controls of the wheelchair. They just stayed, stuck out in front, her fingers clamped to the book that she'd been trying to read. The bell rang again, then the policewoman peered into the room through the lace curtains. When she saw Pam she tapped on the glass. With an effort, Pam managed to press the button that sent a radio message to unlock the front door, and they came in.

The man in plain clothes looked nervous. The policewoman stared straight ahead, not meeting her eye. Had they come about Harry, or was it Lyndsey?

"Mrs. Barratt? I'm Detective Inspector Frank Illiffe, British Transport Police. I'm afraid we have some bad news about Lyndsey." He saw the look on her face. "No, no, she's all right. I mean, she's not . . . she's not dead. She's been the victim of an assault."

"Is your husband at work, Mrs. Barratt?" the policewoman asked.

Pam managed to clear her throat. "Yes."

"Have you his number?" The policewoman wrote it down and handed it to Illiffe. He dialed and asked the switchboard for Mr. Harry Barratt.

It all seemed very efficient to Pam. Calm and efficient. How could they know that every nerve in her body was shrieking a painful protest?

"What happened?"

"As I said, Mrs. Barratt, Lyndsey has been assaulted. She's in very good hands, I assure you. . . . Ah, Mr. Barratt. My name is Illiffe. Detective Inspector Illiffe. I'm speaking from your home, sir. . . . No, your wife is fine. I'll pass you over to her."

Pam tried to take the phone, but the policewoman had to hold it for her.

"Hello, darling. Yes. Something has happened to Lyndsey. . . . No, they've only just got here. But they say she's all right. In good hands. . . . I don't know, Harry. Just get here as quickly as you can, will you.

"It takes him about twenty minutes," she told the police officers. "We have a Space Wagon, so I can get inside, you see."

"Very good, madam," Illiffe said stiffly. He hadn't been prepared for this. Not after seeing that girl lying there like a bloody zombie. Just how much shit can one family take? The WPC excused herself and went into the downstairs toilet by the front door. There was a lot of nose-blowing before she came back out, blinking furiously.

"Sorry, guv," she said.

"That's okay, Alice," he said.

Pam looked at them. She couldn't make any sense of it.

"Has she been mugged, then?" she asked. "We bought her one of those alarm things, but she never wears it. It's supposed to frighten them away, isn't it?"

"It can," Illiffe said. "Trouble is, most people are reluctant to use them until it's too late."

"I don't know what this country's coming to," Pam said. "Lyndsey never carries anything worth stealing. None of her friends do. They even leave their jewelry at home these days. I mean, what's the use of jewelry if you can't wear it?"

"Quite right, Mrs. Barratt," the WPC said.

"Would you like a cup of tea?" Pam asked them.

"That would be very welcome," Illiffe said. "If you're sure it won't be any trouble."

"No trouble at all," Pam said. "Not for me anyway. I got used to our guests helping themselves in the kitchen long ago."

"I'll do it," the WPC said, unable to keep the relief out of her voice. Something to do, anything, to take her mind off what was going to happen when they saw their daughter.

"Everything's marked up on the shelves," Pam called after her.

Harry Barratt arrived home in twelve minutes and squealed into the drive, narrowly missing the police car. He rushed through the door.

"What the Christ has happened?"

"Your daughter has been assaulted, sir," Illiffe told him.

"Assaulted? What d'you mean, assaulted?"

"She's been mugged, Harry," Pam said.

"It's those young bastards from the housing estate, isn't it? They need bloody locking up. Where is she?"

"She's in Hope Green Hospital," Illiffe told him.

"But she's all right. That's what you said."

"The doctors say she's not in a critical condition, but she has been seriously assaulted. We were going to offer you a lift, but your wife—"

"Yes, yes," Harry snapped. "We can manage fine. You lead the way, we'll follow."

Lyndsey was in an intensive care unit. Pam Barratt knew all about intensive care units and so did her husband. But they weren't prepared for the sight of their daughter lying there, her face swollen and bruised, her lips ripped, a plasma feed taped into her arm, oxygen mask clamped to her mouth.

"Holy Christ," Harry Barratt whispered.

Her eyes were slightly open, and her breathing was steady. But she didn't see them.

"Oh, Lyndsey, Lyndsey," her mother said softly. "What have they done to you?"

The door opened, and the WPC came into the room with a woman wearing a white overall, who introduced herself as Dr. Shadri.

"Your daughter is in shock and under sedation, Mr. Barratt," the doctor told him. "In addition to the rape, she appears to be under the influence of a drug, but we won't be able to verify this until we have the results of the blood test. The main thing is—"

"Rape?" Harry said.

The doctor glanced at the inspector, who shrugged his shoulders helplessly. "I'm sorry, Mr. Barratt, I thought you knew."

Pam watched Harry crumple. She'd known all along it wasn't a mugging. The police would have said so right away. They probably found it difficult to tell parents these things, and who could blame them? Easier for them all to go along with a little subterfuge. She thought Harry would have lost control. Exploded. Yelled his anger and defiance. He usually did, over quite little things. And here comes a really big thing, and he just stands there holding on to the door handle, looking like an old, old man. Poor, dear Harry.

"When did it happen?" Harry managed to say at last.

"Some time between four-sixteen and five-thirty-two this afternoon," Illiffe said.

Harry looked at him speechlessly. The times were incomprehensible.

"Between the time she got on the train and the time it arrived at Hope Green station," Illiffe explained awkwardly.

Harry made an effort to stand upright. "You mean my little girl has been raped. On a train. In broad daylight."

The doctor took control.

"I think it would be a good idea if I discussed the situation with Lyndsey's mother and father in my office, if you don't mind," she said to the detective inspector.

Illiffe nodded. "We'll be in the canteen."

A nurse brought a pot of tea and poured them all a cup. Harry swung Pam's tray from the armrest and put the cup where she could reach it. Dr. Shadri glanced through a file of notes.

"There's only one way I know to deal with this, and that is to give it to you straight," she said. "Lyndsey has suffered multiple rape and indecent assault. She has been injured internally and badly bruised externally, but as far as we can tell at this stage her physical injuries are not serious. Mentally, she has undergone one of the most horrifying ordeals that can happen to any woman. She is going to need all your understanding and strength to help her recover, and you are both going to need professional counseling."

"Who did this?" Harry's voice was so low that she did not hear him. He repeated the question. "I said, who did this?"

"The police are making inquiries, and they will want a statement from your daughter as soon as she recovers consciousness. We'll need her permission to carry out intrusive examination. I'm sure you will appreciate that my concern is solely with Lyndsey's health." The doctor hesitated. "You will have to prepare yourselves for a long period of disruption to your lives. Rape is bad enough, but many people feel that the aftermath is worse. . . ."

"You used the word 'multiple,' Doctor," Pam said. "What does multiple mean?"

Dr. Shadri looked at the notes again.

"Preliminary indications are that at least half a dozen people were involved. We will know more after further tests. Now, perhaps you would like to see Lyndsey again before the police escort you home."

*   *   *

"Hope FM News at nine. Rush-hour trains were delayed this after-noon because of an incident at Hope Green station. Services in the region have been delayed by up to twenty minutes . . . "

The Winstanton cricket team sat in silence as Porgy Weston turned off his radio. Harry Squires reached into his bedside cupboard and threw cans of lager to everyone. They sat drinking for a while, then Timmo Smythe said with a mixture of awe and boastfulness, "Twenty minutes. Wow!"

"Come off it, Timmo. This could get serious," Thumper Hodgkins said.

After another silence, Nig Odonga said, "We did go rather over the top, wouldn't you say?"

"Yes, you could say that, Nig," Weston said. "On the other hand, you could also say it was the most successful groining ever. Not just twos and threes, but the whole fucking lot of us in one go. Now that's what I call fucking teamwork. And I do mean fucking teamwork. Two at a time, hey, Shackers!"

"Shackle*ton,* up her bum!" Alan Peters chanted.

The smiles and chuckles told Weston that the comradeship and the discipline he'd worked so hard to build were holding true.

"It's all right for you," Thumper said, "but I left my blazer on the train. How am I going to get it back, now there's all this fuss about train delays?"

"Try Lost Property," Oak Elmwood told him with a snigger.

"And I left my tie. I think I did, anyway," Peters said. "I was flying too fucking high to bother about ties, believe me."

"Not a problem," Weston assured him.

"Well, if it's on the train, and if they find it, and if that arty-farty actress goes yapping her mouth off, I'll be in deep shit because it's got my name in it."

"All our ties have got our names on. I'm telling you, it's not a problem," Weston insisted. "Don't worry about it."

"I think I might have left mine on the train, as well," Nezzer Nesbit complained.

"For fuck's sake," Weston shouted in mock hysterics. "I left my bloody cricket bag on the luggage rack. It's got my name and address all over the label, but do I look worried? How many times do I have to tell you guys?"

"Fair dos, Porgy," Thumper said. "She's bound to report us or something, isn't she? I mean, we did come on a bit strong, like Nig said."

"So she complains. So what? All we have to do is say she went along with it."

There was a very long silence at this.

"Bloody brilliant," Peters said.

"What if they don't believe us?" Thumper persisted. Weston threw his half-empty can at Thumper and caught him on the forehead. "Shit, Porgy!"

The others started yelling at Thumper.

"It's okay," Weston told them. "Every good team has a dickhead in it, so the others can appreciate how truly magnificent they are."

Even Thumper laughed at that one.

"You really think it'll work?" Nesbit asked.

"Of course it will," Weston told him. "If the silly cow is stupid enough to go blabbing round the place, we just say she egged us on. All we have to do is stick together and say how sorry we are."

"Porgy's right." Ramshir's languid voice sounded for the first time. "You can take it from Tiger."

"And what makes you so confident, you Asian arsehole?" Thumper asked agitatedly.

"Because, my dear Thumper, I took the precaution of secreting a joint into the dear girl's briefcase. If she goes to the police and they find that there, just who do you think they'll believe?"

Weston knew when to give credit where due. "A stroke of genius." He retrieved his can. "I call a toast, to Tiger, the genius of Colombo."

"Hope FM News at nine. Rush-hour trains were delayed this afternoon because of an incident at Hope Green station. Services in the region have been delayed by up to twenty minutes. In an incident believed to be connected with these disruptions, a railway cleaner found a young woman who appeared to have been the victim of an assault in an empty compartment on the three oh seven from Waterloo to Hope Green. Police are appealing for witnesses to come forward. They are particularly anxious to interview a young man who is believed to have taken photographs at or near the incident. . . . "

* * *

The color prints of the girl in the train coach came out brilliantly. In the old days you could wait a week for color prints and get black-and-white processed the same day. Now it was the other way around. The color labs took an hour and the black-and-white labs took days. So if you wanted it quick, you did it yourself. The photographer stared at the contacts through his magnifier. Not very pretty, but if Hope Radio news was anything to go by the pigs were making a big thing out of the incident, and he might have a salable commodity here. He decided to make some enlargements. There was nothing quite like producing your own black-and-white prints the old-fashioned way. None of that computer enhancing for him. He could eliminate highlights and bring out underexposed areas by working the enlarger like a conductor working an orchestra, right down to the smallest grain. Meanwhile, if the police wanted to talk to him, let them bloody well find him.

In twenty minutes he was pulling the first full-sized print from the glazing drum, and two objects immediately caught his eye. The first was Lyndsey's crumpled and stained diploma. The second was his business card, lying a few inches from it.

"Oh shit," he said. "Oh shit shit shit!"

In another thirty minutes he had an enlargement of one of the shots he'd taken of the girl at the school, and he used the magnifier to examine the light summer dress she'd been wearing. It matched the stained and crumpled dress of the girl in the train.

He picked up the telephone and slammed it down several times indecisively, then looked feverishly through his address book until he found a name and number. . . .

"Yes, yes," he said breathlessly when the switchboard answered. "*Clarion* news desk, please."

"News desk. Mike Willis." The voice was worldly-wise. And Scottish. Why were all the bloody Scots working on English news-papers?

"This is Dave Edwards. I'm a freelance photographer. I filed some piccies of the tug-of-love story at Wolverhampton last year. I've got something for you. Exclusive."

"What's the story, Dave?"

Story? Jesus, did he have a story! He could see his pictures on front pages all over the motherfucking world. "Honors student Lyndsey— before and after she met the school cricket team!" Only he was not about to get ripped off, was he? The problem was that he hadn't ever had anything like this before, and he wasn't sure how to play it. He forced himself to slow down.

"Yes," he said. "There's been a rape, and I've got the pictures."

"When did you say you filed us something?"

What the fuck was this guy on about? What did it matter when he filed anything?

"Last year. July. The Clarkson couple and their Romanian baby. You know, the teenage mother wanted it back. I sent piccies of her landing at Birmingham. You didn't use them."

"Hold on a moment, Mr. Edwards."

Edwards kept the phone clamped to his ear with one hand and sifted through the prints of the train car with the other. They were crisp and clear. He could read the name on the cricket bag label easily. George Weston. The ties were more difficult. He'd need an even bigger enlargement. He pushed the prints into a pile and stuffed them in an envelope with the ones he'd taken at the school. The phone clicked.

"Dave, we'd need to see the prints before making a commitment."

"I could bring them in for you. It'd only take—"

"No time for that, not if we want to make the first editions. You got access to a wire?"

Christ! Was he going to make it into tomorrow's nationals? There was a wire in the *Weekly Argus* offices, if it wasn't too late. He looked at his watch.

"Yes," he said. "I can use the one at the Hope Green *Argus*."

"Can you E-mail the story to us?"

He was a bloody photographer, not a bloody writer. He didn't have a typewriter, never mind a computer.

" 'Fraid not," he said.

"Not to worry, Dave. Give us what you can over the phone, but I'll get a reporter to you as well."

"Hang on," Edwards said. "Someone's at the bloody door." He leaned as far as he could to the window without letting go of the phone and just managed to pull the blinds to one side. "Holy shit. It's the police."

"Why would they be calling on you?" Willis asked.

"I gave the girl my business card earlier today at the school. Maybe they found it on her. What the fuck am I going to do now?"

"Calm down, Dave," Willis said. "Are you in the phone book?"
"Yes."

"Okay. I'm sending Julie Adams to meet you at the *Argus* office. She's working in your area. We've got two hours to make the first edition, and that's plenty of time. If you can wire me the pix, fine. If not, Julie will sort things out tomorrow. We've still got the edge."

The doorbell was accompanied by a very loud banging.

"What about money?" Edwards hissed.

"Usual arrangements," Willis told him. "Just don't panic."

Illiffe was about to bang on the door again when Edwards opened it.

"Detective Inspector Illiffe." He held his badge in the light from the hallway. "This is WPC Hansforth. Are you David Edwards?"

"That's right," Edwards said. "Is something the matter?"

"Perhaps we could come inside, sir," Illiffe said emphatically.

"Well, it's not all that convenient, actually. I was just about to go out."

"It won't take a moment, sir, if you don't mind."

Bloody typical, wasn't it? He was a law-abiding citizen, and this copper was trying to force his way into his bloody flat.

"It's not that I mind, officer, but like I told you, I'm just about to go out. If you could tell me what this is all about . . ."

"We could ask you to accompany us to the station, sir," the WPC said.

"It won't take long, really," Illiffe said.

Edwards stood back as they came inside. He looked at his watch. Had Willis said two hours or three? And what exactly were the "usual arrangements"? Edwards felt the whole thing slipping out of control.

"Would you mind telling me where you were this afternoon between the hours of one o'clock and five o'clock, Mr. Edwards?" Illiffe asked him.

"Ah yes," Edwards said, his mind racing. Best to play along with this one, or he'd be up to his neck in something slimy. "I understand now. It's about that young girl on the train, isn't it?"

"You tell me," Illiffe said blandly.

"Well, I'd been on a shoot this afternoon, see, and I was walking down the platform when this cleaner comes rushing up to me yelling that someone's been hurt. So naturally I went to see if there was anything I could do."

There was a silence.

"And . . ." Illiffe prompted.

"The fact is I'm not much of a hand at first aid. Thought I'd better leave it to the experts."

"And that's it, is it?"

"Absolutely," Edwards said. "How is she doing, then?"

WPC Hansforth muttered something under her breath.

"I'm sorry," Edwards said, "I didn't catch that."

"I said—"

"That's all right, Constable," Illiffe said quickly. "I'm sure Mr. Edwards's concern is genuine, isn't that so, Mr. Edwards?"

"Oh, absolutely."

"In that case, you won't mind handing over the film you took when you were in the compartment, will you, sir?"

Here it was. The end of a dream. But he wasn't giving up without a bloody good fight.

"I'm a professional photographer. You have absolutely no right coming in here without a search warrant and demanding that I hand over my personal property."

Illiffe caught the WPC's eye, and she wandered back into the hallway. He pushed his face toward Edwards.

"You listen hard, you little shit. There's a young girl out there fighting for her life and her sanity. Her parents are distraught. And my colleagues and I are going to try very, very hard to get this thing sorted. If you don't hand over that film willingly, I'll hold you as a material witness if not a downright suspect. After all, you were on the same train as the girl, weren't you? So where the fuck is it?"

He had said "film," hadn't he? That meant he didn't realize it was already developed and printed. And he obviously had no idea about the color prints from the school ceremony.

"I really must object to this," he said.

"I'll give you a receipt," Illiffe said. "And I'll note your objection. If you wish to file a complaint about my action you can get the appropriate form from any British Transport police station."

He followed Edwards into the darkroom and watched as the photographer used a set of sponges to wipe down strips of film negatives that were hanging from a string by metal clips.

"Just developed it," Edwards explained. "They get streaks on if they're not completely dry." He put the negatives in a packet and handed it to Illiffe, who scribbled a receipt. He couldn't resist adding, "I could make some prints now, if you like."

"Won't be necessary, sir," Illiffe said. "I'll get that done at the police labs."

"When do I get them back?" He made his voice sound worried.

"I think the expression is 'In the fullness of time,' Mr. Edwards. I'll expect you at Hope Green Police Station tomorrow to make a statement. Shall we make it noon."

It wasn't a question.

Fifteen minutes after the police had left his studio, Edwards was in the local newspaper office hunched over the machine that could scan photographs and send them along a phone line to a similar machine at the *National Clarion*. Once that was done, he asked for the rewrite desk and dictated his version of the afternoon's events, surprising himself with the amount of detail he remembered, from the speeches at the school to the train journey and the events in the station. By the time he finished, he was whacked out. He stuffed the original prints into his pocket and made his way to the main entrance, where a black-clad motorcyclist with short dark hair was talking into a mobile phone.

"This looks like him now," she said. "I'll check." She turned to Edwards. "You Dave Edwards?" He nodded. "Julie Adams. Mike Willis wants to know if you have a VAT number."

Edwards shook his head.

"No, he doesn't," Julie said into the phone before she turned back to Edwards. "Mike says, will two grand and two percent of the worldwide publication rights be okay?"

Two grand! Sweet Jesus. Edwards had no idea of what 2 percent of the worldwide publication rights would be in hard cash, but two grand on its own was more money than he had ever dreamed possible for a set of shots.

"Yes, that'll be fine," he managed to say.

"That's fine, Mike. . . . Great. I'll tell him." She disconnected.

"Mike says your pix are great. Now we need enough good copy to make a front-page number two."

"I need a drink."

"We haven't got time for a drink," she told him. "This thing's only just beginning. We've got half an hour to get the story down; then I want a thorough backgrounder from you; then we'll plan tomorrow's schedule, beginning with the schoolkid whose name's on that bag. I'll be crashing at your place until I can sort out a hotel, but don't get any funny ideas. I'm a lesbian. That's F-U-C-K O-F-F, lesbian, okay?"

"Hope FM News at nine. Rush-hour trains were delayed this afternoon because of an incident at Hope Green station. Services in the region have been delayed by up to twenty minutes. In an incident believed to be connected with these disruptions, a railway cleaner found a young woman who appeared to have been the victim of an assault in an empty compartment on the three oh seven from Waterloo to Hope Green. Police are appealing for witnesses to come forward. They are particularly anxious to interview a young man who is believed to have taken photographs at or near the incident. It is believed that the victim is a local girl, but the police have so far refused to issue details."

Pam and Harry Barratt sat in the living room holding hands. Neither had spoken a word since the police had escorted the Space Wagon home. Lyndsey's doctor had insisted they meet a counselor before they left the hospital. Harry had no energy to protest, as he would normally have done, for which Pam was grateful. The counselor certainly knew her job, and like Dr. Shadri she didn't pull any punches. Her basic message was that things were going to get worse and they might never get better. In addition to coping with Lyndsey, they'd have to deal with the police, the press, curious neighbors and a ghoulish public. They'd need an experienced lawyer. If they were religious, they'd need to talk with their priest or vicar. Even if they weren't religious they might consider doing so. The counselor could help in a number of ways, some psychological, some practical. Like getting the phone put on intercept immediately. Apparently some people got a kick out of making obscene and abusive phone calls to victims and their relatives, despite the fact that their calls could be traced. No, she agreed, it didn't make sense and it wasn't fair, but it happened, along with a lot more unpleasantness. Her job was not to make soothing noises but to lay things on the line and to encourage them to deal with each problem as it occurred. Too shocked to sleep, they stayed up all night, sitting numb and mostly silent, having the occasional cup of tea.

At eight-thirty in the morning, the doorbell rang. Harry opened it to find Julie Adams and Dave Edwards on the doorstep.

"Good morning, Mr Barratt," Julie said. "We're from the *National Clarion*. We'd like to interview you about the assault on your daughter Lyndsey yesterday." Harry stared at her silently, blinking as Edwards took a photo of him. "Have the doctors given you any indication of when she'll be coming home?"

She stopped as Pam called out, "What is it, Harry? Who are these people?"

The electric wheelchair whined its way to the front door, and Edwards took more photographs.

"We're from the *National Clarion,* Mrs. Barratt. I need to talk about your daughter."

"And why, exactly, do you need to do that, young lady?"

"Because it's my job," Julie said bluntly. "And because I may be able to help you."

Harry's voice was slurred, as if he'd been drinking. "Help? You help?"

"If we could just come in, I can explain."

"Let them in, darling," Pam said tiredly. "We might as well start now as any other time."

"It's like this," Julie said when they were sitting in the living room. "I'm not going into all this rubbish about knowing how you feel, because I don't know how you feel. Nobody does. But what has happened to Lyndsey is front-page news. It sells newspapers, all over the world. And newspapers take sides. I want to be on your side."

Pam was bewildered. "Sides? I don't know what you mean."

"There's always two sides to a rape case, Mrs. Barratt. The alleged victim and the alleged accused, if they ever catch him. And in this case we have several names of people that might be involved. We've already called round to one of the addresses this morning, as a matter of fact. There's going to be a lot of reaction and resistance to any accusation that Lindsey might make."

Harry turned his dull eyes toward her. "You know who did this to my daughter?"

"I didn't say that, Mr. Barratt."

"I still don't understand how you can help us," Pam said quietly.

"My competitors from other newspapers, radio, television, you name it, they'll all be banging on your door." She pulled the *National Clarion* from her pocket. "We're first on the plot, we got it right, and we did it tastefully. Our group companies overseas in print and broadcast will follow our lead. I am authorized to offer Lyndsey one hundred thousand pounds for the world exclusive rights to her story on the condition that neither she nor anyone else in the family communicates with another journalist. There are various other provisos and conditions attached to that, of course, but your solicitor can sort that out for you."

"Get out of my house," Harry said. He didn't raise his voice, and his tone was completely flat, but Pam flinched from the hidden menace. What was worse, she understood what this brash young woman was saying and she agreed with her. Lyndsey was going to need help, even if they were pigheaded enough to refuse, and that kind of money would buy a great deal of it.

"Harry. We must think of Lyndsey. What we feel doesn't matter."

"I can look after my daughter."

"I hate to tell you this, Mr. Barratt, but that's not what my competitors will be saying. They'll be asking why a father didn't attend his daughter's graduation ceremony, so she had to take that train home. I'm looking at your wife in her wheelchair, and I realize that getting to the school was a problem for you. But I can only print that story if I have your exclusive cooperation. When it's published, the others'll have no place to go. We can deal with similar problems the same way. All you have to do is give your word that you'll cooperate with me, and I'll give my word that I'll seek and report everything honestly and positively on behalf of your daughter. My one condition is that you are entirely open and honest with me in return. We can have the contract drawn up and signed by midday. I presume you can arrange for your solicitor to handle this."

When they left the Barratts, Edwards climbed on the back of Julie's motorcycle and closed his eyes in prayer. Earlier that morning, the journey down narrow country lanes to George Weston's family home had been a nightmare. It was a big, detached place, smelling of new money, with plastic lampposts lining the drive. The kid's father had opened the door, wiping bacon and egg from his mouth, a big, burly man, and when Julie started asking questions he bellowed he didn't know anything about any Lyndsey Barratt, that his boy was still at school until the end of term, which was next week, and that his boy would never harm another person and neither would any of his boy's friends. Anyone who said any different would have a libel action on their hands, and if she didn't fuck off he'd set the dogs on her. . . . Julie had calmly stood there with her recorder while he gave her some really good copy. When Edwards blasted off a few shots, the bastard had tried to rip the camera from his neck. It was still sore where the strap had cut into his skin.

"You're a hard-faced bitch, even for a lesbian," he shouted into Julie's ear as they swerved through a traffic circle and back toward town.

"What makes you say that?"

"Well, you took them two in, right and proper. And I thought I was bloody devious—"

He lurched forward into her back as she hit the brakes. Somehow she got off the bike and had it on its stand before he knew what was happening. Next minute she'd whipped off her helmet and was pointing a gloved finger up his visor.

"Now listen to me, you little shit. I meant every goddamn word I said. We're on that family's side through thick and bloody thin, all right? You cross me on this, and you can kiss your two grand farewell. The only paper you'll publish your pix on will be toilet paper. Do I make myself clear?"

He wrenched off his helmet. "Too bloody right, only what would have happened if I'd rung the *Chronicle* instead of the *Clarion*? Whose side would you be on then, Miss High-and-Bloody-Mighty?"

"I'd be signing up Master George Weston and his poisonous little friends. Do you have a problem with that?"

"No, no, that's fine. Just so long as I know where I stand, that's all."

Jesus, what a cow!

As they continued the journey Edwards grudgingly admitted to himself that Julie Adams was not a person he should mess with. He was even more grateful to be on her side when he next met Detective Inspector Illiffe.

Chapter 5

FRANK ILLIFFE HAD WANTED TO BE A POLICEMAN FOR AS long as he could remember, and he also liked trains. As a schoolboy in Swindon, he had an elderly aunt who lived in Brunel's railway village, and from her he had learned of the exciting days when a small farming village was chosen to become a vital maintenance center for the railway system from London to Bristol. She had scrapbooks filled with old sepia photographs taken by her railwayman father of tracks being laid, bridges built over canals and rivers, of engines that pulled the open cars, with smoke and steam belching from their chimneys and pistons. Wonderful stuff for a young lad to soak in. When he graduated with a degree in history and economics from Leeds University, he was about to apply for a job in the regional police force when a friend told him about the British Transport Police. At first he wasn't interested, but then the thought struck him that by joining this police force he'd be killing two birds with one stone: fulfilling his career ambition and keeping close to his beloved railways. As an added bonus, he discovered that the British Transport Police—the BTP—was the only truly national force, covering the complete country. All other police forces were restricted to their respective regions. Not only that, the BTP dealt with every crime committed on trains and railway premises, from theft to murder. And rape.

Illiffe's shift started at eight o'clock in the morning and finished at four in the afternoon. That was the theory. In practice, he and his

colleagues were expected to be flexible, which meant that the
working day was one long shift. He didn't mind. He loved his
work, and putting the hours in was part of the job. The problem
was that the sods who worked out the pay scales didn't see it that
way. He couldn't remember when he had last received any over-
time payment. Still. What was it they said about kitchens and
heat? So here he was, at seven in the morning, in a hospital
where some poor kid was trying to recover from the worst case
of sexual and physical assault he'd ever seen, and there had been
quite a few since he joined the force. He hadn't had much sleep
after seeing young Lyndsey Barratt lying battered in that railway
coach. He tightened his lips and tried to shake the image from his
head as he turned the corner into the intensive care unit. The police officer outside her room was reading a book.

"How is she this morning?"

"No change, guv. I did call in."

"I know. Just thought I'd check things out myself."

He went into the room. A student nurse was sitting by the bed,
gazing at Lyndsey. The name on her badge was Emily Jarvis. She
stood up quickly when Illiffe came in.

"Morning, Emily. Don't mind me."

"I just thought I'd sit with her." She waved her hands at the
monitoring equipment. "It didn't seem right to leave her alone, even
with all this."

"Quite right."

Some of the swelling on Lyndsey's face had subsided, and her eyes
were half open but not looking anywhere.

"Is Dr. Shadri on duty?"

The nurse shook her head. "She's back on this afternoon. Mr.
Tomlinson is in charge of Lyndsey's case. He's the registrar. I can
page him if you like."

"Please," Illiffe said.

As she picked up the house phone, Illiffe heard raised voices outside the door. He opened it to see the policeman standing with his
arms held out, holding back two men, one of whom had a camera.
When Illiffe appeared, the photographer tried to take his photograph,
but somehow the policeman's arm knocked the camera out of
the way.

"You bastard," the man said. "That's assault, that is."

Illiffe pulled out his badge and pushed it in front of their faces.

"Detective Inspector Illiffe, British Transport Police," he said. "And who might you be?"

"Greg Hawkins, *Daily News,*" the other man said, holding out his hand. "Is the girl in there?"

Illiffe ignored the hand, but before he could say anything a large, jolly-looking man came down the corridor.

"You must be DI Illiffe," he said. "My name's Tomlinson." He turned to Hawkins. "And I must ask you gentlemen to lower your voices. This is a place of healing, not a school for all-in wrestlers."

"We were only trying to find out if the rape victim is in there," Hawkins explained, but Tomlinson cut him off.

"Who is in that room is no business of yours. I'd like to remind you that this hospital is private property. Under the circumstances, I must ask this police officer to remove you from the premises."

The police officer looked at Illiffe.

"You heard the doctor."

As they were hustled away, Hawkins called out, "It's okay for the *Clarion* to get the police lowdown, though, isn't it? I'll be getting in touch with the Police Complaints Commission over this, I can promise you."

"What's the fool going on about?" Illiffe muttered testily.

"I take it you haven't seen this, then?"

Mr. Tomlinson pulled the morning's copy of the *National Clarion* from his white gown and handed it to Illiffe. The editor had upgraded the story to the front-page lead, with the headline LYNDSEY'S GRAD-UATION PRESENT. Two photographs were side by side, the stark reality of what multiple rape can do to an attractive, alert young woman who had her life stretching happily in front of her. With mounting anger Illiffe read the story. It ended with a paragraph that said:

> Detective Inspector Frank Illiffe of British Transport Police is
> in charge of the case. He is believed to be anxious to interview
> a group of sixth form students from nearby Winstanton School
> who are believed to have been on the train at the critical time
> and who are believed to be the owners of various articles and

equipment found in the same compartment as young Lyndsey Barratt.

Next to this was one of Edwards's photographs of the school clothing and sports equipment that had been left in the train car, with the names obscured.

His instinct was to roll the paper into a ball and set fire to it. He handed it back to the registrar.

"No," he said calmly enough. "It's probably waiting for me at the station along with the initial forensic report. I came here to see if she was improving."

Tomlinson led him back into the hospital room. "Why don't you get a cup of tea, Emily? We'll hold the fort for a while." When the nurse had gone, he turned to Illiffe. "Her body is recovering, if that's what you mean. She doesn't look too good now, but there is no permanent scarring. Well, none that will be visible. She's still in shock, which is not surprising, everything considered."

"Can she hear us talking?" Illiffe asked in a low voice.

"Maybe," Tomlinson said cheerily. "But if unconscious patients can hear what we say, I came to the decision a long time ago that the last thing they want to hear is someone talking as if they've returned to babyhood."

"Will she be like this for long? The sooner we get a statement, the better."

"I can't say, but I can outline the medical situation for you. The written report will be sent to your office." He picked up the notes from the end of the bed. "All autonomous body functions such as blood pressure, pulse, and reflexes have stabilized. Whatever drug she was taking has almost completely dissipated. For my money it must have been a particularly strong type of cannabis, bearing in mind the short period in which she took it and the high levels of blood toxins."

"We found an unsmoked joint in her briefcase," Illiffe said. "I'll have the report on that by this afternoon, at the latest."

"Good," Tomlinson said. "I'd be interested to know. As far as the assault itself is concerned, I understand your laboratory chap has taken samples of various fluids. Having conducted our own examination on samples found in her vagina, anus, and other locations, I'm reasonably sure that Miss Barratt was sexually assaulted by at least eight men."

"How does eleven grab you?" Illiffe was taken aback by his own vehemence.

"Possibly," Tomlinson said calmly. "Perhaps Lyndsey will tell us when she feels better."

Illiffe bought his own copy of the *National Clarion* in the hospital shop. When he arrived at Hope Green Police Station, he found that he needn't have bothered. Everyone there seemed to be reading the bloody thing. He'd give that little Welsh sod something to think about when he laid hands on him. As he made his way to the general office, the duty sergeant called to him.

"Your guv'nor's up from London, sir. He's in Chief Superintendent Harris's office, along the corridor."

Illiffe found his way to the office, knocked, and walked in. Detective Chief Inspector Keeran was sitting by Harris's desk with another plain-clothed officer, a tall, thin man with a sallow complexion. Keeran looked impassively at Illiffe, his expression giving nothing away. Harris stood up and held out his hand.

"Good morning, Frank. A bad business, this."

"Morning, sir," Illiffe said.

"This is DI Jenkins from SCS at regional HQ," Harris said, indicating the plain-clothed man.

Illiffe nodded to Jenkins, and said, "Good morning, guv," to Keeran.

Andrew Keeran wasn't a bad supervisor. Solidly built and with a well-deserved reputation for pugnacity, he was a career cop who'd made his way through the ranks and via the Force Training Center at Tadworth to his present position. He wouldn't go any higher, but he didn't want to. Illiffe, on the other hand, did. And he had expected the regional Serious Crime Squad to be called in. If Jenkins behaved true to form, they'd duck out soon enough and leave him to get on with it.

"This case is likely to give us aggravation from a number of directions," Keeran told him. "I've arranged with Mr. Harris for you to liaise with DI Jenkins until things have settled down."

"Liaise in what capacity?" Illiffe wondered what Keeran meant about things settling down.

"No problem, Frank," Jenkins said. "You're in command. I'm simply here to make sure you get what you need."

"That won't be a problem, will it, Frank?" Keeran asked.

Illiffe shook his head. "Any help that Region can give, I'm pleased to get. It's just that there are some . . ." He paused, thinking of Lyndsey's parents, the father's defeated eyes, the mother in her wheelchair. The unsmoked joint in Lyndsey's briefcase. "Some sensitivities."

"Glad you see it that way," Jenkins said. "No need to tell you that we've got to play this one by the book. Fair and square. Straight down the line."

What was going on? He'd missed something. Jenkins was feeding him some Masonic bullshit, and they were all looking at him, expecting him to make some kind of response.

"I'm a great believer in playing things straight down the line," he said.

"The chief'll appreciate that, Frank," Harris said.

The chief. Chief Officer Robert Nesbit. Holy, holy shit! Illiffe should have recognized the name on the school tie in the photographs. Winstanton. Nesbit. Of course. So that was how they wanted to play it. Fair and square, meaning get Nesbit's kid off the hook. Keeran stared hard at him. He stared back. Keeran shook his head, ever so slightly. Warning him to back off. Well, Keeran would, wouldn't he. Anything for a quiet life.

"Good." Jenkins sounded relieved. "So long as we understand each other, I'm sure we can get the right result."

Keeran handed Frank a note. It contained the address and phone number of Winstanton School.

"The headmaster's organized an informal meeting at two o'clock this afternoon for parents and any of his boys who might have seen anything. I think the best way to play this is to let them sort things out at the school before you get involved there. My judgment is, it'll make your investigation proceed more smoothly. That's about it, I think."

Illiffe got up to leave. At the door he turned. "In case anyone's wondering, Lyndsey Barratt is still in shock, but I expect your daughters would be too, if they'd had half a pint of mixed semen pumped into them."

The officers exchanged glances as he closed the door, none too gently.

"D'you think he's the right man to handle this?" Harris asked Keeran.

"If I know Frank, he's been up all night worrying about the girl. He'll calm down," Keeran said.

"Go and see if there's anything you can do to help," Harris told Jenkins.

DI Jenkins found Illiffe at the desk he'd commandeered in the general office, reading the forensic report. He waited until Illiffe had finished a page before leaning forward and putting one hand on the papers.

"Bad career move, Frank," he said.

Illiffe looked at the hand. "Oh really? And sticking your nose up your chief constable's arse is a good career move, is it?"

Jenkins kept his voice low as other police officers began staring at them. "Be your age, Frank. Your SOCO report says she had a joint in her briefcase, for fuck's sake. She's just come out of a school where Drug Squad is tracking a dealer. The school sports master has already informed the headmaster that two of the team contacted him last night to explain that the girl offered them drugs. Apparently the kids fell for it, and then she got, you know, randy, so they obliged. The headmaster's having this meeting to help—"

He backed away as Illiffe violently shoved prints taken from Edwards's negatives at him.

"Okay, okay, Frank, I'm just telling you like it is."

"Telling me like it is, you sanctimonious bastard! That's like it is. Go on. Have a look."

Jenkins scanned through the prints. "So they went over the top. We've all gone over the top, one time or another."

"You're absolutely right. Thanks for reminding me, Detective Inspector. Like you said, I intend to play this by the book. Fair and square. Straight down the line. Now piss off. I've got work to do."

Jenkins glared at him, but Illiffe glared back until the DI went back to report the conversation to Harris. Then he picked the phone up and made a call to his transport department.

As WPC Hansforth stopped the car in front of Edwards's studio later that morning, Illiffe noticed a large Kawasaki motorcycle leaning on its stand outside the door. It had London license plates. A few seconds after he rang the bell, a girl opened the door. She was very attractive. Short dark hair, classical features, good figure. A bit hard-looking, but intelligent. She stared him right in the eye, looked the WPC up and down, gave a little smile, and shouted, "It's your friends from the fuzz, Edwards." She opened the door. "Why don't you both come in?"

Dave Edwards had been dreading this meeting. Maybe he hadn't broken any law, not directly, but you didn't have to break a law to get the pigs climbing all over you. He'd basically pulled this pig's chain, and the pig would not be best pleased.

"Good morning, Detective Inspector. I suppose you've come for that statement you wanted." He tried a smile, but it turned itself into a nervous twitch.

"I read most of what you might have to say in this morning's *National Clarion,* so the statement can wait. I'm here to decide whether to charge you with failing to help a police officer with his inquiries when asked to do so, or withholding evidence, or obstructing justice, or all three."

"From what Edwards tells me, I'd say you have no grounds for making any of those charges," the dark-haired girl told him. "He let you into his home, he cooperated fully, and he gave you everything you asked for. He's got your receipt to prove it."

Definitely intelligent. "And who might you be, miss?"

"She's Julie Adams from the *National Clarion,*" Edwards told him. "She wrote the story. And she's a Ms., not a Miss."

Julie smiled again. Illiffe thought smiling softened her face a lot. "He's a great photographer," she said, "but as a human being he leaves a lot to be desired." She turned to Edwards. "Surprisingly enough, one of the things I learned to do when I first took up journalism was how to tell a policeman what my name is. If you could find that brain cell of yours, maybe you could use it to make us a cup of coffee or something."

She really is a bitch, Edwards thought. "I've only got tea."

"So make us all some tea, why don't you? And no spitting in the pot, either."

She is also a fucking mind reader. Edwards scowled at her and went into his kitchen.

"Okay, Detective Inspector Illiffe, let's trade. What have you got that I want, and what have I got that you want?"

Frank Illiffe met various kinds of women in his work and social life. He'd had the usual run of girlfriends, the odd affair with married women, two engagements, one marriage and one fast divorce. Women fascinated him, but they also made him extremely nervous. He didn't think the confusion had anything to do with sex. He'd come to the conclusion that he was a born-again male chauvinist pig and that any woman who was not living a life of traditional female subservience was a threat. He knew it was stupid, never mind politically incorrect. But that's how he felt. And of all the threatening women he had met, Julie Adams seemed set to top the list.

"You seem very sure that I can't touch Edwards," he commented.

"I know you can touch him. What I'm saying is that you haven't got anything that'll stick. And as he is now an indispensable part of the *National Clarion* team, he has the resources of one of the world's largest media groups behind him. Put a foot wrong, and our lawyers will be all over you."

"Maybe," Illiffe said. "But my colleagues and I have the responsibility for solving this and bringing the people who did it to the courts. Two wrong words in a newspaper can screw everything, and I'm not about to let—"

"Who takes sugar and who doesn't?" Edwards shouted from the kitchen.

"One for me and two for DI Illiffe," WPC Hansforth shouted back.

"Black, with lemon," Julie called.

He came in with two mugs in each hand and a plastic lemon clenched in his mouth.

"You really know how to lay on the style, don't you, Edwards," Julie said disgustedly. "Last time I saw one of those, an alleged bank robber had just squeezed it into a bank manager's eyes in Brixton. Has that one got ammonia in it, too?"

"What I'm trying to impress upon you," Illiffe said, "is that I have an investigation to conduct. If I think Mr. Edwards can help me find the people who assaulted Lyndsey Barratt, I'll take Judge's Rules and stick them firmly in his anal orifice if he doesn't cooperate."

"Does that go for me as well, Inspector?" Julie asked curiously.

"I'll think of something a little more refined." He passed Edwards a written request to attend Hope Green Police Station at midday to give his statement. "Be sure to ask for Detective Inspector Jenkins.

You don't have to come, of course," he said. "It's entirely up to you."

"You haven't answered my first question," Julie reminded him.

"Okay," he said. "You have nothing I want, and anything I have that you want will be communicated to you when I decide to hold a press conference. Good morning, Ms. Adams, Mr. Edwards."

As they got back into the police car, WPC Hansforth said, "I liked her article."

"She is obviously a very good journalist," Illiffe said. "She is also perfectly capable of dropping everyone in the brown stuff, just so she can get her byline on the front page. So watch it. Don't get too close."

WPC Hansforth looked at him. "Absolutely not, guv."

Edwards slammed the door after them, made a rude gesture at the yellowed paint, and snarled, "Pigs."

"I thought he was rather nice, myself," Julie told him.

"Don't you mean you thought she was rather nice?"

"Not my type. I'm not into uniforms. Too butch. I'm into lace and femininity. Languid liaisons with adoring partners who lovingly lend me their bodies at playtime."

Edwards stared at her. "Are you taking the piss?"

"Absolutely not," she said seriously. "I've been like this from prep school. We had a gym mistress who—"

"I don't want to hear about your bloody gym mistress," Edwards snapped.

"Suit yourself," she said. "But she was rather gorgeous."

"I thought we were supposed to be at the hospital at eleven to meet the Barratts."

"There's plenty of time," she said. "We're on my Kawasaki, re-member."

Remember! Christ, how could he forget?

Detective Chief Inspector Keeran looked sadly at Illiffe and mo-tioned for him to close the door.

"Sit down, Frank. There's a few things we've got to sort out on this Barratt thing."

"It's all sorted, guv," Illiffe said pleasantly.

"Don't fuck with me, Frank. I'm not in the mood. What's this requisition for two Transits all about?"

"I'm going to Winstanton for this afternoon's meeting. If all eleven of the little shits turn up, I'm taking them into custody."

Keeran sighed. "And what will you charge them with?"

"How does smoking illegal substances on Railtrack property grab you? From what I'm hearing, they've owned up to that one, haven't they?"

"You're being a bit premature. There's no proof anyone except the girl had anything to do with drugs, and she hasn't made a statement yet. For all you know, you could find yourself charging her with possession with intent to supply. If you take those lads in, you might even find yourself facing a charge of false arrest. And then there's the problem of Chief Officer Nesbit. We must consider his position in all this."

"I appreciate that, sir," Illiffe said stiffly. "But I'm sure he wouldn't ask for preferential treatment, just because his boy is involved."

"Might be involved," Keeran snapped at him.

Illiffe leaned forward. "Come off it, Andrew. He's involved up to his adolescent little pubes, along with his pals. All we need is eleven blood tests to prove it, according to the hospital analysis. If you're so bloody concerned, why don't you come with me?"

He knew Keeran would stay out of the front line.

"I think not, Frank. All I'm saying is for you to go carefully. By the book. Don't do anything that would make it difficult for us to pull back. And we have to keep Internal Affairs in mind, too."

"Fair enough, Andrew, but I don't think *anyone* will be able to pull back from this one. Half the national media are trying to book hotel rooms around Hope Green. It's not just Internal Affairs we have to keep our eyes on, wouldn't you say?"

Chapter 6

Dr. Paul Jorgenson cast his scholarly eyes at the paintings of his predecessors that lined the walls of his study. Winstanton had a long and proud tradition of providing a rigorous schooling for the sons of notable people in politics and the military. Lately, like many other public schools, they had been obliged to change their entrance criteria, to accept boys whose families were not quite so well established in the scheme of things. They had to afford the fifty-five-hundred-pound-a-term fees for boarders and incidental expenses, of course. That went without saying. But the most important consideration was whether the boy was the right sort of chap. And that went doubly for the family. In the case of George Weston's father, John, the college could hardly believe otherwise. As soon as the ten-year-old George had a confirmed place, Weston's lawyers set up a one-hundred-thousand-pound deed of covenant toward the new cricket pavilion, not to mention the offer of his firm's construction expertise. Which meant that Weston Construction designed and built the new pavilion, leaving the money from the covenant in the school's general development trust. Most parents found a way to provide benefits, but seldom on such a scale. The governors were duly grateful, and Master George Weston entered the school at the tender age of twelve. As his teachers soon found out, age was the most tender thing about the boy. From the outset he was a difficult pupil. His father gave the school permission to visit corporal punishment on the lad, if needs must, and the staff took Weston senior at his word with almost savage delight. Young George took it all in his stride, and managed to scrape through the academic syllabus each year. But although he proved difficult in class, he thrived at sports. In rugby, cricket, swimming, and other athletics, he made his mark, winning house and school colors and, when he arrived in the sixth form, leading one school team after another to victory over their traditional rivals. Indeed, Jorgenson pondered as he considered the boy's school record, in this his final year at Winstanton he seemed to have settled down remarkably well. He had made many friends who seemed almost to worship him, especially from within the outstanding cricket team. What a victory yesterday over Betherbridge. And now this!

The knock on his door was a physical shock, a summons to deal with one of the most disturbing situations any headmaster could be called upon to face. Jorgenson's scholarly and sensitive soul was not looking forward to this meeting, not one little bit.

"Enter."

The sports master Thomas Haddock came in. "Ah, Headmaster. Not a pretty business."

"Exactly so, Mr. Haddock," Jorgenson agreed nervously. "Are they assembled?"

"All present and correct. Most of the parents managed to make it. Nesbit's father will try to attend, if he can reschedule some meetings. His mother is here, though. And of course, Ramshir's family in Colombo will have to be informed, should anything untoward develop. Same for Odonga. His father is currently appointed to his country's embassy in London. No point in worrying either of them unduly."

"Let us hope we can contain it within the school, Mr. Haddock."

The headmaster stood and made his way to the assembly hall, a room paneled in oak with the names of school captains carved and inlaid with gold leaf, and pews that some said had been used by English knights to pray before the Battle of Agincourt. Jorgenson felt a shudder pass through his gaunt frame, an unwelcome reminder that he was the custodian of centuries of Winstanton tradition and honor that were now under a wholly unexpected and unacceptable threat. He hoped none of his misgivings showed as he faced the boys seated in the front rows, their parents behind them.

"Let me first apologize to parents for this disruption to your busy schedules and also thank you for coming here at such short notice. And let me commend your sons for having the good sense to come forward and report this incident to Mr. Haddock, as they did last night. As I have just said to him, the purpose of this meeting is to get to the bottom of this unfortunate business and to contain any unpleasantness within the school, as far as is possible."

"I take it you have not seen this morning's *National Clarion,* Headmaster." The speaker was Alan Peters's father, a wealthy merchant banker who had also been a pupil at Winstanton.

"I'm afraid I restrict my daily news gathering to *The Times* and Radio Four," the headmaster said, with what he hoped was a nice balance between information and lightheartedness.

It could not have been more badly judged. Peters strode toward his lectern and slammed the newspaper down, then returned to his seat. As Dr. Jorgenson gazed at the two photographs of Lyndsey Barratt, the blood drained from his face. He bit his lips, fighting to maintain control.

"Oh dear," he said at last. "Oh dear."

Haddock leaned forward and muttered to him, "The quicker you ask our boys for an explanation, the quicker we can put this sleazy newspaper reporting in its proper light, Headmaster."

"Right you are, Mr. Haddock." Jorgenson looked at young George Weston. "Weston, perhaps you would be so kind as to tell us what happened, and I will then want each boy to give his own version of events."

Weston stood up, but before he could say anything a good-looking woman wearing a horse-riding outfit put up her hand.

"Yes, Mrs. Nesbit."

"Should we not ask the boys to give their evidence separately, so as to avoid possible collusion?"

He was about to agree, but Weston's father called out irritably, "If they were going to collude, they'd have done it by now. Let's get on with it."

"A fair point, Mrs. Nesbit, but on balance perhaps Mr. Weston is right. I'm sure the boys will point out any inadvertent discrepancies that might arise. Weston . . . ?"

"Well, sir, we trounced Betherbridge, and as you can imagine we were all feeling pretty pleased about that when we got on the train. . . ."

The sound of motor vehicles in the drive made everyone's head turn. Two British Transport Police vans and a patrol car stopped outside the main entrance. A tall man in plain clothes and a uniformed policewoman got out of the car and came into the hall. There was silence as they opened the doors and made their way to the podium. The tall man held his badge toward Dr. Jorgenson and introduced himself.

"I'm Detective Inspector Illiffe, British Transport Police. I take it you are Dr. Jorgenson."

Jorgenson was speechless. This constituted a gross invasion of school privacy. And in front of parents. He struggled to get words out.

"Are you aware, sir, that you have entered private property?"

"Of course, Headmaster, and my colleagues and I will leave immediately, if that's what you want."

His words left Dr. Jorgenson in a complete quandary. Once more, Haddock came to his assistance.

"Perhaps you could inform us of the reason for this intrusion."

"And you are, sir . . . ?"

"Thomas Haddock. Head of sport."

"Well, Mr. Haddock," Illiffe said loudly. "As you might be aware, several articles belonging to pupils of this school were left behind on a train traveling from Waterloo to Hope Green yesterday. I was hoping we might be able to identify the owners and take verbal statements from them in order to assist us in our inquiries with regard to a crime we're investigating. I have the articles in the vans outside."

John Weston stood up angrily. "You need two vans for a couple of cricket bats and school blazers?"

Illiffe turned to him and smiled. "And who might you be, sir?"

"I might be the Archangel Gabriel," Weston snapped. A few of the boys smirked.

Illiffe's smile did not waver. "Let me put it another way, sir. What is your name?"

"John Weston, and I warn you that I am a personal friend of the chief constable, as Mrs. Nesbit here will verify."

"Thank you, Mr. Weston," Illiffe said blandly, then turned back to Dr. Jorgenson. "It's entirely up to you, Headmaster, but it would take just a few minutes of the boys' time . . ."

"Well," Jorgenson said unhappily. "If you must."

"No one is taking any statement from my son without my solicitor being present," John Weston snorted.

"These will be informal witness statements, sir," Illiffe said mildly. "There is a possibility that members of the school cricket team who traveled on the three-oh-seven from Waterloo to Hope Green were witnesses to a criminal act. I'm sure everyone here will be as keen to eliminate the boys from our inquiries as I am."

"It's all right, Dad," Weston junior said. "I can't really remember anything, and I don't suppose anyone else can either, after those cigarettes she gave us to smoke."

Weston looked at his son angrily for a moment, then leaned back in his seat. "Okay, provided you stick to taking witness statements."

Illiffe motioned to WPC Hansforth, and she led the boys to the Transit vans. One or two of the parents followed them, but all Hansforth did was ask each boy if a particular article belonged to him and whether he had taken it onto the train. She filled in a form for each of them and asked the boys concerned to sign. They then trooped back into the hall.

John Weston turned to Illiffe. "You haven't given my lad his cricket bag back. And what about all the other things?"

"Headmaster," Illiffe said politely, "it will help matters if you allow me to address the boys and their parents."

"That would be entirely inappropriate, Inspector. We have convened this meeting to discuss a matter that relates purely to school affairs."

Nice try, Illiffe thought as the boys settled into their pews. They didn't seem quite so sure of themselves.

"As you wish," he said. "But it would save everyone including myself a great deal of time if you would grant me the privilege." He waited, watching Jorgenson tussle with this one. Haddock leaned forward and whispered in the headmaster's ear.

"Very well, Inspector," Jorgenson said, "but please make it brief."

Illiffe mounted the podium and looked round. The boys were shuffling their feet, and the parents were looking at him with undisguised dislike.

"No doubt you are all aware of the incident that took place yesterday on the train that arrived at Hope Green station at seven-fifty-two. An extremely serious crime was committed, and, on the face of the evidence in our possession, several if not all the members of the Winstanton School cricket team may have been witnesses. At the very least, we must take steps to eliminate innocent people from our investigations. To this end we will require a formal statement from each of the boys over the next two days and permission from the parents of those under the age of eighteen to allow us to take a blood sample. For those boys who have reached their majority we do not, of course, require the parents' permission."

Illiffe let this sink in, watching the reactions. The explosion came, as he thought it might, from George Weston's father. The burly man stood up and pointed a quivering finger at him.

"Now you just listen to me, Detective Inspector Illiffe, or whatever your bloody name is. We can settle this thing right now. For one thing, you've only got the word of a bloody little tramp that any crime has been committed in the first place. Tell him, George. You bloody tell him."

His son stood up again. "Well, sir," he said, addressing his words to Jorgenson. "When the girl got on the train, she asked for a light. We said none of us smoked, but she found a match anyway and lit a cigarette. We were all talking away, and she seemed very friendly. We didn't notice that the tobacco had a funny smell, but she offered us all a puff. It seemed fun at the time, so we did. Then she started joking about sex and sort of egging us on. To be quite honest, I'm not quite sure what happened after that, but if any of the chaps did anything wrong, I must accept full responsibility, as their team captain."

Quite a performance for a youngster.

"There you are," Weston senior bellowed. "If anyone broke any law, it was that bloody girl, no matter what she's told you."

"Unfortunately, she has not been able to tell us anything, because she's still in shock. However, even if your son is telling the truth we still have a major problem on our hands."

"Oh yes," Weston senior sneered. "And what might that be?"

"In the first place, sodomy is still a criminal offense in this country, whether the girl gave her consent or not. A blood test will eliminate all these boys from any suggestion that they committed such an offense, should that indeed be the case."

Even the bellicose Weston senior was rendered speechless by this news, and the parents were clearly shocked. When Illiffe stared at the boys he sensed a change in their attitude. They stared straight ahead, not wanting to look at one another, and he wondered which of them it had been.

"You said, 'In the first place,' " the sports master commented. "Are we to presume you have a second point to make?"

"That's correct." Illiffe glanced at young George Weston. "When you referred to smoking cigarettes, did you all join in?"

Ten heads nodded.

"Sort of thing any kid would do," Weston's father snorted irritatedly.

"Were any of you aware that the cigarettes you claim she gave you contained a prohibited substance?"

"Absolutely not, sir." Weston's emphasis was utterly sincere. "None of us are used to smoking, so it seemed like an ordinary one."

"Tell me, George," Illiffe said. "Would you say that you and your fellow team members were a reasonably observant bunch?"

Weston smiled confidently. "Yes, sir. You have to be, if you want a place in the A team."

"So I can take it that you would all have seen at least one of the sixteen NO SMOKING signs that are positioned in prominent places around the compartment."

Silence.

"I really don't see where all this is getting us, Detective Inspector," Jorgenson said agitatedly.

"Let me lay it on the line, Headmaster," Illiffe said coldly. "Eleven of your pupils in the presence of several witnesses have just admitted to breaking Railtrack bylaws. I am therefore taking each of them into custody. They will be charged with this offense at Hope Green police station. After this, I should imagine that the custody officer will agree to their being released into their parents' charge on police bail. My officers will escort the boys into the transport outside the main door. Parents of juveniles will, of course, be allowed to be present during our interviews. The others will be entitled to have a lawyer present. Thank you for your time, Headmaster."

As he and WPC Hansforth left the hall, the silence was absolute.

"Nice one, guv," Hansforth said quietly as they got into the car to watch the cricket team filing into the Transit vans.

"Thank you, Alice," he said. "I thought it went quite well, under the circumstances."

"Up to now, anyway." She nodded toward the school entrance, where several people were struggling with Weston's father as he yelled and gesticulated wildly toward them.

"Someone should tell that idiot about heart attacks," Illiffe muttered. "Let's get the show on the road, shall we?"

As the police vehicles passed the school lodge an unmarked Jaguar turned off the main road into the drive and was forced to wait as they left the grounds. Illiffe saw a uniformed chief constable sitting in the back with Detective Inspector Jenkins. He raised his hand and received a stony stare in return.

"Pull over to the side and let them past," Illiffe told WPC Hansforth, who stopped as ordered and waved the Transit vans on. When they were out of sight he leaned over and sounded the horn briefly. After a few moments Julie Adams's Kawasaki rumbled out of the woods that surrounded the school and stopped in front of the police car. The photographer Edwards was sitting precariously behind her. He noticed the aerial of a digital scanning receiver sticking out of Edwards's jacket.

"I see you've been trespassing, Ms. Adams," he said through the window. "Got what you wanted?"

"Yes, thanks," she told him. "Pity we couldn't hear what went on in the hall. What did you say to them from your lofty position by the headmaster?"

"You know better than to ask a working policeman such things."

"I presume you can at least confirm that you have arrested the team."

"No comment. By the way, you do know it's against the law to scan police broadcasts, don't you?"

"Absolutely, Inspector, " she said, and Edwards grabbed her waist as the big bike surged forward and roared toward Hope Green.

As they followed, Illiffe said to WPC Hansforth, "Pass the mike, will you? I'd better report in."

When Chief Constable Nesbit reached the hall, pandemonium was raging among the parents. Dr. Jorgenson was walking among them, wringing his hands and pleading for order, while Thomas Haddock watched from the stage, his face set in a sardonic smile. Nesbit went to the podium, seized the wooden gavel, and began pounding it on the lectern. When things quieted down, he said loudly, "Will someone kindly tell me what is going on here!"

Jorgenson hurried toward him, gown flowing. "Thank you so much for coming, Chief Constable," he said with relief. "We face a most serious situation, most serious . . . ."

"I'll not have anyone say things like that about my lad," Weston shouted. "I'll sue the bloody police force. . . ."

"Please, Mr. Weston," Jorgenson pleaded. "Let us explain to Mr. Nesbit what has occurred. I'm sure he can help us resolve this unfortunate matter. Mr. Haddock, perhaps you would summarize matters. . . ."

It did not take long for Haddock to outline the events of the past half hour.

"I hope you put that cheeky bastard of yours in his place," Weston shouted to the chief constable. "My lad arrested! This is bloody well intolerable."

"I understand your anger, Mr. Weston," Nesbit told him, "but Detective Inspector Illiffe is a member of the British Transport Police. Because the incident involving that girl took place on Railtrack property, my officers have no direct involvement in the case. Inspector Illiffe's own chief constable is based in London, and we are in contact over this."

"But surely you can do something," one of the other parents called out.

"The inspector is an experienced officer, and I know he will conduct his investigation in a proper manner. I will, of course, keep you all fully informed as to developments, providing always that my counterpart in BTP gives me his blessing. I know you will appreciate that I will not, under any circumstances, do anything to prejudice this matter, one way or another, just because my own son could be involved. The inspector has a very difficult job in front of him, and it would be in your own interests to cooperate fully, despite what you may feel personally."

As he stepped down to have a word with his wife, Dr. Jorgenson took the opportunity to thank him.

"I'm sure we all feel most relieved at these reasonable and balanced views," he announced from the podium.

Reason and balance were the last things George Weston's father wanted to hear.

"You sanctimonious shit," he shouted at Nesbit. "I don't give a fuck which police force that slimy bastard works on. You just sort it out, or I'll throw more lawsuits at you than a dog has fleas."

As the Jaguar purred down the school drive, Nesbit raised the glass partition that isolated the backseat from the driver. "Stupid young bastards," he muttered. "What have we got on the girl?"

"Still in shock. No statement—" Jenkins began.

"Not that," Nesbit said testily. "Has she got any form?"

"Nothing on the sheet, sir."

"What about her friends?"

"We're working on that. DS Atkins is running a snout in the village. There's a pusher operating at the school. One of the students. Nothing big, but steady. Grass, cannabis, crack . . . the usual stuff . . . Drug Squad is trying to get a line on his supplier, so they're just keeping surveillance at the moment."

"Any leverage?"

"There's always leverage, sir," Jenkins said.

At Hope Green police station, the eleven boys were cautioned and Illiffe recorded their statements with WPC Hansforth as his witness, after which the police doctor took blood samples that were sent immediately to laboratories for forensic examination and comparison with the fluid samples taken from Lyndsey Barratt. They were then formally charged with smoking in a prohibited place and released into their parents' custody on bail set at fifteen pounds.

Late that night, the cricket team sat in the school pavilion sipping lager. The general mood was subdued, but by no means depressed. As Nig Odonga put it, "It's eleven to one, don't forget."

"That Illiffe's a bit of a bastard," Shackleton observed. There was a murmur of agreement.

"Nezzer's old man'll sort him out," Peters assured him. "Just so long as we all stick together. Isn't that right, Porgy?"

George Weston had a bad feeling. There had been a look of disgust on his father's face when they drove back to the school. It did not bode well for the Porsche he had been promised. If only that bloody girl had kept her nose out of their compartment, but no! She had to come in and pretend to read her stupid bloody book, crossing and uncrossing her legs. She'd asked for the groining all right, and if they all stuck together there'd be no problem, not unless that ridiculous policeman was right about the sodomy. He looked over at Peter Shackleton. Shackers the arse man.

"Absolutely, Big Pee," he said to Peters. "The worst that can happen is a two-hundred-pound fine for this stupid bylaw thing. The rest of it doesn't matter. She egged us on, and we didn't know what we were doing. End of story. None of that bullshit at the police station makes any difference to that."

There was an appreciative silence, then Thumper Hodgkins said, "Bloody good groining, though, wasn't it?"

"Best ever," Timmo Smythe agreed. "What're you going to lay on next week, Porgy? Can't let the term end without a bang, can we?"

"Porgy'll think of something," Tiger said. "He always does, doesn't he?"

"Porgy," Pain Johnson said softly, waving his can toward Weston. "Porgy, Porgy, Porgy . . ."

The others took up the chant, keeping it quiet so that no one passing the pavilion would hear.

George Weston looked around at the flushed faces of his team. He had never felt so proud. On the other hand, he was also feeling extremely nervous about his father. He had seen him take Smoky Haddock's arm and lead the sports teacher into a corridor, presumably for what the old man called an in-depth bare-chesting. It all heralded a fan being hit by a truckload of shit.

Thomas Haddock had lived through events much, much worse than this in the army and come up smiling. So a bunch of lads had besported themselves with a tart. So what was new? They were only doing what any bunch of lads with any balls would have done. As an amateur military historian and a recently active mercenary, Haddock knew about such things. The Assyrians, the Macedonians, the Romans, the Turks, the SS . . . right down the chain to his snatch squad in Rwandan refugee camps, collecting Hutu war criminals' heads for the Tutsis and grabbing whatever crumpet came within reach. Of course, the circumstances were slightly different, because his experiences were associated with war, not school cricket outings, but the principle was the same. With few exceptions, the most successful soldiers were also the most ruthless and had the biggest appetites for physical gratification. He had observed many times that this rule seemed to prevail in the world of politics and business, too. Not to mention the Church.

Soon after he joined the school's teaching staff, he had seen that young George Weston was in a class by himself when it came to succeeding. Nothing else mattered. He knew all about Porgy's team-building initiatives, the illicit drinking of alcohol on school premises, and the cannabis that Tiger Ramshir's uncle brought into the country. Groining particularly impressed him. At least two team members had to commit a sexual act with a single girl to qualify as groiners. At first it had been groping, but it quickly developed into the achievement of a climax, first through masturbation, then into what the boys called "dry shagging," and finally into penetration. He had discovered the activity when the Winstanton village police chief called him after a late-night party at which three members of the cricket team had been accused of assaulting the sixteen-year-old sister of the young hostess in her back garden. The hostess had seen them from an upstairs window, rolling about on the lawn. At first she thought it had been some kind of game, but later the boys had come back into the house, leaving her sister lying on the grass, her clothes disheveled and too drunk to remember what had happened. She called the local police who took the boys into custody and called the sports master. Haddock arrived at the village police station, and they were released into his care and warned that any repetition of the incident would lead to charges being brought against them. Haddock had stopped in a rest area on the way back to the school.

"All right, Shackleton," he'd said. "What happened?"

He didn't have to threaten or even ask the question twice. Shackleton quietly told him they had been groining. He was privately amused by the explanation of this term, but gave them a fearsome dressing-down for being so careless. He then drove to the house where the party had been and knocked on the door until the elder sister got out of bed and opened it. He introduced himself and informed her that her party had contravened several public health regulations and other laws, not least being the provision of cigarettes and alcohol to underage persons. However, he told her, he had it on good authority that the police would not inform her parents or take further action unless obliged to do so by any other investigation that might take place, such as a complaint of assault by her sister.

To cover himself, the local bobby entered details of the incident into the station logbook, and the information was subsequently entered into the police national computer when the local data officer made his monthly visit to the police station.

Since the event, Haddock had seen the cricket team go from strength to strength, and the boys certainly seemed to keep their extracurricular activities under wraps. But the repercussions of this new exploit would jeopardize the good standing of the school unless something decisive was done about it, and quickly. John Weston had made it clear to Haddock during his private chat that he and the other parents expected the school to do all in its power to present a united front against any accusation from the Barratt girl. He also offered to underwrite any expenses that might be incurred in ensuring a favorable resolution to the unhappy affair. So when Haddock received a call from the detective who had accompanied Chief Constable Nesbit to the parents' meeting, he readily agreed to meet him at a local pub.

DI Jenkins was waiting in the lounge bar when Haddock arrived. After buying him a pint of beer, the detective said, "It's a bad business, this Barratt thing."

Haddock nodded agreement. Kept quiet, waiting for Jenkins.

"So, what made you take up teaching after leaving Number One Para?"

Haddock expected the question. Before joining the army, he had graduated in sports administration from a college near Aldershot, which helped him to get a commission and a subsequent transfer to the Parachute Regiment. He had insisted to the headmaster, of course, that this part of his curriculum vitae remained confidential for security reasons. But the police had their own ways of finding out such information. And rumors abounded in the school. He was ex-SAS, or even ex-SBS. No one had come up with the Parachute Regiment, which pissed him off, because the Paras could shit all over the Hereford mob, big time. But he kept his mouth shut and let the rumors assist in keeping discipline and maintaining order. Not to mention inspiring the lads to excel at their games and sports.

"Is this a job interview, or what?" he asked Jenkins.

"Kind of," Jenkins replied. "The thing is, we have another problem to deal with besides the gangbang."

Haddock waited again.

"Your boys are claiming that Barratt supplied them with roll-ups during the journey. I can tell you in the strictest confidence that the Scene of Crime Office working for the Transport Police found an unsmoked joint in her briefcase."

"That's that, then," Haddock observed.

"Unfortunately not. There might be a suggestion that it was planted there, by one of the boys. That would almost certainly mean an extension of the investigation and a search of the school."

Haddock nodded. "Thanks for the warning."

"Maybe you don't quite realize the position. If any of your lads have got any stuff, it's no good just dumping it. Any competent forensic guy can prove it's been around. That's not the same as possession, but it wouldn't look too good in court. You'd have to incinerate any containers or furniture that any stuff had been in contact with. Get the point?"

Haddock got the point all right. Jenkins was giving him a mega warning, but there was something else. He clamped his mouth shut and waited to be told what it was.

"The thing is, Tom, I know that this cricket team means a lot to you, and to the school. This girl could ruin the lives of all of the lads, and probably finish Winstanton School into the bargain. If what they say is true, she was a willing participant in something that went a bit too far. Seems a shame."

This time it was Jenkins who waited. Haddock knew he was expected to commit himself, but he had no idea to what. He didn't like it.

"Why don't you just get it off your chest, Inspector?"

"Okay," Jenkins said. "Okay. What if I told you the Drug Squad has fingered a pusher at the girl's school? They've begun a surveillance to get a lead to his source. If she's been getting any skag, she's been getting it off him. We'd have to be sure that he was pushing what she was smoking. The source would have to match the supply, if you see what I mean. Of course, we couldn't be directly involved, for obvious reasons."

Haddock saw exactly what he meant. Jenkins was sounding him out on the possibility of getting hold of some of Ramshir's stuff and planting it on the pusher. If this link could be established, there would be no need for the police to turn over the school. Very neat. And he had no problem implementing such a project. All he needed was to know who the pusher was and how he could get hold of him. Jenkins told him.

"A small point," Jenkins said. "I'll need some of the stuff as a backup. Half would do."

"That'll be okay," Haddock said. "Can you meet here, same time, tomorrow?"

"Make it two o'clock," Jenkins said.

When he got back to the school, Haddock called Ramshir to his study.

"What I need," he told Ramshir, "is every last grain of the stuff you were smoking on the train. No questions asked. Is that understood? It would also be a good idea to get rid of anything that's touched it. Change the cabinets around the dormitories if need be. Burn any empty packets or any clothing that's been in contact. Is that clear?"

"Absolutely, sir," Tiger Ramshir said noncommittally. "Perhaps you would like to have a sampling this evening, say around ten o'clock in the cricket pavilion."

Haddock gave Ramshir a smile that combined indulgence with a warning.

"Don't push it, Ramshir. If anyone gets as much as a whisper that you and the others have had drugs in your possession, you could find yourselves facing prison sentences."

The police officer on duty outside Lyndsey's room stood up and opened the door for her parents. Lyndsey appeared to be sleeping as they entered. Dr. Shadri wondered if she would ever get used to her job. Pam Barratt was putting a very brave face on things, but it was obvious that she was utterly distracted by what had happened and finding it difficult to coordinate her movements. Her husband slumped into a chair, clearly exhausted. Quite apart from the trauma of having their daughter raped, they would soon be facing the unremitting attention of the national media. The article in the *National Clarion* was only the beginning.

"Mr. Tomlinson and I are very pleased with Lyndsey's progress," she told them softly. "She's obviously very tired and sleeping a lot, but she looks so much improved, don't you think?"

Harry Barratt looked at the contusions on his daughter's face. "I suppose it depends on your definition of 'improved,' " he said dully.

"I've tried the odd question, but she doesn't seem to want to talk about it yet," the doctor said. "Of course, that's not altogether surprising. Detective Inspector Illiffe is keen to take her statement when she feels up to it. Once he's done that, I suppose we'll have journalists coming out of the woodwork. A reporter is in the hospital right now. I think she's hoping to get a word with Mr. Tomlinson, but he won't discuss the case, naturally."

A glance passed between Lyndsey's parents.

"That would be the person who wrote the article," Pam Barratt said.

"Yes. Julie Adams. Has she been pestering you?"

"Her newspaper wants exclusive rights to Lyndsey's story," Harry said. "Bloody parasites."

"I know Harry's right," his wife said, "but it might help to keep the others away if they knew that Lyndsey wouldn't talk to them. What do you think?"

The doctor could not give advice, but if that poor girl could get something out of this mess, why should she not?

"Is the contract for a reasonable sum of money?" As they hesitated she added, "Don't worry. I'm bound by doctor-patient confidentiality."

"A hundred thousand pounds." Harry Barratt spoke quietly. She thought she had not heard him correctly.

"I beg your pardon."

"A hundred thousand pounds. And that's the problem."

She found it difficult to understand why a hundred thousand pounds should be a problem, unless they wanted more. "What exactly do you mean, Mr. Barratt?"

Harry shrugged. "It'll look as if we're turning this into a business deal. I know Lyndsey would never accept that, and neither would we. . . ."

"On the other hand," his wife said quickly, "why should any girl go through such a dreadful, dreadful ordeal?" She paused, and the doctor waited until she had composed herself. "Why shouldn't someone pay for what has happened? When they catch those animals, will they pay anything? No! They'll be locked away at our expense for a few years and be let out to do the same thing again. It happens all the time, doesn't it?"

It certainly did. The doctor had lost count of the number of times.

"I repeat that I mustn't advise you," she said, "but it seems to me that accepting such an arrangement with one newspaper will solve far more problems than it might cause. Either way, who could possibly argue against your daughter receiving some kind of recompense, from whichever source it might come? I have a ward round now, but do please keep in touch if you think I can help in any way."

Julie Adams made her way to Lyndsey's room. The young police officer by the door stared at her as she sat down. Things were going well at the moment, she thought. The editor liked the way the story was developing and was keen to get more. He had given her considerable latitude in how she achieved this, and had even provided a backup team of researchers and a generous expense account. She'd taken a suite of rooms in the town's only reasonably sized hotel, and an IT team had installed a high-speed data link with the newspaper. She could tap into all kinds of information and send copy and photographs direct to the news desk. A few of the other rooms had been taken by journalists, but that was par for the course during any big story. Most of the hacks knew each other and were able to live together in a reasonably civilized way, until something newsworthy developed, in which case they pulled all kinds of strokes to get an edge on reporting. Julie made sure that Edwards could use the local weekly newspaper's facilities in case anything happened to her own setup. In return, she would give information to its news editor that he could not otherwise get with his limited resources. Yes, she thought, it was all stacking up nicely.

"Are Lyndsey's parents still inside?" she asked the officer.

"Member of the family, are you?"

"Oh no. I'm just helping them to get a few things done, that's all. It's difficult with the wheelchair. Fancy a tea or coffee?"

"Why not? I could do with a cuppa," he said.

Julie smiled brightly. "Milk and sugar?"

"Three lots," he said.

There was a dispensing machine down the corridor, and she was back in a few minutes.

"Must be tough, sitting here all day," she observed.

"Tell me about it," he said, taking a sip of tea. "You live round here then?"

"On and off. Move around a bit. You know the kind of thing."

"Right," he said again. When she didn't offer any more information, he nodded at the door. "Funny old business."

"Absolutely," Julie said. One way of getting answers is never ask the questions. He was dying to tell someone something.

"I mean, no one should go around doing that sort of thing, no matter what."

"I quite agree." She nodded.

"What I mean is, no one should do that to you, even if you are a druggie."

Julie sighed. "I know just what you mean."

"Those lads were probably not used to hash. It does your head in, if you're not used to it."

"I would imagine it does," she said. "Not bad tea, is it?"

"Not bad," he said broodingly. "A nice family like that, too."

"I wonder what they must think."

"Well, they don't know, do they? Parents never do, until it's too late. We find that all the time. Their sweet little girl going around with joints in her briefcase, dishing them out to some lads, and bang! It all goes wrong. What can you do?"

"I don't know," Julie said. "I really don't know."

At that moment, Lyndsey's parents came out of the room. Julie stood up, nodded to the policeman and accompanied them to the hospital parking lot.

"How is Lyndsey?"

"The doctors say she's progressing, but she seems to be sleeping a lot," Pam Barratt said quietly. "She's still too tired to talk."

"I'm sorry to push it, but have you thought about a contract for Lyndsey?"

"The doctor didn't seem to be against the idea," Pam said. "On balance we think it might be the best thing to do."

"I won't have any sensationalism," Harry Barratt said.

Julie looked at him and said candidly, "You already have sensationalism, Mr. Barratt, no matter what I might write. You'll have to live with that. But I promise you that I will tell Lyndsey's side of things accurately and fairly, whatever happens."

"What do you mean, whatever happens?"

"In my experience," she told him, "even a single charge of rape can get very dirty for all concerned. In this case, you'll have the parents of eleven boys swearing blind that they are all little angels who wouldn't harm a fly."

"Maybe," Harry Barratt said, his low voice holding a note of confidence. "But no one who sees your pictures of our daughter is going to take any notice of that kind of thing."

"I sincerely hope not," Julie said.

"The doctor said you can see Lyndsey, once her consultant says she is well enough," Pam Barratt told her, "provided we give our permission." She looked at her husband, who nodded.

"I don't see why not," he said.

Chapter 7

CHAS HARTFIELD'S INCOME FROM SELLING SOFT DRUGS TO his fellow students plummeted every time Hershal Academy closed for vacations. He didn't mind too much, because he retained a few outlets around the village where he rented a room. Only friends and people he knew really well. That way, nothing could go wrong. Caution was Chas's watchword. It had to be, didn't it? Ever since he'd met Black Artie on that trip to Nottingham and found himself floating on cloud sixty-nine with all those girls. That had been a rave and a half, and no mistake. Three of them giving him the business while Black Artie got a hard-on watching. The tall blond one with the big tits was really nice afterward. Couldn't get over the Hartfield charisma and good looks. Made coffee while they all had a chat, recovering from their exertions. When Black Artie found out he was at drama school, well, there was no stopping the guy, was there?

"It's simple, Chas. You won't even have to pay for the stuff. All you need is ten or twelve regular users, and your commission will pay for what you use and more besides. It's a win-win-win situation."

To be honest, he was too shagged out to resist. Anyway, Black Artie had been right. People were always asking around for a smoke or whatever. The whole thing was a walkover. He now had twenty regulars among the students, and to tide things over the vacation he pulled half a dozen of the locals into it as well. A nice touch that.

Plus he had used his head. They all thought he was just another user. He'd set up a system of dead-letter boxes that he'd read about in spy thrillers. Three of them. Behind the trash bins near the school parking lot, in a hollow log by the path through the woods, and (this was best of all) in a gap under the plinth of the statue of Sir Henry Irvine by Hamlet's study. There was an old settee right by it, and all you had to do was sit down and flop your arm over the back. People were always coming and going around there, and no one took any notice of what went on. He worked his distribution on a rotation, so none of the users ever met each other, at least as far as he knew. So long as they never met him dishing the stuff out, that's all. If they ever did, he'd simply claim there'd been a mixup with the supplier. But it hadn't happened yet. It was all working, sweet as a nut. They left the money, and he exchanged it for the skag or the speed or whatever. Black Artie had given him quite a list of products too, so no one was likely to get bored. And as long as he maintained his caution, there was no reason why the arrangement couldn't carry on indefinitely. So when he took the twenty-pound note out of the hollow log in the woods late that afternoon and replaced it with a small packet of crack for that stupid sod from the village, it was all the more shocking to feel a hand smack onto his shoulder and his hair grabbed so he couldn't turn to see what was happening.

The next few hours were terrifying. A black bag was pulled over his head, and he was pummeled and kicked farther into the woods. Something horrid was shoved into his mouth, and he felt his arms being tied around a tree. No one said a word, but it suddenly came to him that this was a rival drug pusher, and his imagination rushed into overdrive. He had read what these people can do to their competition, and images of mangled bodies in blown-up cars or lying bound and bloodstained in lonely places like this had a seriously debilitating effect on his bladder. He heard noises moving away, leaving him to stand there, the wet warmth down his legs quickly turning to cold discomfort. Hours passed, and he lost all track of time. When he heard someone approaching through the undergrowth, he was prepared to welcome the click of the hammer being cocked that would signal the end of his misery.

The bag was ripped off his head and a flashlight blinded him.

"You little shit," a voice said.

He rolled his eyes and desperately tried to cough out the rag that was blocking his mouth. Rough fingers pulled it out for him.

"Here's the deal," the voice said. "You're going to get nicked for possession. If you play it right, you might go down for a month or two, but more likely you'll get a suspended, maybe just a fine. On the other hand, if you fuck this up, you'll get nicked for supplying, and that'll be that. End of promising career as dashing male actor. Are you with me so far?"

Chas nodded. His mouth was far too dry to cope with speech.

"Good. All you have to do is make a statement that you gave Lyndsey Barratt some of your skag. You don't have to say you sold it to her, okay? She asked you for it because her mother has got multiple sclerosis. She said it would help her get over the pain. You gave it to her because you were sorry for her. You've been doing this for weeks. You got that, shithead?"

Chas nodded, too frightened to feel relief that he was still alive. A fist hit him hard in the stomach.

"I asked if you'd got that, shithead?"

"Yes," he gasped. "No problem."

"Let's hear it, then!"

He painfully repeated what he had to do, then felt a hand shove something in his pocket.

"You better have that on you when they pick you up, or you'll be well fucked. Oh, before I forget. I want the name of the fucker who supplies your stuff."

Instinct triumphed over common sense.

"Christ, I can't tell you that. He'd have me bloody killed."

There was a silence. It seemed to go on forever. The dim, bulky shape behind the dazzling light didn't move. Then the voice said, "You're lucky I've got a sense of humor, sunshine. Can you feel this?"

Chas gasped as something needle-sharp pricked the side of his thigh. "Yes!"

"Let me tell you what it is. It's a military dagger made by Heckler and Koch, and it cost me five hundred quid. Tungsten steel. Best in the world. If I push any harder, it'll come out the other side. So don't fuck about. . . ."

The prick turned into a jab, and something warm trickled down Chas's leg for the second time that evening.

He sobbed with fright. "It's a bloke called Black Artie. I met him in the Old Castle in Nottingham."

"How d'you make contact?"

"He's got a mobile . . ."

Another jab elicited the number, then Chas felt the blade slide through the straps that were holding him to the tree and two very strong hands squeezed his shoulders.

"The path's over there. Now fuck off."

As Chas stumbled through the undergrowth, Thomas Haddock used his mobile phone to call Detective Inspector Jenkins.

"He's all yours. And he gets his stuff from a bloke called Black Artie. Works out of the Old Castle in Nottingham."

"Nice one," DI Jenkins said and used his mobile to contact a colleague in the Drug Squad. "Hello, Charlie. Keith Jenkins here. Got a favor to ask you."

"The answer's no," Detective Sergeant Charles Atkins told him.

"Don't be like that. We need to clear up this Barratt case."

"I thought the railway mob were on that one."

"They are, they are, but they need our help. Their SOCO found a joint in the girl's briefcase. We're pretty sure she got it from someone at that drama school you were telling me about. Some prat called Chas Hartfield."

"So?"

"It would be nice to get it checked out, Charlie."

"Not a chance. We know about Hartfield. My guv'nor wants blood on this one, and the drama school kid's our lead."

"All I'm asking is that you give him a pull for possession. If there's nothing in it, let the bugger go. It'll look good for his street cred. Whatever happens, you can go after his supplier later, and I'll owe you one. In fact, I may get the prat to line up the supplier for you."

There was a silence. "What are you up to, Jenkins?"

"You know me, Charlie. Looking after everyone's best interests, including yours."

"I'll think about it."

"Don't take too long, old son. Let me know what happens."

Jenkins disconnected and smiled. Chief Constable Nesbit would soon be able to relax about his divvy of a son. "I'd call that well levered, my son," he said to himself with satisfaction. There's nothing quite like greasing the wheels of promotion with a little after-hours work.

Mr. Tomlinson was pleased with Lyndsey's physical progress. No lasting damage, but his patient's reflexes still seemed slow in responding to various stimuli. When he took her hand and asked, "How are we getting along, Lyndsey?" she quietly whispered something that he realized was "Thirsty." He gave her a sip of weak orange juice and eased her head on the pillows. "Your mother and father have been waiting for you to wake up," he said.

Pam Barratt moved her wheelchair to the bedside. "Hello, darling."

"Hello, Mummy. Are you all right?"

It brought tears. "That's a fine question for one invalid to be asking another."

"Where's Daddy?"

"I'm here, love. Right here."

"I'm so sorry, Daddy," she whispered.

"There, there," Harry said. "There's no need for you to be sorry. It's us should have been there. I let you down again."

She tried to shake her head. "Not your fault."

"Let's not get ourselves all upset," Mr. Tomlinson said. "The main job is to get you back on your feet, young lady, so we can put this matter behind us as soon as possible."

Harry Barratt motioned the consultant to one side. "Is it too soon for her to meet the reporter? I'd like to get that over with, one way or the other."

"I don't see why not," Mr. Tomlinson said. "So long as nothing upsets her. Miss Adams, isn't it?"

"Ms.," Harry said automatically.

The consultant opened the door and looked sternly at Julie. "Two minutes, Ms. Adams. And don't say a thing to upset my patient."

"Lyndsey, darling," her mother said. "There's someone who wants to meet you."

Julie stared at the bandages and tubes, then at the white, bruised face. "Hello, Lyndsey. My name's Julie. I'm a newspaper reporter."

Lyndsey turned to look at her father. Puzzled.

"I'm afraid you're front-page news, love," he told her. "Nothing we can do about that. It's a bit complicated, but we think this young lady can help."

Julie turned to Mr. Tomlinson. "I'd like to ask Lyndsey a question. It's important."

He moved away from the bed. "And what is this important question?" She told him quietly. "Seems all right. But any distress whatsoever, and you leave."

Julie went close to Lyndsey. "Can you tell me what you had in your briefcase when you left the awards ceremony?"

Lyndsey looked puzzled. "I don't understand."

"You had your briefcase on the train yesterday. I just wonder if you can tell me what you had in it."

"The usual things I suppose," she said. "A book, my diary and notebook, a pen, some tissues."

"No makeup, matches, cigarette lighter—?"

"Lyndsey doesn't smoke or wear makeup, Ms. Adams," her mother said.

Julie did not take her eyes away from Lyndsey. "Any cigarettes?"

Lyndsey looked back steadily, puzzled. "They make me choke," she said.

"Me too." Julie smiled at her and got a small smile back.

"That's enough for one day," Mr. Tomlinson said firmly.

It wasn't until Julie was driving back to her hotel that she realized Lyndsey had forgotten to mention her new diploma. It seemed odd, but then she thought that Lyndsey would only tell her about things that she carried most of the time. As far as the joint was concerned, Julie knew there could only be one explanation. The cricket team must have put it there before they got off the train. She was absolutely certain that Lyndsey had nothing to do with drugs, and she made up her mind to tackle Illiffe about it. She thought he was a funny sort of copper. Like the rest of them in some ways, different in others. That bit about the scanning radio, for instance. Did he know she used one? Was he warning her off? She wondered if Edwards had managed to overhear anything useful, anything that she could add to the story she would file later that evening. His prints of the police at

Winstanton School had come out really well, especially the tele-photos. Whatever else, Edwards was a bloody good photographer. Her boss had told her the North American and Far East editors were hungry for more copy, preferably with graphic details of the attack. She had no problem with that. It wouldn't affect the Barratts, unless they had relatives overseas. She made a mental note to check that out, just in case. A productive day all around, she thought. And if Lyndsey were up to it, maybe she would be able to sign the contract tomorrow.

Julie Adams met Lyndsey's parents early next morning at the hospital. Lyndsey had been taken out of intensive care and put into a private room paid for by the *National Clarion*. The same policeman was outside the door, and Dr. Shadri was back on duty, waiting to make sure that Lyndsey felt capable of dealing with visitors, but there seemed to be no problem with the patient. She was propped up, still moving stiffly, but beginning to look much better as the bruises faded and the swelling on her face reduced. The newspaper's lawyers had couriered Julie a standard contract, which Harry Barratt scrutinized. There was nothing in it that caused him any problems, so he didn't bother showing it to his lawyer. He told Julie that, as far as he was concerned, if Lyndsey wanted to sign it, she could. Lyndsey herself clearly trusted her father and didn't even bother to read it before awkwardly scrawling her name on the two copies. Her mother had brought Lyndsey's checkbook containing her account details, so the money could be transferred electronically as soon as the contract had been registered by the newspaper's legal department. Julie said that would take less than twenty-four hours.

"Remember," she said to Lyndsey, "other journalists might try to get you to tell them something. All you have to do is say no. Tell them you're under contract to the National Clarion Group, and they should leave you alone. If you say anything else, my boss could ask for the money back, and none of us would like that to happen, would we?"

Lyndsey attempted to return her smile. Julie had the feeling that she wasn't taking it all in, but that was hardly surprising. She said good-bye to the Barratts and left the hospital. She wanted to see if Edwards had heard anything of interest over the scanner, and she also wanted to know exactly what he had put in his statement to the police.

When she had left the room, Lyndsey said, "She's nice, isn't she?"

Her parents were not too sure how to reply to that. Julie's article that morning had concentrated on events at Winstanton School, with long-distance but clear photographs of the police confronting the boys with the articles found on the train. The main story began with the headline HOWZAT, OFFICER? The subhead posed the question "What does this public school cricket team know about Lyndsey's ordeal?" and the article went on to ask when the police were going to release a statement about possible suspects. Harry Barratt was beginning to wonder if Julie Adams was not whipping up a storm where there might otherwise be calm. Apart from covering Lyndsey's ordeal as a news item, none of the other newspapers gave the story much prominence.

"She seems nice, dear," her mother said diplomatically. "The main thing is to get you better, as soon as possible, and your father and I thought it would be far easier to have just one newspaper to deal with."

"I don't understand." Lyndsey's voice was a whisper, and she drifted off to sleep.

Dr. Shadri thought the Barratts looked exhausted. Harry in particular seemed disoriented, searching for his words. "Why don't the two of you get some rest?" she said. "Lyndsey is settling down well, and the more sleep she gets, the better. Inspector Illiffe wants to take Lyndsey's statement as soon as possible, and if she maintains this rate of recovery he may be able to do so later this afternoon."

She didn't think it would be diplomatic to let them know that the Divisional Police Surgeon would be visiting the hospital too, in the hope that Lyndsey would now be able to give her consent for an intimate examination that would legally establish whether or not penetration had occurred.

Dave Edwards was bored out of his mind. Over the past twenty-four hours, he had scanned dozens of mobile-phone messages and police frequency transmissions. Only one or two conversations contained anything that might relate to their story, but he did not have a tape recorder, so he scribbled notes on a scrap of paper. When Julie arrived, he showed her the one about someone called Keith Jenkins talking to a fellow called Charlie.

"Obviously a couple of pigs. This chap Jenkins mentioned the Barratt case," he told her. "Charlie said something about the railway mob being in charge, and Jenkins said their SOCO found a joint in a briefcase."

Julie had been shocked when the policeman outside Lyndsey's room had mentioned the joint, and that was why she asked Lyndsey about cigarettes. As far as she was concerned, Lyndsey was telling the truth. One of the boys must have planted it there. In the ordinary course of events, Julie felt sure, this would not be a problem. For one thing, whoever had assaulted Lyndsey had tipped out the contents of her briefcase, as Edwards's photographs showed. All a forensic scientist had to do was check the other articles for the presence of drugs. If they had been next to any cannabis, he'd get a positive result. Julie was sure this would not be the case. But what Edwards was saying put things into a new light. A more threatening light.

"I know about the joint," she said. "Did they say anything else?"

Edwards squinted at his scrawl. "Something about a pusher at the school. The Drug Squad are looking into it."

"What exactly did they say?" she insisted.

"Oh for Christ's sake, I'm not a bloody shorthand reporter."

"Come on, Edwards," she said. "It's important."

"I dunno," he said, slightly mollified. "There was something about doing the guy for possession. Jenkins said the other pig would be doing him a big favor."

Julie was puzzled. There was no way that the Drug Squad would agree to arrest a suspected pusher simply for possession. It didn't make sense.

"I want you to time, date and sign that note," she said to Edwards.

"Sure," he said. "But why?"

"If the courts can accept a policeman's contemporaneous notes as evidence, they can accept yours, if push comes to shove."

Edwards didn't like the sound of that one little bit.

Mr. Tomlinson was not very happy, but he knew that the sooner a complete examination of his patient was made, the better. The divisional police surgeon was an experienced woman doctor with an efficient and reassuring manner. She patted Lyndsey's hand and told her exactly what she wanted to do. Lyndsey nodded and remained totally silent as the surgeon examined her vagina and anus, taking swabs from deep inside and noting the abrasions and contusions. Most of the alien fluids would have drained away over the past two days, of course, but the paramedics who had been first on the scene had been extremely thorough in collecting samples, both in the railway car and during the ambulance journey to the hospital. The police surgeon would now be able to testify that vaginal and anal penetration had taken place with extreme violence and many times. All they needed now was a verification from Lyndsey that intercourse had taken place without her consent, and a rape investigation could swing into action officially.

Frank Illiffe looked at Detective Inspector Jenkins in utter disbelief. The Serious Crimes Squad officer shrugged. "That's how it is, Frank. It's out of your hands. We'll caution the girl as soon as we get the okay from the hospital. I'm hoping to hear sometime today."

Illiffe had been on sensitive ground before in his investigations. It happened all the time. But this!

"A routine drug bust, you say."

"That's right. The lad involved is a user. The drama academy has been under surveillance for some weeks now, and one of the Drug Squad saw him picking up a twist of skag. He was arrested, and it all came out when he made a statement. He's been sharing his stuff with the girl. She told him it was to help her mother. We know better now, don't we?"

"You're telling me that the Drug Squad blew their surveillance to pick up a lightweight user. Is that what you're telling me?"

"Looks that way," Jenkins said. "Who knows what those bastards get up to. Anyway, the whole thing has been passed over to SCS."

"Not by me, it hasn't," Illiffe said angrily. "You're taking the word of an admitted druggie without a shred of evidence. If any crime was committed by anyone, it was done on Railtrack property. That remains my responsibility."

"For Christ's sake, Frank, what will it take to convince you? You've got a roll-up from the girl's briefcase, you've got the combined statements from eleven young men with impeccable backgrounds, and on top of that you have the corroborating and totally unconnected statement of one of her fellow students. What more do you want?"

What Illiffe wanted was clarification of his position from head-quarters, and quickly. The whole thing was beginning to fall apart.

Greg Hawkins of the *Daily News* was pissed off. He'd got a dress-ing-down from his news editor for letting Julie Adams get a lead on the Barratt case. Two front-page stories, one of them the main head-line. Professionally he accepted that she'd done a first-class job. So had that photographer Edwards, for a provincial nitwit. For that rea-son he hoped the whole thing would die the death and peter out, so he could get back to the Smoke and get stuck into something more substantial, like his lead on a secret male brothel for woman MPs. He was chomping peanuts in the hotel cocktail bar and watching his photographer Bernie Watts chat up two representatives from a cos-metic company when the waiter told him there was a phone call.

"Hawkins," he said.

"Greg Hawkins, *Daily News*?"

"The very same. And you are . . . ?"

"Never mind who I am. When's your deadline?"

Hawkins sensed something substantial. Only a serious caller would ask a question like that. And only a very serious caller would know where he was. He looked at his watch. "Two hours."

"Be at the main entrance of Hope Green Hospital in thirty minutes."

The caller disconnected. Hawkins went back to the peanuts. The cosmetic reps had already stung Bernie for three gin and tonics each, but he didn't get the point. Thought he was in with a chance.

"Get your gear, matey," Hawkins called. "Something's come up."

Bernie said, "Shit." The girls smiled a lot and kissed Bernie before he left, leaving lipstick all over his face. Hawkins decided not to mention it. Serve the silly sod right.

There was a police car at the hospital entrance. Hawkins noticed it was not a BTP vehicle. The driver was a uniformed PC from the regional police force. He sauntered over. Bernie started unraveling his cameras.

"What's occurring, then?" he asked.

"Fuck off," the driver explained.

"All right if we hang around, is it?"

The driver ignored him. He checked his tape recorder. Five minutes later, Detective Inspector Jenkins and another plainclothes officer came out and made for their car. Hawkins hurried over to them.

"Excuse me, gents," he said. "Greg Hawkins, *Daily News*. Is something happening here we should know about?"

"Are you asking me for a press statement?" Jenkins asked him.

"Well, yes," Hawkins said, wondering what the hell was going on.

Jenkins looked around and positioned himself on the steps, next to the hospital name plaque. He looked pointedly at Bernie Watts, who took several shots. Then he turned to Hawkins.

"I am Detective Inspector Keith Jenkins of the Serious Crime Squad. At nine o'clock this evening I cautioned Lyndsey Barratt of Nineteen Ashtree Crescent, Hope Green, and arrested her for being in possession of a prohibited category C substance contrary to the Misuse of Drugs Act 1971. Barratt, who made no statement, is now in police custody in Hope Green Hospital and will be formally charged on her release from the hospital. Other charges may follow." He looked at Hawkins. "Any questions?"

Hawkins had plenty. "Let's start with these other charges."

"Don't be a prat," Jenkins told him.

Chapter 8

HARRY BARRATT WENT INTO WORK EARLY THE FOL-
lowing morning. He didn't want to, but his wife said it
would help take his mind off things. He could get a morning's work in, then they could go and see Lyndsey in the afternoon,
she said. He drove into the company parking lot at eight o'clock,
feeling tired and empty. Until now he had given no thought as to
how his colleagues at work would be feeling, or how they would
react to Lyndsey's rape. They had always been very supportive about
Pam's condition, and seemed to take his mood swings in their stride.
Performance was not a problem. He was one of their most efficient
programming managers. Once he was in front of a PC, he had no
thought for anything but the job in hand. It took a lot of people that
way. A sort of obsession, pushing out the problems and concerns of
life. There was no way you could write a macro for a data-sorting
process while you were worrying about paying college fees or electric
bills. When Lyndsey was little, he used to take her into his office and
let her play with the keyboard. She had an aptitude for computing.
At one point he thought she might follow in father's footsteps and
take to the world of information technology, but that all came to an
end when she got a part in a school play. He forgot its name, but he
remembered that she'd been very good. Some sort of malevolent cat,
terrorizing other animals. From that day on, she had breathed, slept,
walked, and talked theater. Drama school had been an inevitability.

And he'd been quite interested, too, until this thing with Pamela. That's how he referred to MS. This thing with Pamela. He couldn't bring himself to say either the words or the initials of the distressing complaint.

He walked into the building and swiped his security pass. The guard stared down at his roster sheet and mumbled, "Good morning," and the few people he passed in the corridors gave him an embarrassed greeting. He spent the next hour trying to read his E-mail, with little success. At ten to nine his secretary arrived for work in her usual summer garb of practically no top and practically no skirt and said, "Mr. Barratt! We weren't expecting you today. Are you all right?"

"Not really, Tracy, but sometimes it's best to carry on as normal."

Tracy saw Harry's manager, Tim Hardiman, looking through the partition. He made a drinking motion and jerked his thumb at her.

"I'll get coffee," she said.

"Thanks. That'd be nice."

As she went out, Hardiman came in. "Harry," he said, "for Christ's sake, there's no need for you to come in until all this is cleared up."

"That's all right, Tim. She's got a long way to go, but the doctors are confident that things'll work out. A lot of coming to terms, of course, but she's a strong girl. She'll cope."

"Sure she will." Hardiman had met Lyndsey many times, and liked her a lot. But all this! It made you think. "Kids," he said. "What can you do? You bring them up as best you can, and then they go and do a thing like this."

"They've got a lot to answer for. I hope they lock the little bastards up and let them rot in hell for the rest of their warped little lives. You know, Tim, I never thought of myself as a vindictive or vengeful person, but I can understand now why some societies torture their criminals to death. It's no more than these little swine deserve."

Hardiman thought that was a bit over the top, under the circumstances. Harry was well stressed out, and Hardiman knew it was best to let things lie, but he found himself trying to inject a note of fairness. After all, according to the article in the morning's *Daily News* it must have been six of one and half a dozen of the other in that railway carriage.

"I know how you feel, Harry, but you can't really put it all down to the boys. They're only human."

Harry looked at him. "You're right. Maybe their parents should be banged away as well. A bit more parental discipline is what this bloody world needs."

Hardiman thought this was decidedly off. He'd known Harry for a long time, understood the pressures of having his wife stricken with MS, and now this business of Lyndsey. But the man seemed to be blaming everyone but himself. If he'd kept his act together, maybe his daughter wouldn't be facing a drugs charge. Well, it was not his place to get involved, not unless Harry's work suffered.

"When you've checked your mail, let's get up to speed on the Gable Mining project. They want our side of the process finished in three days flat, and that doesn't give us much time." He grabbed his coffee off the tray as Tracy came back. "I'll have this in my office."

Tracy realized that something had upset Hardiman but could not imagine what it could be. Harry Barratt was the one who was entitled to be upset, after all. Not to mention his poor daughter. And this drugs thing was no big deal. Lots of her friends had been cautioned for smoking. That's usually as far as it went.

"Don't let it worry you, Mr. Barratt," she said. "I'm sure the police will let her off."

The words didn't sink in for a while. Then Harry looked at her and said, "I'm sorry, Tracy?"

"Lots of my friends smoke a bit. It's nothing we can't handle. All she had in her case was one roll-up, and she can say it was for her own use. It might not even get to court."

"What the hell are you talking about?"

Tracy got a shock. Her boss's voice was rasping and his face had turned red.

"I'm sorry, Mr. Barratt, I didn't mean to upset you."

Harry Barratt made a final effort to pull himself together. "What do you mean, all she had in her case was one roll-up?"

His face was now gray, and Tracy was really frightened. He looked really ill. She picked up the phone and keyed Hardiman's extension.

"It's Tracy, Mr. Hardiman. I think Mr. Barratt is poorly. . . ."

Hardiman was there in seconds.

"I knew it was too soon for you to come in, Harry," he said. "Maybe you'd better get along home. I can deal with the Gable Mine people."

"What does she mean, Tim?" Harry asked.

Hardiman had no idea what he was talking about and looked at Tracy.

"I was just saying about that thing in the papers this morning. I didn't mean to upset him."

Hardiman's composure slipped. "For God's sake, Tracy. Mr. Barratt's got enough on his plate without you reminding him that his daughter's a drug addict. . . ."

Harry's phone burbled. He picked it up, moving like a man in a trance, and said, "Barratt." He stood up, listened for a while, and tried to say something, his throat writhing with the effort. Then he slumped forward. Tracy told her friends later that it was like slow motion, but nothing like they show you on films or television. He was making bad smells and a horrible belching noise.

Hardiman motioned frantically to Tracy and hissed, "Call a bloody ambulance, for Christ's sake, will you?" Tracy rushed out in tears, and he picked up the dangling phone and said, "Who's on the line, please? Oh, Mrs. Barratt, can I call you right back? I think Harry's fainted."

The company doctor later told Hardiman that after such a massive thrombosis, Harry was probably dead before he hit the carpet.

Pam Barratt wasn't too surprised to see the police stopping their cars outside again, but there were two cars this time, and the tall detective who had first called around was not among the officers who got out and walked purposefully toward her front door. When she opened it, a lanky man with a sallow face and slicked-back hair held out his warrant card and a sheet of paper.

"Mrs. Pamela Barratt? I am Detective Inspector Keith Jenkins, and I have a warrant to search these premises."

As he was speaking, men and women police officers in overalls were moving past her. Most of them avoided her eyes.

"I don't understand," she said in bewilderment. "There must be a mistake."

"We'll try not to inconvenience you, Mrs. Barratt," Jenkins said. "Perhaps you wouldn't mind telling me which is your daughter's bedroom."

"I must call my husband."

"I'd prefer not, if you don't mind." He motioned for an officer to stand by the wheelchair as Pam moved toward the telephone. "We'll do this as quickly as possible." He wandered through the downstairs rooms, checking on the team that was searching the living room, kitchen, and downstairs toilet. "Is that your daughter's, Mrs. Barratt?" he asked, pointing at a designer jacket hanging from a hook under the stairs. When she nodded, he took it into the kitchen and put it on the table. "Check that out too," he said to the officer who was looking into jars and pots taken from the cupboards.

A woman officer came out of the living room and shook her head at Jenkins before going upstairs to continue the search. After a few moments, the officer downstairs called, "Something here, guv."

Jenkins went into the kitchen and found him holding Lyndsey's jacket in one hand and a small paper packet in the other. Jenkins smelled it. "Okay. Bag it," he said, then turned to Mrs. Barratt. "You can call your husband now, Mrs. Barratt."

Julie Adams was sitting on her Kawasaki outside Hope Green Police Station when Illiffe came out. When he saw her, he hesitated, then walked over and nodded a curt greeting. "Ms. Adams."

"Inspector. We need to talk." She held out a spare helmet.

Illiffe knew his regional colleagues would notice, but after his meeting with Chief Superintendent Harris, he was in no mood to care.

"We all regret this kind of thing, Frank," Harris had said. "No one likes having an investigation pulled, but under these circumstances we had no alternative. Mr. Barratt's death is a tragedy, but it is not, repeat, not our responsibility. The substantive point is that a prohibited substance was found in Lyndsey Barratt's home. That's a regional matter."

"I'll need to discuss this with my colleagues, Chief Superintendent," Illiffe had said carefully, "but as I see it, I still have an investigation on my hands. Several crimes have been committed in BTP jurisdiction, and until I receive a written order to the contrary from my superior I'm still on the job."

He hadn't meant to slam Harris's door, but his frustration exploded, and it was still in top gear as Julie gave him the helmet. She took him on a high-speed journey out of town and into country lanes that led to a pub by a canal. He was still struggling to get the helmet off when Julie vanished into the pub. She returned with two pints of bitter and some chips and put them on a wooden table a few feet from the towpath.

"This is a rotten business," Illiffe said. "How is anyone going to tell that kid about her father?"

"Her mother's with her now," Julie said. "She'll find a way."

"And how do you feel about it?" Illiffe asked bluntly.

She gazed at two swans that were looking for tidbits.

"It's good copy, and it'll sell newspapers."

"Is that it?"

"Yes, Inspector, that's it. What do you want me to say, for God's sake? Of course it's a rotten business. If you're not very careful you'll end up thinking that the whole of life is a rotten business. You want to know what I was doing last week? I was standing in a cellar with damp running down the walls looking at five children lying on one piss-soaked mattress. Their mother was slumped against the wall with a broken needle sticking out of her arm. That was the arm that hadn't been broken by her pimp. And we're not talking about Romania or Bosnia here. We're talking about a mainline British city that's won a European Community award for civic achievement. Stories like that sell newspapers and keep people glued to their TV. Successful manufacturing industry stories don't."

"And that's okay with you?" He didn't mean to ask, but he was still riled about Harris.

Julie glared at him. "That's none of your business," she said, "As far as my newspaper is concerned, Lyndsey represents a large financial investment. Besides, our group is pitching for a cable franchise, and we want to appear socially concerned. On the side of law and order."

"Sounds like you operate in the same crock of shit as me," he observed sourly.

"Let's go back to the beginning," she said, when they had both taken a drink. "What have I got that you want, and what have you got that I want?"

"I'm not at liberty to discuss police business," he said.

Julie stared at him. He was very attractive. She thought he looked stressed. Funnily enough, it made him look younger. A bit vulnerable, but that was probably misleading. You didn't get to be a detective inspector by being vulnerable.

"Bullshit," she said.

"Don't hold yourself back," he said. "Just come right out and say what you think."

When she grinned, she seemed like another person. The brittleness vanished, but he reminded himself that this was a determined and very professional journalist.

"Right," she said. "What I think is that one or more of your colleagues in the regional force is guilty of corruption and conspiracy to pervert the course of justice. A student called Chas Hartfield is involved. I think that the joint you found in Lyndsey's briefcase was planted there by one of the cricket team. If you can lay your hands on any of Hartfield's hash, you'll find it's totally unlike the stuff in the roll-up. And according to what Dave Edwards told me immediately after it all happened, the boys were out of their minds well before Lyndsey got on their train. He got a good look into their compartment as the train came into the station, and they were making one hell of a racket. So, I think it's a setup. There's no way Lyndsey was involved with drugs."

Illiffe wondered if she knew that Hartfield had already been arrested. He put the pint on the wooden table and stared at it. If he had any sense he'd walk away from this. On the other hand, who was he fooling? There was no way that Lyndsey Barratt used drugs. Julie Adams was absolutely right, but the idea of getting involved in an internal investigation into fellow officers was every policeman's nightmare.

"Your photographer friend didn't mention any of that in his statement," he said. "But even if he's right, it's not going to be easy to prove."

"I don't see why not."

He wondered how much he should tell her and decided he could cover things that she was likely to figure out for herself anyway.

"Hartfield had already been busted. I'm not saying I agree with you but, speaking off the record, anyone playing around like that is not going to overlook the weaknesses. They'd have to make sure that the roll-up in Lyndsey's briefcase will match what they found when they arrested him."

"Maybe, but which way will they play it? Their best bet would be to quietly get hold of some of the stuff the team was smoking and dump it on Hartfield so it matches, right? If they did it the other way round, they'd have to implicate the school."

She was as quick as a whip. She'd come to the same conclusion as Illiffe, with far less to go on.

"You might as well know that Region has started its own proceedings against Lyndsey. I'm going to have a hell of a job sorting this out."

"Try the weakest link," she suggested. "Lean on Hartfield. If someone is setting Lyndsey up, he must be directly involved."

He didn't have enough evidence to go to Internal Affairs, but the idea of doing a solo number was definitely dodgy. He could end up waving a pink slip and looking for a job as a nightwatchman.

"I'll have to think about it," he said. Julie threw the transcript of Edwards's eavesdropping in front of him.

"That should help to make up your mind."

The name did not surprise him. In fact, he'd simply avoided bringing it to the front of his mind. But DI Jenkins would not have acted without the nod from a higher authority, and it didn't take the Brain of Britain to work out who that was. Nesbit.

"Shit," he said.

"So who's this Keith guy that gets Charlie to do favors for him?"

"You don't really expect an answer to that."

"Not yet, I don't, but he'll emerge from the woodwork eventually." She dangled the motorcycle key in front of him. "You drive a bike?" He nodded. "Let's go back to work," she said.

He'd spent six months in the BTP motorcycle unit, but the Kawasaki's 1,100-cc engine was bigger than his BMW's had been, and the bike was heavier. Still, it felt good to grip the controls and feel the starter whine the engine into action. Julie swung up behind him, balancing her weight so that the bike hardly moved. Then her arms slid around him. He felt the softness of her breasts, even beneath her leather jacket, and it took all his concentration to make it back to her hotel.

John Weston gazed out of his office window as George came into the room. Thomas Haddock had given Weston some interesting information about his son during their little chat the other day. Kind of a confidential school report, and it wasn't half bad, either. To be perfectly honest, Weston was proud of George. The kid had been a total wimp when he was a nipper. Always clinging to his mother's skirts. Always wanting to be picked up. She'd taken the boy to see a child psychologist without telling John, then returned with some crap about little George being frightened of his father. John had been scandalized. Okay, so he had a bit of a temper on him, but you didn't get far in the construction industry by being a conciliatory yes-man. So he shouted a lot. So what! The silly cow was living in the lap of bloody luxury and biting the hand that fed her. The divorce had been almost brutally quick. She got more money than she deserved, plus a warning that any fucking about with future claims against her ex-husband would mean more grief than she'd know what to do with. He got custody of George.

"All right, you little shit," he said. "Tell me what really happened, and I mean really."

George's father had many faults, but dishonesty was not on the list. For one thing, he was too arrogant to lie about anything. For another, he was so wealthy he didn't need to bother. George had no problems with lying when it suited him, but he had a shrewd idea that his father already knew pretty well what had happened on the train. In this case, the truth was called for. Not all the truth, of course.

"It all happened pretty much like we told Jorgenson," he began. His father stared at him without comment. "I saw this girl on the station platform, and she walked quite a long way to get into our compartment. She sat on the end seat, right in the middle, so we could get a good look down the aisle. We were all feeling a bit frisky, you know how you do after winning a match, so Tiger asked if she wanted a smoke."

"So she didn't have the cannabis?"

"I've no idea. She might have had her own, but she certainly smoked ours."

"Tell me about groining," his father said.

George blinked. How did the sod know about that? And what did he know?

"It's a game we play," he said. "Kind of like an initiation ceremony for the team." His father's face was like a stone carving. "The idea is, instead of just one of us dating a girl, it has to be two or three. Then, whatever one does, the others have to as well."

"That's it?" his father asked.

"Yes," George said.

"The girls don't mind?"

"Not usually. We'd never do anything they really don't want us to, but you know what girls are like. Say no when they mean yes."

"And this Lyndsey Barratt. Did she say no when she meant yes?"

"We thought she was enjoying it. Specially at first, but we were all a bit on the high side. Lots of girls change their minds, but by that time it's not always easy to stop. I'm sorry she seemed to have been roughed up a bit, but we're very much into the work-hard-play-hard thing. You know how it is."

John Weston knew exactly how it was. At worst, the entire incident had been a misunderstanding among a group of high-spirited young people, and the little bitch had probably asked for it. But there was one factor he couldn't accept. Something that was alien to him.

"There's only one thing I want to know from you, George. Did you give her one up the arse?"

So that was it. That's what the old man was worried about. Porgy breathed a sigh of relief.

"Christ no, Dad."

John Weston pushed his face nearer. "You're sure?"

"Absolutely. First thing she did was go down on me. After that, I wasn't much good for anything else. I'd never dream of doing anything like that. It's . . . it's animalistic, isn't it?"

The fact was that he dreamed of doing things like that all the time, but you can't control your dreams, can you?

"It certainly is," his father agreed. "But don't think I'm letting you get away with this incident. Whatever else, all this drugs and booze is no bloody good for you, so I'm bringing everything forward."

George looked worried. "What does that mean?"

"You can forget college. If you get up to these things at school, Christ alone knows what'll happen if you get mixed up with all those degenerate students. I need you here in the business. I want to retire to some bloody sunshine paradise in five years, and I'm not having some jumped-up corporate shithead running this business into the ground when I do. I want you here, working your swollen little bollocks off so I can pass my days in idle, early retirement. You understand me?"

George managed to look crestfallen, which was quite an achievement. He didn't want to go to college. He viewed it as a waste of time, but not for the same reasons as his father. Too much brainwork involved, with fuck-all to show that was any use to anyone.

"That's not fair, Dad," he complained.

"Screw fair. You're starting here on August the first, and you can forget that Porsche you've been on about."

This time George didn't need to pretend to look crestfallen. He really was pissed off. His father threw a set of keys at him.

"You'll need something a bloody sight more practical than a Targa, working for a national construction company. It's in the basement. That's at the bottom of these offices, where you'll be starting work, like I did."

He watched as his son and heir took the keys with an ill-concealed bad grace and was well satisfied. Young George was an ambitious, selfish, ruthless and conniving, hard-nosed little shit. Just the right kind of qualities to succeed in an industry that reels before, during, and after every economic recession.

For once Mr. Tomlinson failed to look his usual jolly self as Pam Barratt came into his consulting room. He had offered to visit her at home, but she had insisted on coming to the hospital, despite all that was happening. Her determination to carry on was quite extraordinary. He looked through Lyndsey's file, sighed, rubbed his eyes, and pushed it away. Until that appalling policeman had put in an appearance, Lyndsey had been recovering steadily; still a little vague and unsure of herself, but that was only to be expected. Now, she was altogether too quiet. He wouldn't go so far as to call it a relapse. Not yet. But it was worrying.

"Lyndsey seems a little tired today," he said. "But that's hardly surprising under the circumstances."

Tired? Aren't we all, Pam thought sadly. She had lost count of the times that persuasive inner voice had whispered to her to give up the unequal fight and join her beloved, unhappy Harry. But Lyndsey needed her more than he did, and she had no intention of letting down her daughter. None.

"She doesn't seem to know what's been happening," she said. "It's almost as if she's a baby again."

"I should never have let that policeman in," Mr. Tomlinson muttered. "You can rest assured that I will be submitting a formal complaint. Right now, all I can do is ensure that there is no relapse, though I must say she is still making a good recovery from her injuries. We must draw some comfort from that."

Chas Hartfield sat in a corner of his local pub, knocking back lagers and feeling pretty shitty. His case was coming up before the magistrates in two weeks. The copper who'd arrested him had only charged him with possession, like that bastard in the woods had said, so he figured that maybe the magistrates would take a lenient view as it was his first offense. Sometimes people didn't even go to court. It was no big deal. He'd phoned Black Artie's mobile, taking care to make the call from a public phone box, and Black Artie had been quite impressed. "You just keep it buttoned, my man," he'd said, "and you could come up smelling Moroccan brown." So there wasn't a problem in that area. No. He was feeling shitty because he was being used by someone. Fuck knows what was going on, but someone wanted Lyndsey Barratt dropped in the crapper. As if she wasn't already round the U-bend! He couldn't figure it out, and it pissed him off. Plus he still felt nervous. The bastard in the woods had made it clear he would be watched to make sure he didn't do anything stupid. The trouble was, he didn't know what the bastard meant by stupid. Or who might be watching. All he knew was that his stomach still ached from the punch, and he wanted no more of that, thank you very much. He'd keep his head down until the court appearance and hope things would get back to normal, and fast. So he wasn't too pleased when the tall man in the old-fashioned sports jacket got a pint from the bar and came to sit at his table. "Filth" was written all over him. Chas drained his glass and stood up.

"Fancy another?"

"No thanks," Chas said.

"It wasn't a question." The copper slid a fiver at him and waited until he came back with another lager. "Keep the change," the copper said.

Chas sat down nervously as the copper pushed a chair toward him. Just what the fuck was going on?

"So, where d'you get the stuff?"

"What?" Chas said.

The copper sighed. "I suppose you're going to tell me that one of the school's other kids gets hold of it for you, but you're not sure who, because you never actually see who it is."

"I don't know what you're on about."

"Fair enough, Chas. But whatever kind of deal you've been offered over this Lyndsey Barratt thing is going to blow up in your face."

"Who the fuck are you, anyway?"

"I know for a fact that your case will be pulled. The Crown won't offer evidence, so you'll walk. Then one of my colleagues will pull your friend Black Artie. . . . They want his supplier, of course. They'll make him cough easily enough. You know how?"

Hartfield licked his lips and tried to swallow.

"They'll get him rattled, to start with. They'll tell him you cooperated with them. That's why you walked, and so can he. He can cooperate and cop a short prison sentence in an easy nick. He'll probably go along with it, but once it's all over it'll be a case of farewell Chas Hartfield. That's how it works."

Chas felt really sick. Like he was in the jaws of some bloody nutcracker and some bastard was squeezing harder and harder. How could things have gone so horribly wrong?

"Everything okay, Chas?" the bartender called. Over the past few months Hartfield had become a regular customer. Lots of cash to spend, and this tall guy seemed to be hassling him.

Chas nodded. "No problems."

"Full marks for optimism," the copper said calmly. "Now what I want you to do is this. I want you to come voluntarily to my office tomorrow morning to give me a statement." He slid his card across to Chas, who stared at it like it was primed Semtex. "You do that for me, Chas, and I'll forget all about Black Artie and you being a pusher."

"What kind of statement?"

"The kind where you tell the truth. And we both know what that'll be, don't we?"

"Listen," Chas said desperately. "There's some very heavy people in all this. What guarantees have I got?"

"None, except if you don't come to my office tomorrow you'll end up deeper in the shit than you knew was possible. In any case,

I'd advise you never to call that mobile number again. That's how I got on to you, and so did my colleagues in the Drug Squad. No one can promise anything, but you've got a chance of getting out of the business if you drop it all now. It'll be up to you.''

Something bad had happened. Something very, very bad. She could tell by the way people talked quietly when they were in her room. Her mum and dad were terribly upset when they came to see her, and she made an effort to cheer them up, but it wasn't easy. Mum seemed particularly sad today, and Dad hadn't come to see her. Probably too busy. Poor Dad. And poor Mum, too. And they still hadn't told her what had happened. She hurt somewhere inside. Deep inside, but she was not sure where. Sometimes it seemed to be in her stomach. At other times, in her backside. Why would that be? Worst of all, her head hurt. No. That was wrong. It didn't hurt. Not exactly hurt. More like an empty, buzzing ache. Lots of people came in and out of her room, and some of them made the ache feel better. Like the nurse who came and sat with her. Emily. And a man they called Mr. Tomlinson who seemed jolly and nice. And Dr. Shadri, who was very efficient and gentle. She was puzzled about the first policeman and the newspaper reporter called Julie who said she was getting a lot of money. That was how she knew something bad had happened. You don't get all this fuss with hospitals and policemen and newspapers without a good reason. But the second policeman, the one who called himself Jenkins, he had really confused her. He had made her head ache a lot worse. He seemed to believe that whatever had happened was her fault. She dimly remembered him saying something about arresting her, but that couldn't be right. Why would anyone want to arrest her? But maybe the bad thing that had happened was her fault. When she could remember what it was, she might know the answer. Meanwhile she thought that what Mr. Tomlinson had told her mother and father made a lot of sense. She must get better, no matter what. But it wasn't easy, because she did not know what she had to get better from. Her face was stiff and sore, for some reason, so she spent a lot of time trying to relax the stiffness, tightening her expression into a frown, then changing it to a smile. For days she knew this wasn't working, because it hurt too much. But eventually the pain began to subside, and the frowns and smiles were easier. If only the empty, buzzing ache in her brain would go away. She wished her dad had come today, but her mum came and cried. She always knew when Mum was crying, even though she never made a sound. Poor Dad. Poor Mum. If only she could help them. The lady with

the soft Scottish voice wanted her to help them. She and the jolly man Mr.
Tomlinson said that Lyndsey must try to be strong and to get over what had
happened so that they could put all this behind them and be a happy family
again. But Dad hadn't come today, and Mum was so desperately unhappy.
Perhaps she could get better and help them, but she didn't know what she
had to get better from, and when she tried to remember her head began to
ache again. More than ache. It was a burning, unbearable pain, and she
would have screamed if she could, but the pain froze her heart and her throat
and her lungs, so she couldn't make a sound. Despite this, Lyndsey knew
one thing very clearly indeed. No matter how unbearable, she had to under-
stand what was going on. While she was puzzling over this, someone came
and stood by her bed.

"Hello, little sister."

Linda! At last Linda was back! Lyndsey made a huge effort to forget
the pain. What a lovely surprise. Thank heavens she had practiced
smiling, because a really big one came along. And so did some tears,
but they were of pure happiness. She held out her hand and felt it
being squeezed.

"They really made a mess of you, didn't they?"

"I still don't know what's happened. I've been so confused."

"Of course you have. That's why I'm here. I'm the only one who
really understands."

"How did you get in? Everyone has to see Mr. Tomlinson, and
there's a policeman outside."

"I sneaked in when he wasn't looking. I think he's asleep, actually.
Look, we've got to get you out of here. We need to get together
properly and have a good old chat."

"I don't think I'm well enough, yet."

"Nonsense. You look as fit as a fiddle to me."

"Will you be coming back home with me?"

" 'Fraid not, little sister. And you can't go home. Not yet, anyway.
There are some things we need to sort out first."

"What kind of things?"

Linda smiled at her. "Don't worry your head about that just now.
Just get yourself up and out of here. Don't forget all your things. I'll
be waiting outside."

"Can't I come with you now?"

"No, no, that wouldn't do. We mustn't be seen together or it would give the game away. Don't worry. And be careful."

Nurse Emily Jarvis had taken time off her tea break, to read *The Wind in the Willows* at Lyndsey's bedside. It was one of her favorite books, and she hoped Lyndsey liked it, too. When she first arrived at Hope Green Hospital, the older nurses warned her not to become too involved with patients, but no one seemed to mind her slipping into Lyndsey's room to spend some time there. They seemed to understand that it was more out of respect and a wish to support the patient than sympathy. Every now and again, she would catch Lyndsey looking at her, or perhaps through her, but never saying anything. She had strict instructions to call the duty nurse if Lyndsey should speak to her.

" 'Chapter One. The Riverbank,' " she read. " 'The Mole had been working very hard all morning, spring-cleaning his little home. First with brooms, then with dusters; then on ladders and steps and chairs, with a brush and a pail of whitewash; till he had dust in his throat and eyes, and splashes of whitewash all over his black fur, and an aching back and weary arms. Spring was moving in the air above and in the earth below and around him, penetrating even his dark and lowly little house with its spirit of divine discontent and longing. It was small wonder, then, that he suddenly flung down his brush on the floor, said—' "

" 'Bother!' and 'O blow!' and also 'Hang spring-cleaning!' "

Emily gave a jump at Lyndsey's whisper.

"And he bolted out of his house without even waiting to put on his coat, didn't he?"

"Yes, yes he did. 'Something up above was calling him imperiously, and he made for the steep little tunnel which answered in his case to the graveled carriage-drive owned by animals whose residences are nearer to the sun and air . . .' "

Lyndsey smiled at her. "It's my very favorite book."

"Mine too," Emily said.

"You've been coming here quite a lot to sit with me, haven't you?"

"Yes, but I didn't think you knew."

"I've been dreaming about my mum and dad. At least I thought I was dreaming, but they've really been here, haven't they?"

The nurse nodded and looked at the bell push on the wall. "I'm supposed to call Sister if you start talking again."

"Please don't," Lyndsey pleaded. "I don't want them to come back, asking questions. I couldn't stand it."

"But your mother will want to know that you're getting better."

"No, it's the others I mean. That nasty policeman who said he was arresting me, and I don't even know what I've done."

"I really should call someone." Emily looked nervously at the door again in case the policeman on duty in the corridor could hear.

"Can't you tell me what I've done, Emily? Please. I really need to know, or I think I'll go mad."

"You haven't done anything." Emily was torn between anger and tears. "It's those little bastards from Winstanton School who should be bloody well arrested and locked up."

"Why should anyone be locked up?"

"Can't you remember anything?"

Lyndsey shook her head. "All I can remember is waking up here and feeling awful. Really, really awful. And seeing my parents crying."

"Not even the train?"

The train? Yes, there was a train, and someone was having a party, and she got in their compartment and then . . .

"No," she said firmly. "No."

Emily closed her book and stood up. "I must call Sister. I'll get into trouble."

Lyndsey pushed herself into a sitting position. "I know you want to help me, but I really couldn't face anyone right now. I need to have a little time to myself. I'm sure I'll feel much better. Anyway, I have to go to the loo."

Emily stooped under the bed and produced a bedpan. Lyndsey stared at it blankly.

"Oh dear," she said. "I haven't been using that, have I?"

"You haven't been able to move."

Lyndsey began swinging her legs out of bed. It was painful, but she managed. Emily hovered indecisively.

"You shouldn't get up. Anyway, I'm not sure that the policeman will let you. They're waiting to take your statement."

Lyndsey gave a sudden giggle. "How can I give a statement? I don't remember anything. Look. I must go. I'm desperate. You'll have to take me to the loo."

"I can't do that. What if Sister sees us?"

"I'm going to wet myself." Lyndsey was still giggling and whispering. "You've got to. Go on. I'll only be a minute. Where's my bag?" She pulled it out of the bedside cabinet. Her clothes were there too, folded up neatly. She began putting them on. Her mother had brought a clean blouse, and when she buttoned it up, she got the buttons in the wrong holes.

Emily began to catch the giggles too. "Here," she said. "You've done it all wrong." She rebuttoned the blouse and stepped back to check. "There," she said.

"You'll have to come with me, or I'll get lost."

As they stepped into the corridor, the police officer on duty looked up.

"It's all right. Lyndsey's feeling much better, but she has to go to the toilet."

"I'll have to accompany you," he said.

It set them giggling again.

"Well, if you must," Emily told him. "But we'll only be a few minutes."

"All right, but I'll have to let my inspector know." He pressed a button on his radio. "November Charlie to control . . . November Charlie to control . . . Are you reading, over . . . ?"

"Quick," Lyndsey said. "I'm really desperate."

They left the policeman trying to make radio contact. The women's lavatory was down several corridors, and Lyndsey was leaning quite hard on Emily's shoulder by the time they reached it. When she came out a few minutes later, she looked decidedly relieved.

"That's better," she said. "Is there anywhere we can get a cup of coffee and a snack before we go back? I'm absolutely ravenous."

Emily looked at her watch. The hospital cafeteria was on the ground floor. It would still be open, and Sister wasn't likely to see them. After all the excitement, she thought a coffee was a very good idea.

"All right, but we mustn't be long."

They went down in the porter's lift, and Emily picked up a tray as Lyndsey peered at the food counter and took some money from her purse.

"A coffee and one of those lovely cheese and pickle rolls, and whatever you're having," she said.

Emily made her way down the serving counter. When she paid and turned to see which table Lyndsey was at, her patient had vanished.

Chapter 9

LYNDSEY'S DISAPPEARANCE CREATED CHAOS IN AN AL-ready chaotic situation, and the unfortunate Nurse Jarvis took the initial brunt of the storm before her union representative stepped in to insist she be given a chance to explain matters in a more settled environment. The hospital governors announced that there would be an inquiry that would involve asking the police some pointed questions about the manner in which they began proceedings against a suspect in hospital care. Friends and family rallied around Pam Barratt, who found an inner strength to remain calm amid the frantic activity surrounding her. The parents of the cricket team found they had another problem to worry about, with more unwelcome publicity about the Barratt case, the possible involvement of their sons, and "the questions that need to be answered," as the journalists put it.

The *National Clarion* tried to recoup some of its investment in the story by mounting a "Have you seen Lyndsey?" campaign with a ten-thousand-pound reward. But there was no trace of Lyndsey until Detective Inspector Illiffe suggested taking a look at her bank account. The day after walking out of her room in Hope Green Hospital, Lyndsey had closed her account and withdrawn all her money as cash at a branch in London.

Illiffe met Julie Adams for a farewell lunchtime drink in the pub by the canal. He arrived early and ordered two pints of bitter and packets of plain potato chips. The same family of swans was drifting beside the towpath, waiting for a contribution. He obliged, flicking chips into the water and watching as the graceful necks undulated and the golden beaks chattered the chips into edible mushy fragments.

The Kawasaki grumbled into the parking lot right on time, and Julie walked toward him. She grabbed a pint and downed it in one gulp.

"You look absolutely shagged out," she told him.

"Thanks a lot."

She gave him that dazzling smile. "You know me. Tell it like it is. So, what are you going to do now?"

"Besides generating a mountain of reports, you mean?"

"Yeah. What's going to happen to the bad guys?"

"Nothing, until we find Lyndsey and she prefers charges. I'll push the case for breaching Railtrack bylaws by smoking, but apart from your photographer's statement there's no evidence for any other charges, and what he says doesn't amount to much." He didn't tell her he intended to make an official complaint against Detective Inspector Keith Jenkins. That was internal police business.

"No," she said. "I don't suppose it does."

"What about you?"

"My editor wants me to do an in-depth piece on multiple rapes. You know. Victims of the gang bang: Where are they now? It'll keep the pot boiling until Lyndsey turns up."

"Jesus."

"That's what I thought, but it's a living. After that, I don't know. There's an offer on the table from a TV company."

"What kind of offer?"

"Action TV," she explained. "They're starting a new series of investigative programs next year, and they need a presenter."

"I think you'd make a very good presenter," he told her.

"So do I." The smile hit him again. "I'll get us another pint."

He watched as she went into the pub. What a waste of a good woman. Sod that Dave Edwards, he thought bitterly. On the other hand, if the loathsome photographer hadn't told him about Julie's sexual orientation, he could have made a real fool of himself. Then he realized that it wasn't only sex. Julie had got to him in other ways. He liked her vitality and her directness. He even liked her insults. In fact, he liked every damned thing about her. Probably the best thing he could do was take off while she was in the pub and let her drink the beer on her own. But when she came into the sunlight carrying the pints, her eyes met his, and it was too late. He had a funny feeling that she was reading his thoughts.

She put the pint in front of him, turning the glass so he could easily take the handle. "There," she said.

"Thanks."

"You're looking pretty serious."

"Tough day. Tough week."

She nodded, then said, "Edwards told you, didn't he?"

"Told me what?"

"Don't play games, Frank."

"Yes, he told me. The trouble is I'm trying not to play games. You've no idea how hard I'm trying. God dammit!"

Edwards had been very specific. Spitefully specific, as if he knew that Illiffe's interest in Julie was changing from the professional into something more personal.

"The woman's a dyke, boyo," he'd said. "I mean, I spotted it right off, didn't I? I'd have been in like Flynn otherwise, I can tell you. In fact, if she'd stayed at my place a bit longer, I might have turned the bloody tables. She was definitely beginning to fancy me. Definitely."

"You don't want to believe everything a newspaperman tells you," Julie said solemnly to Illiffe. "Especially a prat like Dave Edwards."

He took a deep breath. "So why did he tell me? What was the point?"

"Because I told him I was. It's the best way I know to keep dick-heads like Edwards at arm's length. Works every time."

"Does 'dickhead' include coppers?"

"If the cap fits."

It caught them on a nerve, and they both needed a bloody good laugh. Other drinkers looked around good-naturedly. It took five minutes before they could settle down, wipe their eyes, get back to being serious.

"What are we going to do now?" he wondered.

"I think you've forgotten how to pull, Detective Inspector," she said. "You're supposed to make me an offer that I don't want to refuse."

She was right. He couldn't remember the last time anything like this had happened. A long time ago.

"Have you booked out of your hotel yet?"

"I thought you'd never ask," she said. "I've booked out, but we can always book back in."

He followed her into the hotel foyer and up to the reception desk. The clerk made a point of not looking at either of them as she swiped Illiffe's credit card through her machine and activated a security key for a room. Illiffe felt as guilty as sin. Julie told him later that he looked that way as well. They raided the autobar and emptied it of its half bottles of champagne at ludicrous prices, poured the first one into plastic cups, took a gulp, and made love. Only it was by no means as quick as that. They both found themselves unaccountably shy. So kissing was a good way to start, tasting the lust in each other's mouth, sliding lips over faces and down necks, feeling hands moving nervously toward secret places and moving back as if, somehow, to touch would shatter this incredible feeling. And she began to moan. It was such a basic noise that the hairs on the back of his neck bristled. The hands became more directed, more determined, fumbled with zips and buttons, tore at shirt and underwear, until they were both wrestling naked on the bed, frantic to couple, until she managed to slow herself down, slow him down, push him back to gaze at his body and let his eyes feast on hers. After that everything seemed to be in slow and very deliberate motion, with fingers, lips and tongues exploring everything that possibly could be explored. When he entered her they tried to maintain this sensual composure, tried to move in such a way that each could feel every tiny part of the other, prolonging the sheer ecstasy of intercourse. Afterward, they lay like two exhausted animals, incapable of anything except taking in great gulps of air.

Later, she snuggled into him and lay very quietly. He knew she was thinking of Lyndsey Barratt because he was thinking of Lyndsey too. Sex for her had been a calamity. Not like this.

"What happens if no one ever finds her?" Julie asked. "There's lots of runaways who are never found. What happens to your case?"

"What case?" he asked wryly. "She never did make a formal complaint of rape. Until she turns up and makes a statement, the whole thing goes on the shelf."

"You mean, those little shits will get away with it."

"Yes," he said. "Apart from the loose ends, they'll be home and dry."

Part II

HEATHSIDE

Chapter 10

JULY. UNSEASONABLY DAMP. COOL WINDS FORECAST. DEB-orah Lambert walked down the tree-lined road from the bus stop, looking at the entrances to the houses. Steps of Portland stone leading up from the sidewalk to tiled porches with time-pocked marble balustrades. Almost all the huge buildings had the multiple doorbell and intercom assemblies that denoted their conversion from Victorian, single-family dwellings into flats and maisonettes. A few had been taken over by businesses, and she could see people sitting hunched in front of computer screens. Heathside seemed quite an expensive area, but the rent for the room would be within her means if she landed the project with the car dealership. If not, well, there were lots of opportunities for her skills in a city like London. The property agent in Chester had checked her references and taken a deposit against breakages and a nonrefundable commission. He said she was exactly the kind of tenant that the landlady had specified. Miss Marshall was not too sure of her movements that day, so Deb-orah had to pick up the keys from the agent's Baker Street office and let herself into the flat.

Deborah wondered what Miss Marshall would be like, whether the room would be suitable, if they would get on well together. Well, here she was, and there was only one way to find out. She walked up the steps of number sixteen, opened the front door, and took the lift to the third floor. One flat per landing. That was good. More privacy. Some of the places she'd stayed in had been most unsuitable. Noisy, sharing common facilities, dowdy. But this was a decided improvement.

She used the Banham security key and found herself in a luxuriously appointed hallway. Nothing flashy or overdone. In fact, quite discreet, but if she wasn't very much mistaken there were several original paintings hanging under tiny spotlights. She peered at one closely. The signature looked like Degas. My God, it must be worth a fortune. No wonder there were deadlocks and hinge bolts in the door. There were also alarm sensors blinking red at her from vantage points in the ceiling.

The hallway was T-shaped, and the hardwood doors leading off it were all closed. Each one had a label. The first door on the left was the living room. The one on the right was the cloakroom. The second on the left was the dining room, and the kitchen was opposite. The main bathroom was around the corner, to the right, and at the end of the corridor the label on the door said "Sister's Room." The room directly facing the front door was "Linda's Room." Next to that was the utility room, and at the end of that bit of corridor, facing Sister's Room, was "Flatmate's Room." All the doors were fitted with expensive mortice locks.

The agent had told her that if Miss Marshall was out she should wait in the kitchen for her to arrive. It seemed an odd arrangement, but who was she to object? She put her bags down in the hall and found her way to the kitchen. It had every conceivable gadget to make life easy, from an electric can opener to a microwave oven, large fridge-freezer, dishwasher, washer-dryer, and an oven with eye-level grill and self-igniting gas burners.

There was a note on the table: *"Miss Lambert. Please make yourself at home. Help yourself to tea or whatever you fancy. Shouldn't be too long. Linda Marshall."* For a while she felt too embarrassed to accept the invitation, but eventually she found some tea bags and sweetener in a cupboard and a carton of semiskimmed milk in the fridge. Miss Marshall had obviously been out shopping, she thought, because none of the items had been opened. In fact nothing in the food cupboards or fridge had been used at all.

There was a small radio set on a shelf, and when the tea was ready she turned it on in time to hear the last twenty minutes of a program about Schubert's songs. Very pleasant and relaxing, after tramping around London.

"Well, at least you're punctual. Don't just sit there. Come in and help me."

The voice came from Linda's Room. The door was unlocked, so she pushed it open and went in. It wasn't exactly a bedroom, although a large four-poster bed dominated the far wall. Deborah's first impression was of a studio of some kind, with video equipment, lighting and backdrops of exotic tropical scenes. On closer examination she realized that these were tapestries, executed in remarkable detail and obviously worth a great deal of money. They were also erotic rather than exotic, depicting groupings of humans and animals in positions that would tax the skills of a circus contortionist. Deborah felt her cheeks turning red.

"Does this suit me?" the voice said. "I've been to one of those color charting gurus, and I'm not sure if they're talking crap or not. What do you think?"

Miss Marshall walked from behind a screen wearing a dress that swirled in the air and then clung tantalizingly to her body like a gown of gossamer worn by a fantasy heroine. She was outstandingly beautiful. Her dark hair fell lightly to finely sculpted shoulders. Her lips were blue, outlined in black, and her eyes were shaded in opal green. On anyone else the combination would have looked dreadful. On her it looked wonderful.

"I think . . . I think it's beautiful."

"I know it's beautiful," Miss Marshall said testily. "What I want to know is whether it suits me or not."

"Oh yes," Deborah said, nodding vigorously.

"Well, I'm not so sure. My normal colors are sort of bluey and greeny. This is sort of browny."

She turned around, and the dress swirled and settled again on a figure that made Deborah feel like a frump.

"I'm just not sure," Miss Marshall said again.

"Perhaps . . ." Deborah said, then stopped.

"Perhaps what?" Miss Marshall demanded. "Dear God, I hope you're not one of those awful little people who can't say boo to a gander."

"I was just going to say that perhaps you should change your lipstick. You're wearing blue . . . and your eye shadow is green. . . ."

Miss Marshall glared at her, then vanished behind her screen.

"Pour us a drink, will you? The bar's over there."

It's funny how some people always assume you know what they mean when they say "Over there," Deborah thought. She also thought Miss Marshall was a bit overwhelming. Not what she had expected. Not what she liked.

The bar was in a recess behind ornate wicker folding doors. It contained more kinds of drinks than a hotel cocktail lounge. There was even a carbonation machine for homemade tonic water and an ice machine with an electrically powered crusher.

"Mix me a Sicilian," Miss Marshall called.

Deborah was about to tell her that she had no idea what a Sicilian or any other kind of cocktail was, but she spotted a row of books, one of which promised to turn the reader into the second-best cocktail shaker in the world (the author claimed pride of place). She searched for the ingredients, which included tequila and bitters, and tried the ice-crushing machine. It made such an appalling racket that she almost leaped backward. She shook the mixture, poured it into a cocktail glass, and added the finishing touch. An anchovy and a black olive skewered on a cocktail stick. It smelled dreadful.

As she stood holding the glass, Miss Marshall came into the room again. The striking makeup had been replaced by altogether softer, warmer colors that blended in with the dress in such a way that its fine material lent an even more sensual air to its wearer than before. The dark hair must have been a wig, because she was now a gorgeous shade of honey blond, fine hair hanging as straight as only natural hair can. The effect was devastating. Deborah thought she was the most beautiful woman she had ever seen in her life.

"Oh, that's lovely."

"My name's Linda." Miss Marshall held her hand out for the drink. "I'll call you Deborah. And you can forget about all this 'tenant' stuff. I'm looking for a flatmate, and you were highly recommended. You were right about the lipstick. You haven't got yourself a drink. What'll you have?"

"Sorry. Just an orange juice, please."

"Carton's in the fridge. Get a glass and come and tell me about yourself."

Linda floated to a chaise longue and draped herself along it. Deborah sat in an upright chair, sipping her drink nervously.

"Well?"

"I'm looking for work and I need a place to stay."

"What kind of work?"

"I'm a freelance programmer."

"How very exciting. I used to work in television too, but that was way back, of course. In the young, heady days. It was fun then, I can tell you. No one gave a shit, and everyone had money. Not like now. Everyone's so concerned, aren't they? I mean, they're concerned with pollution, they're concerned with infant-mortality rates, they're concerned with senile dementia. Dear God, is there anything they're not concerned about, I ask you? Is that the kind of program you work on?"

Deborah shook her head. "No, I mean, I'm not actually in television. I write programs for computers."

Linda stared at her blankly. "Well, never mind. Have you got any other peculiar habits? You know, snoring or something? You can hear snoring through six-foot walls."

Deborah shook her head again. "I don't think so."

"Well, I have. For one thing I sleep during the day and have a bloody good time at night. The neighbors think I'm a bit, you know"—she twirled a finger—"so I keep myself to myself. Course, I've made a few friends since I moved in. People like myself, mainly. People who don't give a shit. I'm rather hoping I can find someone who can handle all that. You know, cope with it. Maybe help out with a bit of shopping here and there. I mean, if you sleep all day, it's not easy to stock up with the right kind of food, is it?"

She stared at Deborah and Deborah stared at the floor, not knowing what to say. This wasn't at all what she had expected. She felt completely out of her depth and wished she could be out on the street with her bags looking for somewhere else.

"How easy is it to get your kind of work?"

"There's a lot of good programmers on the market."

"So it's not easy."

"No. Not very. But they're looking for someone at a car company near here."

There was a pause.

Linda said, "You don't have very much to say for yourself, do you?"

Deborah put her glass firmly on a table and stood up. "I'm not at all sure this would work out for me."

"At least have a look at the room while you're here. If you don't like me, that might not be a problem, because we won't see too much of each other. If you don't like the room, well, fair enough."

Perhaps it was tiredness, or the uncertainty of trying to find somewhere to work on a project-by-project basis and somewhere to live as one job finishes and another begins, but when Deborah opened the door to Flatmate's Room her eyes filled with tears. It was a bed/sitting room, with a lovely big bed, a settee that looked like a put-you-up so a friend could stay, TV and music center in one corner. Linda had lit a few aromatic candles and put flowers in vases on tables and the mantelpiece. The pictures on the walls were prints taken from children's stories: Toad and Moly, Peter Rabbit, and Black Beauty. A pine bookcase was full of classics and reference books on travel, animals, and a host of other subjects that Deborah loved. The wallpaper was a cheerful shade of rose that blended with the window drapes and the bedspread. Around the corner she could see the entrance to an en-suite bathroom, and she was unable to resist tiptoeing over the deep carpet to take a peek. Everything was a soft peach color. She looked at the bath and wished she could just peel her clothes off and jump into a warm, embracing mountain of bubbles.

"What d'you think?" Linda's voice sounded gently in her ear.

"It's lovely," she breathed. "Really lovely."

"I know I'm a bit of a bitch, but I really do think we'd get on famously."

Deborah felt herself weakening. "It's all a bit grander than I was looking for."

"If you're worried about the rent while you're looking for work, we can always put things on hold until you find something. It's not so much the money I'm looking for. It's a bit of company. You know, someone to shout at if there're no more anchovies for my Sicilians."

Deborah's shoulders began to shake, and she felt two arms take hold of her in a nice, huggy kind of way. She turned around and sank her face into the designer dress, feeling her tears soaking into the fabric, feeling Linda's hands stroking her hair.

"I take it that's a yes," Linda said softly.

While Deborah unpacked, Linda ordered a takeout from a nearby French restaurant whose manager normally refused such a service but was happy to accept a twenty-pound inducement. When the bell rang, Linda gave Deborah seventy pounds.

"Tell Joel he can keep the change," she said.

Deborah released the front door catch and waited for the lift to arrive. A young waiter stepped out and looked surprised to see her waiting.

"I have an order for Miss Marshall."

"Yes," she said, handing him the money. "She said you can keep the change."

He looked embarrassed. "But it is too much. The bill is for sixty-two pounds, with service included. Perhaps she has made a mistake?"

"I don't think Miss Marshall is the kind of person who makes mistakes like that," Deborah said.

It was a splendid meal, during which Linda laid down a few house rules. The hall, kitchen, and dining room were common ground. The put-you-up could be used if Deborah wanted a friend to stay. Their own bedrooms were off-limits to each other, except by invitation. Sister's Room was off-limits no matter what! She'd suffered a dreadful experience and needed absolute privacy whenever she visited. There was no problem about Deborah using her portable computer and modem. Any extra phone charges would be shown on the bill, and they could settle up then.

Linda said she'd seen an ad by a local car showroom. Shackleton Motors, she thought it was.

That was the one, Deborah told her. Someone at her previous job in Chester had slipped her a note about it when her project there had finished.

If she didn't make it with the car company, Linda said, the local paper usually had lots of jobs.

Deborah said she'd get a paper in the morning and have a look. She also said she wouldn't mind taking over the shopping. It was the least she could do in view of Linda's generosity about the rent. So it seemed they were off to a flying start. Deborah wondered what would go wrong. Something always did, in her experience. But right now everything was fine, but she was feeling really, really tired. After a couple of wide yawns, she declared that she was ready for bed.

When Deborah had gone to her bedroom, Linda returned to her own room. It was a few minutes to ten o'clock. At ten precisely the phone rang. She carried it to her chaise longue and made herself comfortable before answering it.

"Hello, Pimples," she said. "Have you been a bad boy again? No, I don't want you to come round tonight. I know you need spanking, darling. But I don't feel like it. Of course there's no one else here. Nursey only spanks Pimples, doesn't she? If you whine like that, I'm going to become really angry with you. Spanking will be far too good for you. I'll have to tie you up and punish you with my little leather strap. You're such a bad boy. Oh, all right then. You'd better come round right away, so Nurse can deal with you."

She put the phone down, went behind the screen, and came out after a few minutes wearing a nurse's uniform that was short and tight, showing a glimpse of thigh and black stocking tops. Her breasts were straining against the blue tunic under the white apron. Her hair was pulled back severely and tucked under a starched cap. When the buzzer sounded she glanced at the TV security screen and pressed the front-door-release button before opening the flat door and returning to her room.

The man who came in a few moments later was elderly and well dressed. Without a word he handed Linda an envelope, which she opened to check the contents. When she was satisfied she threw it carelessly onto a table.

"Nurse is very, very angry with you, Pimples."

"I'm sorry. I'm so sorry," he said. "I'll do anything to make up. Anything."

"I need to examine you. You must take off all your clothes before I decide what to do with you."

He began undressing, while Linda strode up and down, staring at him and cracking a leather strap into the palm of her hand. When he was naked she looked at his penis.

"You naughty, naughty boy. Nurse will have to teach you a lesson that you'll never forget. Never, ever."

"Oh please, Nursey," he said in a high-pitched voice.

She walked across the room to a wooden frame. "Come over here, you bad, wicked little boy."

He obediently placed his arms and legs against the wooden supports, and she began tying him to the frame with Velcro straps, crooning to him. "Wicked boy, bad boy. Been having naughty thoughts about Nurse, have you? Yes, I can see you have. What a naughty boy you are. We'll have to beat you, and beat you . . ."

She began caressing his legs and arms with her strap, flicking them occasionally, with increasing speed. He groaned.

"Please, Nursey, I can't help it."

"You can't help it?" The sound of the leather hitting his body became sharper. "I'll teach you to think naughty thoughts, you little bastard. I'll teach you to stand there with your prick swelling like that. Want to put it near me, don't you?"

"Oh yes, yes," he moaned.

"He's another naughty little man, isn't he? I'll have to tie him up as well."

She took a silk cord from her waist and pulled a loop around his penis until it had almost doubled in size. She then began to strip off her uniform, easing and teasing it over her body until she was wearing only a G-string and halter.

"You'd like Nurse to lick your naughty lollipop, wouldn't you, Pimples? Well, I'm not going to. You've been such a bad, bad, wicked little boy. But just as a tiny little treat, I might press my breasts into it. You'd like that, wouldn't you?"

He was almost fainting with lust, incapable of a coherent reply.

"But five hundred pounds isn't enough for Nurse. You've been so very, very bad. Nurse wants more. She wants a lot more. That's all right, isn't it, Pimples?"

He nodded frantically, and she swayed over to his jacket and took out his wallet.

"Fifty, one hundred, one hundred and fifty, two hundred, three, and fifty more because you've been so terribly naughty. . . ."

His body was arching toward her as she threw the money onto the table and knelt in front of him, cupping her breasts in her hands and rolling them into his testicles.

"Oh my," she said, "Oh my, what a lovely, lovely lollipop."

Her mouth slipped over the end of his penis and began sucking, feeling the pulsing begin, taking his ejaculations into her mouth, and when he had finished she stood up and spat the semen into his face.

"You wicked, wicked boy. Look what you made Nurse do. Shame on you."

She flipped the restraints from his wrists and vanished behind her screen with the money. She did not come out until she heard the front door close. Then she lounged back on her seat and waited for the phone to ring again. Her next appointment was for twelve o'clock. She always gave herself plenty of time to recover her composure and settle into the next role. Two hours between each of her nocturnal clients.

In the morning, Deborah woke up to the refreshing smell of lavender and the wonderful relaxed feeling that follows a truly restful sleep. It was ten minutes before her alarm was due to warble, but she canceled it and got out of bed anyway, letting her toes dig into the pile. In two minutes she was treating herself to a bubble bath, eyes closed. As she lay there she heard a door slam, but thought nothing of it. Probably a neighbor going to work, which reminded her that she had to find out about the job at the car showroom, and quickly.

On her way to the kitchen she saw that Linda had stuck an envelope to her bedroom door. It said: "*Good luck with job. Use enclosed to get anchovies and whatever else you fancy. May see you this evening.*" There were two fifty-pound notes inside the envelope. She went quietly to the kitchen and found some cornflakes, munching them while the kettle came to the boil, then made herself some black coffee. It seemed a good time to get to know the kitchen, so she fetched a notebook from her room and began checking what was in the cupboards and fridge-freezer.

Whatever else, it was clear that Linda was not a vegetarian. Boxes of fillet steaks, lamb chops, and other meats took up both the bottom racks. Frozen gourmet meals-in-boxes took up the rest of the freezer space. In the cupboards she found pulses of all kinds, pasta, sauces, herbs and spices. The only things missing were everyday consumables, such as milk, bread, and eggs. She put them on her list and wondered if Linda had been serious about the anchovies, but there was no way of checking that without going into her room, so she put one tin on the list. When she could think of nothing else she put the list in her bag and checked her purse. She had fifteen pounds and a few pence, more than enough to buy a bunch of flowers as a present for Linda out of her own money, without going to a bank. Not that there was much in the bank to go for. She had to find work, and for her particular talents the best places were small companies run by people who needed computer systems but knew little or nothing about them.

As she sat and sipped her coffee, she wondered if she had made a mistake in accepting the room. Everything seemed perfect, although there was the problem of Linda herself. The woman was highly strung, to say the least, very artistic, and Deborah was not sure she could cope with that. But the thought of going back to the grubby hotel she'd been staying in, then back to the rental agent and starting the whole rigmarole over again was too much to bear. It was up to her to find work so she could start paying her rent, saving money, and settling down. She scribbled a note in case Linda got up before she returned, put on her hat and coat, and went to explore the neighborhood.

In a small street leading up a hill off the main road, Deborah found a parade of well-appointed shops, including a cosy-looking pub called the White Swan, a shop stocked with wonderful old items of brass and leather, an art gallery with strange shapes in stone and wood, a newsstand and stationer, a bookshop, an upscale food store and l'Étoile au Printemps, the French restaurant and wine bar from which Linda had ordered last night's takeout. The young waiter who had brought the meal was unstacking plastic tables and arranging them on the patio. As she passed, he looked up and gave her a shy smile. The newsstand next to the café was open, and she bought a local paper. Back on the sidewalk, she opened the paper to the jobs section, battling a little against the slight breeze.

"Perhaps you would like a coffee?" The waiter was smiling at her and indicating one of the tables. "It would be easier to read your newspaper."

She shook her head, shyly. "Thanks all the same. I have some shopping to do."

"The shops don't open until nine o'clock," he said. "The boss doesn't mind people coming here for an early-morning coffee and croissant. 'Why not?' he says. 'Good for business.' So people come and read their newspapers while I get ready."

"If you're sure it's no trouble."

He smiled and held a chair for her. "No trouble."

As she sat scanning the jobs column a man with gray hair and a warm, lived-in face nodded to her pleasantly and sat at a nearby table with a copy of the *Guardian*.

"Morning, Joel," he called. "Large black, please. Very large." He leaned toward Deborah conspiratorially and whispered, "Bit of a night last night, I'm afraid. Book got published. Very exciting."

"Oh," she said, but that didn't seem an appropriate response to someone who had just had a book published. "Was it your first one?"

"First one to be published." He nodded. "Fiction, that is. Written a few tomes on engineering. Passion of mine, engineering. You mustn't get me started, or I'll be telling you about the foundations of the BT tower and how the pillars of the Humber Bridge are further apart at the top than they are at the bottom because of the curvature of the earth. There you are: I'm off already. . . . By the way, the name's Leo Chindwall."

His smile was infectious.

"Deborah Lambert."

He took her hand and shook it warmly. "Moved into our enclave, or just passing through?"

"Moved in. I've taken a room round the corner."

The waiter, Joel, brought out three coffees and put the third on another table. The author looked at his watch and began an ostentatious countdown.

"Ten, nine, eight, seven, six, five, four, three, two, one, zero!"

A few seconds later an elderly woman with a bichon frise arrived. The dog stared at Deborah and growled.

"You're late, Marge," the author scolded.

"Get away with you! Joel, I'll have a pain au chocolat this morning, heated up in that contraption thing of yours. And bring one for Wilfred."

"Certainly, Mrs. Harrison."

The newcomer looked at Deborah while the dog sniffed tentatively at her ankles and growled again. "Oh do shut up, Wilfred. And what's your name, young lady?"

"It's Deborah Lambert," Leo told her. "A new neighbor."

Wilfred started barking.

"Shut up, Wilfred. I don't know what's got into you this morning. Nice to meet you, Deborah. I'm Marge Harrison. Have you explained the ground rules, Leo?"

"Marge," Leo protested, "this young lady was just sitting here when I arrived. She isn't interested in how we Heathsiders begin our daily grind."

"Nonsense. If she's a resident that's the first thing she'll want to know. How to get on with all the new people she'll meet. Such as her new landlady, the mysterious Miss Marshall. Am I not right, my dear?"

Deborah was greatly surprised. How did this little old lady know where she was now living? The question showed on her face.

"A simple enough deduction," Marge explained proudly. "Mrs. Patel has taken Miss Marshall's advertisement out of her window, and she told me that she had a new customer this morning, a nice young lady wearing a dark coat and a woolly hat who had just that minute bought the local rag. Presto!"

Deborah laughed. "Are there no secrets?"

"Not in Heathside," Leo sighed. "And certainly not within a mile of our Mrs. Harrison, with the possible exception of your Miss Marshall."

"Why did you call her mysterious?" Deborah asked them. "She's very charming."

"She comes, she goes," Marge said. "Never to the High Street, though. Out of the door, into a cab, and off into the night. Never gets close enough to say hello—"

"Marge, really!" Leo interrupted. "Here we are, gossiping about this young lady's new landlady! I apologize, Miss Lambert, for our unfeeling crassness. And Marge does too, don't you, Marge? Will you ever forgive us?"

Two real characters! Deborah couldn't remember when she'd had such a surprising morning, and a pleasant one. Who would have expected such an easygoing atmosphere in a city? Well, yes, they were not exactly in the city itself; more on the gentrified outskirts, but even so.

"Of course I do. But only on condition that you tell me about these ground rules of yours."

"There's only one, and it's not mine," he protested. "Nothing to do with me. Ask Marge."

"Reprobate!" Marge snorted the epithet. "You see, my dear Miss Lambert, how he behaves. If we didn't have some rules, we'd never get anywhere. It's very simple. We arrive here, and Joel serves coffee. If it's cold, we sit inside. If it's fine, like today, we sit on the patio. Very pleasant. And we talk. Or, rather, Leo talks. And if we let him carry on, we'd never get to read our newspapers. So we allow ten minutes for talking and ten for reading, and so on. That way we at least get to know what's going on in the world, and have a modicum of fruitful discussion about important issues, without this incessant chatter about bridges and bending moments and other such nonsense."

"And she says *I* talk a lot," Leo observed indulgently.

"So, what do you think of this rule of ours, Miss Lambert?" Marge inquired.

"I think it's quite sensible, really. I mean, it's lovely to talk with someone, but I have to start looking for a job, so ten minutes on and ten minutes off would be exactly right for me, wouldn't it? And please call me Deborah."

"You don't say," Leo said. "And what sort of job are you looking for?"

"Something in business administration," she told him. "I'm particularly interested in computing systems. The last job I had was setting up a system in a car showroom in Chester, and there's another one near here that's been advertising for the same kind of thing."

"That'd probably be Shackleton Motors," Leo observed. "It's run by a friend of mine, as a matter of fact. Peter Shackleton. They're always on the lookout for good people. I take it you are a good person, Deborah."

"I'm sure Deborah is excellent at whatever she turns her hand to," Marge observed.

"I've had a quick look in the paper, and they seem to have stopped advertising," Deborah said.

"No problem," Leo said emphatically. "I know for a fact they've not taken on any new staff. You've got to get in there before they advertise again. Young Peter's always complaining they can't keep up with developments in this and developments in that. Why not give him a call? Tell him Leo said you should. In fact, I'll ring him myself to break the ice."

"No, really . . ." she began, but Leo had already dragged a mobile phone from his pocket and jabbed the buttons.

"Hello, Peter. It's Leo . . . Fine, fine . . . Thanks very much. It's in the bookshops today. The only thing to worry about now is if the bloody thing sells or not. . . . Yes . . . Look, old man. Got a young neighbor here who's looking for a job. . . . Now hold on. You're always bleating on about your bloody computers, aren't you? She's a computer whiz kid." He covered the mouthpiece and hissed, "You are a computer whiz kid, aren't you?"

"Well . . ."

"She says she is," Leo bellowed down the phone. "So what's it going to cost you to have a chat? . . . Of course she's attractive. You don't think I'd be spending all this time talking about someone who wouldn't do you credit, do you? . . . Right, I'll send her round. . . . Half an hour." He disconnected. "There you are. All set up."

"But I'm not dressed for an interview."

"Fiddlesticks and tosh. What do you think, Marge?"

Marge looked up from her paper and smiled at Deborah. "You look perfectly charming, my dear. I've always liked woolly hats, my-self."

Peter Shackleton put down the phone and glared at the computer console on his desk. To be fair to the computer, it wasn't the only piece of equipment that was causing concern. There were the telephones and the fax machines. Shackleton Motors had eight branches, each with a manager who had been given responsibility over the years for building up an administrative system suitable for his particular area of the market. None of these systems could work with each other. In addition, the company had several motor franchises, and each motor manufacturer ran a data system that was incompatible with the others. This meant that each branch was locked into a particular

manufacturer, a cause of considerable annoyance to Shackleton, because he wanted to juggle things around with the franchises, to get
a leverage on the manufacturers, to squeeze more margins and pro-
motional budgets out of them. What made everything even more
complicated was the plethora of cable companies offering alternative telecommunication systems to the managers in the various
branches. The cable sales representatives were all blandly confident
that this would cause no problem, but at the very least it would
mean eight different sets of phone bills at a time when Shackleton
was trying to consolidate services into the main office where he
worked.

Three months ago, his father had introduced a firm of consultants
who claimed they could provide a central solution, but all they did
was listen hard to the problem and submit a lengthy and expensive
report many weeks later telling him what the problem was. Jesus!

It was kind of old Leo to phone him about this girl he'd met.
Probably a waste of time. The man was nobody's fool, but inclined
to let his enthusiasm run away with things. But like Leo said, what
did Shackleton have to lose by seeing her?

When his secretary showed Deborah into his office, he gave an
inward sigh. What he had to lose was time, and this frumpy little
thing seemed all set to lose it for him. She was wearing a long baggy
coat and a shapeless, knitted woollen hat and was clutching a plastic
shopping bag.

He stood up and gestured to a chair. "Do come in. I'm afraid Leo
didn't give me your name."

She sat down and put the shopping bag carefully on the floor, only
for it to collapse and send a cabbage and several apples rolling across
the floor. She gathered them together, face turning red.

"Deborah Lambert," she said. "Sorry . . ."

"Don't worry about it," he told her, looking at his watch. "Look,
I don't know if Leo bothered to tell you anything about our IT
problems, but they're fairly substantial. What kind of experience have
you got?"

She had managed to scan one of his company's brochures in the
waiting room, and she could make a shrewd guess at some of his
problem areas.

"Mainly business computing and data networks," she said. "I've also been involved in setting up voice and data telecom systems for conferencing and telemarketing. But most of the problems I solve are pretty basic."

"You don't say. What about faxes?"

The question took her by surprise. A fax is a fax is a fax.

"I'm not sure what you mean."

"This thing here is what I mean," he said. "Half the time my managers try to phone me, this bloody machine turns itself on, and the phone's bloody useless. It's got so that when they want to talk to me they have to send a fax and I ring 'em back, for God's sake."

She leaned forward to see, then got out of her chair and crawled under his desk to look at the wiring.

"You're running your phone and fax on the same line, with a fax switch, aren't you?"

He nodded. "Saves having a separate line."

"And you're on a BT circuit, and these managers are on a mix of cable and mobile."

"No idea." He shrugged.

"I think you'll find they are," she said, crawling back to her chair. "Some calls are preceded by a tone frequency of one thousand one hundred and eleven cycles per second, which is exactly the same tone that some of the older fax machines generate to tell other fax machines they're calling. Your fax switch is designed to switch all calls starting with that tone to the fax. That's why your managers can't always get through."

He stared blankly. "You don't say," he said again.

"You can either ask the carriers to switch the tone off at their exchange, or you can standardize your equipment. The new combined phone, fax, and answering machines have software that solves the problem, and they have other advantages as well."

"Would you like a cup of tea, or coffee, Miss, er . . ."

"Lambert. No thanks. I've just had breakfast."

"Have you got a CV with you?"

"I'm sorry, I haven't," she said. "I actually came out to do some shopping before looking for work, but I can send one later if you want."

"Well . . ." Shackleton said thoughtfully, "I'm not taking on extra staff at the moment."

"That's all right," she said. "I work on contract. If I do my job properly, you won't need me after a few weeks."

He was intrigued by this approach. "Why not?"

"I fix systems so they're easy to run and maintain," she said. "That's what you want, isn't it?"

Was it ever what he wanted! She might look like a vague weirdo, but she knew what she was talking about. She'd made more sense in five minutes than his father's consultants had made in five weeks.

"What's your day rate?" he asked.

Deborah knew what she was worth but always found if difficult to talk about money. She supposed it was her middle-class background. If she had been an ICL consultant the company would be charging her out at around a thousand pounds a day and paying her the salary equivalent of one-fifty. The last client had agreed to pay her two hundred pounds a day but had argued about her invoice and refused to pay her after the job was complete. They'd been in the middle of an increasingly tense letter-writing campaign when he'd been killed by a hit-and-run driver and his deputy had not unnaturally asked if she wouldn't mind waiting for a few weeks while he sorted things out. Which was why she was having to watch the pennies.

"I charge thirty-five pounds an hour," she told Shackleton.

He sucked in his cheeks and did some rapid calculations. "That's over a hundred grand a year!"

They all did it! They all assumed she could work an eight-hour day, three hundred and sixty-five days a year, then compared that figure with their own salary. They didn't give a damn about the times she didn't work, or the equipment she had to buy, or the holidays she cut short because something came up that she couldn't afford to turn away.

"I wish!" she said politely. "Last year my earnings grossed rather less than a fifth of that, and I spend quite a lot on running my business, like you do. I think thirty-five pounds an hour is really quite reasonable."

It was more than reasonable. The consultants had charged a day rate of six hundred pounds. Their bill for a load of crap had come to more than eight thousand pounds.

"If you can convince me that you can handle our problems, I'll pay you twenty-five pounds an hour on an agreed schedule of work."

She knew she was unlikely to get a better offer without spending days or even weeks looking around.

"You already know I can cope. You've got a network and data distribution problem. I can make recommendations for the cheapest and most effective way to sort it out and allow for future growth. That's what you'll be paying me for. It would be a help to have an inventory of your existing systems and a clear statement of what you are trying to achieve."

Bingo! He dragged the consultant's report from a cabinet. It contained a very thorough description of the computers and telecommunications at each of the showrooms.

"I need to be able to contact my managers at any time by phone and fax," he said. "We need more coordination. Once we sort out the voice comms, I want to look at data comms. Ideally, I'd like to see a central accounts system, but all the product information comes from a variety of sources, and it's constantly changing. It's a bugger's muddle to be honest."

She glanced at the report and flicked through the pages. "I can do this in two stages," she told him. "The first stage will create an IT strategy that fits your corporate objectives. The second will be a blueprint for detailed implementation. If you like, I can also oversee suppliers and contractors, as a third stage."

"Fair enough," he said. "How soon can you get a proposal to me?"

"I'll fax it with the CV tomorrow morning. I'll need you to sign it if you want me to do the work."

"Of course," he said. She might look like a bloody Womble, but she talked business like Sir John Harvey Jones.

When she left his office he called Leo Chindwall. "Where on earth did you find that one?"

"She's joined our early-morning coffee club," Leo said. "She's sharing a flat round the corner from here with that sexy number I told you about. Is she any good?"

"You old bugger," Shackleton laughed. "You're the one who gave her the glowing reference. I should have known it was all bullshit. Yes, she's good. I'd say she was very good indeed."

*   *   *

Deborah hurried back to the flat, eager to tell Linda that she might have found a job already. Her note was lying untouched on the kitchen table, and there wasn't a sound coming from Linda's room. Clearly, her new landlady was the night owl she claimed to be. She made herself a snack, then went to her room to read the consultants' report on Shackleton Motors. In the afternoon she phoned some local firms that supplied IT equipment to get a feel for the kind of hardware options she would be able to include in her proposal. She worked hard on getting the document together, and by early evening she had finished it.

The work involved in stage one would take her an estimated forty hours, so if Shackleton signed her proposal she would earn a thousand pounds. Stage two would bring her a fee of five times that amount. At least. Plus the installation and set-up costs. The entire project would cost Shackleton Motors around fifty thousand. That averaged just under six thousand per site. She wondered if he'd go for it. There was no doubt it was value for money. Doing it through a conventional systems company would cost two or three times that amount. She clicked the button that would send her documents to Shackleton's fax direct from her computer and looked at her watch. Seven o'clock. It had been a long day after the previous day of upheaval, and she felt very tired. There was still no sound from Linda's room— the mysterious Miss Marshall, as Leo the writing engineer called her. Deborah wrote another brief note, outlining the day's events, and left it on the kitchen table. Then she went back to her room that smelled of lavender and roses and fell fast asleep.

That evening, Leo Chindwall was feeling very expansive. His novel had been well reviewed on Radio 4 and in the *Daily Mail,* and his agent was hopeful that at least two of the Sundays would include it in their books section. Initial orders from booksellers were more than anticipated, and all was well with the world. All that remained for total satisfaction was for the book-buying public to grab it from the shelves to keep the royalties rolling in. Meanwhile, having a few glasses of bubbly with his cronies in his local was a perfect way to end a perfect day. He was particularly pleased when young Peter Shackleton arrived to join the celebrations on his way home from the office.

"Can't stay long, old man," Shackleton said. "Already late. More than my life's worth."

"The delectable Louise wielding the old rolling pin, is she?" Leo asked in a theatrical whisper. "Well, never mind. Get some of this down you."

"This" was a glass of reasonably cold Moët. Shackleton took it and swallowed a large gulp. "Wonderful. Just what the doctor ordered. And congratulations again. Bloody good show."

"I agree," said Leo. "And you know what? It couldn't have happened to a nicer guy. Same again, Ronnie," he said, waving the empty bottle at the barman.

"Pushing the boat out, aren't you?" Shackleton said.

"Well, you don't get to be an overnight publishing success every day, y'know. And it's been a long time coming, I can tell you." Leo pushed his face toward Shackleton. "Y'know when I wrote my first work of truly creative fiction, hm? It was my first income tax return as a self-employed businessman."

At that moment Ronnie the barman popped the new bottle of champagne, and Linda Marshall walked in. She was wearing black, skin-tight leggings and a black leather jacket, opened to show a fine, hand-crocheted smock that managed to hide and reveal her figure at the same time. Her honey-blond hair was flowing loose, framing her perfect features. She was delicately made up in a way that looked cold but suggested warmth. The effect was stunning, and the barman let several fluid ounces of Moët foam vigorously onto the bar before Leo said, "Watch it, Ronnie!" and thrust his glass under the bottle neck. Peter Shackleton simply said "Jesus!" under his breath.

"Evening, miss," Ronnie said. "What can I get you?"

"What you're holding will be fine," Linda said in her husky voice.

Ronnie looked inquiringly at Leo, who was galvanized into action.

"Allow me to share my happiness with you, dear lady," he said ponderously and with a slight belch. "I have achieved a modicum of success with a new work of fiction that I wrote, and my friends and I are celebrating."

"That's very kind, but I wouldn't like to intrude." Linda turned to Ronnie. "Another bottle of Moët, please."

"This is the lady about whom I was telling you," Leo said to Shackleton carefully and solemnly. "You know. Miss Marshall, from around the corner. She wouldn't be intruding, would she, Peter?"

Shackleton shook his head. "No," he said. "No, she wouldn't be intruding."

A pair of purple eyes flecked with a lighter blue glanced at him briefly, and a slight smile took coldness away from those unbelievably sensual lips. That's all it took. The urge to sweep everything to one side and have this woman hit his senses like a line of smack.

"Thanks all the same," Linda said. "But I just stopped in to have a few quiet minutes on my own, before I start work. You know how it is." She turned to the barman. "I'll take it in the lounge."

As she walked away, Leo hissed to Shackleton. "She's what's-her-name's landlady. You know: that little girl I sent round today."

"Deborah Lambert," Shackleton said, staring helplessly after Linda. "Is that a fact?"

Chapter 11

DEBORAH DID NOT SEE LINDA FOR SEVERAL DAYS, DURING which time they communicated by leaving notes on the kitchen table. The arrangement suited Deborah. Peter Shackleton had accepted her proposal, and by the end of the week she was working very hard on the first stage, traveling between the branches of Shackleton Motors, checking the inventory of IT equipment listed in the previous consultants' report, just to be on the safe side, and discussing with the branch managers exactly how they perceived their side of the business developing. It was all going very well, but the work was tiring.

Peter Shackleton turned out to be a moody taskmaster. He started each day pleasantly enough, but then he would become critical of her progress, finding fault with niggling details, questioning why she did this and when she would finish that. He also began telling her about the problems he had at home with his wife, Louise. All very tedious, but she felt obliged to listen.

The day she handed in her proposal he invited her to lunch at l'Étoile au Printemps. What could she do? She felt very vulnerable when she passed her work to a client. There were so many ways they could find fault, and it often ended up in her having to do more work at no extra cost, just because they claimed she had not given them what they had expected. But she was always meticulous, always delivered the goods. If she turned Shackleton down, who knew what would happen. So she said yes.

Joel the waiter gave her a friendly smile as he showed them to a table and greeted Shackleton by name. The owner hurried across.

"Mr. Shackleton, how good to see you again. And welcome to l'Étoile au Printemps, young lady. May I get you both an aperitif, with my compliments?"

"Thanks, Michael. I'll have a large whiskey, and Miss Lambert will have . . . ?"

"An orange juice would be nice."

"An orange juice it shall be," Shackleton said, "and you'd better bring a bottle of the '89 Chablis, if you have any left. You will have some wine, Deborah?"

"Well, maybe just a glass," she said.

"The '89 Chablis, certainly," the owner said. Joel gave them each an oversized, handwritten menu.

"Try the fillet," Shackleton advised. "Michael chooses it himself once a week at Smithfield."

"Well, actually," Deborah said, "I'm rather going off meat. A vegetarian meal would be nice."

"In that case, may I recommend the mushroom lasagne?"

"Yes, it looks very nice," Deborah agreed, peering at the French description.

They ordered, and Shackleton settled back in his chair, sipping the whiskey.

"I brought Louise here once," he said. "She didn't like it. I think she was just being awkward. I think she's decided that anything I like, she doesn't. Christ knows why, but that's the way she is these days. Does that make any kind of sense?"

"Well, I don't really know," Deborah said politely.

"It gets right up my nose, I can tell you. And I'm still supposed to be the loving husband. You know. Remember the birthday. Don't forget to bring flowers from time to time to surprise her. And she's got all bloody day to swan around in a new car, with a nanny looking after the bloody kids." He motioned for Joel to bring another whiskey. "On top of that, it's always no-nooky time. Jesus, I can't remember the last time we had a shag."

For as long as she could remember, anything to do with sex made Deborah feel utterly embarrassed. It wasn't anything to do with being a prude. God knows you couldn't be a prude with explicit sex acts dominating half the movies, and naked men and women in most of the magazines you saw in the newsstands. It was just that she felt sex was so . . . so personal. Something you should never talk about with anyone else. Not ever. And here was her client, someone to whom she had to present an invoice for one thousand pounds, embroiling her in the most intimate details about his marriage.

"Sorry to dump all this on you," he said. "Sometimes it's good to let things out to a sympathetic ear."

Or any kind of ear, she thought, provided it's on someone who can't afford to walk away.

"Most people seem to have problems, these days," she said. She would like to have added, But they don't thrust them onto comparative strangers.

"What about you?" he said suddenly.

It was the first time he had asked her any kind of question about herself that was not related to work. She had no idea how to respond.

"Me?"

"Yes. Since you walked into my office the other day, you've been Miss Perfect, haven't you? Never flustered. Never put a foot wrong. Got on with the job. Met your deadline. It's all too good to be true, wouldn't you say? There's got to be a problem or two lurking in the background. Having rows with your landlady, maybe."

Deborah wondered what on earth made him say that.

"I don't really know her. She keeps herself to herself."

"So I've noticed." He remembered Linda taking the bottle of Moët from Ronnie the barman and walking into the lounge. Away from him. The physical longing to touch her hit him again, and he finished the second whiskey in one draft.

"I'm sorry," Deborah said. "I didn't realize you knew Miss Marshall."

"I don't," he said. "She came into the pub over the road the other night. I was having a drink to celebrate Leo's book being published."

She seized on a common, neutral subject. "Yes, he was ever so pleased. But he didn't tell me what it was about."

He ignored the implicit question, not so much because he didn't know what Leo's book was about either, but because he had not been able to get the image of Linda Marshall out of his head for much longer than a few minutes at a time. It had been years since he'd been aroused like this.

"You've settled in well, then."

"I'm very happy there," she told him.

Joel brought their starters, vegetable soup for her and smoked salmon for him.

"She seems to be quite a character," he persisted.

"She's been very kind to me."

"Really? In what way?"

None of his business, was it?

"Helping me to settle in." Not to mention providing a room that was perfect and being so understanding about the rent. She was beginning to detest this man and his stupid questions. But she needed him to approve her proposal and move into the second stage; otherwise she would have to start looking for work all over again. "She's very nice, but as I said I don't see very much of her . . ."

At that point, Shackleton's pocket bleeped, and he pulled out a mobile phone. "Shackleton . . . Yes, Alan . . . No, you did the right thing. Call you back in a minute."

"Shit," he muttered, looking through the window. Joel was opening the door to greet an attractive, well-dressed woman. "It's my wife." He stood up as Louise Shackleton came to the table.

"Your secretary said I'd find you here. That bloody BMW's acting up and I need a car. I've got a golf match with Ann Evans." She looked pointedly at Deborah.

"Of course, darling," he said. "Where's the car now?"

"At your showroom, naturally. That little shit you call a showroom manager said he'd have to check with you before he could let me take another one. He was going to call you, but I told him I'd come and see how the boss takes his lunches."

"I'll sort it," he said, taking out his mobile phone again. "Hello, Doreen. I want Alan. Alan? What's all this about a car for Mrs. Shackleton? I see," he nodded. "So what's wrong with the 735? Okay. She'll take that one. Yes. See that it's topped up, will you?" He clicked off the phone. "Sorted," he said. "Most of the cars are due out this afternoon, but you can have one of the 735s."

"Aren't you going to introduce me to your friend?"

"This is, er, Miss Lambert. She's a computer consultant."

"Really?" The word was drawn out. "Well, don't let me interrupt anything, will you?"

"For Christ's sake, Louise," he hissed angrily. "She really is a computer consultant."

"Is that what you are?" Louise asked Deborah.

"Yes. I'm working on—"

"The last one was a PR consultant," Shackleton's wife told her. "And the one before that was a doctor's wife."

Deborah noticed that other people in the restaurant were devoting their attention to their plates.

"I really am a computer consultant," she said.

"Well, bully for you. We must compare notes some time. You tell me about his computers, and I'll tell you about his less agreeable habits, unless you've already found out about them for yourself."

Shackleton's jaw muscles bulged as his wife stalked out of the restaurant. Deborah took a determined sip of white wine.

"Okay, all of you. Show's over," Shackleton said in a loud voice.

"Can I pour you some more wine, sir?" Joel asked.

"Yes, you can. And you can bring another bottle of the same."

The lunch had its good side. Shackleton insisted that Deborah accompany him back to the showroom, where he promptly wrote her a check for one thousand pounds and signed the proposal committing him to her plans for development. She wondered whether he did this for business reasons or because it was a way of asserting himself. Either way, it was an unexpected and very pleasant surprise, marred only by his clumsy attempt to hold her when they shook hands. She stood very still and stiff until he awkwardly let her go.

"Right," he said, looking flushed. "I'll let everyone know you're on the job and leave the rest to you."

She took a bus into the city so that she could put the check into her bank. She was even more pleased to see that the money from the Chester job had been credited to her account. After that she called on several of the equipment suppliers she had contacted by phone during her initial research. She had long since learned that any fool can supply equipment: What mattered was how they would shape up for after-sales service and maintenance, how many technically qualified staff they had on the payroll, and whether they were up to date in filing company accounts at Swansea. She was made welcome everywhere she went and, apart from one firm, was pleased to discover a generally high level of service capability.

She got back just after six o'clock, to find a large bunch of flowers in the entrance hall with an envelope addressed to her containing an invitation from Peter Shackleton. A handwritten note from the ground-floor neighbor said that he had answered the door to stop whoever was ringing so persistently on all the bells from disturbing everyone. She guessed that would be Shackleton himself, rather than a delivery man.

His short letter contained an apology for the scene his wife had caused as well as the invitation: *"Louise and I would like to make amends by inviting you to a drinks party on Sunday evening at 8:30. Please bring your landlady, if she would like to come."*

How strange, she thought as she went into the lift. Why does he want Linda to come?

When she opened the door to the flat she knew by the peaceful silence that Linda was still in bed. The central heating was switched on, and there was a warm smell of lavender and rose. It was good to come home to such a welcoming place. She quickly settled into what had become a pleasant routine and made herself a cup of herbal tea, which she sipped to the sound of Capital Radio. A good way to relax and keep up with the news, and as usual she had almost dozed off when Linda called from her room.

"So there you are! I thought self-employed computer people only worked till noon. What time do you call this?"

Deborah tapped on Linda's bedroom door and went in to find Linda mixing drinks at the bar.

"Look at these," she said, holding out the bouquet. "Aren't they lovely?"

Linda turned and stared appraisingly at the flowers.

"A secret admirer?"

"They're from my new client. The man in the downstairs flat let him leave them in the hall."

"So that's what all the bloody noise was about! You can give him a piece of my mind when you see him again, assuming that you are going to see him again. How did the proposal go? Are the flowers condolences or congratulations?"

Deborah wondered why Linda had not answered the door when Shackleton had rung the bell. She could be such a strange person at times. "He signed the contract and paid me for the work I've done this week," she said. "I can give you a check for the rent now."

"No rush," Linda told her. "Have an orange juice and tell me what sort of day you've had."

Deborah found it difficult to talk to people about her work, and particularly about other people's behavior, but she found herself recounting how Peter Shackleton had taken her to lunch at the French restaurant to tell her the most personal things, and how his wife Louise had come in and embarrassed everyone, and how he had tried to embrace her in his office.

"I don't think he meant any harm, though," she said. "I think he was just a bit upset."

"It's not for me to destroy your illusions about men," Linda told her, "but in my experience they are at their most dangerous when they're upset. You should have given him a swift knee in the balls."

Deborah giggled. "He'd just given me a check."

"Kick them in the balls, and they'll end up doubling your money. Believe me, I know," Linda murmured.

"Anyway," Deborah said, "he's invited me to a party at his house next Sunday. He said you could come as well, if you wanted. In fact, I've a funny feeling that he would quite like you to go."

"Why should he want me to go, for God's sake? I've never met the man."

"Perhaps he thinks I wouldn't like to go on my own. He said he saw you in the pub the other night when he was having a drink with one of his friends. I told you about him—Leo, the one who's just had his book published."

"Oh yes." Linda nodded. "There was a guy there. Mid-twenties. Quite tasty in a tough-shit kind of way. Black wavy hair. Good build. That him?"

Deborah nodded.

"Are you going to his party or not?"

"I don't think so. I don't like to socialize with my clients."

"Why not? All part of the business, isn't it?"

"It makes me feel uncomfortable. And I don't think I'd like to meet his wife again. She was very aggressive."

"She's probably got reason to be aggressive, married to a good-looking bastard like that. I bet all the girls are after him, or maybe it's the other way round."

Deborah thought it probably was, but felt it would be indiscreet to say so.

"I think we should go," Linda said. "I could do with a little fun."

"You go," Deborah told her. "I really wouldn't enjoy myself."

Louise Shackleton stared at her husband contemptuously. "You've invited that mousy little computer thing and her landlady! What the fuck for, might I ask? Or have I just answered my own question?"

"I just thought she'd like to come, that's all. She doesn't know many people, so I invited her landlady too, okay?"

"No, it's not bloody well okay. You might have checked with me."

"I'm checking with you now," he said.

"You know, Peter, you can be a real arsehole at times."

"It takes one to know one, darling," he said. In his anger he recalled what she'd been like when they'd first met. Couldn't get enough of it. And when she found he liked it the other way, she couldn't get enough of that, either. Squealed and squirmed and clenched those fantastic buttocks on his prick so that his orgasm practically blew itself out of his head. But when they'd married and had the kids, all that vanished. Puff. Gone, in one of the world's most extended postnatal freeze-outs.

"I hated all that, you bastard."

"The hell you did. It's not my fault you went through a premature menopause. Why not have a fucking hysterectomy while you're at it?"

She took a deep breath, exhaled slowly. Smiled. "You know, I really loathe you, you perverted shit."

"Really," he said. "And what about all the money, the cars . . . hate them as well, do you?"

"Oh no, I love all that."

Leo Chindwall prided himself on being a precise and accurate observer of all things natural, including human behavior. As an engineering student he had excelled in understanding such phenomena as why the tensile strength of mild steel increased and decreased with changes in temperature and crystalline structure, and the effect of random loading in the stress-corrosion cycle of offshore production platforms. To him, people were no different from engineering structures. They worked fine, if they stayed within their operating parameters, but Christ help them if they strayed outside their natural limits. Psychiatrists called it mental breakdown. Leo called it fatigue failure. His novel was about a highly stressed, unhappily married career executive who turned to crime when he met a petty criminal. He had based his two main characters on Peter and Louise Shackleton. Not that they knew. Even if they ever read the book (which they wouldn't), he doubted if they would recognize themselves. People never seemed to know when someone was mimicking them. Maybe the penny would eventually drop, but even then they would be reluctant to accept that they had been the subject of scrutiny, parody, or ridicule. So over the months of writing, he had come to know Peter Shackleton very well indeed, and, although he had been more than the worse for wear, when Linda Marshall walked into the pub and refused his glass of Moët he had been keenly aware of Peter's reaction. Smitten with the Thunderbolt! When he learned that the Shackletons had invited funny little Deborah Lambert and her glamorous landlady to the Sunday party, Leo had been intrigued. Not a function to miss, he thought, as he cradled his drink and looked around. And who knew, he might come up with a subject for his second novel.

He knew several of the Shackletons' guests. Some were from the motor trade, and some were neighbors. Half a dozen of the company's customers had been invited, the kind who bought big BMWs as a second car. A pop star and his Page Three girlfriend. The editor of a motor magazine and his wife. Not a bad mixture. He noticed that every time the doorbell rang to announce a newcomer, Peter Shackleton made sure he was near enough to answer it. Louise mingled efficiently, keeping the waiters on their toes, so that everyone had enough to nibble and drink.

By ten o'clock, Peter was looking frayed, as if the whole business was an anticlimax for him. No. Not an anticlimax. It was something different. It was more like he was experiencing a terrible loss.

At ten-thirty, the doorbell rang again, and Leo saw Peter turn white. He made no move to answer the bell this time, and the pop star opened the door. It was Linda, on her own. She smiled at the pop star and gazed around. She saw Leo and smiled again. He waved and grabbed a glass of champagne from a passing tray.

"Nice to see you," he said after battling through the dancers. "Hope you're not too busy to drink this."

"Certainly not," she said. "I was rather abrupt the other evening, so I thought I'd better come along and make amends. Would you introduce me to Peter?"

"Sure." He took her arm and guided her through the crowd. "Peter, I don't believe you've met Deborah's landlady. Linda Marshall, Peter Shackleton."

Very few women understand the madness that can engulf a man when he sees a woman he wants. They know it's there, this madness. They play with it. They use it. They may get damaged by it. But very, very few of them understand it. Linda was one of the few. She knew that Peter Shackleton wanted her with the manic helplessness of a heroin addict. She'd seen it in his eyes in the pub, and she saw it here, in his drained expression. He was a man whose life was driven by physical passion, and he saw in her something that could satisfy his drive. She knew all this, because that was how she survived.

"I don't believe we've met." Louise Shackleton was staring at Linda with undisguised dislike. A threat.

"I'm Linda Marshall. I'm afraid Deborah wasn't able to come, but she insisted I do. I hope you don't mind."

"Mind? Why should I mind? It's only a party, for God's sake, not some bloody diplomatic function. Make yourself at home, why don't you?"

Louise went to join a crowd of her golfing friends, and Peter cleared his throat.

"I'm sorry Deborah couldn't make it. She's all right, is she?"

"Oh yes," Linda said. "Apparently she has a client who's making her jump through hoops. She's a little tired, that's all."

"Her client is very inconsiderate," Peter said. "I must have a word with myself."

"I wouldn't worry too much. I think Deborah is tougher than she appears." She looked about the room. "Quite a gathering. Is it in aid of anything special?"

"Not until you arrived," Peter said. He hadn't meant to say anything so trite, but the words expressed exactly how he felt. No more, no less.

"Are you going to monopolize Miss Marshall, old boy, or can the world's most recently published author get a look-in?" Leo asked casually. He recognized a ticking bomb when he saw one. "I'll introduce Linda to a few people so she can get her bearings." He guided Linda away, leaving Peter standing awkwardly. Louise joined him. They both stared after Linda.

"You bastard," she said quietly.

"I don't need a scene," he said. "Not now."

"Oh, don't worry," she told him. "I'm beyond making scenes. But get a bloody grip on yourself. You're looking at her like a love-sick adolescent. Don't you dare embarrass me in front of my friends."

Shackleton made a valiant attempt to ignore Linda, but every few seconds his eyes let him down and he watched helplessly as she talked to people, laughing, animated, with a natural grace and charm that turned his insane lust into an equally mad jealousy. Eventually, a residue of reason led him out of the room and onto the darkening patio, where he leaned on the stone balustrade, shivering occasionally, listening to the disco music, knowing that she was hearing it too, maybe dancing with someone, knowing that if she didn't come outside he would quite literally go mad. But it wasn't Linda who joined him, it was Louise, and she lit a cigarette and blew smoke at the moon and said, "You know, Peter, I almost feel sorry for you. You haven't a hope in hell, you poor sod. That's a truly professional bitch. And before you say it again, let me say it for you. It takes one to know one."

He stayed on the patio, forcing himself to chat to the people who came outside for a breath of air, trying to behave normally, taking the drinks that good old Leo brought out to him from time to time, feeling himself slip lower and lower into a dismal limbo. And then he felt her hand on his arm. He didn't need to look. It was her hand all right. Her perfume. Her body warmth.

"Thank you for the party," she said. "I have to go now."

"Right," he said. "Glad you could come."

She leaned toward him, reached up, and kissed him on the cheek. "Good-bye, Peter."

He wanted to say something, anything, to stop her going. Above all he wanted to know when he would see her again. If he would see her again. But he couldn't get the words out. She moved toward the party, then glanced back at him. He was looking about as miserable as a man can look without actually crying. She went back to him and pushed a visiting card into his hand.

"Phone me. Ten o'clock. Friday evening."

Sweet Jesus. That was five days away. How was he going to survive?

Leo Chindwall was disappointed that the party passed without any undue excitement. There were, of course, the undercurrents. Louise had emitted negative energies that would have set an atomic clock running in reverse. As for Peter, well . . . The Shackletons' marriage was a busted flush, and all their friends knew it, but the pretense continued. Partly habit, partly expediency. It wasn't that Leo wanted a scene to develop; he was much too kind a person for that. But the Peter Shackleton of his novel (aka Harry Foster, angry motor–dealer–turned–master–criminal) would never have behaved as the real–life Peter had done. Much as Leo liked the young feller, he'd turned a particularly wobbly shade of jelly as soon as the mysterious Linda Marshall had arrived, and he'd stayed that way after she'd left. I mean, bloody hell, she's only another bloody woman, Leo said to himself. Yes, she was attractive. Okay, she was gorgeous. But that was no reason to go mooning around like a star-struck undergraduate. He expected more from his characters than that.

Chapter 12

THE MORNING AFTER THE PARTY, LEO WENT TO L'ÉTOILE au Printemps at his usual time. Marge Harrison and Wilfred were already at their table, the dog finishing off a chocolate éclair. As Leo said hello and sat down, Wilfred suddenly began growling and showing his teeth. He looked up and was delighted to see young Deborah Lambert approach with her copy of the *Independent*. Talking with Marge was interesting enough, but Deborah was on another level altogether. He thought it was a pity she hadn't gone in for engineering, instead of computing and this newfangled information-technology rubbish. The engineering institutions were opening their chauvinist doors increasingly these days, and more women were competing with their male counterparts in civil, electrical, and mechanical projects. Leo was scandalized at the instability of it all.

Wilfred barked sharply and backed under Marge's table as Deborah came in.

"Wilfred, where are your manners this morning?" Marge said, giving his lead a sharp tug.

"Good morning, my dear," Leo said. "I see you have a spring in your step and a sparkle in your eyes. Would that be because of your newfound work with my friend Peter, or perhaps you've heard an account of his exciting party from your mysterious landlady?"

"Good morning, Marge. Good morning, Leo," she said. "No, I

don't think it's either of those things. Work's a necessary evil, as usual, and I haven't seen Linda yet. She'll probably sleep through the day, so maybe she'll tell me about it this evening."

"You missed some excellent food, and the company wasn't bad. I was just telling Marge."

"He was boring me to death," Marge said. "Except for the bit about your Miss Marshall making rather an impact with the men and therefore upsetting the wives."

"She is extremely attractive," Deborah said. "People are bound to notice."

"They noticed, right enough," Leo chuckled. "In fact, I don't think I'm revealing too much of a confidence when I say that young Peter was particularly smitten."

"Well if he was, no good'll come of it," Marge sniffed. "He's a married man, after all. He should keep his slippers under his own bed."

"What a delightful notion," Leo observed. "But rest assured. The redoubtable Louise has the task in hand. I'd say that Peter is in for a particularly rough ride."

Leo's observation was an understatement. Peter Shackleton was living through one of the worst weeks of his life, his concentration centered around the day and the time when he would hear Linda's voice again. He made everyone around him share in his distress, too. Naturally, he didn't notice. Junior sales staff melted into the nearest corner when they saw him approaching. Managers found other things to do when he drifted into their offices. And as the days went by and his tension increased, he began to find fault with everything, from the sales area to the parts department and the workshops. He even found time to criticize one of the lads who jockeyed cars around in the service area for wasting the space reserved for customers. This turned out to be a bad move, because the lad was a local hard case on a misguided job placement scheme, and Shackleton found himself slammed up against a wall with an oily finger wagging in front of his nose and a severely ripped jacket and shirt. Only the swift intervention of the shop manager stopped this from escalating into a full-scale row, in which Shackleton would have been more than capable of inflicting serious injury on the lad, who was promptly sent back to the Job Center.

He was particularly hard on Deborah. Nothing she did was satisfactory. When she managed to get a consensus from all eight of his branch managers on a particular point, he vetoed it. She gave him a plan for establishing a data line from each of the car manufacturers that fed into a dedicated local area network (so solving one of his main development problems), but he pushed it to one side and told her it wasn't convincing. On Thursday, he refused to see her at all. He said she could take the Friday off and talk to him on Monday.

Deborah was confused by all this, and on several occasions was reduced to tears. She knew that there was nothing wrong with her work, but confidence can be undermined by constant rejection. She couldn't confide in Linda, as she might well have done given an opportunity, because her landlady was never around in the daytime, or when she came home at the end of the day, and they were conducting what little relationship they had by note. Her morning coffees with Leo and Marge at l'Étoile au Printemps became a lifeline, a breathing space to retain her composure and carry on. Marge was fairly offhand about it all, but Leo was rather more sympathetic, despite his tendency to make excuses for Shackleton's behavior.

"There's always a lot of pressure in the motor trade, especially building up to the August sales," he said during their Friday get-together. "Peter gets a bit scratchy this time of year. He'll bounce out of it."

"It's more than just scratchy," Deborah told him. "He's almost irrational, not like when I first went there."

"Trouble at home, I dare say," Marge said. "That wife of his isn't the most compliant of creatures. Cracks the whip a bit, so I'm told. Too much independence, if you ask me."

That was part of it, of course, Leo thought. Louise could be a real bitch. But that had nothing to do with it, and neither did the pressure of work. Peter's reaction to Deborah's landlady was like a nuclear reactor going critical. The moment he'd laid eyes on her in the pub, he was hooked, and when she turned up at his party he was doomed. Leo had never seen anyone looking so smitten. And he had noted the brief but intense interchange between Peter and Linda as she left the party. Something very basic and very primitive was starting between them. Half of Leo envied Peter: few experiences can bring a man so vigorously to life. But the side effects were generally catastrophic. Peter's wife might overlook the occasional infidelity, but the idea of another woman becoming in any way serious, let alone an obsession, would not be tolerated. Louise had far too much to lose. And here was little Deborah, an innocent caught in the crossfire. It had all the ingredients of a major screwup.

"Maybe you should have a word with your landlady about it all," he said. "Peter seemed to be quite taken with her last Sunday. Perhaps she knows why he's so out of sorts."

Deborah looked surprised. "Why on earth would Linda know anything?"

"Well," he said cautiously, anxious not to imply something improper might be taking place. "You know how some people get on famously immediately they meet. It just seemed a bit like that to me. Peter's rather impulsive, and maybe he, you know, maybe he . . ."

"I'm sure Deborah can work it out for herself, Leo," Marge said impatiently. "The truth is, my dear, that young Mr. Shackleton has been mightily smitten by the mysterious Miss Marshall. All this about pressure at work is fiddlesticks. What Leo is trying to suggest is that Peter's poor behavior toward you and your work is a symptom of something altogether different. *Cherchez la femme!*" she added with a degree of satisfaction and finality.

Broaching such a subject with Linda would be completely out of the question for Deborah, and if her new client was attracted to another woman it was not her business, whoever that woman might be. But Leo and Marge were making her very uneasy. She had been banking on a satisfactory project with final payment in three or four weeks. That would give her a welcome credit balance to enable her to look for more work without worrying about rent and bills and living expenses.

She spent the rest of the day in her room developing a computer spreadsheet that would show how the total cost of the project for Shackleton Motors would vary with alternative types of equipment and network services. At about seven o'clock she was feeling really tired when she heard Linda calling, "Anyone at home for a refreshing cup of black coffee laced with best-quality malt whiskey?"

It was a good time to take a break. She went into the kitchen, where Linda was filling the kettle.

"Hi," Linda said. "You've been keeping yourself quiet these days.

You're never around when I get up, so I thought I'd better alter my abominable habit and rise early. Early for me, that is. So how does a Scotch whisky without cream sound?"

"I bought some cream the other day," Deborah said.

"I know. Saw it in the fridge. But it does rather distract from the malt. Mind you, some might say that the coffee detracts from the malt as well. It's up to you."

"I'll try it your way," Deborah said. "It'll probably help me to unwind."

"Busy day at the keyboard?"

Deborah nodded. "Busy day, busy week."

"Hope you don't mind my saying so, but you look a teensy bit frazzled. Everything okay?"

Depends how you look at it, Deborah thought. The project itself couldn't be in a better shape. The Shackleton managers were becoming more and more enthusiastic about her plans as the benefits became clearer. The only real problem was Peter Shackleton himself.

"Everything's fine," she lied.

Linda looked at her, then poured the hot water into the *cafetière*. "A little bird told me that all was not well *chez* Shackleton. Would that be true?"

"I really couldn't say," Deborah told her. "I'm just getting on with my work as best I can."

"So there is something wrong."

Deborah hadn't meant to say anything that could lead to a discussion, but Linda was too quick.

"It's been a bit difficult getting things approved," she said.

"Getting Peter Shackleton to approve things, you mean. Is there anything wrong with what you're doing?"

Deborah shook her head emphatically. "Absolutely not. It's all knitting together very well, but he finds fault with everything. It's not just me. He's jumping all over the staff and he almost had a fight with a boy who'd come from the Job Center. Leo, you know, the writer you saw in the White Swan, well he thinks it's something to do with pressure at work."

"Is that what you think?"

It wasn't what Deborah thought, at all. She was pretty sure that Leo was right. Linda was so beautiful that it wasn't surprising someone like Peter Shackleton was attracted to her. And she found herself adding the notion that having a wife like Louise didn't help matters.

"Things are getting pretty busy," she said. "They're building up to the August sales."

"Right," Linda said. "The August sales. I've never understood all that crap about registration letters, myself. Bloody silly, if you ask me. I once tried to sell a car, and this idiot on the phone kept asking was it a late M–reg or an early M–reg. I mean, for God's sake." She pushed the plunger and poured an equal amount of coffee and Jamieson into two mugs. "There. Get your digestive system round that. The magic elixir. Wakes you up when you get up. Zonks you out when you go to bed. Must be something to do with the caffeine and the alcohol."

Deborah sipped it. "Mmm. It's nice."

"Good," Linda said. "D'you fancy something to eat? I see you've got suitable noncarnivore provisions in stock."

Deborah yawned. "Excuse me! No, thank you. Maybe I'll get a snack later."

"There you are," Linda said with satisfaction. "You're zonked out, and I'm getting all feisty. Told you."

"You certainly did," Deborah said. "I really feel as if I should get my head down. Would you mind?"

"Mind? Why should I mind? Me landlady, you tenant. You can do exactly what you want."

As Deborah finished her coffee and whisky, Linda's mood changed subtly.

"It really *is* like we're becoming flatmates, isn't it? Not landlady and tenant."

Deborah smiled. "Yes. Much more like flatmates."

Deborah was dozing in her room a little later when she thought she heard voices, low and murmuring, but conveying the impression of a disagreement. Women's voices. Linda, of course, with someone younger. For a while she tried to hear what was being said, but sleep overtook her.

Chapter 13

IT WAS NINE-THIRTY, FRIDAY EVENING. SHACKLETON slammed the front door on Louise's harangue and immobilized the alarm on the BMW 750 parked in his driveway. His hands were shaking as he fumbled with the key and climbed into the car. Thirty minutes before he made his phone call to Linda. Twenty-nine minutes. Twenty-eight. He took a deep breath and started the car, slipped it into gear, eased it onto the road. He had no idea where he was going, as long as it was away from Louise and nearer to Linda Marshall. The big engine sighed as he hit the accelerator and surged toward Heathside. Being in a car like this helped. He felt enclosed by excellence, pampered. Above all, he felt in charge. The BMW was responsive to every whim, every command. It was a sexual thing. Being able to dominate, always with the understanding that the beast in the car was more than capable of turning the tables on him, of providing more power than he or anyone else could possibly use and get away with it. That's how he felt when he looked at Linda. Her slight, full-breasted, sensuous body would be able to take everything he could deliver, from violence to a marathon groining, and still come back for more, and more. . . . He could see it in her eyes. And he knew she understood it, too. Their being together was inevitable. Nothing could come between them. Nothing could interfere.

So why was he so terrified that it wouldn't happen?

After driving for fifteen minutes he found himself on the common

overlooking Heathside, with the lights of the city beyond beginning
to twinkle in the dusk. She was down there. If he reached out an
arm he could pluck her from the humdrum streets and elevate her
to be with him, here, above it all. Above all the shit. He turned on
the radio and scanned the wave bands, listening impatiently to the
banal chattering and the equally banal music on each station for a few
seconds before hitting the search button again. Nine-fifty-five. Jesus
Christ. He got out of the car and stood taking deep breaths. It didn't
help. He got back in the car and reached under the dash. There was
enough for three lines in the packet of cocaine, and his hand shook
again as he held it to his nose. If it had been anyone else but Linda,
he would have been in there. But there was a very strong primitive
reluctance not to be under any kind of influence when he spoke to
her. That made sense. A feeling like this didn't need any stimulant.
Christ, wasn't that marvelous! Nine-fifty-eight. He got out his mobile phone and pressed the memory button for her number. That
had been the first thing he'd done when the party was over last
Sunday. Programmed her number into his mobile.

Nine-fifty-nine.

An overwhelming resentment came rushing out of nowhere. Just
who the fuck was this, making him sit here like a fucking schoolkid
counting the fucking minutes to a fucking phone call? Who the fuck
did she think she was? He'd bloody well keep her waiting, like she'd
kept him waiting.

He put the phone on the dashboard and stared at the clock,
watched the seconds tick to the hour, watched them go past it and
travel toward the next minute, and the next, and the next. At five
minutes past ten, he picked up the phone and keyed Linda's number.

It was busy.

It is possible that no one was ever more astounded or outraged to
hear those innocuous pips. Possible, but not probable.

Feeling dizzy, he pushed open the car door and swung his legs out
to sit with his head between his legs, sucking in air. When he'd
recovered, he got back in the car and tried again. Linda's line was
still busy. He called again every minute, on the minute until, at ten-
twenty-two, he got a ringing tone. When his call was answered he
heard Linda say, "Hello?"

Hello? Just like that? Hello? A cold, neutral voice: Who the fuck
are you, phoning me like this? He couldn't believe it.

"Hi," he said. "It's Peter."

"Peter?"

"Peter Shackleton. You said I should call you."

"Oh, Peter, of course. How are you?"

If Shackleton had a sense of humor, it might have allowed him to see the funny side. But he didn't. It took all his control to try to keep his voice steady. He wasn't sure if he succeeded.

"Fine," he said. "I was hoping we could get together."

"That would be nice," Linda said. "When did you have in mind?"

This was a joke. She had to be joking.

"I was hoping you could make it this evening," he said.

"Oh dear," she said. "I wish you'd called earlier. I've just made arrangements."

She made him fill the silence.

"That's a pity."

"Maybe some other time. Next week perhaps. Give me a call about the same time on Monday."

"Right," he said. "Speak to you on Monday, then."

"Must go," she said. "Someone at the door. Good-bye, Peter."

Linda put the phone down, pressed the outside-entry release, and smoothed her nurse's uniform, making sure that the white apron was tight over her clean, tight, blue overall, pressing her bra gently up to emphasize her breasts. She heard her front door open and close quietly, and, as she started the video cameras, Pimples came into her room. He handed her his envelope and stood in silence as she counted the money and then threw it carelessly onto a table.

"Nurse is very, very angry with you, Pimples."

"I'm sorry. I'm so sorry," he said. "I'll do anything to make up. Anything. . . ."

Peter Shackleton sat in his car, trembling uncontrollably. It was rage, mainly. Rage coupled with an underlying fear. If she would only call him back, he'd be around to her flat like a whipped poodle. The thought infuriated him. But it also frightened him. No one should have this kind of hold over someone. No one. He reached under the dash again, brought out the packet of cocaine, with the smooth piece of card and the clean plastic straw. In less than a minute he'd cut himself a line and sniffed half into each nostril, waiting for it to hit him. It didn't. Not the way it usually did. More of a slow warmth than a fiery takeoff. Too slow. He cut another line. That was better. Much better. Why couldn't it always be like this? He could handle anything. Especially pretentious, manipulating bitches who didn't recognize an opportunity when they saw one. Christ, he could give that Linda Marshall a good time in more ways than one. But first things first, or rather thirst things first. Snow always made him thirsty. A beeline for the White Swan was the order of the day. Day and night. Bet old Leo would be there. Good old Leo. Clever old Leo. Writing a book like that. Must read it sometime.

Luckily the BMW knew its way to the pub, because his mind was on higher things than mere driving. And Leo was there, with the usual gang of locals. Local yokels. Well-meaning bastards, by and large. Friendly enough. Certainly generous with the offerings. But they weren't the only ones. Old Shackers could stand a round with anyone and everyone. And the great thing was, no one knew his secret. No one knew what he had up the old olfactory organ, something that was making him buzz and feel good.

"You're looking more like your old self, tonight, Peter," Leo said.

"Been rather preoccupied lately, Leo. Lots on the old plate. You know how it is."

"Coming up to your busy time, too, isn't it?"

"Absolutely. But we've got it by the balls this year. Already met most of our targets. We'll cruise home on the new registrations."

"What about this reorganization of yours?"

Peter had to think about that one.

"Reorganization?"

"You know. This new system that Deborah's putting in for you."

"Oh, right. Tell the truth, I've not been too happy about all that. Not sure it'll do the trick."

"You know best, old son. But I'm sure she knows her stuff."

Primpy little slut. Coming in and telling him how to run his bloody business. He must have been mad, letting her sweet-talk him into it. He shook his head.

"Nah. I'm going to blow her out on Monday. Waste of bloody money."

Leo felt quite uncomfortable about this, as he was the one who had sent Deborah along to Shackleton Motors in the first place. But it wasn't any of his business.

"Have another drink anyway," he said.

"My shout," Shackleton said firmly. "Another pint?"

"Make it a small Scotch."

Shackleton pushed his way to the bar and waved a twenty-pound note to attract the barman's attention.

"Over here, Ronnie, when you've got a minute."

One of the people he pushed looked up at him. It was the youth with whom he had rowed in the showroom parking lot. Shackleton didn't recognize him.

"Wait your fucking turn," the youth said. "You and your fucking money."

Shackleton ignored him. The youth turned to a friend.

"This is the shithouse I was telling you about. Only lost me my fucking job, didn't he."

"That right?" his friend said.

Their conversation began to percolate through Shackleton's newly acquired euphoria. He smiled benignly.

"Is there a problem?"

"There wasn't till you came poncing in," the youth said.

"Two large malts, Ronnie," Shackleton said.

"Sorry, Peter, these two gentlemen are top of the list. Yes, lads . . ."

Shackleton put the twenty-pound note on the bar and said, "Make that two very large malts, Ronnie."

The barman kept his gaze on the youth and his friend.

"Two pints," the youth said.

It seemed to Peter Shackleton that things were about as wrong as they could be. These two little shits were asking for trouble.

"Why don't you take your grubby money back to wherever it is you crawled from and leave this pub for the people who can appreciate it," he said.

"You what?" the youth's friend said. "Who is this ponce, Gary?"

"I told you. The bloke who gave me the sack. Mr. Peter Bloody Shackleton."

"Two pints coming up, lads," the barman said nervously.

"It's two triple malts, and one for yourself," Shackleton said in a loud voice.

People were beginning to give them sideways glances. Leo came over.

"Everything all right, Peter?"

"Everything is splendid," Peter said. "At least it will be when these two snots piss off and leave us to drink in peace."

"That'll do, Mr. Shackleton," Ronnie said.

"Right. That's fucking it!" the youth shouted. Before anyone could stop him he smashed his pint glass on the edge of the bar and swung it at Shackleton, who blocked it easily and punched the lad in the center of his face. There was a noise like a plastic cup rupturing, and the youth lurched back into his friend, blood spurting from his nose and mouth.

"Fucking hell, you've fucking killed him, you bastard," the friend shouted.

"Let's hope so," Shackleton said. "One less of the dirty ungodly to worry about."

Ronnie took a quick but experienced look at the youth, who was lying motionless on the floor with his friend trying to keep his head upright.

"Get an ambulance, Rose, and phone the police!" he called to one of the bar staff. "Right, ladies and gentlemen, I'm shutting the bar, and I'd be grateful if you'd all stay here until we can sort this. . . ."

Several people quickly drained their glasses and scurried out.

"I believe I placed my order before you called time, Ronnie," Shackleton said.

Leo pulled his arm. "For pity's sake, Peter. Did you have to hit him so hard?"

"Hard?" Shackleton said calmly. "That wasn't hard. I'll show you what hard is." He grabbed the friend's hair and hauled him to his feet. Leo managed to hook his elbow round Shackleton's arm. Shackleton chuckled. "Only joking," he said, letting go of the friend's hair.

"Give me your car keys," Leo whispered in his ear. "I'll say you came here in a taxi, with me."

"Good old Leo," Shackleton observed. Leo led him to a corner seat.

One of the people who had stayed behind was kneeling by the youth, easing him into a more comfortable position and clearing his breathing passages.

"He's all right," he told the friend. "Probably concussed, that's all."

"You're dead," the friend shouted at Shackleton. "You're fucking dead, you are."

Shackleton surged toward him, scattering people and tables. The friend cowered back, but Shackleton grabbed him and began banging his head against the bar as Leo and several others desperately tried to drag him off. They were still struggling when the sirens shrieked into the street and the police arrived to sort things out.

Officers moved among the debris, noting the damage, taking names and addresses, questioning people about what had happened. Then an ambulance turned up, and the crew eased the youth onto a stretcher. The youth's friend tried to follow the paramedics back to the ambulance. A police officer stopped him.

"Sorry, sir. I'm afraid we need to take a statement."

"Fucking statement," the friend shouted, pointing at Shackleton. "Take his fucking statement, the bastard. You're fucking dead, mate!"

He tried to push past the policeman.

"Right," the cop said. "You're nicked, sunshine."

Another policeman joined in the brief struggle and took the friend outside to a police car.

The senior policeman finished talking to the barman and went over to Shackleton, notebook at the ready.

"If I could have your name and address, sir." Shackleton obliged, and the policeman wrote it down slowly. "According to the barman, you were involved in a misunderstanding at the bar with the gentleman who was injured. Can you tell me what happened?"

"Yes," Shackleton said. "I tried to order a drink, and the little sod pushed in front of me."

"So you have been drinking?"

"One usually drinks in places like these, Officer. That's what they're for, believe it or not."

"Did you hit the gentleman who was injured, sir?" the policeman asked tiredly.

"Not immediately. I hit him after he tried to hit me with his glass. Then his friend threatened me, and I hit him."

"So you do admit to hitting, er, Gary Shotton and, er, Arthur Williams."

"Absolutely, if that's what their names are."

"After Gary Shotton threatened you with a broken glass . . ."

"He didn't threaten me, Officer, he tried to hit me with it. I was defending myself. The other one threatened me, as one of your colleagues heard."

"Right, sir. As things stand, Mr. Shotton might wish to prefer charges against you, in which case you'll be asked to make a statement. In the meantime, might I suggest that you do not drive home; otherwise you may well be guilty of an offense."

"He's taking a taxi, with me," Leo said.

When the police had left, Shackleton looked around at the shambles and took several notes out of his wallet. "This ought to cover everything," he said to the barman.

Ronnie shook his head. "No, thanks, Mr. Shackleton. I don't want your money, and I don't want your custom. You're barred."

Shackleton looked at him, eyes narrowed. "You what?"

"It's all right, Peter," Leo said, pulling at his arm. "Let's get you home. We can sort all this out later."

Saturday is always a busy time in a successful car showroom, and this Saturday was no exception at Shackleton Motors. Time wasters, upwardly mobiles, seriously interesteds, and one or two genuine punters with actual money came and went. Not to mention the parts department and the service bays. The staff were all very busy coping, and if they thought Peter Shackleton had been bad during the week, they were searching for a new description as the day wore on. He shut himself in his office and began going through files, and every time he found something that didn't fit in or that had not been updated, someone got a severe dressing-down. They were approaching a state of mutiny when they were saved by the bell, or rather by the warbling sound of Shackleton's mobile phone. They couldn't hear it, of course, but it saved them nevertheless.

"Shackleton," he snapped.

"Peter. Hello. It's Linda Marshall."

He held the phone tighter.

"Hello. Are you still there, Peter?"

"Yes," he said.

"I wanted to apologize about last night. I'd been looking forward to seeing you again, but so many things cropped up at the last minute. You know how it is."

"Yes," he said again. Just listening to her was soothing away the throbbing headache. How could a voice do that? He cleared his throat. "I'd been looking forward to seeing you as well."

"I'm glad. Are you free this evening? I'm meeting a couple of chums at the Piedmont Club at nine. It would be wonderful if you could join us."

Louise had already organized his night, as usual. They were supposed to go around to her mother's for dinner.

"No problem."

"Nine o'clock, then." She disconnected.

He put his phone back in his pocket and began returning the files to their respective cabinets. He'd be sharing her with her friends, but so what. He could handle that. As long as he had a chance to be with her. Talk. Maybe touch. . . . He made a phone call to his usual liquor store, then picked up the intercom and buzzed his sales manager.

"Alan. Get in here, will you." When the manager arrived, looking justifiably nervous, he said, "There's two cases of champagne at Harry's, plus glasses. Send someone to pick 'em up. Everyone gets two glasses if they're driving and as much as they like if they're not. Any punter comes through the door gets a glass. If you run short, get back to Harry. Okay?"

"Okay," the manager said, surprised and relieved by this turn of events. "Fine. I'll send Martin. What's the celebration?"

Shackleton shrugged. "I've been dishing the shit lately. Not that you all haven't needed it. But I know we've got a good team out there, and I just thought I'd let them all know that I know."

The Piedmont Club was seriously exclusive. Not snobbishly exclusive. Seriously exclusive. It was an institution of very long standing whose members enjoyed a considerable respect in the community, coupled, it has to be said, with a certain reputation for fast living and scandalous behavior. Not exactly a latter-day Hellfire Club, but definitely hinting at the libertine rather than the liberal. Membership was not for ordinary mortals. You needed a great deal of money and you needed to know the right people to become a member. Trouble was, no one really knew who the right people were. It was like a closed society. A magistrate here, a judge there. Someone big in TV. A pop star, maybe. Perhaps some old bloke who didn't look as if he had all his marbles but who'd been around since Lord knows when. Plus it admitted women. Shackleton knew the lady town clerk was a member. But no one seemed to know who was on the membership committee, or even if there was a membership committee. He'd put his name down years ago, but whenever he phoned to see how it was progressing someone told him there was still a long waiting list. As he drove through the heavily wooded estate and into the parking lot, he wondered which of Linda's friends had cracked it. His big BMW was almost out of place among a clutch of Bentleys, Rolls-Royces, Ferraris, and other top-end motors. He parked it between a Mercedes SL and a Lamborghini and made his way to the entrance, a solid oak door with an equally solid security guard in front of it.

"Good evening, Mr. Shackleton," the guard said.

"Evening." Peter wondered how the man knew his name, then guessed that all invited guests were expected. Impressive.

The door swung open as he approached, and a very attractive woman in a smart business suit greeted him.

"Good evening, Mr. Shackleton. I'm Joan Harvey. Miss Marshall has arrived. She's in the cocktail bar with Mr. and Mrs. Daniels."

She led the way and stepped back as he went in. Linda was sitting at the bar, her back to him, legs wrapped around the stool, her arm raised as she sipped her drink. He didn't even notice who she was with as he went across, but they stopped talking and looked at him. So did Linda, turning, and smiling, putting down her drink and holding out her hand, pulling him gently close so she could breathe a kiss on his cheek, envelop him with her perfume.

"Peter," she said. "I want you to meet Walter and Sylvia. They're from somewhere in Texas. Walter owns the Piedmont chain of clubs."

Walter stuck out his hand and Sylvia smiled.

"Howdy, Pete. Walt Daniels. Welcome to the club. Call me Walt. Everybody does, except Linda. What a kidder. She says it makes me sound like some Bob Newhart character. Y'know, the fellah who discovered tobacco. This is my lifetime partner, Sylvia."

"Nice to meet you, Pete," Sylvia said. "We're from Valley Mills on the North Bosque River. Have you ever been there? It's barely ten miles from Crawford. That's on the Middle Bosque River."

Under normal circumstances, it would have been nice to meet her too. Despite being pissed out of her skull, she was a very foxy lady. But there was only one person in the bar that mattered to Shackleton.

"Good evening," Peter said. "Er, no, I can't say that I have."

"What would you like to drink?" Linda asked. "And before you go all macho on me, guests aren't allowed to buy drinks. Something to do with the licensing laws, isn't that right, Walter?"

"This is a crazy country," Walt sighed. "Ain't it, babe?"

"It sure is," Sylvia said, looking straight at Peter.

"I'll have what you're having," Peter told Linda.

The bargirl was already waiting. "Another Sicilian, Mary, please."

"What business you in, Pete?"

Two of the things Shackleton disliked most about Americans was their habit of truncating names on first acquaintance and their vulgar curiosity. Next thing, the bastard would be asking how much he earned.

"Motor trade. Various dealerships: BMW, Nissan, Mercedes . . . nine showrooms," he said, then found himself adding, "Turnover's just over ten million."

"Jesus," Walt whistled. "That's a lot of vee-heh-culls."

"I think he means ten million pounds, Walter," Linda said.

"I knew that." Walt grinned. "Just fooling around."

"So, how long have you been in the club business, Walt?" Shackleton asked. He frankly didn't give a fuck how long the obnoxious bastard had been in anything, but he had to make an effort at polite conversation to avoid upsetting Linda.

"Actually, Walt and me are in the pornographic industry," Sylvia said, pronouncing each syllable very carefully. "The clubs are just a sideline."

"Now, darlin'," Walt said warningly.

"They are so!" Sylvia pouted. "Walt calls it exotic publishing, but all it does is make big guys like you get a hard-on."

"My lovely wife is exceedingly forthright," Walt said unnecessarily.

Shackleton's drink arrived, complete with skewered anchovy and black olive. He took a swallow and almost gagged.

"Bloody hell," he said. "What's in this?"

"Mainly tequila and salt," Linda said. "Don't you like it?"

"Well, it's here, and I like that, and it contains alcohol, and I like that. It'll do."

"You Britishers," Walt said. "Goddam, I like it here. You two people must allow my lovely wife and myself the honor of buying you dinner."

Shackleton was irritated beyond belief. He wanted Linda on her own, and the idea of spending another minute with the garrulous Walt and the vampish Sylvia was mind-numbing. But Linda smiled at them and at him and said how wonderful that would be and squeezed his arm secretly as if to say that she understood his feelings, so he bottled them up and carried on forcing his mouth to smile. When the headwaiter eventually called them to the dining room, he found himself placed opposite Linda, with Walt on his left and Sylvia on his right. A number of the diners acknowledged Linda, who smiled back. The food was wonderful and the wine was excellent and Shackleton was going out of his mind. At one point an elderly man with a heavily pockmarked face sent a bottle of fine claret to their table. Walt nodded benignly and Linda waved a thank-you.

It was all very amiable, but not what Shackleton wanted. The only consolation was that he was beginning to feel quite nicely pissed. Finally, he slid off his shoe and extended his leg toward Linda, feeling like a bloody juvenile, hoping for just one brief touch, however momentary. He was rewarded by yielding flesh that responded to his pressure. It sent a delightful shiver through him, and he ran his foot up and down her leg, trying to convey everything he was feeling and wanting through this woefully inadequate point of contact. He realized just how woeful and inadequate it was when Linda excused herself and went to the ladies' room, leaving him still pressing a leg, Sylvia smiling like a cat.

As Walt continued his monologue, Shackleton stood up in a desperate attempt to escape the deluge and said he needed to go to the loo as well. He waited for Linda to come out of the ladies' room and stood in front of her.

"I need to be with you," he said.

She looked at him, calmly. "I know."

"For Christ's sake, this is killing me. I mean, your friends are very nice, but I'm going off my skull. I just need to be with you."

The manager approached them. "Is everything all right, Miss Marshall?"

"Everything is perfect, Joan, thank you."

"Your guest left this under your table," the manageress said, holding out Shackleton's shoe.

"So that's where it was," Shackleton said.

"Yes, sir. I know Mr. Daniels is most relaxed about things, but Piedmont clubs have strict rules concerning dress, I'm afraid, and one of the members noticed that you were walking in rather an odd manner."

"Bang goes the old application," he said.

"Not necessarily," the manageress said with a slight smile.

He put on the shoe, and they made their way back to the table.

"You didn't mention you'd applied for membership," Linda said as they joined the others.

"It hasn't exactly been top of my mind."

"We're into all that, aren't we, hon?" Walt said, smiling amiably at them. "Top of the mind."

"We sure are," Sylvia agreed. "Saved a fortune on psychiatrist bills." She put the emphasis on the "a," but as neither Linda nor Shackleton knew what they were talking about it didn't seem to matter.

"Mind-mapping," Walt explained. "You take a sheet of paper, see, and you take a pen, and you—"

"I know what mind mapping is, Walter," Linda said firmly.

"—and you write down all the things that are troubling you," Sylvia said, "and you put little circles around them, and join them all up. . . ."

"I think Linda and Peter have the point, lover," Walt said.

"Time for us to be on our way, I'm afraid," Linda said. "Lots of things to do. Thanks very much for your hospitality, Walter. You too, Sylvia."

"It's been a pleasure, Linda. You and your friends are always welcome in my clubs. Anytime. You know that."

Sylvia nodded and squeezed Shackleton's buttock. "Linda is our best freelance contributor, isn't she, Walt?"

"She most surely is." He became conspiratorial, leaning over to Shackleton. "Her stuff is a-mazing. Ve-ry realistic. Sells all over the world, for big, big bucks. We generally find that ladies make the best videos, same as they write the best love stories. Just look at *Gone With the Wind,* for Christ's sake. We reckon maybe some of them do it to get one over on hubby, don't we, dear heart?"

"There's nothing a lady likes better than to get one over on her husband," Sylvia agreed sweetly.

Sylvia's obvious and pointed remark was accompanied by a surreptitious but deft rub of her hand over Shackleton's crotch as they all stood up. He hardly noticed. The thought of being alone with Linda was utterly intoxicating, and he was even more excited at the mention of pornography. He hadn't felt as turned on as this since being a teenager.

The manageress came to the table and handed a small card to Walt.

"Mr. Shackleton's membership, Mr. Daniels. Perhaps you could approve it so he can join immediately."

"No problem," Walt said, signing the card with a flourish.

"Hey, that's great," Shackleton said.

"Wait until you read the conditions," Linda told him wryly. "It's basically a direct-debit mandate for a minimum of two hundred pounds a month plus whatever else you rack up."

"Not a problem."

"You Britishers," Walt said. "Jeez, some kinda style."

"Can you give me a lift home, Peter? I came in a taxi."

"I think I can manage that."

Linda said nothing as Shackleton took the road to the common. He parked the car where he had stopped the evening before and switched off the ignition. Quiet though the engine had been, the silence that followed was absolute. He felt incapable of making a move, in case it broke something irreparable, but eventually he forced his hand across the car and put it on her thigh, amazed at the softness of her flesh. She took hold of it and placed it firmly on his own leg.

"I'm worth more than a grope in a car, don't you think, Peter?"

There was no answer to that. Of course she was, but he was helpless in his need for sexual release.

"Don't think I don't understand," she told him. "I do, but there's a time and a place for what we feel, isn't there?"

The time is now. The place is now.

"You don't know what it feels like," he said miserably. At that moment he hated her for reducing him to this.

"Perhaps not," she said softly. "Why don't you show me?" He thought he had misheard her, but she reached over and found his penis, swelling hard in his trousers. Squeezed it gently for a moment. "This. Show me."

She leaned back, and he pulled his belt open and yanked his zipper down.

"Oh, that's lovely," she murmured. "Is that what you want to give me?" He turned clumsily toward her, but she pushed him away. "Not yet, not yet. It's far too soon. I want to see you play with yourself."

He made a few more attempts, but she kept him at arm's length, putting his hand back on his penis and moving it for him until he kept it moving himself, groaning slightly, moving faster and faster and suddenly exploding into his climax, shooting spunk into the air and onto the steering wheel and the dashboard in a huge white stream until he slumped back, exhausted.

"There," she said, and moved her head down a little. "There. Wasn't that nice? It looked nice. It made me all wet inside." She moved her head a little closer, and closer again, until her lips were touching the still pulsing flesh, tongue flicking out to taste. "Ah," she said. "That's so good."

He lay quivering and helpless as she sucked and licked him clean, like an animal.

"I want you to do that every night until we see each other again," she breathed. "When you come inside me, I don't want it to be too quick. I want it long and slow and fierce. Will you promise me that, Peter?"

He nodded his head.

"Cross your heart and hope to die?"

He nodded again. "When . . . ?"

"That all depends," she said. "I hear you've been a bad little boy at work. A real crosspatch. Shouting at everyone. Frightening everyone. Specially my friend Deborah. She's trying very hard, you know. But you've been a bad boy, haven't you? Haven't you?"

Another nod.

"I want to hear you say it: 'I've been a bad boy.' "

"I've been a bad boy."

"There," she said. "That was easy, wasn't it? And you'll be kind to Deborah. Yes?"

"Yes, I'll be kind to Deborah."

"Well then," she said. "Why don't you take me home?"

On Monday, Deborah found Shackleton almost pathetically eager to please. He insisted that all his managers attend an afternoon meeting to agree on the final strategy for the telecommunications network and computer system. After that it was simply a matter of costing out the equipment. Deborah's spreadsheet made this a simple, fast exercise. By the end of the week everything was finalized and agreed on with the suppliers. The weekend came and went, with no phone call from Linda, but in a way Shackleton didn't mind. He wanted the project finished, and he knew that she would call him when it was.

Installation began the following week. Deborah did some hard negotiating with the cable companies and arranged discounts on line usage and call times. As a bonus, one of them offered the Shackleton Motors branch in its area ten hours a week of free video films for the customer waiting room. Two hours later, Deborah got the same deal with the others. The managers were delighted, and so was Shackleton. When Deborah came to him and announced that she'd just worked herself out of another job, he wrote a check for ten thousand pounds on the spot and told her she was worth every penny. His temper had improved to such an extent that even his wife was impressed. But still Linda didn't phone. He knew that something must be out of balance, and he racked his brains trying to think what it was. Then he remembered the pub and the fight. Did she know about that? Certainly she did. Everybody in the neighborhood knew about it. He checked with the police and learned that young bastard Gary What's-his-name was still in hospital. They'd had to rebuild his nose and half his sinuses. Serve the little fucker right, but Shackleton went to the hospital all the same, said sorry, and handed the shit a check for a grand. Then he went to the White Swan and apologized to Ronnie, who said it was okay and he could drink there anytime provided he behaved himself. He sent Leo Chindwall a case of Glenlivet for being such a good sport.

Still the phone didn't ring. By Friday he was beginning to become desperate again, until he discovered that he hadn't recharged its battery. When he did, he discovered on the pager that Linda had called twice, leaving him messages to call back.

"I thought you'd forgotten me," she told him.

"The battery was flat on this bloody phone," he said. "I thought it was you that forgot me!"

"How are you?" she asked.

"I'm fine. Everything's fine. Sorted, like you wanted."

"It certainly seems so, and I want to see you. Would you be free tomorrow?"

He didn't have to think very hard about it. "Yes."

"Why don't we meet in the evening at the White Swan at, say, seven-thirty," she said. "We can grab something to eat, or go straight to my place and eat later."

The prospect made him feel dizzy. After all the shit and the turmoil, it was finally about to happen.

Linda left Deborah a note asking if she wouldn't mind staying out for Saturday evening, as she had asked Peter Shackleton around and she was a bit concerned about any possible embarrassment. Deborah had scribbled: *"Of course. Could do with a night off. Probably hire a car and drive to the country. Stay in a B&B. Have a walk in the hills. Deborah."*

Sensible girl! Linda looked around her room, checking that everything was in order, and smiled. Perfect. It would be a night to remember. She made sure that drinks were ready and that all the bar equipment worked. Made final adjustments to the video cameras.

Deborah had a wonderful day on Saturday. She enjoyed the hired car, a new Renault Clio with all the trimmings, and in the afternoon she drove around London to do some much-needed shopping. By the time the shops were closing, though, the hard work of the past few days caught up with her, and she decided to take a snooze in the car before heading west to the Cotswolds, one of her favorite places.

Linda stepped out of the shower and heard Lyndsey singing softly in her room. She hoped her little sister wasn't upset again. Not at this stage of the game. Linda loved Lyndsey's room. It was so pure. Just like Lyndsey. Whenever she went inside, it made her all the more determined to continue her work. She pulled on her bathrobe and found Lyndsey sitting cross-legged on the floor, her back to the door, like last time.

"Hello, little sister."

The singing continued, a gentle, wordless song, like a lullaby.

"You really mustn't worry. It's for your own good."

The singing stopped.

"I don't want you to. I never wanted you to. It's very wicked."

"I'm protecting you. How can that be wicked?"

"But you're keeping me safe anyway. You are protecting me, without . . . without . . ."

"You don't want it to happen to you again, do you? Not again?"

There was a sniffle; then Lyndsey shook her head.

"Well then, you must trust me. You do trust me, don't you?"

A little nod, but a nod, all the same.

"Of course you do. Now, you know it's not safe for you to come here when I'm busy. Why don't you go back home, and I'll see you later?"

When Lyndsey stood up, they gave each other a little hug, and Linda wiped her sister's tears away.

"Right then, off you go."

Linda was sure that Walter and Sylvia would be thrilled with this one. She'd put a lot of preparation into it. But then, she'd get a lot back out of it. And it wasn't just the money. In fact, she didn't really need the money. It was the satisfaction of a creative job of work well done. She wasn't due to meet Peter for an hour, and she had a thought. Why not say hello to Walt and Sylvia on the videotape. It would be a nice touch, and they could always edit it out. She stood in front of a camera and flicked the remote record.

"Hello, Walter. Hello, Sylvia. I think you'll really like this one. You remember Peter from the other night? Well, he's in it. We've got an absolutely super script and some really incredible special effects. You'll not believe it isn't really happening. Oh, and thanks for the last royalty credit. It's good to know one's work is appreciated."

She switched off the equipment and had a drink. At a quarter past seven she slipped a jacket over her chemise and walked the short distance to the pub. Peter Shackleton was standing at the bar with his friend Leo, the writer. He must have come straight from work, she thought. Still wearing his suit. He seemed intensely animated and waved vigorously when she came through the door.

"Hello," he called out. "Just in time for an ice-cold glass of bubbly. You remember Leo, don't you?"

Linda exchanged greetings with the writer and held her glass out as Shackleton popped the cork and directed the champagne into it.

"This looks like a special occasion for you two," Leo observed.

"It's a special occasion for everybody," Shackleton enthused. "Ronnie, set old Leo up, will you, and one for yourself."

The barman handed Leo a glass. "Not for me, thanks, Peter. Champagne makes me burp."

"It's supposed to make you burp, you silly bugger. That's what it's all about, isn't it, Linda?"

"Absolutely." She smiled. "It's the one drink that allows you to burp without offending everyone. Doesn't work with beer, somehow."

Her reply sent Shackleton off into a burst of chuckles.

"Doesn't work with beer! That's a bloody good one. Must remember that. She's right, though, isn't she, Leo?"

"Now you come to mention it, yes," Leo said. "Although I could split a point here and say that no one actually burps after drinking eight pints of bitter. They belch. They eruct. They fart. But never a burp. Burps are reserved exclusively for the product of *la méthode champenoise.*"

"Bloody hell," Shackleton spluttered. "*La méthode champenoise.* Never took you for a linguist, old man."

Leo gave Linda an old-fashioned look. "I really don't know what's got into him tonight."

That sent Shackleton off into more laughter. What had got into him was a couple of lines of high-grade cocaine. He was ready to take on the world, not to mention the utterly groinworthy Miss Linda Marshall. And the sooner they got out of this bloody pub and onto the job, the better.

Shackleton closed the lift doors and followed Linda into her flat. He was impressed by the décor, as Deborah had been. Not to mention the slight smell of incense. If he wasn't mistaken, it didn't come from any ordinary joss sticks, either. Not a bad start. There was a pulse of New Age music and a soft, warm light coming from the room at the end of the hall. Linda took his hand and led him there. Once inside, she closed the door and slipped off her jacket to reveal a thin, clinging blouse of shiny, translucent material that molded itself to her perfect breasts like a second skin. She was the distilled essence of sexuality.

"Just one thing," she said. "I don't want us to rush this. I want us to be slow, and careful. I want it to last forever. I want to start with champagne, and I want us to finish by sucking each other and fucking each other until we can't suck or fuck anymore. How does that sound?"

"It sounds fucking marvelous," he said. "Truly fucking marvelous."

"I'll get the bubbly," she said. "You'll find something much more comfortable to wear behind the screen over there. It'll turn you on. It turns me on."

It was a Roman-style tunic of pure silk and a black leather harness with chains swinging from metal rings. Not his style, but what the hell. If it turned her on, that was okay by him. He took off his suit and shirt, paused, then removed his underclothes too. No point being constrained by Jockey shorts at this stage of the game. When he emerged, she was holding out his glass. He drained it, and she filled it again for him without a word. Then another, and she laughed.

"I'd call that quite a thirst you've got there."

"This is good stuff," he said, holding his glass for more. Life was a series of fairy lights, a theme park, a universal fucking galaxy. "Love the incense. Very Moroccan."

"Nothing but the best tonight, Peter. I want to start by showing you some very, very sexy movies. Just lie on the bed, and I'll set them up."

He lay down and watched as she moved to a video player, the material flowing over her breasts and buttocks. Christ, he was going to teach this bitch a lesson she'd never forget. He was going to fuck her till her teeth rattled. He was going to do it so well that no one else would be able to make it happen for her. And when he'd done that, he'd give her a taste of her own bloody medicine. He'd make her wait for it, day after day. . . . She came and stood at the foot of the bed, looking at the rising mound under his tunic.

"Did you do it to yourself every night, like we agreed?" she asked. He nodded. And he had, too. No problem. Just thinking about her was enough to get a stonker going. "It doesn't seem that way to me," she said. "Just look at it, all ready for action!"

He couldn't avoid looking at it, upright like a bloody fist. He wanted to grab hold of her and shove it into her until she was bow-legged. But he could play the bitch's game.

"Here," she said. "Give me your hands. If anyone's going to play with him, it's going to be me. I'm going to drive you crazy, playing with him. And if you're a good boy, I'll let you put it anywhere you like."

"I'm not into all this tie-up stuff," he told her. He tried to pull his hands away, but she was surprisingly strong as she reached over him and pulled the chains toward the corners of the bed.

"You will be after tonight," she breathed. "Believe me. Oh Christ, I can feel him between my legs. Don't make me come, not yet. . . ."

He wasn't sure how it happened, but as she squirmed over him the chains on his leggings became caught up in something as well. When he looked down, he saw they were locked into pulleys. And so were the chains on his hands.

"Fuck it," he said angrily. "I told you I wasn't into all this."

"It's just a bit of fun, Peter. And it's a real turn-on. I'm surprised you haven't tried it before. It's going to blow your mind, so relax." She leaned across and poured another glass of champagne, helping him to drink it down. "Look, I'll show you." She slid along his body until her mouth was level with his crotch and began nibbling his penis playfully. Every now and again she gave it a tiny nip, which made him yelp and struggle with the chains. Then she pumped his foreskin up and down a few times with her hand, letting her fingers slide over the wetness.

When she stopped he gasped. "Jesus Christ. Don't. Keep doing it . . ."

"See what I mean. If those big hands of yours had been free, you'd have stopped me doing that yourself, wouldn't you, you bad, bad boy? Now settle back and watch the movies."

The screen was already showing a typical love nest, a guy with a hood strapped to a padded whipping block and a piano tinkling a Mozart background. He'd seen this sort of crap a hundred times, and it never did anything for him. Then a woman appeared, dressed in black rubber and a mask, holding a whip. She strutted around the hooded guy, saying things like "What have we here, then?" and "It looks like you want punishing, my lad." And the guy in the hood was turning this way and that to try and see where the voice was coming from. She went through the usual routine of flicking his dick and giving him a hard-on. Sucking, wanking. Then a break in the routine for a whipping, although Shackleton had to admit she did lay into the guy a bit, and then she straddled herself over him for a right good humping, and grunts and shouts. It was quite horny, but it wasn't the finale. Not quite. The woman climbed off the guy and pulled her mask away, smiled into the camera.

"Bloody hell," Shackleton said. "That's you."

"One of my first roles," Linda admitted. "Now watch this. I think you'll find it truly amazing, like Walter said."

The woman on the video used a remote control to zoom the camera into the whipping block, then reached to her belt and pulled out a short kitchen knife. Without a pause she pulled the guy's head back and began cutting his throat. His body lurched this way and that as he tried to get away, but she kept at it as blood jetted up her arms and down the rubber catsuit. She kept cutting until his head came away from his neck and fell out of the hood, and then she used the remote control to get a close-up.

"Oh fuck," Shackleton said in a sick voice, recognizing who it was.

"Tara!" Linda shouted. "And there you have him, ladies and gentlemen, the one, the only, the erstwhile . . . Michael Nesbit!" She put her hand on Shackleton's now flaccid penis and waggled it around. "What d'you think of your old cricket chum, lover? Did old Nezzer die happy, or what?"

Shackleton was terrified and confused. He was very dizzy, couldn't move or shout.

"Let's watch some more," Linda said, pointing the infrared controller at the video player. "People pay fortunes to see this kind of stuff. We may as well enjoy it."

The next half hour was a nightmare for Shackleton. He saw old schoolmates start off in what seemed reasonably innocent encounters with Linda, only to end up suffering violent and very painful deaths in front of hidden cameras. Tiger Ramshir's handsome face changing from ecstasy to agony as a pair of female hands pushed a hypodermic needle into his arm and then deep into his urethra. Hodgkins and Odonga fighting desperately to get out of a small cinema auditorium as a fire took hold of the seating and enveloped the space with smoke and flame. Johnson and Smythe tied up and being fucked by Linda as she pressed popper after popper into their noses until their backs were arching to breaking point. Alan Peters spread-eagled in the cockpit of a yacht while she teased him, before butchering him with an ax. A final clip, taken through the windscreen of a car at night, showed Harry Squires crossing a road and turning to face the vehicle as a blinding light lit him. The picture lurched as he was flung over the windscreen, and lurched again and again as the car was reversed and driven over the body several times.

"I was hoping to have your friend Elmwood in the can, too, but someone got to the bastard first," Linda said. "Never mind. You'll help me to make up for that."

Shackleton's wrists and ankles were weeping blood as he tried feebly to pull his arms and legs out of the manacles.

"Why?" he managed to gasp.

"I would have thought that was obvious," Linda smiled. "It's what you and your friends did to my little sister. Remember Lyndsey and your romp in that shitty railway carriage with your chums? She had the whole world in front of her, until you did what you did. She's still dreadfully shocked, you know. Can hardly do a thing for herself anymore, so I decided to come home and look after her, keep her safe. And one day I thought, Why should those dreadful boys get away with it? It's hardly fair, is it? So here we are. It works out very well for me. I needed to spice up my professional output, and I get rid of some perfectly despicable people at the same time."

"You've got to stop this," he whispered.

"I'll bet that was just what Lyndsey was thinking when you all started in on her." Linda's voice was chillingly conversational.

"I'm sorry." He was sobbing now. "Please."

"I'll tell you what we're going to do," Linda said. "We need to make you a lot more comfortable. Or, if you prefer, a lot less comfortable."

She began turning a handle, and Shackleton's arms, legs, and neck were pulled tight into the bed frame so he could hardly move.

"There," she said. "Howzat? And the great thing about all this is, no matter how you feel right now, King Dick won't let us down. Isn't that remarkable?" She began to squeeze her breasts through the thin material until her nipples stood proud, then she rubbed them on Shackleton's penis, which immediately began swelling again. "There. You see that. Good old King Dick. You must be very proud of him. He's a bloody hero, and you know what heroes get? They get what they fucking well like, Peter. And I know what this hero likes, don't I? Oh yes. My sister Lyndsey told me. The big one with the freckles likes it up the arse, she told me. Poor little thing. You ruined her life, you know that? You and your Winstanton chums."

Linda turned, pirouetted slowly, pushing her buttocks toward him and slipping her gown onto the floor. He watched helplessly as she squeezed a tube of KY jelly into her hands and rubbed it into her backside, then over his penis. "No point in me going through all that pain, is there? We know better now, don't we? Spermicidal non-staining water-based lubricant. Lovely! Now you just lie back and enjoy yourself. Leave it all to me."

She maneuvered herself astride him and eased herself up and down so that he was penetrating her. She pushed on his shoulders as she moved, digging her nails into his flesh, letting her breasts brush his mouth, murmuring to him all the time, slipping her hand back and beneath every now and again so she could play with his testicles while the sweat gathered on his brow and in his eyes and he erupted into her again and again and again, until she slowed her movements and clenched him hard one last time to make sure that he'd finished.

"Good boy," she said breathlessly as she rolled away. "Give me a minute, then it's your turn."

"Listen," he whispered painfully. "For Christ's sake, we were just a bunch of kids. . . . We thought she was hot for it. . . ."

"I know you were only kids, lover, and don't think I'm not taking that into account."

She disappeared from view, and he tried desperately to pull his arms free again, but everything was locked solid and the effort exhausted him. She must have put something in his champagne. What with that, the incense and the coke . . . If only he could just get one hand free, he'd bloody well show her.

When she came back she waved a large plastic dildo attached to a rubber tube in front of his face, swaying to the music. "Party time!"

She smeared the dildo with jelly and fumbled under his tunic to locate his anus, then began pushing it inside. He tried to scream, but his throat was too dry. When the dildo was driven in hard she covered it with binding tape, wrapping it around the tube and around his buttocks to make sure it would stay in place.

"Just think, Shackers, if it hurts with all this lovely jelly on, just think how Lyndsey felt when you began stuffing your big cock into her while one of those other bastards was giving it to her up the front. Pretty grim, I should imagine. But don't you worry. The best is yet to come."

She began arranging one of the video cameras so it was directed down at him.

"Walter and Sylvia edit all this. They're very good at it, too. Funny thing is, they think all my lovely special effects really are special effects. They think I switch from the real thing to latex dummies. You've got to laugh. There's all these fake snuff movies being made with latex so the punters think they're the real thing, and here's me doing the real thing and making them think it's latex. Am I good, or what? Oh, I almost forgot, we need sound effects for this one." She poured some more champagne into his mouth. "There, that should loosen the tonsils for you. Everyone's out for the evening, so don't let me down. Give it everything you've got."

"Let me go, for Christ's sake," he mumbled.

"This tube," she said, "runs over to the bar. You might have noticed a small cylinder of gas. Well, I say small, but it's big enough. I'm going to turn it on, ever such a little, then it's over to you. There's things I have to do around the place. Tidy up . . . pack. . . ."

He watched, struggling frantically, as she bent behind the bar. He wasn't sure when the pain from the gas began, because he was hurting anyway. But it slowly began hurting more.

Linda was in the shower when the screaming began, carefully cleaning herself, under the nails, in all the private parts, using a douche, medicated shampoo, antiseptic soap. It didn't sound much like a human scream. More like an emergency siren, rising and falling

for ages . . . until there was a very strange thumping noise, and silence.

Time to collect the cassettes, Linda thought with a satisfied smile,
as she dried herself.

Deborah woke up in the car with a start to find she'd had decidedly
more than a catnap. In fact it was almost midnight, and she had at
least sixty miles to drive. But at least she'd missed the heavy traffic.
She made good time, and on the road between Burford and Stow-
on-the-Wold she saw a sign pointing to a bed-and-breakfast farm
down a lane. Although it was late, the people still had the lights on,
and they made her feel welcome.

In the morning, after a good breakfast, she set off for nowhere in
particular, following her nose until she reached a lane leading to a
Roman villa. She parked up against a hedge and began walking. The
air was clear and fresh, and the clear summer sun had begun to burn
the morning mists from the low ground. The villa itself was not very
grand, not like the one at Fishbourne with the wonderful mosaics.
Here were just the foundations, lying square in the earth as they had
for over fifteen centuries. But it was wonderful to sit, imagining what
it had been like all those years ago.

A few ramblers appeared across the fields and made their way to
the site, smiling greetings, exchanging a few words about the
weather, directing her to a walk across the hills, where she could get
views over the River Severn and the Black Mountains, if the air
stayed clear. And if she turned north, then east, and followed her
nose, she'd end up back where the car was parked, passing an ancient
country pub on the way.

It was too good to resist.

She drove back to the city at the end of the afternoon, checked
the car in, and took a bus back to Heathside, very tired, but very
happy and not a little hungry after the day's exertions. She wondered
if Linda would like one of those French meals they'd had together,
the night she had arrived.

She realized that something was not quite right the moment she
opened the door. Despite the warm day, the flat felt cold, and there
was a musty smell like rotten drains. Then she saw that Linda's paint-

ings had been taken from the walls, and ornaments were missing from alcoves and shelves. She hurried to the kitchen where they left messages for each other and saw a bulky envelope on the table. It contained a large amount of money, some documents, and a letter.

Dear Deborah,

Sorry to leave you to pick up the pieces like this, but the money may help. All the bills are paid, and there's a ninety-five-year lease on the flat which I've transferred to you. Sell it, if you want.

Bit of a mess in my room, I'm afraid. Probably best if you don't go in. Call the police and let them sort it out. That's what we pay taxes for, after all. I'd like to say I'll keep in touch, but you know how it is.

Love,
Linda

P.S. Don't worry about Peter Shackleton. He was a bastard, but then you knew that, didn't you?

What did it all mean? Why had Linda gone off like this, leaving her money, transferring the lease . . . ? And what was all this about the police? What was a "bit of a mess"? She left the kitchen and tried Linda's door. It swung open, and the musty, rotten smell rolled into the hall.

The thing on the bed looked like a rag doll with the stuffing burst out. It was only when she moved closer that she saw the congealed wetness and the indescribable things that were sticking to the walls and the ceiling. They seemed to be moving, and she saw they were covered with flies. She backed out of the room, fighting an impulse to vomit, feeling her way along the hall and into the lift, fumbling for the ground-floor button. Somehow she managed to reach the neighbor's door, and she banged on it with her fists until he answered. Then she fainted.

Part III

FRIDAY
THE THIRTEENTH

Chapter 14

AUGUST, A HOT SUNDAY, AND THE GARDEN WAS STILL looking good after the warm, wet spring. Not that Detective Superintendent Frank Illiffe could take much credit for that. Life in the investigative arm of the British Transport Police was not conducive to sweeping up leaves, trimming borders, and planting hardy perennials. That had been up to his wife, Jean. He looked fondly at her as she took advantage of the weather and dozed in the sun by the side of the small outdoor swimming pool. Things were developing well, according to her ultrascan, and they were both hoping that this time would be the big one. Boy or girl, it didn't matter, just so long as they could keep it. It was one of those things that only rest could sort out, Jean's gynecologist Dr. Elman had said. So despite her protests, Illiffe advertised in the local paper for a part-time gardener to come in during the week to keep everything under control, and old Albert had proved to be a blessing in more ways than one. Ex-army and a strict disciplinarian. Once on the premises, he wouldn't even let Jean make a cup of tea, never mind see her scrambling about the grounds with a trug and a pair of pruning shears. So Illiffe could set off to work at six-thirty every morning reasonably sure that his wife would be obliged to stay off her feet for most of the day as the gynecologist had advised. He bent down and kissed her forehead.

"Mmmmm," she murmured contentedly.

"Fancy a swim?"

"Too comfortable. Go away."

"Gentle exercise, Dr. Elman said. Swimming is the best gentle exercise you can get. You lie out here all day, and you'll get fat."

"I want to get fat," she said. "Big and fat and pregnant."

"Wrong sort of fat," he told her seriously.

"Maybe later, but only if you promise not to splash me."

"Would I ever do such a thing?"

"All the time. You're a proper pest."

As the morning went by, a few clouds made a brief, threatening appearance but were moved on by the southerly wind. Jean was eventually persuaded to have a swim in the heated pool and began moving from one end to the other with a lazy sidestroke, while Frank made inroads into a carton of Ruddles beer and caught up with a week's supply of newspapers. And then the doorbell rang. Unusual. It was usually Frank's mobile phone or pager that interrupted their time together.

"You're not expecting anyone, are you?" he called to Jean.

"What?" she asked, shaking water out of her ears.

"Someone's at the front door. Are you expecting anyone?"

"Absolutely not. Don't answer it."

Illiffe frowned and stood up. "Could be one of the neighbors, I suppose."

It was Julie Adams.

Apart from watching her documentaries and news reports on television, it was the first time he'd seen her since their evening together in the hotel at Hope Green all those years ago. Must be six at least, maybe seven. They had planned to meet for lunch once or twice in the weeks that followed, but his duties and her assignments always got in the way. She took a correspondent's job reporting conflicts in the Balkans, and he was posted to Northwestern Area Headquarters in Manchester, where he met Jean. After that, they lost touch.

"Hello, Frank." She was looking straight into his eyes, the remembered smile upturning the corners of her mouth.

It came rushing back, a jumble of Lyndsey Barratt lying in a hospital bed, and passion in Julie's hotel, and the horrendous cleaning up of the mess created by that bent DI Jenkins, and the worse mess created by young Lyndsey vanishing from the hospital. It had taken weeks to sort out the paperwork, not to mention the time wasted in dealing with the irate families of eleven schoolboys, full of injured parental innocence and accusations of police harassment. He still thought about Lyndsey, wondered what had happened to her, even after all these years.

"Hello, Julie," he said, conscious that he was wearing only his bathing shorts. And that she was using the same perfume. Plus, she was wearing one of those silk chemise things that emphasized the feminine curve of her body. He was holding his arm across the doorway, like a barrier.

"Sorry about dropping in on you like this, but we need to talk."

"You'd better come in." He wondered how she'd got his address; why she'd come; how he should introduce her to Jean.

"We're in the back. Come and say hello."

She followed him through the house to the swimming pool, where Jean was toweling herself dry.

"Darling, this is Julie Adams. We met on that Lyndsey Barratt case I told you about."

"Yes, I watch your program," Jean said politely. "How do you do?"

"I do apologize for the intrusion, Mrs. Illiffe. But something's cropped up, and I need a word with your husband."

"Will you have something to drink?" Jean asked politely.

"That's very kind," Julie said, "but I really just need a quick word, and then I'll be off."

Illiffe pulled on a robe. "Okay," he said shortly. "We'll go inside." He led the way to the living room. "What's this all about? How did you get my address?"

Julie shrugged. "The complete UK phone list is on the Internet, ex-directory numbers and all. The hard bit was coming here. It's been a long time."

"Never mind the long time, Julie. What's up?"

She gave him a Metropolitan Police press statement, issued three days previously.

The body of a man was discovered today in a flat in the Heath-side area of North London. Police are anxious to interview the owner of the flat, who may be able to help them with their inquiries.

"Not my patch. If you want to know anything about that, try the Met."

"I did try the Met, and they're bloody useless." She handed him another paper containing a list of names. "Remember that lot?"

He scanned down the list. Selik Ramshir. James Odonga. Alan Peters. Michael Nesbit. Harry Squires. How could he forget! Ramshir with his diplomatic connections and an insider route to soft drugs, Nesbit and his chief constable father. A thoroughly nasty bunch.

The names reminded him that there was an outstanding drug charge against Lyndsey that needed formal winding up. His own British Transport Police investigation was on the back burner because the men on the list and their cricketing chums could not be charged unless she came back and filed a complaint against them. If she ever did, Illiffe would take great pleasure in reopening the case. Meanwhile, he had tidied up what loose ends he could. Before his promotion to detective superintendent, he began the procedures that led to an internal inquiry against Detective Inspector Jenkins of the regional force. He had faced considerable resistance from the man's colleagues, including several warnings that his career prospects would be severely damaged if he persisted. Fortunately, this particular brand of freemasonry was contained in the region, and despite its influence Jenkins had his rank reduced to detective sergeant, after which he resigned. Thomas Haddock, the sports master of the school, had been sacked and missed facing a criminal charge because someone in the Ministry of Defense pulled in a favor. A rotten business all around.

All these memories, conjured up by a piece of paper. He handed it back. "What's the point?"

"The point is, they're all dead. That's why I wanted to see you. I found out yesterday that Peter Shackleton was the man in the Heathside flat."

Illiffe stared at her. Thinking. And the first thing he thought was that this was bad arithmetic. Six young men out of a group of eleven from the same school, the same cricket team. Very bad arithmetic.

"How come you've got the list in the first place?"

"Violent or unusual death is something we keep our eyes on to see if anything can be used in a program," Julie told him. "Sometimes I file things away, specially if I recognize the names, like with this lot. So when the Met released Shackleton's name I began a few inquiries. They're keeping the lid on the details, but the neighbors are muttering about a sadomasochistic love nest. Then I remembered that Nesbit had been killed during sex-related activities. There was nothing to show if his death had been deliberate, and the coroner recorded an open verdict. Squires was killed by a hit-and-run driver, and the same verdict was brought, although whoever hit him and ran managed to roll over the body a couple of times. Ramshir OD'd in a Mayfair hotel, and Odonga died in a fire in a Guildford cinema club. Well, I thought, bloody good riddance. But it seemed more than a little strange. An elongated arm of coincidence. So I spent this morning on the phone. I checked with the bursar at Winstanton School, and he very kindly gave me the last known addresses of the other members of the cricket team. George Weston is running his father's construction business somewhere near High Wycombe. The others have all moved away, and I haven't been able to track them down. I was hoping you'd help me."

"Out of the question."

"Crap. You and I both know that the first thing you're going to do when you get back to your office is run a check on this. At the very least you can let me know where they are and exactly how their teammates handed in their tallies. That's a matter of public record, so you won't be committing a felony, will you? You'd save me a hell of a lot of time. It's just a question of bringing it all together."

"Quite," he said dryly. "And, assuming it comes together in a reasonably newsworthy way, I'd have you running a media circus all over me. Forget it."

"You sound like a bloody policeman."

"I am a bloody policeman."

"Yes, but you didn't always sound like one. I remember . . ."

"I don't," he lied. "And I really must get back to my wife."

"Yes, I'm sorry to disturb you both, but I thought this would be important for you as well as me."

It was.

"You're looking too hard for a story. Forget it."

"That's my job. At least you can remember that, can't you?"

How could he forget? And he still couldn't figure out why she'd spent that afternoon with him at the hotel. Was it professional or personal?

She closed her briefcase. "I half expected to see you at the funeral."

"What funeral?"

Those dark eyes again, straight at him. "Lyndsey's mother. You mean you didn't know?"

He shook his head.

"Four years ago. They said she died of pneumonia. Couldn't fight it because of the MS. Personally, I reckon the whole thing just broke her heart. Two clodhopping CID men were lurking in the churchyard in case Lyndsey turned up."

"Isn't that why you were there?"

"Absolutely. Got some good shots of them leaning against the gravestones. Anyway, you proved that sod Jenkins was bent, so what were they doing there?"

A good point, but the brotherhood never gave up on its own. Jenkins might have taken the rap for planting drugs at Lyndsey's home, but everyone knew that Chief Constable Nesbit had given the nod and the wink. If they could get their hands on Lyndsey, they'd try to stick something else on her. Call it revenge; call it persistence. That's the way it works.

"I've no idea," he said.

"This case is going to wake up one day, and I'm going to nail down every loose bloody plank in it."

"Meaning?"

"Come off it, Frank. Lyndsey Barratt is either dead or hiding away. I don't subscribe to the death theory, and no one can hide away forever."

"Meanwhile you're perfectly happy to collect information and jump to some unsupportable conclusions."

"What conclusions? Did I say I'd jumped to any conclusions?"

As he watched her walk down the path to her car, he knew she had manipulated him, just as she planned to do. The first thing in the morning he was going to make inquiries about every single member of that rotten bunch of prep school shits.

When he returned to the back garden, Jean rather pointedly asked no questions, but the atmosphere had changed, no longer relaxed and carefree. He slipped into the pool and swam several lengths, pushing strongly at each turn, enjoying the flow of water and concentrating on making himself as streamlined as possible. Push, glide, break surface, two strokes, turn, push, glide . . . When he finally hauled himself onto the poolside, Jean was waiting with a towel.

"You've slept with her, haven't you?"

Anger welled up quickly. How did they always know? "It was a long time ago."

"The question is, are you going to sleep with her again?"

"Bloody hell," he muttered furiously. "It was before I met you. And no, I will not sleep with her again. It obviously escapes your notice, but I love you, and I want you to have this baby. I want you to have a lot of babies."

She blinked and turned away, busied herself tidying and polishing, until he pushed her into a chair in front of the TV and did the chores himself. When he came back from the kitchen, the chair was empty. He looked into the garden to see if she was putting away the sun loungers. There was no sign of her there, so he did the job himself. When he went back into the living room she was by the drinks cupboard pouring two glasses of champagne. She was wearing a silk robe with nothing underneath.

"I'd forgotten how much you like me in this," she said, holding out a glass.

He took it and drank slowly. "I hadn't."

She moved closer. "Dammit, Frank. I've been ignoring you. I've been so bloody selfish."

She smelled wonderful. Clean, warm. The smell of Jean.

"Leave it out. Dr. Elman—"

"A very professional man. Unfortunately, not altogether wise, or practical. There's more than one way to make love, isn't there?"

She pushed his robe aside and pressed herself into him. His reaction was immediate, and she reached between his legs and smiled.

"Why don't you lie down and let me take care of this?"

She began massaging his neck and his shoulders, his arms and legs, and his buttocks, then turned him over so she could run her hands more gently over his stomach. Whenever he tried to move, she pushed him down, so that in the end he was content to lie there while she caressed and kissed him to a climax, and then she put his hand into the warmth between her legs so he could feel her climaxing too. It was several minutes before he could catch his breath.

"Look. About Julie Adams—"

She leaned over and kissed his mouth gently. "I know all about Julie Adams. I've known ever since the day I caught you watching her program with that nostalgic look on your face. Don't forget how perceptive we women can be, and how nosy we are. I've read every newspaper clipping about you and your cases. She seems to have written a good many of them. She's very good."

"Well then—" he began, but she stopped him again.

"I should never have put you on the spot like that. But Julie coming here made me realize that I couldn't sit back and forget that I'm married to a handsome, fit, and very sexy bloke. If I lose you to an attractive lady like Julie Adams, I'll only have myself to blame."

"So, you agree she's attractive," he said mischievously.

"Oh yes," Jean said seriously. "In fact, under any other circumstances, I think I might quite like her."

Chapter 15

FIRST THING ON MONDAY MORNING, ILLIFFE CALLED DEtective Superintendent Harry Branskill, an old friend who worked at the Police National Computer Bureau at Hendon in North London, the PNC.

"Harry, it's Frank Illiffe. I need a favor."

"If it's unauthorized access, the answer's no," Branskill said emphatically.

"Definitely authorized," Illiffe assured him, blandly. "I've got a list of eleven names. They all had files opened in July '88. The fourteenth. If our regional data officers have been doing their jobs, you'll have updates."

"Eleven names and what else . . . ?"

"Just the names, plus they were all aged roughly the same. Born between August '69 and July '70."

"We'll need more than that."

"I'm told you have some very clever people working up there. I'll fax the list to you."

Harry's voice was resigned. "I'll see what we can do. But that's another you owe me."

"It's on the fax right now. Appreciate a fast response. The press are nosing about. Oh, and keep the lid on this, will you?"

Illiffe grinned as he disconnected from the grumble. He and Harry went back a long way. Owed each other many favors.

*   *   *

Two days later a civilian member of the PNC staff, Susan York, phoned him to arrange a meeting. She arrived in his office dressed in a smart suit, blond hair tied back, black-rimmed spectacles firmly in place. Strictly no makeup. Very businesslike. Politely refused his offer of coffee. Straight down to business.

"I thought you'd like to see this summary, sir. I can leave you my files, if you like."

Illiffe looked at the list of dates and names.

4/19/90 Selik Ramshir: Deceased. Drug overdose; Mayfair

2/1/92 Alan Hodgkins: Deceased. Fire; Guildford

2/1/92 James Odonga: Deceased. Fire; Guildford

9/18/93 Ainslie Johnson: Deceased. SIHA; Macclesfield

10/17/94 Michael Nesbit: Deceased. Sadomasochistic incident; Gloucester

5/15/95 Jonathan Elmwood: Deceased. Stabbed in mugging; West End

8/8/95 Alan Peters: Deceased. Sailing incident; Solent

12/12/95 Timothy Smythe: Deceased. SIHA; Stevenage

5/24/96 Harry Squires: Deceased. Hit-and-run victim; Chester

8/26/96 Peter Shackleton: Deceased. Sadomasochistic incident; Heathside

He stared at it, and the hair at the back of his neck bristled. Ten out of eleven, a coincidence?

"Apart from the stabbing, there's no indication of foul play. The assumption for the others is accidental death, so all the coroners recorded open verdicts," Susan said.

"SIHA?" he asked.

"Sexually induced heart attack, sir. The postmortems suggested that large amounts of a heart stimulant had been ingested. Probably amyl nitrate. The postmortem on Nesbit showed traces of Pavulon. It's a curare-type relaxant. There were also marks on the arms and legs. You know the kind of thing."

He shook his head. Ten members of a school cricket team dying in such a short period of time was definitely odd, but apart from Elmwood's stabbing there was nothing on the list to arouse suspicion of foul play. Ramshir was a sybaritic little sod who would have overdosed sooner or later. Presumably Hodgkins and Odonga kept in touch after leaving school and were involved in a fire together. Probably an accident, but it could have been a grudge arson attack against the club. Two SIHAs among such a perverted group was hardly surprising. The final four deaths were a stabbing, a sailing incident, a hit-and-run, and finally Shackleton, another victim of a sadomasochistic event. Apart from their cricket team membership, there was no connection and certainly no distinctive modus operandi. But Julie Adams was right. It was difficult to put so many deaths down to coincidence, bearing in mind all the circumstances.

"These SM victims," he said. "What's that all about?"

"Michael Nesbit was found in a hotel room that had been rented out to a prostitute. She left him tied to a whipping frame with his head severed. Decapitation and other mutilations are increasing in this kind of thing, apparently. The coroner recorded a verdict of death by person or persons unknown, because there was no evidence to indicate that it had been deliberate rather than a drugs party that went wildly over the top. Probably murder, but that would almost certainly be reduced to a plea of manslaughter on the grounds of diminished responsibility. You probably know about Shackleton."

"Not the details."

"Someone used him as a party balloon. Very unpleasant."

"Any result on the investigation?"

"It's not on the computer yet."

She could have sent all this information through the internal post. Illiffe had the feeling she wanted to tell him something.

"Did Harry Branskill ask you to report in person?"

"No, but he said you wanted to keep the lid on your query, so I thought it best to meet." He let the silence develop, and she began to fidget. Finally: "You're looking for a common factor, aren't you, sir?"

"Why don't you call me Frank?" he said. "And there is a common factor. In fact, there are quite a few. The sex angle, the age, the school . . ."

She nodded. "And the woman."

"What woman?"

"When Harry asked me to run these names through the computer, I used your query to test a program we're developing. It shows there's always a woman involved in some way."

"Sorry. You just lost me."

"It's a new data–mining application."

He noticed that her eyes were beginning to take on an evangelical glaze behind her spectacles. He'd seen that kind of look before, when experts get carried away by their own enthusiasm.

"Susan," he said firmly. "I do not speak computer. You'll have to translate."

She needed no more encouragement, and Illiffe was treated to a discourse on how huge amounts of information in a computer database contained patterns and connections that normal inquiry procedures would miss.

"It's a bit like not seeing the wood for the trees. BT used the method to nail a team of telephone fraudsters using call centers with Premium Line numbers. They got away with around two million pounds before they were caught. Basically, you make the computer ask itself questions about the data that you wouldn't have thought of."

"I see," Illiffe lied. The finer points of computing were a mystery to him. "So what about this woman?"

"In eight of the cases, a female witness mentioned the presence of a woman being with the victims just before they died. When the investigating officers tried to renew contact with these witnesses, they'd all moved and were untraceable. A woman was with Shackleton when he died and another woman reported his death. She's the only one who hasn't disappeared. She gave a statement and is still available for questioning."

"Who's in charge?"

She glanced at her notes. "DI Terence Chesterton. Number One Area."

He scribbled the name down. "What d'you make of it all?"

"It's another common factor. There may or may not be something significant. There may be other common factors."

"You've gone to a helluva lot of trouble, to come up with that kind of conclusion." He was unable to keep a note of irritation out of his voice.

"All I'm saying, sir, is that I'd need more than this to come to any firm conclusions."

"How about some unfirm conclusions? And call me Frank, will you, for heaven's sake?"

She looked unhappy. "We can only get out of the PNC what the duty data officers feed into it, and that's usually just a synopsis. The next logical step would be to make a manual check of the complete files for each case. Ideally, we'd feed the information from all of them into the computer and do another pass with the data-mining program."

"Failing that," he asked as patiently as he could, "what do you think?"

"I ran a statistical analysis on the variables. The chances of these deaths containing all the known common factors are several billion to one."

"Indulge me," he persisted. "Cut out the arithmetic and talk English."

For several seconds she sat squeezing her fingers together. Nervous. Not wanting to believe what she was about to say.

"The computer is telling us that at least nine of the deaths are connected."

There was another silence. Illiffe didn't want to believe what he had just heard.

Susan pointed at another heading. "You took statements from each of the deceased following an assault on a young actress on a train. Lyndsey Barratt. The record shows that no charges were brought."

"The girl disappeared from hospital," Illiffe said heavily. "She'd been drugged, raped, sodomized, indecently assaulted, and beaten. The medical staff thought she showed signs of amnesia during treatment. The school cricket team admitted having sexual intercourse with her but alleged that she had given them the drugs and initiated the incident. As if that wasn't bad enough, her father had a fatal heart attack while all this was going on. I learned recently that her mother died, probably as a consequence of what happened."

"Were the boys telling the truth?" Susan asked him.

"No way. If I could have got her statement on record, we would have brought rape charges against all eleven of them. On top of that, at least one policeman, a teacher at the school, and one of the students at Lyndsey's college conspired to pervert the course of justice by planting drugs and tampering with evidence."

"Well," Susan said briskly. "It presents you with two alternatives. Either we're looking at an amazing coincidence or at the work of a serial killer."

She was right about any coincidence being amazing. There was no way that ten fit young men from the same school could possibly have met violent deaths at random in so short a time period. Julie Adams suspected it when she found out about five of the deaths. That's why she had sought him out and given him the list in the first place. He suspected it, and that's why he had called Harry Branskill at Hendon. Susan York suspected it, too, and that was why she was giving it her best shot. But suspicion and surmise are poor reasons to start what might become a major investigation or a major screwup. He needed to see the individual files on the deaths: witness statements, SOCO and coroners' reports. The trouble was, if the BTP put in official requests to get case information from the regional forces involved, not least the Met, people would wonder if an internal investigation was under way. It would become very complicated. On the other hand . . .

"How is your development work funded?"

Susan looked puzzled. "We're part of the Home Office. The PNC bureau director works out the central budgets, and we're assigned the money. In the regions, each chief constable is responsible for peripheral funding and data input."

"I've got a small operational budget," Illiffe told her. "If I squared it with Harry, how would you feel about continuing this testing you were talking about?"

"The data-mining project? That would be very helpful. We're always short of resources."

"Okay. Put in a request for the files on these deaths as a follow-up to your development work. If there's anything there to substantiate the serial-killer theory, I'll pass it along the line to the national coordinator at the regional Crime Squad."

Julie Adams called Illiffe the next day. He had expected her to chase things up, but was not sure how to handle it. His problem was not made any easier by the fact that, despite his assurances to Jean, he still felt the old thump in the guts when he thought of Julie.

"Hello. What can I do for you?" No point in asking how she had the number of his direct line at Tavistock Place.

"Lunch," she said. "I'm buying."

"You know I can't do that."

"So you buy it."

"That's not what I mean. It's out of the question."

There was a silence. "You know, Frank, when I got those names I used them as an excuse to see you again. There's other coppers I could have gone to."

He still wondered why Julie had gone to bed with him. As the job they'd been working on had more or less finished at the time, he liked to think it had been personal, but he'd never been sure. He was even less sure now. But whatever else was true, she had brought him a list of names that might well open the door to a major murder inquiry.

"There's no need to bullshit me," he told her. "If anything comes out of your list you'll be informed through the proper channels."

"So you are investigating it then?"

He'd forgotten how quick she was. "I didn't say that."

She created a moment's silence; then, "Why are you being so confrontational, Frank?"

"Am I? I wasn't aware of it."

"Fair enough. I'll do my own thing on this one. But don't blame me if the headline includes something about police incompetence." She disconnected.

Three days later, Susan York piled ten dossiers on Illiffe's desk together with another of her funny-looking charts with key words printed in boxes. It was a fast result, by any standards. She told him she hadn't had much sleep, and he believed her. She'd spent a great deal of time traveling to the regions in which the deaths occurred and tracking down coroners' court records and other public documents.

"One day we'll be able to do all this with a computer terminal," she said seriously. "At the moment, it's quicker by train. The good news is that I was able to sift through the files and prioritize the contents. I was then able to scan in the most important reports, run the TIFF files through an OCR routine, add the text files to the PNC database, and run the results through the new program again. It'll help you when you go through the files in detail. You'll know what to look out for."

He had no idea what she was talking about, but her chart was interesting, all the same. It showed the same links as the one she had first shown him between the men's dates of birth, regions of birth, education, sporting affiliations, and Illiffe's witness statements from the Lyndsey Barratt case. But there were some additional boxes.

Estimated time of death between 8:00 P.M. and 6:00 A.M. × 10

Maximum time between deaths: 129 weeks

Minimum time between deaths: 13 weeks

Average time between deaths: 42 weeks

Video equipment found at or near scene × 5

High luminosity at scene of death × 4

Woman companion at scene of death × 8

Witness (female) at scene of death × 9

Witness available (female) × 1

Witness unavailable (female) × 8

Illiffe pointed at the box containing the phrase *"Woman companion at scene of death × 8."*

"That said four last time," he noted.

"Data officers don't always put consistent information from the witness statements into the computer. I did, and that's where our new program scores," Susan said animatedly. "In eight of the deaths there were reports of the deceased men being with a woman before they died.

"The key witnesses in nine of the cases were also women, and until Shackleton none of these women have been available to make a court statement following their verbal statements. Ramshir had been to a gambling club with a blond woman. A taxi driver said he took Hodgkins and Odonga to a pornographic cinema club in Guildford with a dark-haired woman he thought was a prostitute. Six other people died in the fire, but none of the corpses was a woman. The Fire Brigade was unsure how the fire started.

"Alan Peters kept a yacht at Poole Harbour and went on a two-day sail with an attractive woman. The empty yacht was picked up by the coast guard in the Channel after they failed to return to the harbor. His body was caught up in some ropes underneath the boat but hers was never recovered.

"Harry Squires was hit by a car late one night as he left his office. Apparently the vehicle reversed over him when the driver tried to back away. The witness who said she saw the car leaving the scene described the driver as being slightly built, with long blond hair, but she only got a glimpse."

"What's all this about luminosity?" Illiffe asked.

She shrugged. "No idea. You might get more information when you read the files. If I were you, I'd start with the Shackleton case, because it's up and running. We have a witness who was very close to the people involved, and she's still available."

"You've done a remarkable job," he told Susan. "Maybe it's all coincidence, but I can't get my head round that."

When she left he called his boss, Detective Chief Superintendent Mark Villiers, a shrewd copper who had worked with the Met before taking his position as head of the BTP's internal investigation unit.

"I need a couple of days off."

"Really?" The voice was not surprised. Just cynical.

"Yes." Illiffe had never asked for favors and reckoned he was owed one now.

"And if I asked if you were up-to-date with the caseload, you'd tell me everything was on schedule, right?"

"Right. And when I come back, I might be asking for a temporary transfer to SCS."

"Just like that?"

"Thanks, guv."

If Illiffe was heading for the kind of investigation he thought he was, he'd need to liaise closely with the regional police forces involved, and that meant working with the Serious Crime Squad. He put the phone down with a smile and waited. Two minutes later Villiers came into his office, his hook nose thrust belligerently forward.

"Show me."

Illiffe pointed at the dossiers. "I need to go through that lot immediately, and it'll take at least two days, solid, no interruptions. If it throws up what I think it'll throw up, we have a serial killer on our hands."

Villiers flipped through the pile, noting the locality of the various deaths.

"Christ, Frank, this is well off our patch. What's your interest?"

"Lyndsey Barratt. Have I got those days off, or what?"

A pause. Keen brain behind hook nose weighs the pros and cons. Little to lose, maybe something to gain.

"Unless something crops up, you've got Thursday, Friday, and the weekend. Report to me first thing Monday. Give my best to Jean."

By Sunday morning, Jean Illiffe was beginning to think that having a husband working at home wasn't such a good idea. Illiffe had worked almost around the clock, reading, making notes, and telephoning people all over the country. Her hot meals became cold snacks, nibbled absentmindedly as the mountain of paper on the dining room table grew higher.

Despite all this, Illiffe was no nearer a conclusion as to whether or not the ten deaths had been caused by the same person or a number of people who were connected in some way or were even—despite the odds—unrelated. The arson victims, Hodgkins and Odonga, could well have been innocent bystanders in rivalry involving pornography gangs. The hit-and-run case involving Harry Squires fitted into no obvious category that related to any of the other deaths, but a Ms. Bronwyn Williams, who came forward after the police had asked for witnesses, stated that she saw a powerful white light shining out of the car just before she heard the impact. A local car-hire company reported a missing vehicle three days later, and a sample of paint taken from the victim's trousers matched the color and make of the missing car, which was eventually discovered parked in a little-used side street three miles from the incident. The woman who hired the car no longer lived at the address on her driver's license, and despite extensive inquiries the police had been unable to trace her.

Jonathan Elmwood was stabbed late at night on Frith Street in Soho. One witness (a doorman for a nearby strip club) said he had seen Elmwood go into a Greek restaurant opposite Ronnie Scott's jazz club with a blond woman and come out on his own a few minutes later. As he crossed the road a group of muggers stampeded around the corner and tried to grab his wallet. A moment later, Elmwood was crouched in the road with blood pumping from his stomach. He died on his way to hospital. One of the Greek waiters confirmed that Elmwood had arrived with a woman but had a row with her before they reached the table. The waiter's English was poor, and he was not able to add anything more substantial to his statement. Still, Illiffe thought, it added one more woman to the mystery.

Johnson and Smythe had been found dead in hotels used by prostitutes and homosexuals. One of the night porters remembered Smythe arriving with a woman, but again there was nothing more definite to go on.

The case of Alan Peters was well documented, partly because of the natural tendency of yachting types to notice the movements of other yachting types, and partly because the coast guardsmen involved had submitted a very detailed report. Peters left his moorings in Poole Harbour about ten o'clock one Saturday morning in August on his Contessa 36, *Tiger Shark*. The evening before, he had agreed to take an attractive woman for a sail. Several yachtsmen said they saw *Tiger Shark* motoring its way past the chain ferry at the mouth of the harbor and setting sail into the bay. Another yachtsman said he saw them at anchor in Binnel Bay in the Isle of Wight at around one thirty in the afternoon, and later they were seen in Chapman's Pool. Nothing more was seen of the boat until next morning, when a windsurfer saw it drifting off Lulworth Cove. There was no sign of anyone on board, so he attracted the skipper of a motor cruiser who radioed the coast guard. Peters was discovered caught by a broken safety line, disemboweled and castrated by the propeller. The pathologist's report said he had died of heart failure. His clothing and a woman's outfit were discovered in the cabin. The coast guard compiled an inventory of the articles on the yacht. The coroner recorded an open verdict but commented that the case would be closed when the woman's body was discovered.

Illiffe phoned the Portsmouth coast guard and asked to speak to the officer who had investigated the death yacht, Jim Hetherington. The duty officer said he was on leave and gave him Hetherington's home phone number.

"Sorry to interrupt your weekend," Illiffe said after he had introduced himself, "but I'm checking through the *Tiger Shark* incident, and I wonder if there's any chance we could get together sometime today."

Hetherington agreed to meet Illiffe at the boatyard in Poole where *Tiger Shark* was laid up.

It took Illiffe two hours to motor down the M3, through the New Forest to the boatyard. When he arrived, the tide was in, and dinghy enthusiasts were racing madly across the navigation channels under the bows of larger yachts trying to tack their way against a steady breeze to the harbor mouth. Air horns sounded constantly as irate skippers jibed to avoid collisions.

Hetherington was waiting for him at the security gates, a ruddy, down-to-earth man who scrutinized Illiffe's warrant card before saying a word.

"Just checking through the incident, I believe you told me, Superintendent," he said in a soft country accent.

"That's right."

"How can I help?"

"To be honest, I've no idea. I've checked through your report, and everything seems in order, but I have this feeling that there's something missing."

"You wouldn't be wrong there, sir. For one thing, that young lady is missing. I know these waters, and I've not known anyone drown in that sector without the body appearing within a few days, somewhere along the coast. 'Course, she could be tangled up in some old anchor lines. Happens sometimes, but I'd have expected a scuba diver to have found her by now. Then again, *Tiger Shark* started the evening at anchor in Chapman's Pool, but moved on shortly after, according to one of the skippers who spent the night there."

"I didn't see anything about that in your report." Illiffe got his notebook out.

"Well," Hetherington said in his south country drawl. "They didn't have anything to add to what we already knew, so I didn't bother. Chap by the name of Jack Holton. Local man."

"So, how d'you feel about the incident after all this time?"

"Same as I did then. It's tidy and it's untidy. On one hand, it looks like a typical accident at sea, a couple of amateurs larking around. His safety line gets tangled up in the propeller, and hers is somehow snapped off at the waterline. It happens. On the other hand, there's the way he was cut up by the propeller. Could have happened that way, I suppose. Those bronze blades can make a hell of a mess. But some of the cuts seemed a bit too neat, for my liking. Like they'd been done with something a bit sharper or maybe heavier than a propeller blade. I talked to the pathologist about it, but he wasn't convinced. He reckoned they were floating high on drugs when Peters fell overboard and she jumped in to save him. Snap! Mangle! End of story. Till she turns up, we'll never know."

"Any chance I could take a look on board?"

"No problem."

Illiffe followed Hetherington up the ladder and down into the boat's cabin, well equipped with modern navigation and communication equipment. The furnishings were expensive and designed as much for pleasure as for serious sailing. Everything seemed perfectly normal. He was about to leave when he noticed a videocassette lying on the video recorder.

What had Susan's printout said? Something to do with videos in five of the cases. He picked up the cassette and read the title: *Let's Romp in the Water. A Walt Daniels Production.*

And now there were six. Illiffe wrote the title and company name in his notebook.

"I've got a chum in Customs who knows that company," Hetherington informed him. "Very, very saucy and quite nasty too, so he says."

"So what do you make of it all, Jim?"

"I don't like guessing games, Mr. Illiffe. Seen too many funny things happen at sea."

"But if you had to come up with an explanation?"

"Well, putting all things together, I'd say we had a couple of young people on a night cruise, messing with drugs and intent on an orgy, and it all went wrong for them. Maybe she was trying to get his cock out, and one way or the other he gets chopped up. She could have drowned, but like I say, where's the body? On the other hand, she could have made it to the shore, buggered off, and kept her mouth shut."

"While I'm down here, I'd like to have a word with Holton," Illiffe told him as they clambered off the boat.

"That's easy. He'll be in the Anchor, round the corner on the right as you go out of the yard."

"You've been very helpful."

"I hope so," Hetherington said. "I'd appreciate a call, mind, if you turn anything up."

Illiffe already had turned something up. Something small, maybe trivial. Something he might never have seen, but for Susan's report. The video connection.

In many investigations there comes a time when you know exactly what the answer is. As far as Illiffe was concerned, he was on the track of a serial killer, and all the signs pointed to Lyndsey Barratt or someone connected with her.

The problem was, a hunch based on this common factor was one thing; proving it would be another. And then he realized that he had something else to worry about: George Weston.

The Anchor was a modern pub designed to look like a very old pub, with timber mezzanines, dark wooden beams, brass portholes, binnacles, pulleys, chains, ropes, and other marine equipment hanging from walls and hooks and scattered in corners. A fire burned in a large open grate, radiating an almost unbearable heat. Illiffe ordered a half pint of Guinness and turned to look at the customers. Very much a yachting lot, he decided.

"You'll be Frank Illiffe," the barman said as he handed Illiffe the Guinness.

"Is that right?" News obviously traveled fast in Poole.

"No offense. Jim called to say you wanted a word with Jack Holton.

"There was no need for him to go to any trouble."

"Maybe not, but he said we should make you feel at home, so I'll take you across to Jack. Otherwise you might not get very much cooperation. He's over by the window."

Illiffe followed the barman to a table where a large, jolly man with a booming voice was sitting among a group of young women.

"This is Detective Superintendent Illiffe, Jack. He wants a word. Jim Hetherington says he's okay."

"Welcome aboard, Mr. Illiffe," Holton roared. "What can we do for you?"

"You don't look like a policeman," one of the girls said.

"I'm never quite sure how to take that kind of remark." Illiffe smiled.

"Definitely a compliment. What kind of policeman are you?"

"British Transport Police."

There was a short silence while they pondered the significance of having a British Transport policeman at their table.

"Don't tell me one of you young ladies has been jumping over ticket barriers again," Holton said mischievously.

"I wouldn't mind jumping over his barrier, I can tell you," another girl said.

"You watch your manners, young Helen," Holton said. "Tell you what, Mr. Illiffe, why don't you and I have a chat outside? I could do with a breath of air."

They made their way through the crowd to the back veranda, overlooking the harbor. The light wind had dropped and the sea reflected all the lights from the opposite shore like a mirror. Here and there small boats disturbed the water, making the reflections shimmer up and down.

"I've lived round these parts all my life, Mr. Illiffe. Some funny things happen."

Illiffe let the silence develop.

"I don't believe you explained to Jim what a transport policeman is doing round here, asking about a marine incident."

"It's a long story."

"Is there a short version?"

"Not at this stage. I just need to get a feeling for what's been reduced to a pile of papers."

"Fair enough. How can I help?"

"The girl's name was Eileen. You said you introduced her to Alan Peters. Apart from that, you didn't say much else. Do you know her second name?"

"No, I'm afraid not."

"Bit unusual. After all, the report says she sailed with you the weekend before."

"I sail with a lot of people. I often don't know their second names, or anything else, except whether they make a good crew."

"Did Eileen make a good crew?"

"Not at first. She was all thumbs. But I've never seen anyone learn so fast. After two days she sailed my boat in and out of harbor like she'd done it all her life."

"How long had you known her?"

"She just turned up that weekend. Lots do. There's all kinds. Girls who fancy the sailorman. Girls who want a bit of fun in the clean fresh air. Eileen wanted to make some videos."

Video again.

"Did she make any when she was with you?"

"No. She was too busy learning the ropes. But she saw Alan getting under way the Sunday before it happened, and she asked me if I thought she could get some shots of him sailing."

"Why not you, if she'd spent all this time learning about your boat?"

"Did you ever meet Alan Peters, Mr. Illiffe?" The question was rhetorical. "Handsome young beggar. Take a look at me. Eileen and I had a couple of good sailing days together, and that was all there was to it."

"You were sailing too, that weekend?"

"Absolutely, with young Helen. I told the coast guard that we last saw *Tiger Shark* in Chapman's Pool before Alan upped anchor. After that we had other things to think about."

Illiffe wondered what he meant by that and cocked his head inquiringly.

"No, no, everything was perfectly proper, but she got the shakes over some damn animal caught in a snare. Least, that's what I thought it was. Never heard such a racket."

Illiffe got that bristling feeling again. "What animal?"

"Sounded like a hare. They can make a hell of a racket. One of the other skippers thought it was gulls fighting over something. Whatever it was, Helen won't go near the place."

Holton looked at his empty glass and opened the door to the bar.

"By the way, when are you chaps going to do something about Eileen's car? It's still parked behind where my boat is laid up at the end of the season. No one seems to know what to do with it."

Car? No one had said anything about a bloody car. Illiffe sighed inwardly. He pulled his mobile phone from his pocket.

"Have you got a berth number?"

"Fifteen. Next to the landing craft by the slipway. You can't miss it."

"Thanks for your help, Mr. Holton."

"You're more than welcome. I hope you find what you're looking for."

Illiffe stayed on the veranda and put a call through to the local police station.

"Duty Sergeant? Good evening. This is Detective Superintendent Frank Illiffe of the British Transport Police. Could I speak to the duty CID sergeant please?"

All this time, a car belonging to a missing person who might have been involved in a serious crime was sitting in a private boatyard, with no mention of it in the report. How sloppy can you get?

"DS Miller," a voice said. "What can we do for you, Detective Superintendent?"

"Can you contact the owner of Brownsea boatyard and get a forensic team, an incident unit and a car transporter down to Bay fifteen in thirty minutes?"

There was a silence.

"Is this a wind-up?"

"No, DS Miller, it's not a wind-up. It's something you people should have done a year ago. I'm in Poole on BTP business, and I'd appreciate the assistance. Check it out with Tavistock Place and meet me there in . . . twenty-nine minutes."

He disconnected.

It was a yellow B-Reg VW Polo with absolutely nothing to distinguish it from any other yellow B-Reg VW Polo, apart from its covering of salt and rainborne dust particles. DS Miller had arrived in his car with a small man carrying a fingerprint outfit. He was followed by a patrol car. No incident van. No lights. Illiffe decided to go ahead with what he'd got.

Miller looked at the Polo in disgust and then looked at Illiffe in disgust.

"Do what?"

"Treat it as if it contained a murder victim. Full examination."

Miller glanced at the small man, who shook his head.

"Not likely to get anything usable from the outside, not after all this time. I'll give the handles a go, then your uniformed lads can open her up."

They watched as he dabbed at the car's door handles and boot lock with his brush. After ten minutes he gave up.

"Nothing except smudges. I'll have a go inside."

He used a high-intensity flashlight to examine the inside of the car.

"No stains, no damage, no cigarette ash," he called. "I'll try for prints, then vacuum it for fibers, okay?"

"That'll be fine," Illiffe said.

Miller strode off and sat on a bollard, staring at the harbor. It took thirty minutes for the small man to check the interior, trunk, and engine compartment.

"Okay, Sergeant," he called. "Done what I can. The only thing resembling a print is a smudge on the oil filler cap. There's a few smudges in the trunk. Absolutely nothing in the car itself. Clean as a whistle. We'll get a report on fibers in the next few days, depending how busy the lab is."

Illiffe smiled. "Thanks, but don't bother with that."

"Another total fucking waste of police time." Miller tried to make his voice jokey, and failed.

"Not at all, Sergeant. Your colleague has been very helpful indeed. And so have you, although I must say if you'd done this last August you might have played things differently in the coroner's court."

He got in his car and drove away, leaving Miller looking utterly pissed off.

He arrived home well after midnight. Jean had gone to bed but left a small light on for him. She didn't move as he came into the room, but he knew she was still awake. He suddenly remembered she had an appointment with the gynecologist in the morning, that she must be worrying herself sick about the possibility of losing another baby, and he'd shut himself in his study for the past four days, not to mention returning from Poole at one o'clock in the morning.

"For what it's worth," he said at last, "I feel like a real shit."

She still didn't move, didn't say anything, and he got a sick feeling in his stomach that the whole policeman thing had gone too far. She wouldn't be the first copper's wife to pull out of an unrewarding relationship.

"There's a flask of coffee in the kitchen," she told him.

"Right," he said. "D'you want a cup?"

She shook her head. "Not on my menu."

He should have remembered. "The thing is, something's cropped up that's going to take a lot of cracking. I'm right in the middle of it."

"Yes," she said. Then after another silence, "Do you still love me, Frank?"

It was one of those questions a man can dread. He should say yes, without any hesitation. But, if he did love her, how could he do this bloody awful job? How could he still feel a longing to make love with Julie Adams? How could he feel scared about starting a family?

"Yes," he said without any hesitation. "I love you very, very much."

Chapter 16

DETECTIVE CHIEF SUPERINTENDENT MARK VILLIERS stared thoughtfully at his younger colleague. Frank Illiffe was an excellent policeman and a good detective, thorough and not given to speculation. He was on track for further promotion and, like every policeman, knew the value of keeping his head down to avoid the shrapnel that constantly flies around all police stations. At least, until now. His unofficial sortie into a regional force coupled with this fanciful report could blow all that away. The one thing Villiers hated was a colleague who indulged in flights of fancy. In his long experience, the application of surmise or imagination to police work tended to undermine the painstaking work undertaken by the vast majority of the Force, twenty-four hours a day, three hundred and sixty-five days a year. A creative copper was a dangerous copper. On the other hand, there were times when you let the horse have its head. Villiers followed the management rule that subordinates should be managed to provide maximum credit to the boss if things went right. If things went wrong, the subordinate carried the can. Easy to say, not so easy to do. He'd have to be careful. Tackle the phone call he'd received from the Dorset constabulary concerning a heavy-handed visit from a BTP detective superintendent.

"You should know better, Frank. You put their detective sergeant in a difficult position. Used their resources, and came up with nothing."

"Is that what they said?"

"More or less. The forces need each other's trust and cooperation. You've jeopardized that."

"I disagree. Last August there was a serious incident in their area which they failed to investigate. If they had investigated it, the coroner involved might have returned a different verdict. I haven't jeopardized anything. They screwed up."

"Really!" Villiers did not like the direction this was going one little bit.

"Their forensic man found no prints in the car used by the missing girl, Eileen. They didn't even bother to check Swansea for the owner's name and address, believe it or not."

"I agree that's sloppy, but what's your point?"

"The last person known to have driven that car was Eileen. Before she left it to go sailing with Alan Peters she wiped it clean. That's point one. Point two is, she paid cash for the car at a dealer in Commercial Road and gave them a name and address that doesn't exist. That means she was about to do something naughty and made sure there'd be no trace. She maneuvers herself into a sail with Peters. He ends up dead. She disappears. The coastguardsman says he expected her body to have been found within days. It never was."

"You're saying this was a murder."

"Yes."

"And you're suggesting that there may be others, are you, Frank?"

"Yes, guv, but not just me. This new system at Hendon indicates that there are factors that can't be explained by coincidence. It's against the odds. I believe we should reopen these cases and inform the DI in charge of the Shackleton inquiry, Terry Chesterton."

"You understand the implications."

Illiffe understood them only too well. It would take manpower the force could ill afford, and it would take a large chunk out of already stretched budgets to reopen nine other cases in seven police regions and link them with his BTP investigation. Then there was the public-relations aspect. They would be trying to establish the existence of a serial killer, possibly but not necessarily Lyndsey Barratt. Maybe someone connected with her. Maybe someone else entirely, but he didn't think so. Whichever way it went, Julie Adams was already nosing about and other journalists would follow. The last thing the BTP needed was a media circus. None of them did. And, if he was right about all this, he had the eleventh man to consider. George Weston, captain of the team. Next on a list? The sooner they got this thing sorted, the better.

"We can start the ball rolling by assigning a project-development budget to Harry Branskill's team at Hendon," he said. "I'm sure he'd go for it. We can save time and money by using their new system to reexamine existing statements and forensic reports from the cases. If need be, we can reinterview a few key witnesses. . . ."

"Sorry, Frank. I'm not denying you put up a good case for connectivity, but it's totally circumstantial. And I'm definitely not sold on the serial-killer theory. There's no modus operandi, is there? I mean, all the deaths are different. On top of that, I can't afford to let you slip behind on your workload."

Illiffe himself had been perplexed about the variety in the actual method of death. He was aware that one of the factors shared by most serial murderers was a consistency in the manner of their killings. In any case, only Jonathan Elmwood's stabbing in the West End was recorded as a murder. The other coroners recorded open verdicts, as there was no evidence to show that the killings had been deliberate acts. Shackleton's death could well have been a fetish gone wrong, as could that of Nesbit. But stack the lot of them together, and you had to come to the conclusion that the ex-members of Winstanton School's cricket team had been singled out for extermination.

"I can take some more leave."

Villiers sighed. "It's too flimsy, Frank."

"Give me two weeks. Open the routes for me, and let me check what DI Chesterton has come up with. We can't ignore the fact that there's one member of that cricket team who is still around. If these are serial killings, he's a target. The problem is that at least one journalist knows that we have this information. If anything happens to George Weston, we'll be hung out to dry."

It was a good argument. "Put that in writing, Frank, and I'll see what I can do."

The last thing Detective Inspector Terry Chesterton needed was a visit by a rubber-soled merchant from British Transport Police.

He'd heard of Frank Illiffe and his work in uncovering corrupt coppers, and the man's presence within a hundred miles of a case spelled trouble for someone. So he and his colleagues were icily polite to the detective superintendent from BTP, despite the fact that Illiffe was at pains to point out that he was engaged in a separate investigation which he wasn't at liberty to discuss.

Chesterton explained that the house in Heathside in which Peter Shackleton had come to such a grotesque and painful end had been given a thorough examination and cleared by the investigating team. The young woman who had found the body, Deborah Lambert, was the new owner of the flat's ninety-five-year lease, and she had hired decorators to refurbish the room in which the death had occurred.

"They've taken it back to the brickwork," Chesterton told Illiffe. "Can't say I blame her. Never seen such a mess. Blood and guts all over the place."

"I see you haven't put in your report."

Chesterton shook his head. "Not yet. I've told the coroner we'll finish our initial inquiries next week, and he'll hold his inquest a couple of days after that. The place was set up as a pornographic video studio. Stocks, whips, you name it. The postmortem showed that Shackleton was high on a right old mixture. Smack, alcohol, and a particularly strong brand of Thai resin, plus residual traces of an alkaloid that forensics couldn't identify. This Linda Marshall was probably high as well. My bet is they went for some kind of anal kick, and when it all went wrong she did a runner."

Illiffe remembered what the coastguardsman had told him about Eileen. The more he delved into these cases, the more common factors he found.

"D'you think that's likely?"

"Why not? I mean, there was no obvious reason why she would have done him in. She was working as a hooker, very high class, and according to some of the neighbors he was infatuated with her. They'd been seen at the local weird club, and he'd just taken up a membership there."

"What weird club?" Illiffe asked.

"The Piedmont. It's part of a group, owned by an American called Daniels. Bit on the lines of the old Hellfire Club, far as I can tell. Naughty and not very nice, but it costs a bundle to join. They're into these kinky scenes, so it's not surprising if some of them come a cropper every now and then. Serves them bloody well right, if you ask me."

The name Daniels rang a bell, but not very loudly. He'd seen it somewhere recently. "So you don't think it was deliberate?"

"Well, if you call chaining a guy to a bed and stuffing his arse with carbon dioxide until he explodes over the ceiling 'not deliberate,' no. But there's nothing to show that she meant to kill him. I only wish we could lay our hands on her, but there's no trace."

"No trace?"

"She's disappeared. We've checked back through the solicitor she used to buy the place, and he said they'd done everything over the phone and through the post. He never saw her. Her references seemed okay, but they turned out to be people in the same position as the solicitor. We checked her bank account, but that was closed down the day Shackleton died. One blank after another. Not too surprising, if she's on the game."

"And this Deborah Lambert can't help?"

"Can't or won't. We've checked back with a number of her clients, and she seems to be a reliable citizen. Pays her taxes, registered for VAT, good credit rating, but there's something odd about the lady."

"What kind of odd?"

Chesterton hesitated. "It's the way she talks about this Marshall woman. Can't put my finger on it, but she just seems very vague. And there's one really funny thing. Marshall arranged for Lambert to take over the lease of the flat, and she signed the documents a few days before Shackleton copped his lot. I'd like to know why."

"What's your impression of Miss Lambert?"

"In a word, mousy. Bright enough, by all accounts. But mousy. Unassuming."

"I take it you'd have no objection if I called on her, Terry?"

"Not at all, sir," Chesterton lied. He wondered what the hell was going on. There was no indication, as yet, that he was under any kind of personal scrutiny. But you never knew, not with internal investigators, no matter which force they came from. Bastards.

The builders were replastering the walls of Linda's room when Illiffe phoned. Deborah took the call in the kitchen. When he asked if she would be available at lunchtime, she said one o'clock would be convenient. He arrived in Heathside with time to spare, passing Shackleton Motors, where everything seemed to be operating as normal after the untimely death of the proprietor. The village-type Main Street, with its boutiques, French restaurant and pub, had a number of empty parking spaces, and on impulse he stopped his car outside the pub, ordered a pint, and sat at a table by the window. There was a fair amount of passing trade, plus the usual collection of regular drinkers. By relaxing and listening he learned that the head barman was called Ronnie, and the distinguished man at the next table reading the newspaper was called Leo. As he drained his pint, Ronnie appeared at the table, casually, ready to take the glass away.

"Everything all right, sir?"

"Everything's fine, thank you," Illiffe said. "Nice pint."

"It's all in the cellar work," Ronnie said, wiping the table with his cloth. "Haven't seen you in here before. In Heathside on business?"

"You know I am." Illiffe gave him a slight smile, an acknowledgment that one professional had recognized another.

"Ah, yes," the barman said. "Mr. Shackleton. A bad business, that."

The distinguished man stopped reading his newspaper.

"Very unfortunate," Illiffe agreed.

"Bit of a mystery, all round."

"Definitely a mystery."

"Yes, there was a Detective Inspector Chesterton round here just the other day, checking out the lie of the land."

"You don't say. Well, we've all got our jobs to do. So, how d'you think the land lies?"

Ronnie gave the table another wipe. "From what I gather, things went a bit too far in the love nest, but no one round here really knows very much about it. We incline to the view that least said, soonest mended. There's a family to consider."

"Perhaps you're right." Illiffe stood up and held out his business card. "If you think of anything that might throw more light on things, give me a call."

Deborah was becoming quite used to strangers visiting the flat. Apart from the police, she'd had disturbances from journalists sensing a story, plus the builders tramping in and out. No matter how many coverings she put on the carpets and furniture, there was always a thin film of dust or a smear of dirt on everything. But the important thing was that all traces of Linda were being removed. And this was vital if Deborah was to settle down there and expunge the awful memory of the bloodstained room. To be honest, she wasn't sure if she could make it, but the property market was slow, so she wouldn't be able to sell the lease very easily, and she needed a place to live. She had to be practical.

The doorbell sounded, and she let Detective Superintendent Frank Illiffe into the building. He looked nice. The other policeman, Detective Inspector Chesterton, had been very aggressive. Not at all sympathetic, considering what she was going through. This one smiled and shook her hand, waited for her to make the moves. She wondered if his rank was above the other policeman's.

"Would you like a cup of tea or coffee?"

"Whatever you're having."

"I'll make some tea. The kitchen's the cleanest place at the moment. Would it be all right if we talked in there?"

"No problem." He glanced around, noting the layout. A radio was playing Capital Radio very loudly behind the door at the end of the hallway. "Miss Marshall's room, I presume."

"Yes," Deborah said seriously. "They don't seem to be able to put a nail in a wall without that row blasting away. In the end you don't notice it."

He watched as she heated the water and opened a cupboard to reveal a collection of tea boxes.

"I don't have any ordinary tea. Only herbal infusions."

"Coffee would be fine."

"Decaffeinated?"

"Maybe I'll have an herbal infusion."

"This camomile and peppermint one is nice. It's good for the circulation."

"Let's try some of that then."

She busied herself getting the cups and dangling a sachet into each of them. The task engrossed her completely. When she passed his cup over, he sniffed it suspiciously before taking a cautious sip.

"Not bad," he said when she gave him a worried look.

"It's also supposed to be relaxing and good for the digestion."

"Mmmm," he said. "It's certainly different."

She thought he was different too. He hadn't asked a single question about what had happened. But no doubt he would.

"I understand you work with computers, Miss Lambert. Exactly what d'you do?"

"I design commercial systems, mostly. Administration, communications, security, that sort of thing. I also write source code for games and simulation exercises."

Frank wondered what she meant. "That must be very interesting."

"I suppose it is," she said, as if the idea that her job might be interesting was a new one to consider.

"I'm not a computer person, myself. I appreciate what they do, though. I mean, what would we do without them?"

"Most businesses would come to a complete standstill."

"I suppose they would. D'you get a lot of work?"

Deborah gave that some thought. "When you work for yourself you always get gaps between projects, so it sometimes seems there's nothing much to do. But I've had a few really good commissions recently."

"It might be helpful if I could have a note of your clients over the last year or two," Illiffe said, watching her reaction carefully. It didn't seem to bother her.

"I can print you a list now," she told him.

She went to her room, and Illiffe heard the gentle buzz of an ink-jet printer. It wasn't a very long list. He scanned it quickly. In addition to Shackleton Motors there was a car firm in Chester, a plastics company in Birmingham, an HVG tractor agency in Shropshire, an estate in Gloucestershire, a holiday tour firm in East London, and a housing association in Liverpool. She'd included phone numbers. It seemed perfectly straightforward, but he wondered if Susan York could throw something up with her newfangled computer system.

"Mind if I touch base with them?"

"If it's going to help, of course not." She seemed eager to please, not bothered why he might want to do so.

"I wouldn't mind a look around, too. Only if you agree. I'm not officially on the case, but it's sometimes good to get a look at things firsthand."

"Of course not. Would you like to wander around, or shall I . . . ?"

"Why don't you show me?"

She gave him a little smile and led the way down the corridor to the dining room, the sitting room, and then to her own room.

"I do like this," he said. "Very warm. Very . . . feminine."

"Linda made it like this. She said she wanted whoever stayed here to feel at home."

"And do you?"

"Oh yes, yes, I do."

A hint of animation. Then a shadow. Sadness.

They reached Linda's old room, and she pushed the door open. Capital Radio came tumbling out. A young lad was carefully painting the baseboard, tongue jutting from the side of his mouth. He took no notice of them.

Deborah was about to go back into the kitchen.

"One more to go." Illiffe nodded at the door at the end of the corridor.

"Gosh, yes. Sorry, only I never go in there. It's Linda's sister's room."

Click. Another tumbler dropping into place?

She took a key from a drawer in a small dresser and unlocked the door. The room they entered was startlingly white and bare. Ceiling, walls, woodwork, and even the floor. White gloss.

"You say you've not been in here?"

"Linda showed me once, but I didn't go inside, no."

"And the decorators?"

"Why would they?"

Why indeed? The whole thing was beginning to look very weird to Illiffe. Did Chesterton know about this sister? Had he taken steps to find and interview her? They went back into the kitchen, and he sipped his tea.

"So you've been working on a system for Shackleton Motors?"

"Yes. I finished just before . . ." She waved her hands, unable to say the words.

"And you'd stopped working for Peter Shackleton when this thing happened?"

"That's right."

"Bit of a coincidence, wasn't it?"

"I'm sorry?" she said.

"A coincidence; you working for Peter Shackleton and your flat-mate knowing him."

"I suppose it was." Deborah nodded. "Linda knew about Shackleton Motors needing someone to work in the office, but I don't think she'd met Peter then. She told me she saw him in the pub a few days after I started working for him."

"That'd be the White Swan."

"Yes."

"Have you any idea how they got to know each other?"

"I think he must have fallen for her. He invited us both to a party. I didn't go, but Linda did. She got the impression that he was getting interested. He began phoning her, so he probably was."

"Have you any idea why Linda might have wanted to harm Shackleton?"

Deborah bit her lip. She seemed near to tears.

"Oh no. She's a very kind person. Very kind. I don't think she could ever hurt anybody."

"Well she certainly hurt Shackleton, by all accounts."

"It must have been an accident," she whispered. "A lot of people . . . a lot of men used to come round. I think they liked to do things like that."

"You mean sadomasochistic things."

The words embarrassed her. "Yes."

"Fair enough. But what I don't understand is why she disappeared if she hadn't done anything wrong, and why she transferred ownership of the flat to you before she did. Don't you find that strange?"

Deborah was silent for some moments, then she said, "She put on this hard exterior, but when I first came here, to see the room she wanted to rent out, she . . . she seemed to want to look after me. And I'm sure that she told Peter Shackleton to stop being horrid at work."

"What do you mean, horrid?"

"He wasn't very easy to work with. He criticized everything I did. And not just me, either. He was horrid to everybody. But he had a date with Linda, and I'm sure she had a go at him. Afterward he began being nice to everyone. When I finished the installation, he paid my check even before I sent him an invoice."

"Did she ever say anything to you about her sister?"

"No. Only that she came to stay every now and again."

"What about friends, like these men you mentioned?"

"Not really. She sometimes told me that she'd had a good time at a club with someone or other from time to time."

Illiffe remembered what DI Chesterton had told him.

"The Piedmont Club?"

"Yes. She knew the people who owned it, I think. I'm not sure. She seemed to know a lot of people."

Illiffe had conducted many interviews, but he had never felt so strongly that he was spiraling around and getting nowhere. Deborah Lambert was obviously trying to help, but there were blank spots in every direction he took. There was nothing specific, but he began to understand why DI Chesterton had found Deborah so peculiar. Maybe he could jog her memory. He took out the list of names that Julie Adams had given him and the ones Susan had found.

"What about these people—did she ever mention any of them to you?"

Deborah read down the list. As he watched, he saw her body tense. "No." It came out as another whisper.

Illiffe kept quiet and waited.

"What is this list?"

"I'm not at liberty to say, Miss Lambert. Why do you ask?"

"I knew Mr. Squires. He was killed a few weeks ago. I'd been doing some work for him when I was in Chester, and he was knocked down by a hit-and-run driver."

Illiffe felt another of those strange sensations that arrive out of nowhere and play havoc with hair follicles. Not another coincidence—no way! He tried to carry on the interview, but Deborah either wouldn't or couldn't say any more about Linda. She withdrew into a kind of dazed silence. As he was leaving he asked one more question, more from curiosity than with any sense of purpose.

"What about this chap Squires? Did you do the same kind of work for him as you did for Shackleton?"

"Yes. He wanted to improve his office communications, too. Lots of small companies need to do that."

"And you solved his problems for him, did you?"

"Yes. At least I did my best. He said I'd not done a very good job, and he wouldn't pay me."

Again that chill trickle ran up Illiffe's neck.

"So you were having problems with him, like you had with Shackleton?"

She nodded, then looked at the floor. She seemed frightened. "They did pay me though," she added quickly.

So did Shackleton Motors, he thought. What the hell was going on? Was Deborah Lambert involved?

When he got back to his office there was a note on his desk from DI Chesterton, saying that the coroner had recorded an open verdict on Shackleton's death. That wasn't altogether a surprise. Until the investigation team found Linda Marshall and got her statement, they'd never know what happened, or why. He tapped Chesterton's number and got an answering machine.

"It's Frank Illiffe, Terry. Got your message, thanks. I need to look at everything SOCO got on the Shackleton case. Can you call me please?"

He then rang Susan York at the Police National Computer Bureau in Hendon and asked what she knew about serial killers.

"Not an awful lot. There's a professor at Sussex University who's an expert on offender profiling, and I read a paper by a visiting professor there who's worked with the FBI on serial killing. That list of yours doesn't conform to what they said about it."

"Why not?"

"Well, almost all serial killers kill the same way, over and over again, and the deaths are often personalized."

"How d'you mean, personalized?"

"Mutilation, rape, sodomy, cannibalism. Either way, it's obvious that the victim has been murdered."

"There are at least four, maybe five sex-related deaths here," he said with a growing frustration, "not to mention that the victims were very definitely the same kind of people. They all went to the same school, played for the same cricket team, and got involved in a drugged-up gangbang on one of my bloody trains." There was a pause. "Sorry, Susan. It's just that this whole thing is throwing up weird problems by the minute."

"That's all right, Mr. Illiffe, er, sorry, Frank," she said. "If it's any

consolation, I think they're connected too. But it's still all circumstantial. We can't operate on hunches, can we?"

The hell we can't, he thought. The day a copper couldn't use his
intuition was the day he'd go for early retirement.

"Of course not," he lied. "And that's why I'd like you to phone
the universities and see if we can arrange a meeting with one of your
experts."

Professor David Cantor was unavailable, traveling on a lecture
tour, but Professor Bill Taylor, the American psychologist who had
written the paper on serial killers, was still at Sussex University, half-
way through a sabbatical year of study. He agreed to see them in
London the following day in the coffee bar of the British Museum.

Taylor arrived five minutes after the appointed time, a tall, balding,
vigorous man in his sixties, with keen blue eyes and a nose that
showed signs of multiple contact with boxing gloves. Illiffe saw him
gazing among the tables and lifted an arm.

"Hi," he said, hurrying to their table and holding out his hand.
"Bill Taylor. You must be Frank . . . and Susan. Sorry I'm late."

They all shook hands. Taylor had a grip like a vise. Fit. Bronzed.
Steady eyes that looked you right in the face. A man who could take
care of himself. Not your typical academic.

"Let me get you a coffee, Professor," Susan said.

"Call me Bill. I'm surrounded by professors. It gets so no one can
tell who you mean."

"It's good of you to meet us at such short notice," Illiffe told him.

"I can always spare a couple of hours when I'm in London. In fact
I got here an hour ago, but managed to lose track of time in the
Assyrian halls. I get carried away by all that stuff. How about you
guys?"

"Actually, it's the first time I've been here," Susan said.

"Me too," Illiffe confessed.

"I can't keep out of places like this," Taylor said. "I'm reading
about your explorer Sir Henry Austin Layard whenever I have a
moment. What a guy! Makes Indiana Jones look like a Venture
Scout. He discovered Nineveh, y'know."

Illiffe decided it would save time if he didn't make any more con-
fessions. He had never heard of Sir Henry Austin Layard.

"We don't want to keep you from your studies, Professor Taylor . . . er, Bill . . . but I have a problem, and you may be able to help me."

"Yeah. You want the lowdown on serials. I've brought you copies of all my Quantico papers, plus a few book references. But I'd better warn you. There aren't too many ready answers."

"I suppose not," Illiffe said. "What's Quantico?"

"It's the FBI's behavioral science unit in Virginia. I work on their Profiler system. You'd be interested in that, Susan. Big system, lots of data, lots of analysis. And it gets results, too."

"Sounds a bit like the crime-pattern-analysis feature we've developed on the PNC," Susan said enthusiastically.

"Before you two get into the technology," Illiffe said hurriedly, "I'd better explain that computers leave me a fraction below freezing point. I've simply got this problem of ten deaths that could be related, and I need to have some background understanding of serial killers before I can make an informed judgment."

"Fair enough," Taylor said, winking at Susan. "Where do you want me to start?"

"Right at square one. What exactly is a serial killer?"

"Well now, opinions vary, but a useful definition is, anyone in civilian life who kills a large number of people to satisfy basic urges, such as sex, the need for self-esteem, or to establish ultimate power over their victims. On top of that you have all kinds of nasty stuff, like sadism, cannibalism and necrophilia."

"What about revenge?"

"Sure, revenge," Taylor said. "You can break it down into all kinds of subcategories. Revenge against parents, revenge against society, revenge against God. You name it, the killer kills for it."

Illiffe nodded. "So, what kind of people end up as serial killers?"

"The short answer is, anybody. But many serials show signs in early childhood, like bed-wetting, arson, bullying, that kind of thing. Truth is, they come in all sizes."

"You said in your paper that serial killing wasn't anything new," Susan commented.

"That's right. The phrase itself was coined by an FBI agent in the seventies, but serial killing is no way an American thing like some people think. It's probably been around as long as humans. If you take sadists and sex killers, the earliest known examples include Roman emperors. You Britishers have Jack the Ripper in the 1880s. He knocked over five prostitutes. Ten years later, the French gave us Joseph Vacher. He raped and disemboweled eleven people, including three young boys. In this century a guy in Ecuador called Lopez is reckoned to have raped, strangled, and mutilated around three hundred and fifty young girls. Ted Bundy owned up to twenty-three killings. Charlie Manson and his young ladies may have more than thirty deaths to their credit. And these are just the sex weirdos. On both sides of the Atlantic we've got the crazies who shoot up a bunch of people just for the hell of it, and then blow their own brains out. But your true serial hardly ever commits suicide, and their murders take place over periods of time. The theory is, this gives them time to cool off before the killing bug hits them again. Quite often, the period between the killings gets shorter and shorter and then they stop, and no one ever knows who or why."

"Some of the people I've talked to think that the MO is very important," Illiffe said. "Do serial killers always stick to the same pattern?"

"Most of them do, but there are exceptions," Taylor said. "Some of the clever ones move around and kill their victims in different ways, but they eventually create a pattern or fit into one that we've already figured out. That means we can often create an accurate profile of a particular killer at an early stage in the game."

"What kind of profiles do you come up with?" Illiffe asked. He was beginning to see a dim light at the end of a very murky tunnel.

"Typically where they might live, what kind of person they are, sometimes what race they might be."

"All the cases you quote are men," Susan said. "There must be cases involving women."

"There sure are. The most notorious are loners who used poison. There was a Frenchwoman in the 1850s called Hélène Jegard who wiped out twenty-three people with arsenic she got from boiling up flypaper. Lots of women get involved as part of a team, though. The dominant partner is usually a man, but there are exceptions. A few years ago in Vienna, four women nurses were charged with murdering around fifty elderly patients."

"Were they mercy killings?" Susan wanted to know.

"That's what the nurses claimed, but they drowned some of the patients by holding their noses and pouring water down their throats. Very painful, but many elderly people die with water in their lungs, so it seemed that death was due to natural causes. This was one of those cases where the killers changed the modus operandi to avoid arousing suspicion. They injected a variety of drugs, for example."

"So why did they do it?" Illiffe asked.

"The hospital chief reckoned they enjoyed watching people die. It gave them a sense of power."

Susan shivered. "It's too awful to take in."

"We live in a grim old world," Taylor agreed. "I hope all this is helpful."

"To be honest, it's too early to say," Illiffe said. "We've got a succession of deaths, but only one of them is listed officially as a murder. The others are open verdicts."

"There are some killings that start off looking accidental or natural," Taylor said, "but when others are discovered and common factors linked together, the truth comes out. You had a case like this in South London in 1986. A guy called Erskine strangled seven old-age pensioners, maybe more. The first one looked like she died in her sleep because he tidied up her room. Unfortunately for him, he also stole her TV, so she was examined more closely. As a result, her death was linked to the others that followed."

Illiffe was convinced that the deaths of the cricket team, perhaps with one or two exceptions, were murders. But suspicions were all very well. The one thing that might persuade Mark Villiers to give the go-ahead for an investigation would be expert advice. From Bill Taylor. He took the list from his pocket.

"I'm going to need your help. I've got these names—"

"Ramshir, Hodgkins, Odonga, Johnson, Nesbit . . ." Taylor intoned. "Don't look so startled, Frank. I had a visit from Julie Adams a couple of days ago. Her company has retained me to advise on a TV program she's doing on the case. She said you'd probably be getting in touch."

"Oh, did she!" Illiffe said angrily.

Taylor smiled. "I'll do all I can to help you, of course, but I have a confidentiality clause, not to mention my code of professional standards. Julie said you'd understand."

Illiffe understood only too well. Julie Adams had pulled a stroke on him. It was her way of retaliating for his lack of cooperation.

"A TV program, you said?"

"That's right. The line she's taking is to ask how ten people from the same background and the same cricket team could die violent deaths without someone noticing."

"Meaning without someone in the police noticing."

"She's got a point," Susan York said, undiplomatically. Illiffe gave her an exasperated look, but she stuck to her guns. "Well, here we are, trying to develop data systems that can reveal these patterns, and not only are we grossly underfunded but when someone like you does turn something up, we get a bureaucratic handoff from our elders and betters, not to mention the difficulties in liaising between all the regions. Maybe this will shake things up a bit."

"I think that's a fair comment, don't you, Frank?" Taylor said.

He did, but he did not take kindly to police matters being discussed in front of a civilian. Especially a smug American academic who was cooperating in a TV program that could create a raft of problems for any possible investigation. But before he could say anything, Taylor took the initiative.

"Julie sees it this way. Some years ago her company invested a great deal in the Lyndsey Barratt case in the reasonable expectation that they'd get a return on their money. They didn't. But almost all that school cricket team has been wiped out. Even if it's got nothing to do with the Barratt girl, it's a major story. I agreed to consult on the program, but that doesn't stop me making a few observations that might help you guys."

"Such as?" Illiffe wondered why Taylor irritated him so much.

"One of the major successes in the FBI's VCAP work—that's their violent criminal apprehension program—is offender profiling. Basically it extends the notion of the modus operandi and adds unseen aspects of a killing that the forensic boys don't pick up. They're interested in this at Sussex University, and that's why I'm in England."

"Not everyone over here goes along with offender profiling," Illiffe observed.

"Yeah." Taylor nodded. "Maybe that's because some people expect too much from it. It's generally seen as another tool against crime that may produce good results."

"What do you mean by unseen aspects?" Susan asked.

"It's a different way of looking at things. Your Scene of Crime officers are trained to make a thorough examination of the killing ground. They're looking for physical clues, like fingerprints, footprints, weapons, and bloodstains. What the FBI figured some time ago is that with serial killers the mere location of the crime is a clue. So is the particular method of killing, the sex and age of the victim, the time of day, the frequency of killings, and so on. Over the years, they've built up a database of this kind of information at Quantico, and it's helped them to identify and apprehend some serials real quick."

"You said in your paper that they use a particular technique to get these details," Susan said.

Taylor nodded. "The trick is to be systematic, to know what you're looking for, and to tie everything in with what you know about previous killers."

Illiffe prodded the list. "As far as I'm concerned, that's unnecessary. I'm convinced that most if not all these men were killed because of Lyndsey Barratt. All we have to do is find her."

"That's a hunch, Frank," Taylor said calmly. "You may well be right, but anyone with a grudge against this group of people could be responsible. From what Julie told me about the case, Lyndsey wasn't the only one who ended up with a grievance. That cop Jenkins lost his job and got a suspended prison sentence. The sports coach lost his job too. You could even add the captain of the team for good measure."

Illiffe was astonished. "George Weston? If I'm right about a serial killer, he's next on the list."

"Not if he is your killer."

"What on earth would be his motive?"

"He might think that his cricketing chums had let him down in some way. They all left the school under a pretty heavy kind of cloud. Maybe he blamed them."

"Surely that's not logical," Susan said.

"Where is it written that serial killers are logical? They latch onto something, and off they go."

"So where do the reports about a woman fit in?" Illiffe asked cynically.

"She could be his accomplice. Remember the Moors Murders?"

Illiffe recalled the crimes committed by Ian Brady and Myra Hindley in the 1960s. One theory was that Hindley had been led astray by her boyfriend. Illiffe did not subscribe to it.

"No way. I can't accept that."

Taylor looked at his watch, then took a printed form from his case. "One thing I've learned in this business is to keep an open mind. If I were you, I'd go carefully through all the files on these killings of yours and look for more commonality. If you can fill this out for all of them, it may help me to produce the killer's profile."

"Hang on," Illiffe said. "You're working for Julie Adams, remember?"

"Once her program is broadcast I'm a free agent," Taylor said. "This case is interesting, so I'd be happy to stick around. Maybe work with Susan." He gave her a big smile, and she blushed. "But it's up to you. Now, I'm afraid I have to get on with my book larnin'. Nice to meet you both. And good luck."

When he'd shaken hands and gone, Susan fiddled with her glasses for a minute, then looked through the form.

"I can fill in most of this for each death from what we have on file. But we'd need to check back with the investigating officers to get some of the other details."

"It's a bloody waste of time." Illiffe decided the reason Taylor made him irritated was that the man was too cocky, too sure of himself.

"I'll have it on your desk on Friday. What have we got to lose?"

Illiffe stared at her. When Taylor had been talking, she'd focused on him like a cult worshiper.

"Make sure you get the okay from Harry Branskill." Illiffe had other problems to deal with besides filling in this Yank's bloody forms. One of them was Julie Adams.

They met in the upstairs bar of the Blue Posts on Rupert Street. Illiffe suggested the venue. It was small, cozy and generally quiet in the afternoon. When Illiffe arrived it was almost empty. A young man in jeans was reading a newspaper, an expensive-looking leather briefcase standing upright on his table. Julie was sitting by a window with a short, wiry man aged around forty, sporting an unkempt shock of red hair.

"This is Donald Cameron, my program editor," she told Illiffe.

"He knows the background. I'm still hoping you can give us a brief-ing on all this."

"On all what?" Illiffe asked blandly.

Cameron leaped in before she could answer. An intolerant Glas-wegian accent. "Come on, Detective Superintendent, let's not fart around. The Met's press office is blanking us, and it's getting right up my nose. You are a senior officer involved in a case of multiple deaths, and we want you on camera explaining why the police of this country failed to notice that these young men were being sys-tematically wiped out."

Illiffe took a deep breath and forced himself to relax.

"I wanted an informal meeting with you to see if an exchange of views would be of mutual benefit," he said to Julie. "I'm not going to put up with your colleague's ranting."

"I asked for your help the other day, remember?" Julie said. "I don't need help anymore. I need your response to some questions. For example, ten members of a school cricket team have suffered violent deaths over a six-year period. Why have the police failed to take action?"

"You know I can't give you any response."

"Look, pal," Cameron said, "you interviewed every one of these guys when you were investigating a case of multiple rape. There are questions that you have to answer. . . ."

"Hold it right there," Illiffe told him angrily. "If you're going to cover that story, you'd better get your facts right, or you'll be the one answering questions."

Cameron glared at him, then turned to Julie. "What's he mean?"

"Lyndsey never made a formal complaint or even a statement. So, no rape. Not even alleged rape."

"Oh really?" Cameron sneered. "And the moon's made of fucking green cheese."

Illiffe stood up. "I see no point in continuing this," he said. On his way out, he stopped at the young man's table. "If you broadcast any of this, you'd better make sure it's not edited or altered in any way; otherwise you'll be hearing from a very hard-nosed team of police solicitors."

"Shit, Arny. You blew it," Cameron said to the young man with the briefcase as Illiffe disappeared down the stairs.

"*I* blew it!" Arny snapped. "If you'd let me take the shine off this case, he'd never have noticed. The bloody thing stands out like a knob at a eunuch's wedding."

"At the risk of starting World War Four," Julie said, "I must say you weren't much help, Don. If you hadn't interrupted, I'd have got more footage out of it. As it is, we might just be able to use that one question. It shows their lack of cooperation."

"There was no way that guy was going to give us anything but a hard time," Cameron said.

"That's for me to say, isn't it?"

"For Christ's sake, Julie. As soon as he walked in, I had it sussed."

"Had what sussed?"

"You can hardly conduct a reliable or objective interview with that man. This meeting was a waste of bloody time. We'll run with what we've got, and let Detective Super-bloody-intendent Frank Illiffe and his snotty Metropolitan chums sort it out afterwards."

"What the hell do you mean, I can't conduct a reliable or objective interview?"

"You've got the hots for each other."

"How dare you, you obnoxious little Glaswegian prat!"

"I dare because I'm an obnoxious little Glaswegian prat," he said, grinning. "And that's also why I'm the senior editor of 'your' investigative program. We don't need Illiffe. When this goes out, it'll frighten the shit out of everybody, including the dozy bastards who are supposed to be responsible for law and order. Plus, it'll help our lords and masters to get some return on that hundred grand they forked out to the comatose and well-fucked Miss Barratt all those years ago."

"Christ, and I thought I was hard," Julie said. "That's a disgusting thing to say. The poor kid never had a chance. They raped her, they sodomized her, they beat her half to death. No wonder she cracked up. God knows whatever happened to her."

"Cracked up, she may have been," Cameron said laconically, "but she wasn't so cracked up that she didn't know how to make one hundred thousand pounds disappear from her bank account."

"Fuck you, Donald," Julie snapped.

"If only you would, darling. I've got the hots for you too, or hadn't you noticed?"

She glared at him, and he smiled benignly.

"Don't worry about Mr. Plod. It's time to get your investigatory little teeth into your old chum George Weston."

"You can be a patronizing bastard, sometimes," she told him.

"Only sometimes? I must be slipping."

Illiffe was suffering from what vaudeville artists called the slow burn. The more he thought about the list that Julie Adams had dumped on him, the angrier he was becoming. He was angry with himself for reacting the way he had when she walked into his house. He was angry with her for trying to use him. He was angry with his boss and a police system that could slow something down from a crawl to a coma in less time than it took to say, "Fill that in, in triplicate." Most of all he was angry with the cricket team, who had committed a brutal crime, sent an innocent young girl over the edge, and who were now, posthumously, set to turn what should have been a low-key investigation into another media circus.

By the time he got back to his office at Tavistock Place, DI Chesterton's copy of a report from the Met's Scene of Crime officer who had examined the flat in Heathside was on his desk. It made grim reading, with a detailed description of what happens to a body when gas under pressure is fed into the lower intestine. He was scanning the inventory of items found in the room when he came to a section headed "Video Equipment." In addition to stands, lighting, and cables, a dozen cassettes had been found in a cupboard. Two of the containers had been empty. He picked up his phone.

"DI Chesterton."

"It's Frank Illiffe, Terry. Thanks for the report. Can you tell me where the things in the Heathfield flat were taken?"

"The human remains are at the path labs. The other stuff is in central storage."

"Any chance you can meet me there in about an hour?"

"No problem, sir," Chesterton said in a monotone.

Illiffe put down the phone and permitted himself a small smile. Chesterton's attitude was understandable. It was time to take the man into his confidence, some of the way at least.

Chesterton was already at the depository when Illiffe arrived. The DI managed to look noncommittal and pissed off at the same time.

"Hello, Terry. Thanks for coming."

"How can I help, sir?"

"First off, let me clear one thing for you. My interest in the Shackleton case has absolutely nothing to do with any internal investigation. It goes back a long way, to my time as a DI. There was a gang rape on one of our trains. A young girl and a school cricket team."

"Lyndsey Barratt."

"That's right." Illiffe had not expected Chesterton to know that.

Chesterton's expression changed almost imperceptibly from pissed-off to smug. "I thought it would be prudent to see why things were stacking up the way they were."

"Come to any conclusions?"

"Absolutely not." Smug smoothed its way to blank.

"Fair enough. I asked you here because if I find what I think I'll find, I'll have enough to convince my guv'nor in BTP that we've got a serial killer on our hands. In which case, you'll find yourself involved in the biggest murder hunt you're ever likely to see in your working lifetime, involving other regions besides the Met."

Chesterton followed him into the depository and through the racks of labeled bags and articles from dozens of solved and unsolved crimes. On a shelf labeled "Shackleton, Heathside" he found twelve videocassette cases. Ten of them contained blank cassettes with a label overprinted with the name Walt Daniels Productions.

Click. Daniels. Piedmont Club. *Let's Romp in the Water.*

"I have no jurisdiction over your current inquiries, Terry," Illiffe said. "But if I were you, I'd check this lot out. Whoever killed Shackleton made a video of it, and so did whoever killed Alan Peters. There's some indication that the same thing happened with other members of the cricket team."

Detective Chief Superintendent Mark Villiers was holding meetings in the districts and was unavailable for all but the most urgent business until the morning. "Urgent" meant that the entire BTP force had been caught taking bribes from independent bus companies to help them blow up mainline stations. That Illiffe had uncovered one link too many for anyone to continue to support the coincidence hypothesis about a deceased cricket team did not qualify as "Urgent."

Nor did the fact that Julie Adams had dragged in an American psychiatrist to help her prepare a TV program that was likely to ask some embarrassing questions about police competence.

Faced with an atypical pause in the pace of his work, Illiffe decided to leave his office at the official time of five-thirty and spend an evening with his long-suffering wife. There was nothing further he could do without his chief's permission, which he was not sure would be forthcoming, despite this compelling if circumstantial evidence.

Jean was standing on a chair in the kitchen cleaning cupboards when he got home. She looked at him guiltily as he stood in the doorway glaring at her.

"Where's Albert? He should be doing that."

"I sent him home. It's all right. I feel fine. Dr. Elman says the baby's perfectly okay. Just a few more weeks, and we're out of the danger zone, but I can't sit around here doing nothing all day, Frank. It's driving me bonkers."

She looked and sounded like a naughty schoolgirl caught stealing cookies. He grinned and helped her down.

"It's one thing not sitting around. It's another tempting fate. If I catch you playing any more gravity-defying tricks like this, I'll get Albert to move in and do the housework as well as the garden."

"Give us a kiss. It's good to have you home so early. Why are you home so early, by the way?"

He spent a moment taking advantage of her offer. "Aw, you don't want to hear all my troubles, lady."

"Yes, I do," she said firmly. "You sit down, and I'll make us a nice cuppa."

"Not a chance. You sit down there, and I'll make us a nice cuppa."

"Let's compromise. Why don't we both sit down there, and we'll both make us a nice cuppa?"

As a joke, it wasn't exactly Rowan and Martin, but it made them both relax. "You know." He held her close again. "When I came through that front door just now I was thinking what an unlucky bastard I am. Ten seconds with you, and I'm thinking what a lucky bastard I am. What d'you make of that?"

She moved closer. "I think that's very sweet, Frank." There was the trace of a snuffle in her voice. "But I'd still like to know what's wrong."

He told her, pulling together the salient points, highlighting past events, expressing his fear that the police system wasn't keeping on top of serious crime. Above all the growing likelihood that he was becoming involved with what could well be one of the worst cases of multiple murder in British criminal history.

"If Julie Adams does the kind of job she's all too capable of doing, the ordure will impact the air-conditioning system and be spread on whoever is standing within a mile," he said. "And I'm well inside the killing zone."

"That's not fair," Jean protested. "You've done everything you can to bring it to their attention."

"There's nothing in my contract of service about fair. They'll say I didn't do enough, and they'll be right."

"But what else could you have done?"

"I have no idea," he said tiredly. "All I know is that tonight I'm going to sit in front of the telly with my gorgeously pregnant wife, get very cuddly, and have an early night. What's more, I'm taking the morning off."

Chapter 17

EAMONN GRADY, WESTON CONSTRUCTION'S MOST EXPE-
rienced site engineer, stared belligerently at the small man in
the suit and green Wellington boots who was scrambling up
the slope toward him, slipping every now and again on the wet earth.
The visitor was either from the Department of Transport or the Department of the Environment, or maybe he was the new site inspector
from the consulting engineers who had designed the overpass. Pricks.
They'd got the soil mechanics all wrong, and now they'd want to
blame it on Weston Construction. Well, we'd see about that.

"Are you Grady?" the visitor called. He was seriously out of
breath. Grady put him down as a consulting engineer. Half the bastards died of heart attacks in the field.

"That's right, sorr. Eamonn Grady at your sorrvice." He exagger-
ated the Irish accent.

"My name's Pickford. I'm from Haslins Riddle and Partners.
There seems to be something wrong with your mobile phone, so I
decided to come here in person."

"There's nothing wrong with the phone at all, Mr. Pickford. I
keep it turned off. Stops all those nuisance calls."

"Rather defeats the object, doesn't it?" Pickford didn't try to hide
his annoyance.

"Well, you could say that. On the other hand, I don't take instructions over the telephone, so I don't care about calls coming my way,

d'you see? If I need something, I switch on the phone and get it. So, what can I do for you, Mr. Pickford?"

"We received a call from the Department of Transport that you'd stopped working on this section yesterday afternoon. I want to know why."

Pickford was new to the project, but he'd certainly have briefed himself from the files. He'd know that the bore holes used to investigate the soil strength had been drilled at regular intervals across the area and that the pattern had straddled the course of an underground stream. When Grady's team had started hammering in the steel piling, the site foreman had noticed that one of the piles was entering the ground too easily. It was Grady's guess that either the stream had been wrongly surveyed or it had changed its course. Either way, he decided to stop pile-driving to avoid problems. The company's chief executive, George Weston, had backed his action. If he was right, carrying on could lead to expensive and possibly disastrous consequences. If he was wrong, he'd get chewed out. Old John Weston would probably have carried on, gambling on getting the contract extended if they laid foundations that later proved to be faulty. Young George was smarter than his father. He'd worked out that contract extensions seldom made a profit for the company because too many subcontractors were involved in sorting things out. They were far better off spotting mistakes in other people's work at an early stage and negotiating an increase in fees. The consulting engineers knew all about this and tried everything in the book to avoid it. Like bringing in a new man to make sure that no cozy arrangements existed that could prejudice the outcome. Pickford had come to the site with the sole objective of ensuring that blame for any fault was directed away from the engineers. Grady's job was to do the same for Weston Construction. In this particular case, he felt certain that the chartered surveyors were the ones who would get it in the neck, if his hunch about the underground stream was right. There was only one way to find out, and he needed Pickford's cooperation.

"Look, Mr. Pickford," he said. "Let's not get off on the wrong foot. Now you're here I can show you the piling reports and how this particular location is different. It may be simply an alteration in the relative depth of clay and gravel, but my guess is that it's more serious than that. My chief executive agrees. If you like, I can get him over here while you and I take a look."

"I haven't got all day," Pickford said.

"Sure, and that's not a problem. Mr. Weston can be here in less than thirty minutes." He turned on the mobile phone and keyed a number. "Grady here, Mr. Weston. We have a gentleman from Haslins Riddle on site. A Mr. Pickford. . . . Yes, sir. I'm going to show him where the problem is, but I'd appreciate it if you could come over and discuss matters with him direct. . . . Right. I'll let him know." He turned to Pickford. "He'll meet us down there."

"I don't see how he'll make it through the traffic," Pickford observed as they climbed into a Shogun. "I'm running late as it is."

"Don't you worry about that," Grady said. "Mr. Weston is not one for letting a little thing like traffic get in the way."

Pickford ran a practiced eye over the piling reports and noted how the suspect pile had indeed been driven into the ground at more than twice the rate of the others with the same degree of force from the hydraulic hammer. He was examining the pile itself when George Weston's Jet Ranger whirred its way over the site and landed within a few yards, scattering sand and gravel over them. Pickford looked annoyed and impressed at the same time, as the handsome, well-built figure of Weston Construction's young chief executive strode toward them, holding out his hand.

"George Weston. Hope I didn't keep you waiting, Mr. Pickford."

"Not at all, Mr. Weston. Mr. Grady here was just briefing me on the situation."

"I had a word with your senior partner on the way over," Weston told him. "I said that I had every faith in my project manager, and Tony said he had every faith in you. I'd say that made for a positive start, wouldn't you?"

Grady hid a grin. Bullshit had its place. Pickford was as susceptible as anyone else when it came to a little judicious flattery. And having a man like Weston arrive to see you in a private helicopter was nothing if not flattering.

"You'll understand that we don't want to go jumping to any conclusions," Pickford said. "It wouldn't be the first time I'd seen an accidental increase in hydraulic power produce results like these."

"I know what you mean." Weston nodded sympathetically. "But I can put your mind totally at rest. Our own surveyors blitzed the local authority records this morning, and two maps of this area pro-

duced by the Ordnance Survey over a twenty-year period show that
the stream that runs under the reclaimed land changed its course by
several meters. My guess is that it still hasn't stabilized."

Pickford's mind raced. This contractor was pulling some kind of
a scam. He'd probably known about the stream since the independent
survey team had investigated the site, but kept his mouth shut so that
he could capitalize on the situation. No one would be able to prove
anything without going to a lot of trouble and stirring up waters that
were already well and truly muddied. The worst thing was that the
man had not actually done anything wrong. But the whole thing
stank of opportunism, and it offended Pickford's sense of professional
rectitude.

"We'll get the survey company back immediately," he said.
"They'll need to cover this section again to locate the source of the
problem. Then we'll have to see what changes must be made to the
piling specifications, if any."

"No need for that," Weston told him. "We've got coring equipment on site, and I can get our mobile soil lab here within three
hours."

So that was it! The bastard has seen this coming and had set things
up so that his company was the only one in a position to fix the
problem within the contract timetables. Pickford was impressed, and
even more irritated.

"I'm not sure we can go down that route without making further
investigations," he said.

"You take as long as you like." Weston smiled. "I'll leave the
chopper here so you can get back to London at speed if you like.
You'll find all the documentation that supports our capability to do
this work in the cabin, including our professional indemnity insurance certificate for a cover of a hundred million. All right if I take
the Shogun, Eamonn?"

As far as Grady was concerned, Weston could take Concorde or
a bloody NASA space shuttle. It was a privilege to watch the man
operate.

Weston arrived back at his firm's head office by car two hours later
in a very good mood; so much so that the sight of a TV crew waiting
outside the security gates failed to alert him as it might otherwise

have done. When the butch-looking female with the short hair and big tits waved at him, he lowered the window and smiled as she approached his vehicle.

"Good afternoon, Mr. Weston. I'm Julie Adams from Action TV . . ."

His smile faded as he recognized her. "I know where you're from, Miss Adams."

". . . and I'd like to interview you about the deaths of your friends from the Winstanton School cricket team."

The Shogun surged forward and sped into the company parking lot. Then its brakes locked, and it broadsided to a halt. Julie and the TV sound-cameraman waited as Weston strode back down the drive toward them.

"Get rid of him," he said, pointing at Arny.

"Sure," Julie said. "Piss off, Arny."

"He can wait in the guards' cabin. They'll give him a cup of tea. You can come inside and explain what the hell you're talking about."

"And you'll give me an interview?"

"Take your chances," Weston said coldly. He led the way into the building and to his top-floor office without saying another word. He sat at his desk, ordered two coffees from his secretary and waited silently until they arrived, eyes fixed unwaveringly on Julie, who gazed calmly back. "Want something in it?" he asked. "I'm having a Grant's."

"That'll do nicely."

He poured generous measures and took a gulp from his, waiting until Julie had taken a few sips. She could almost see his mind changing gears.

"Right. Tell me again what you said at the gate."

"We'd like to interview you about the deaths of the other members of your old school cricket team."

"Is this some sort of doomsday joke, or what?"

"Are you telling me that you didn't know that they were dead?"

"I know Alan Hodgkins and Nig Odonga copped it in a fire a couple of years ago. It was all over the bloody newspapers."

"What about Selik Ramshir, Ainslie Johnson, and the others? Nesbit, Elmwood, Peters, Smythe, Squires, Shackleton?"

"We lost touch. You know why."

"There was a report in the press about Shackleton just two weeks ago. Didn't you see it?"

He was still staring. She couldn't make out if he was seeing her as a rabbit or whether he was beginning to treat her like a fellow snake.

"I don't read gutter press. Takes all my time to keep up with construction-industry journals. Are you telling me they're all dead?"

She nodded.

"How?"

"Most of the coroners recorded open verdicts, but apart from Ramshir, which seems like a straightforward overdose, there was a degree of violence involved in all of the deaths. I can show you a report if you like."

"Never mind your bloody report. Why do you want to interview me?"

"I would have thought that's obvious. If someone has put your old cricket team on a death list, you're the only one left. You're next."

He stood up and went to the window. "And you are making one of your famous television programs about it all."

"That's right."

"Maybe I should see your report."

She handed it to him. He scanned it and keyed the intercom.

"Sandy, ask Charles to come in, will you."

He sat and stared at Julie again, until the door opened and an elderly man with a wrinkled, worldly-wise face came in.

"Miss Adams, this is Charles Ruslin, our group legal director. Charles, this is Miss Adams, whose face you no doubt recognize."

"Good afternoon, Miss Adams."

"Mr. Ruslin."

"We have a problem, Charles. Miss Adams has presented me with a list of the old school cricket team. She claims that they are all dead. She says that I might be next in some kind of line. She wants to interview me for a program she intends to produce on the matter. Your recommendations, please."

Ruslin didn't hesitate. "We will apply for an injunction prohibiting the mention of Weston Construction or any of its trading subsidiaries on your program, Miss Adams, on the grounds that nothing related to your list has any relevance to the group or its activities and that any adverse publicity or the coupling of the name in any context with such a program as you plan would be both defamatory and damaging. I must also caution you that I am familiar with the history of the cricket team and with your own coverage of that unfortunate incident. I am sure you are as familiar with the law of libel from your standpoint as I am from mine."

"I know enough to get by," Julie said.

"Mr. Weston will not, of course, be giving you an interview, and any attempt on your part or on the part of any of your colleagues to obtain one will be treated as an intrusion of privacy and referred to the courts."

"It's okay, Charles," Weston said. "I'll give her an interview, once you've checked the names on this list."

"I really must advise most strongly against such a course of action," Ruslin said.

"Phone our police chum. Shouldn't take more than a few minutes for him to check things out."

Ruslin sighed and took the list of names out of the room. Weston turned to Julie.

"He's right about the company name. It has no relevance to anything you want to cover. Just to make sure, I want you to sign an agreement that it won't appear anywhere in the program."

"That's not a problem," Julie said. She wondered why he was willing to cooperate; then she remembered what Frank Illiffe had said about him after he'd visited the boys at their school. Ballsy. Not the kind of chap who would run away from a problem, our George.

Arny set up his camera in the drive leading to the Weston building from the main road, and Julie asked Weston to point out his office window. Arny took an establishing shot, zooming into the window, zooming out and panning around the building, careful to avoid the company flags. A few minutes later, Weston came out of the main entrance on cue and walked toward the camera, taking up a position with the building as a backdrop. Julie stood next to him, and Arny took a sound check on her radio microphone.

"All set," he said to Julie.

"George Weston is the only surviving member of the ill-fated Winstanton School cricket team," she said to camera, then turned to

Weston. "Mr. Weston, have you any idea why so many of your ex-teammates have met violent deaths in the past few years?"

"No," he said, looking confidently into the lens.

There was a long silence.

"Cut that," Julie told Arny. "Mr. Weston, it will help if you respond just as you would in a normal conversation."

"You mean, if I said something like 'No, I have no idea whatsoever'?"

"Clever dick," Arny muttered, loud enough for the others to hear.

Weston gave him a surprisingly amiable look. "It's new to me, all this."

"Let's try again, can we?" Julie said. "Mr. Weston, have you any idea why so many of your ex-teammates have met violent deaths in the past few years?"

"No. I have no idea whatsoever."

"But you would agree that ten such deaths cannot be put down to coincidence?"

"I'm not so sure. We were all very active. Worked hard, played hard. Didn't mind taking a chance or two. But we'd lost touch with each other, so I don't think there's much point in speculating."

"But if we assume that the deaths can't be put down to coincidence, then we must draw the conclusion that they are connected in some way."

Weston nodded. "If we make that assumption, yes."

"Which means that as the only surviving member of the team, your own life may be in jeopardy."

"Yet another assumption, Miss Adams, but yes again."

"Have the police made any kind of contact with you over this matter?"

"Absolutely not."

"Do you think they should have done?"

"That's something you'd better ask the police."

Arny, watching through the viewfinder, saw Julie's expression change to the serious look she had when she was about to stick it to someone. He wondered how Weston would react.

"You see, Mr. Weston, people who remember the incident involving your school cricket team and a young girl called Lyndsey Barratt might come to the conclusion that these deaths are connected with that incident. Would you think that's a possibility?"

"I don't see why," Weston said. "We were just a bunch of kids at the time. Lyndsey was what we used to call a real raver. That's no excuse for going over the top, of course, but these things sometimes get out of hand. We all regretted it very much, as you know."

Clever dick and clever bastard, Arny thought. Come on, Julie. Do your stuff. But to his consternation she took an atypical softly-softly approach.

"So you put it all down to youthful high spirits?"

He nodded, smiled sadly into the camera. "Exactly. Not that we should use that as an excuse. We behaved badly, and we paid the price. Lyndsey. All of us."

Julie let the camera run for the statutory few seconds, then asked Weston to walk up and down for the cut-ins before she thanked him and did a few setting-up shots.

"Let him right off the bloody hook, didn't you?" Arny asked as they were driving back to London.

"On the contrary. I put him on the hook," she said.

Arny looked puzzled. "I don't get it."

"That's what makes you a good TV person and me a great one," she said, grinning at him. "Now let's get back to the studio and make sure that Glaswegian twit can splice this in time."

Charles Ruslin met Weston in the entrance lobby, looking very agitated. "That was most unwise, Mr. George, most unwise."

Weston glared at him and pulled him into a corner. "Never mind that bitch and her fucking TV program. For Christ's sake, Charles, what's going on around here? How the fuck didn't anyone notice what was happening? Some bloody lunatic wipes out my bloody cricket team, and no one notices! Jesus H. Christ. Get on to Farthingale Security. I want full cover on the house and all company sites until we get to the bottom of this. Get on the phone again and ask what the fuck the police are up to. I can't believe this is happening. . . ."

Julie Adams's program was broadcast that evening in its late-night slot, half an hour before midnight. Not peak viewing time, but Action TV achieved viewing figures much envied by producers of other investigative programs. Snug and safe in her hideaway, Lyndsey Barratt watched the credits scroll up the screen, her young face smoothly expressionless. She rewound the video, found the section with George Weston's interview and watched it again, and again.

"What a bad man," she said in her little girl voice.

"You mustn't let him upset you," Linda said gently. "I'll make sure he doesn't upset you again. Not ever."

"You're going away from me again, aren't you?"

"Only for a little while, I promise. There's someone I must see."

"I don't want you to go."

"It's someone who can help me. Someone who can help us. Someone we can trust. She's my flatmate."

"Please don't go, Linda, please don't. I know they were all bad people, but I'm frightened. I don't want you to go."

"It'll be all right, it really will, and when it's all over you can leave here, and there'll be no one to hurt you, no one to tell lies."

Thomas Haddock watched the broadcast too. Television and radio were his links to the news of the day, as the postman always brought the newspapers from the day before to the remote quarry in the Black Mountains. He watched as George Weston faced the world and stated his case, aware that few people would find any sympathy for this kind of self-justification. But it was exactly what Haddock would have expected Weston to do. Face it out. Fight back. Play your hand as hard as you can. Even so, was the program right about all those deaths? Was that slip of a girl out there, getting her own back on the cricket team? No. Inconceivable. Haddock switched off the set and poured himself the usual good-night Otard, swishing the golden liquid in the palm of his hand. No way. Absolutely not.

Deborah woke up. Not the fuzzy half-consciousness that leaves you wondering for a moment if you're asleep or awake. She was totally awake, and she knew someone else was in her room. Someone with a fragrance she recognized. She was so afraid that none of her muscles would work. Her arms refused to reach out and turn on the light, and her legs remained stuck under the sheets like sacks of sand. She could hear a hoarse panting in the darkness that she suddenly recognized was her own breath. She had never been so frightened, not even when she walked into Linda's room that awful day.

"Who's there?" she managed to whisper. But she already knew who it was.

"Hello, Deborah." Linda's voice was calm, confident.

"How did you get in?"

"This used to be my place, remember? The locksmiths send copies of any new keys to another address that I have."

Deborah tried to sit up.

"No. Don't get up," Linda commanded. "I won't stay long."

"The police are looking for you. What happened with Peter? What went wrong?"

There was a sound like a satisfied cat stretching and purring after a good meal.

"Mmmm. Nothing went wrong. In fact, it all went according to plan, thanks to you."

"I don't understand."

"That's why I'm here. To help you to understand. Peter Shackleton was a bad man, and so were the others. They hurt my little sister, Lyndsey. They hurt her very badly, Deborah, so very badly."

"What others?" Deborah asked.

"You knew one of them. Harry Squires."

"But he was run over in Chester. . . ."

"Wasn't he just. I'd been after him for several weeks. I had another flatmate who was supposed to help me, but she . . . Oh, I don't know. People are so unreliable. She wasn't there when I needed her, but you were."

"I still don't understand."

"How could you? But you were part of it, all the same."

Deborah was now confused as well as frightened. What had she been a part of? She bit the question back. She didn't want to know. She had to get Linda to talk about something else.

"These men. What did they do to your sister?"

There was a silence. "It's more a case of what they didn't do. Let's just say I'm helping her to come to terms with what happened, in my own rather special way. When I've finished, she'll be safe from all of them. She'll be able to forget what happened and live a normal life."

"Where is she?" Deborah asked.

She could sense Linda's smile in the dark.

"She's safe, I've made sure of that. She's somewhere she can stay until I've dealt with them. But I need your help, Deborah. I need someone to get close to these people, don't you see?"

"No, I don't see." Deborah was near to tears.

"It's obvious, darling. I mean, I don't exactly blend into the crowd, do I? And on top of that, as you say, the police are looking for me. The less I'm in the open, the safer I'll be, and the safer Lyndsey will be. Simple."

"But I can't do anything. I won't do anything."

"That's the beauty of it. You don't actually have to do anything. Not really. Just carry on with your life and your computer projects. I'll do the rest. That's how we dealt with Peter Shackleton and good old Harry Squires, you and me. You remember how Harry wasn't going to pay you and you phoned him and had that argument about getting a check that evening or else?"

"Of course I do."

"Well, the row made him stay late at the office, trying to sort out what you had and hadn't done. You gave me just the chance I needed. By the time he left, I was waiting outside in my car, and POW! Got the whole thing on video, too."

"I don't know what you're talking about. I want you to go away and leave me alone."

"I'm afraid I can't do that, Debs. I need you. Lyndsey needs you. And you need me."

"No, I don't."

"Of course you do. How else will you find new clients?"

"I don't need you to find my clients for me, thank you very much!"

"Maybe not, but having good leads put your way makes life a lot easier. Who d'you think sent you that job ad for Shackleton Motors just as you were finishing in Chester? Who d'you think arranged for the estate agents to send you here, so you could be my flatmate?"

Deborah found a lot of things slipping into place. Work had certainly gone smoothly for her in the past few weeks, but she could not accept that this manipulative woman had been the cause. She wondered if there was some way she could get up and phone the detective who'd come to see her. The nice one who'd left his card. She sat up and groped for the light switch.

"I'd like a cup of tea."

"Not yet," Linda said firmly. "You can have one after I've gone. There's just one more thing."

Deborah felt her coming closer, the perfume growing stronger. It was like the feeling she'd had when she had first come to see her room, and Linda had held her gently. Unsettling, frightening, but somehow exciting.

"I know your little secret."

"I don't know what you mean."

"Yes you do, because I have the same secret, and it binds us together, closer than any man and woman. We need each other, you and I."

Deborah froze as Linda slid into bed beside her, feeling the warmth of legs and thighs and breasts and arms that were too strong to struggle against.

"Oh Jesus, please don't do this to me. Please, Linda."

"My little virgin," Linda whispered in her ear. "I knew that you were, the moment we met. You've never had a man, nor a woman, have you? You've been too frightened, but there's no need to be frightened now. No need . . ."

"I don't want this," Deborah gasped. "Leave me alone."

"I understand," Linda murmured. "I felt like that at first, and then I realized I didn't have to be frightened if I accepted what I am. That's all you have to do. Accept what you are. Accept me."

Despite her fear and her tears, Deborah could not help responding to what Linda was doing, feeling her nipples harden as Linda sucked and licked one breast and teased the other with her fingers. She felt a strange, burning pain in her vagina, even before Linda pressed her hand down there. She tried desperately to hold her legs closed, but it was impossible to resist, and her fear turned into wave after wave of pleasure.

"We are bound together," she heard Linda say in the darkness, before she passed out. "That's why I gave you the lease. They'll come to you to find a way to me. And I'll be watching."

She felt exhausted when she woke up next morning, and at first she didn't know why. Then she began to remember the dream, bit by bit. Linda. What she had said. What she had done. She felt dampness in the sheets and then wrinkled her nose in disgust when she detected her own body smells. Quickly she scrambled out of bed and tore off the sheets, wrapping them in a bundle and stuffing them in the washing machine, scrabbling at the controls for a hot wash, then stumbling into the shower to swill the smells away. As the water jetted down, she wondered if it had been a dream. It was so real. Bad but real. She'd heard of dreams like that. Men had them too, she'd been told. Wet dreams. Shameful dreams. But it had been so believable. Then she remembered what Linda had said about the locks, and she rushed out of the shower to the front door, almost slipping on the wet tiles in her eagerness. And yes. The chain lock was securely fixed in its slot. There was no way anyone could get in and out without a key. But Linda said she had one. All so confusing. Stressful. It wasn't surprising her mind might be playing tricks. It had indeed been a terrible dream. She hoped fervently that it never happened again. She was so shaken by her nightmare that she decided to have breakfast at l'Étoile in the hope that Leo or Marge would be there. She badly needed to be with normal people.

When she arrived, she saw them talking to an attractive young woman seated at the table where she usually sat. Joel the waiter smiled and set a plate and napkin at an adjoining table. Leo looked up and smiled a greeting.

"Talk of the devil."

Marge poked him. "That's not a very nice thing to say."

"Good morning," Deborah said, already feeling better for her walk to the restaurant.

"This is Julie Adams, my dear," Leo told her. "You probably saw her television program last night."

"Hello," Julie said.

"I'm afraid I don't watch television very much," Deborah said, feeling embarrassed.

"We covered what happened here the other week," Julie said. "I'm glad to have bumped into you like this. I was hoping we could have a chat."

Deborah felt a sense of panic. She had been looking forward so much to relaxing with Leo and Marge, and all of a sudden the events that she was trying to forget were being pushed at her.

"I'm sorry," she said. "All I came for was a little breakfast. . . ."

Leo had sensed her discomfort.

"Of course, Deborah. It was most thoughtless of us to bring it up like this. But I must confess to being an admirer of Miss Adams, and here she is, in the flesh. Far too good an opportunity to miss, I'm afraid."

"Of course. I'm sorry."

"So am I," Julie said, standing up. "I didn't mean to upset you."

Deborah was in a quandary. Leo and Marge were enjoying themselves so much with Julie Adams it seemed churlish to spoil their fun.

"I'm just being silly," she said bravely. "I've got to put all that behind me."

"Quite right, Deborah," Marge said. "I'm sure Miss Adams appreciates that, don't you, Miss Adams?"

"Of course I do."

"Apparently this thing with Peter is linked to a chain of other deaths," Leo said. "It seems to have started a long time ago, that's what you were saying, isn't it, Miss Adams?"

"That's right. With a young girl called Lyndsey Barratt."

"You must know the name, Deborah," Marge said. "It was in all the papers at the time, wasn't it, Leo?"

Deborah felt the panic again. In her dream last night, Linda had told her about her little sister, Lyndsey. How could a dream do that? Maybe she had read something about Lyndsey Barratt in the papers, and it came together, all jumbled up.

"Yes," she said. "I think I remember. Actually, I did know someone else who was killed, that Peter knew. In a car accident, it was, a few months before Peter."

"You *have* been having a bad time, dear," Marge sympathized.

"He was in the same cricket team, I think."

"You knew Harry Squires?" Julie asked, trying to keep her voice neutral. This was a discovery, and no mistake. She wondered how she could get this mousy little thing to stand in camera and say all this, but the girl looked as if she were about to fade away with embarrassment. Or fright.

"I didn't really know him. I did some work for his company, that's all."

"But you know he was in the school cricket team, like the others?"

"Yes, well, I think so." Linda had told her about Harry Squires. But that had been a dream, hadn't it? Linda hadn't really been there. Or did the police tell her? Her eyes filled with tears and she stood up, just as Joel was bringing her coffee and croissants, almost knocking him over in her rush to get out. She left a very uncomfortable silence behind.

"I really don't think there was any need to press the point, Miss Adams," Leo said stiffly.

"I quite agree," Marge said.

It wasn't the first time Julie had upset people during research.

"How do you think we get the kind of programs that you like so much without pressing points, Mr. Chindwall? I'm sorry if you're upset, but there's something very odd about this, and that's not my fault. I think your Miss Lambert knows a lot more than she's letting on, and it's my job to find out what it is."

Illiffe's phone rang. He and Jean had fallen into such a deep sleep that they didn't wake up. The phone rang again, several times. At nine o'clock an unmarked police car drove up to their house, and a young police officer got out and rang the doorbell, then hammered on the door until Frank came down in his dressing gown and opened it, bleary eyed.

"Detective Superintendent Illiffe?"

He nodded, and the young policeman held out a Metropolitan Police warrant card.

"Detective Constable Rogers, sir. Your guv'nor wants you at Victoria Street right away."

Victoria Street. New Scotland Yard. What was Villiers doing there?

"Give me ten minutes. Want a coffee?"

"No thank you, sir. I'll wait in the car, if you don't mind."

Illiffe had a cold shower, a cold shave, and a gulp of cold coffee. He had to wrench himself away from Jean's warm lips and an almost overwhelming desire to say "Fuck it!" and crawl back into bed beside her. But as the car made its way into central London, the old spark came back. At heart, he was a simple, effective thief-taker. A tracker of villains, outside the Force or inside. A scourge of the ungodly. It was what he loved, and he was going to march right in there and tell those sanctimonious bastards just that.

The sanctimonious bastards were waiting for him in a TV viewing theater in the basement of New Scotland Yard. Mark Villiers raised a quizzical eyebrow before introducing him to a number of senior policemen from the Met, including Commander Geoff Perkins from the Serious Crime Squad, a gaunt man with deep-set eyes. Illiffe knew about Perkins. Not a man to cross if you wanted to stay on your career path.

"Glad you could make it, Frank," Perkins said in a carefully blank voice.

There was a time to keep your mouth shut, and this was it. Illiffe said nothing.

"I take it you saw the Action TV program last night," Villiers said.

So that was what this was all about. Damn. He had no idea it would be broadcast so soon.

"No, sir," he said.

"We'd better watch it now, then, hadn't we?" Villiers said.

No one spoke as the half-hour documentary hammered out the story of Lyndsey Barratt, her disappearance from the hospital while under police custody, the deaths of the school cricket team and the coincidences involved. Julie Adams scrupulously avoided even a hint of editorializing. The word rape was never mentioned. The word murder was never mentioned. The phrase serial killer was never used. But by the time George Weston was looking confidently and calmly out of the screen, Illiffe would have taken an odds-on bet that 99 percent of the viewers would be thinking that Weston's ex-teammates had got no more than they deserved, however they died, and that handsome George was probably next on someone's hit list. His smug reference to Lyndsey as a "raver" did nothing to arouse any sympathy about the plight he might be in, not after the audience had seen the archive photographs of Lyndsey in the train and the hospital. Then the worst bit: Illiffe sitting at the table in the Blue Posts with Julie Adams and refusing to answer questions.

"Any comments?" Villiers asked, looking directly at Illiffe.

"No, sir." Illiffe wondered why they weren't jumping all over him. It had been a calculated risk to meet Julie Adams, but the way he saw it he had had no alternative. He was a working copper, despite their brief relationship, and she had an interest in a case. He hoped his seniors saw it that way. No doubt they'd let him know, once the immediate issues were out of the way.

"If I were to guarantee that this is an unofficial meeting, just to chew the fat, would that help?" Commander Perkins asked.

"Okay, sir," Illiffe said. "One comment I'll make is that someone, somewhere on the Force, should have identified these deaths as a possible series months if not years ago. I thought the PNC did that, but apparently it needs considerable updating. Even the new Home Office systems aren't set up for that kind of thing. When we did identify the possibility of a series of related deaths, the Met and the regional forces aren't set up to respond quickly enough. Neither is NCIS. These are not criticisms, sir. They are comments made with the benefit of hindsight."

"And what would you suggest, if we were to accept your comments in that spirit?"

"DCS Villiers gave me a chance to look into the situation in my own time," Illiffe said diplomatically. "I've linked up with the PNC people, and I've seen how the FBI deals with this kind of crime. I can't claim to understand their procedure, but it starts off with a collection of standard information about every murder, and it ends up with a special kind of computer system that can search for common factors, identify a possible serial situation, and come up with suspect profiles. It's very efficient. There's only about a dozen people looking after the whole shebang, although they do use psychologists and other eggheads to interpret what the computer throws up. There are people in UK universities who could do the same thing for us. Maybe we could adapt some of their methods on the PNC."

"I'm sure we've got people in NCIS who are on top of that, Frank. The point is, that's long-term. What about short-term? What about the Winstanton cricket team?"

"Let me set up an independent, cross-force investigation. Give me Susan York from Harry Branskill's civilian staff and the DC who drove me here. His name's Rogers. I'll need an operational budget of five hundred a week, a free hand, and no one climbing over me. I also need authority to open the cases again."

Villiers looked at him. It sounded as if Frank Illiffe had planned the thing well in advance.

"Why the DC? You've only just met him."

"No preconceptions. I need someone fresh and bright who can kick my . . . who can advise me if he feels I'm going down a wrong route."

"Your time frame?" Perkins asked.

This was the one question Illiffe had been dreading. No one liked starting an open-ended investigation, but he had no idea what he was getting into. He decided a white lie would be in order.

"According to the experts, the frequency of the incidents is important. The consensus is that we've got between two and four weeks before anything else happens."

"Meaning before someone has a crack at George Weston," Villiers said.

"Give us five minutes, will you, Frank," Perkins said. When Illiffe had left the room he turned to the other officers. "Your comments please, gentlemen. You first, Mark."

Mark Villiers saw all the signs of a public relations disaster unless the Met and the regional forces involved in the deaths did something positive, and quickly. What Frank Illiffe had suggested was not only reasonable, it was essential. He could release one officer on temporary assignment without too much trouble, but of course it was never wise to say so. That was the road to cuts in the budget.

"Illiffe's got a considerable workload, sir," he said, "but his suggestion is sound. A small task force could achieve a great deal in a short time, given cooperation from the regions, and maybe NCIS."

Commander Perkins looked around the table and saw there was general agreement among the other officers. He did not think the National Criminal Intelligence Service would be much help. On the other hand, Illiffe would need all the cooperation he could get from the regions.

"No need to bring NCIS into it at this stage, Mark. I presume Illiffe will arrange security for this chap Weston."

Chapter 18

GEORGE WESTON SAT DOWN TO BREAKFAST AT AN EMPTY table. His wife, Janet, had left the living room without speaking to him immediately after last night's Action TV program. When he heard her making up a bed in one of the spare rooms, he wasn't too worried. She threw a paddy like this every now and again. It lasted a few days, but she always came around. Too fond of King Dick. Anyway, the program was a load of rubbish. If his erstwhile schoolmates had come croppers, it would have been their own bloody stupid faults. Good team players, but not one of them had any real balls. No real initiative. Not like Weston.

George thought he'd come across looking bloody good on the program. Told it like it was. No horseshit. A crowd of kids going a bit over the top. That's how it was, no matter what that butch TV presenter said about it. He buttered some toast and was spreading marmalade on it when Janet came downstairs. She poured herself a large gin and tonic.

"I don't know what you're all huffy about," he said, looking at her rigid back. "It was a long time ago."

"What has a long time ago got to do with you being a thorough bastard?"

"Jesus," he muttered. "Are we going through all that again?"

"You'll go through it as many bloody times as I want you to go through it. You fuck my sister, my best friend, and Christ knows how many others, and there you are looking as if butter wouldn't melt, trying to convince everybody that you and ten other bastards were only doing what that poor little cow wanted you to."

"You can think what you like. She had it coming."

"Didn't we all, sweetheart?" She finished her drink, poured another one, and started out of the room.

"Where d'you think you're going?" he demanded.

"Golf, as if you care."

"Frankly, my dear, I don't give a shit. Only it splits the security team."

"You see, darling, that's exactly what I don't understand. If Lyndsey Barratt egged you on, the way you say she did, how come you've hired Rent-a-Thug? How come all your little willow and leather chums are history? And how come you're so bloody scared?"

"Don't be so fucking ridiculous. I'm just taking sensible precautions. Charles insisted on it, as a matter of fact."

"Charles couldn't insist on putting milk in tea. You're scared shitless."

"Crap," he said.

"No need to be coy, lover." She leaned toward him and spoke very carefully. "If one tenth of what Julie Adams said is true, you're entitled to be scared shitless. I only hope your life insurances are in order. I'd hate to be left a poor widow."

Weston lurched across the table and grabbed her throat. "You absolute bitch."

They struggled for a moment, and then Janet smashed the marmalade pot into his head. He staggered back, blood streaming down his shirt.

"Christ, now look what you've done."

Despite her own pain, Janet began to laugh hysterically.

"That's bloody typical. It's always someone else's fault, isn't it? Well, if you are next on someone's shit list, you've only yourself to blame. Don't come looking to me for sympathy."

Illiffe arrived at Weston Construction's head office near High Wycombe unannounced and found himself flashing his credentials at four very hostile close-protection security guards, who looked as if they'd be more at home pulling the heads off chickens than stuck on gate duty.

"I don't give a shit who you are, pal," one of them told him. "You don't get in there unless Mr. Weston gives the okay."

Illiffe said, "I could get a warrant."

"Oh really?" the guard said. "And how exactly would you manage with your warrant stuck up your arse?"

"You're not threatening a policeman, are you?"

The man ignored him and muttered a few words into a radio. "Mr. Weston says you can go up," he told Illiffe disgustedly. Pulling the heads off policemen was clearly a more desirable activity than doing the same thing to chickens.

They directed him to a parking space and one of them escorted him to the top floor and into George Weston's office. Charles Ruslin was also there.

"It's all right, Del," Weston told the guard. "Mr. Illiffe and I are old friends, aren't we, Frank?"

"I wouldn't have put it like that, myself," Illiffe said equitably as the guard withdrew from the office. "I think you're an arsehole."

As Ruslin began to splutter, Weston said, "For Christ's sake, Charles, at least we know where we stand with Mr. Illiffe. He doesn't like me, and I don't like him. But that's beside the point, isn't it, Detective Superintendent?"

"Unfortunately." Illiffe wondered why Weston had a piece of surgical plaster on the side of his head. "I take it you know why I'm here."

"Not really," Weston said venomously. "I mean, why bother? You didn't bother with Peter Shackleton or Harry Squires or any of the others. To what, exactly, do I owe the honor?"

"This is merely an informal interview, Mr. Weston, to establish where you were on these dates." Illiffe pushed the list of the dates on which Weston's former team members had come to their untimely ends.

"Do what!" Weston's astonishment was quickly replaced by rage. "You're asking me where I was, like I'm a fucking suspect."

"You don't have to answer that question, or any others, George," Ruslin said quickly. He turned to Illiffe. "You'd better leave, Mr. Illiffe, and come back either with an arrest warrant or a search warrant."

"For heaven's sake," Illiffe said exasperatedly, "this is just routine. I'm not here to accuse Mr. Weston of anything, but at the very least we need to get some facts together. I might say that someone who has a lot more experience than I do in this kind of thing pointed out that if all these deaths are connected, as they surely seem to be, then several people might have motives. I think he was just being academic. I think that Lyndsey Barratt is involved, and possibly someone else. I think that you, Mr. Weston, are next on that someone's list, but if I didn't do my job properly and cover all the shots, you'd be the first to level a complaint, am I right?"

Weston stared at him belligerently, then nodded. Illiffe thought he looked suddenly tired, as if it was getting to him.

"So, where do I stand?"

"From what I can see, you're starting the right way with this increase in personal security, but it can't stop there. We're dealing with a very cunning and very ruthless serial killer, but she—or he—is now working under a distinct disadvantage."

"Perhaps you could explain," Ruslin said.

"What he means, Charles, is that we know who the next target is, don't we, Mr. Illiffe?"

"That's right." Illiffe noted Weston's quick grasp of the situation. The man was no dummy. "Serial killers have their own warped logic, but, until we know what this logic is, it looks as if they're working at random. There's no way we can protect likely victims because we've no idea where they'll strike next. This is different."

"Are you saying that you can protect Mr. Weston?" Ruslin asked.

"Of course," Illiffe said. "The problem is, what level of protection will be effective, and what level you would accept."

"I presume you have completed a threat analysis," Weston said.

"We're working on that."

"Really!" Sarcasm oozed out of the word. "Do let me know when you've figured it out, won't you?"

"I don't think you quite understand the extent of the problem," Illiffe told him patiently. "For one thing, everything we have to date is circumstantial. Apart from one of the deaths, the coroners recorded open verdicts, which means that officially there are no murders. They could have been accidents. It's only when you put them all together that the accident theory doesn't stack up. We're having the cases reopened, of course."

"I don't need your theory crap," Weston said angrily. "I need a precise briefing on what I'm protecting myself against."

Fair enough, Illiffe thought, but he couldn't do that for Weston until he had a better understanding of how the killer or killers were operating. Professor Taylor could help. He was also banking that Linda Marshall's flatmate could throw more light on the subject. Deborah Lambert had lived with the woman, after all, and there was definitely some kind of connection. At the very least, she should be able to recognize Linda if she got near to Weston. He and Weston would have to cooperate on this, and the only way that would happen was if Weston was brought totally into the picture.

"I'd like to set up a meeting tomorrow with someone I think can help to do that," he said.

Professor Taylor roared up to the security gate of Weston Construction the next day on a well-tuned Harley-Davidson. One of the guards came out and looked at him aggressively, noting the bald head, the broken nose. All he needed was a tattoo and chains over the shoulder, and the guy would be a perfect Hell's Angel.

"Private property, mate," he said.

"My name's Taylor. I've got an appointment with George Weston in five minutes."

"If you're Taylor, where's your ID?"

"I wasn't aware that any ID was necessary," Taylor said mildly.

Another guard joined them. "Something up, Del?"

"This hippie thinks he's got an appointment with the boss. No ID."

"No ID, no entry. Piss off."

"If Detective Superintendent Illiffe has arrived, he can vouch for me," Taylor told them.

"It's none of your business who the fuck has arrived, pal. Piss off like I said. If you're Taylor, bring ID."

Taylor slipped off the saddle, and the two guards immediately adopted a combat attitude, watching to see if he would make any moves that they could interpret as a threat.

"If Illiffe hasn't arrived, I'll wait."

The guard called Del seemed astonished. "You got trouble hearing, or what!"

"I'm not causing any trouble," Taylor said reasonably. "Maybe you'd better check with your client."

"You don't get it, do you?" Del said. "No one but no one gets in here without ID, especially no one looking like a sack of shit tied in the middle like you do. Get the fuck out of here."

"You know," Taylor said. "I could get awful tired listening to your crap. All I'm asking you to do is make a phone call. If you can't get your pea brains round that one, you're in the wrong business."

"Right," Del said nastily. "You're nicked."

He grabbed Taylor's arm and swung him into his friend, who grabbed the other arm and caught hold of Taylor's neck, jerking his head back to restrict his movements. Del managed to elbow his stomach at the same time. It was a blow that would have brought most people to their knees. Taylor just said, "I think you really ought to make that phone call," in a voice that was totally unaffected by what they were doing. The two guards merely held him tighter, as Del's mate thumbed his shoulder radio.

"Alpha Charlie. Gatehouse. Code Nine."

"Oh, for heaven's sake," Taylor said, and slid out of their grasp.

"Shit," Del said, and grabbed for him again. It was like grabbing at a shadow.

Taylor caught his hand and dug his fingernails into nerves. Del screamed and dropped to his knees. His mate made another call, but this time it was Code Ten, whatever that was.

Taylor moved toward him, but stopped when he saw Illiffe's car approaching. Del was still screaming. Illiffe slowed and opened his window.

"What's going on?"

"Hello, Frank. Maybe you wouldn't mind informing these misfits who I am."

Two more guards arrived at the run. One of them unhooked an extended truncheon from his belt and swung it at Taylor who blocked the blow almost carelessly with his forearm, with no apparent effort. Illiffe got out of his car hurriedly and flashed his badge.

"Okay, okay, that's enough," he shouted. "Hold up or I'll arrest the lot of you and bang you away till Christmas."

*　　*　　*

"I'm sorry, Frank," Taylor said good-naturedly as they took the lift to Weston's floor. "I don't usually let people like that get to me."

Illiffe grunted. "Just as well for the close-protection industry, I'd say."

Taylor laughed, then said, "I've been doing some digging and come up with a few notions. I need to work with your Miss York on a couple of things. You want a briefing before we meet Weston?"

"I don't think so. If we get onto sensitive ground I'll kick your leg."

Weston was waiting for them. Angry.

"What was all that about?"

"Just a little misunderstanding," Illiffe told him. "Professor Taylor sorted it."

"How d'you do?" Taylor said, holding out his hand.

Weston didn't return the courtesy. "Just so long as they don't hit me for danger money. I'm getting bloody sick of all this, I can tell you."

Taylor smiled. "I can understand that. I hope I can help."

"You can help if you can tell me what the fuck I'm supposed to do when someone decides to whack me out."

"Did Frank explain my position?" Taylor asked.

"What position?"

"I'm currently involved in profiling serial killers with the FBI and some colleagues at Sussex University, which is why he thinks I may be some assistance to you."

George Weston sneered. "Assistance? Very good of you. What do you suggest?"

"It depends very much on Frank and his colleagues, but my recommendation is that we follow two lines of attack, or maybe I should say one line of attack and one of defense. The way I see it, we must assume Lyndsey Barratt is connected with most if not all of the deaths of your former cricketing pals. We also know that this Linda Marshall woman was involved with Shackleton's killing. The obvious implication is that she is helping Lyndsey."

"And why might she do that?" Weston asked.

Taylor shrugged. "There are several factors that may help to sort things out."

"May help?" Weston asked acidly.

"Mr. Weston," Taylor said, patience a tad under strain. "You just said you're getting sick of all this. Well, I'm getting sick of your hostility. If what I'm told is true, there's a lot of folk out there who'd be delighted if a rape victim managed to get her own back, so why don't you keep a lid on it?"

Illiffe hid a smile as Weston stared at Taylor with a look of near hatred.

"When Lyndsey disappeared from hospital, I reckon she went to ground both mentally and physically to distance herself from what happened on the train," Taylor said. "My first thought was that we look for Linda and we look for Lyndsey. Sounds obvious, but that approach would need two separate, side-by-side investigations. On the other hand, we know quite a lot about the kind of environment that Linda prefers, from Deborah Lambert's statement. Secure, good communications, well appointed, good quality stuff around the place, good taste, pure foods. And it struck me that Lyndsey would also want security, and privacy.

"I ran a check through the Profiler computer in Quantico, and there was a remarkable overlap on psychological and physical requirements. My best guess is that they have the same bolthole. Linda comes out when necessary and does the business. Pow! Exit one rapist, then back to the hideaway. Lyndsey gets revenge, and Linda gets her kicks. What we do is, we find that bolthole."

Illiffe was disappointed by this analysis. They could spend weeks looking for boltholes. On the other hand, it was almost certain that someone would have a go at Weston. That was where to focus resources. In addition to that, Linda obviously kept in touch with the people who produced these videos. He wondered if he should brief Taylor about Walt Daniels Productions, but decided not to, at least until DI Chesterton had given him more information about the firm.

"Even if you're right," he said, "I don't see how that takes us any further forward. She could be anywhere."

"I agree. But we can narrow the search for the bolthole considerably. I don't think Lyndsey would be happy in a city, not after the physical violation that happened. She'd want to get away from people. Think countryside, remote, probably isolated. Then there's the defensive dimension. Above all, she'll want to feel totally and absolutely protected."

"How about a lighthouse?" Weston suggested. "The bitch would love that."

Illiffe raised a questioning eyebrow.

"Mr. Weston is suggesting a phallic association," Taylor said blandly. "I doubt if that would be attractive to her."

After a pause, Illiffe said, "So it has to be somewhere defensible? An old fort, or a manor house?"

Taylor shook his head. "I followed the defensible theory for a while, but it doesn't go far enough. Lindsey would look for a place that couldn't even be attacked effectively."

"What about RSGs?" Weston muttered after a pause.

"Regional Seats of Government," Illiffe explained to Taylor. "Underground bunkers, constructed in the cold war to protect bigwigs from nuclear attack, so they could emerge and run the country after the radioactivity had halved its life and the charred corpses had been disposed of by Mother Nature."

Taylor grinned. "You got those places too?"

"My old man built a couple in the sixties," Weston said. "Made a bundle out of it. There's a property agency in Bristol selling them off. Maybe they can help."

Weston was certainly no slouch, however unlikable.

"I'd also run checks on any local upscale supplier of works of art, antiques, furnishing, that kind of thing," Taylor added. "Your witness to the Shackleton killing should be able to help there. She knows the kind of thing Linda goes for."

"Not a problem," Illiffe assured him. He made a mental note to get Terry Chesterton on to it.

"So while your merry men are out there looking for a homicidal duo, what the fuck am I supposed to do in the meantime?" Weston asked.

"All the signs are that the victims had no idea they were in any danger," Taylor reassured him. "You do know. This gives you an edge. Best thing is, maintain your current level of security, but carry on living and working as normal. Vary any routine stuff, like routes to work or visits to your golf club or whatever. We're dealing with a very cunning lady here, but there's a limit to her ability to approach someone who is aware of the threat. I guess Frank will be taking steps to assign officers to your case."

Illiffe nodded. "I've authorized round-the-clock protection at your home as of this morning, and we'll screen your staff and associates here."

"What have my associates got to do with anything?" Weston asked with some irritation.

"As I explained before, Mr. Weston, we don't want to miss any shots by sloppy police work. For all we know, Linda Marshall might already have made contact with someone in your firm. Maybe she's someone's new girlfriend. Maybe she's even got a job in your organization under another name. Just let me have details of any recent appointments, say over the past three months, and we'll look into it for you."

"I'll instruct our personnel department right away," Charles Ruslin said.

As Illiffe and Taylor left the Weston building, Illiffe said, "That was very constructive. Thanks."

"It's a start," Taylor said. "We had to give him something to work on. He's under a lot of strain. I don't think it's all to do with the killings, though. He's got personal problems. Someone's taken a swing at him recently. Probably a woman, or there'd be a bigger bruise. My guess is, his wife."

"Serves the son of a bitch right, whatever," Illiffe muttered. Taylor was still getting on his nerves.

Taylor made no comment. He had learned long ago that people had their own ways of letting off steam, and there was no point of making an issue out of throwaway remarks. He didn't think for a moment that Frank Illiffe would let his personal feelings toward Weston cloud his judgment. He could see that Illiffe was also having problems with his own way of working, but he was used to that too.

"Of course," he said, "the bolthole theory could get us nowhere. It's merely a sensible deduction from all the factors we have at hand. We may be able to make improved deductions with more information."

Illiffe remembered Lyndsey lying in the hospital bed, damaged, maybe beyond repair.

"RSGs are the most unattackable places we've got," he said. "If she can afford it, that's the kind of place she'd be."

Taylor shook his head. "It's a line of inquiry, that's all. The human mind is a funny thing. She might find a place that no one else could possibly imagine."

Chapter 19

DI TERRY CHESTERTON TRACKED WALT DANIELS PRO-ductions to an office in Amsterdam and from there to a number of exclusive sex clubs in the UK and other European cities. The focus of the enterprise was in the USA, at a town called Valley Mills in Texas. No attempt had been made to hide the links, and all the companies were registered with the authorities as providers of adult entertainment including soft porn, S and M, and phony snuff videos. No kiddy stuff. Nothing with animals. The general feeling in the trade was that Walt Daniels was an okay guy, and his products were better than average. If he didn't do it, someone else would, only they wouldn't stick to the same standards as Walt. Better the devil you know, so they left him alone.

Chesterton wasn't about to leave anyone alone if their name came up during a case he was working on. He reported his findings to Frank Illiffe.

"I phoned this Valley Mills place, and when I asked to speak to Mr. Walt Daniels a kid with a cornpone accent gave me her boss's itinerary, just like that. Daniels and his wife, Sylvia, are in Saigon at the moment; then they're flying to Hamburg, and then they're drop-ping into the UK to do the rounds of the clubs they own here. They'll be in London next Tuesday, and the kid asked me if I would like an appointment. I said yes. We're booked into the Piedmont Club at nine in the evening."

"Nice one, Terry," Illiffe told him, pleased. "Good result. We'll take Susan along. By the way, did you mention you were a copper?"

"She didn't ask."

"Fair enough. Let's stay close to this. In the meantime, there's a possible lead to Lyndsey Barratt. Can you track down any sales of nuclear bunkers starting from her disappearance? If anything turns up, run another check on the local delivery people. See what the owners have been taking in."

"Nuclear bunkers? I don't get it."

"It's Professor Taylor's theory. He reckons Lyndsey and her friend Linda would want a bolthole that couldn't even be attacked, never mind one that could be defended. George Weston suggested RSGs." He sensed disapproval in the silence. "Any problems with that?"

"The prevailing theory within the Force, guv, is that all this offender profiling is a load of crap."

"Don't beat around the bush, Terry. Tell me what you really think."

The viewing theater in the Piedmont Club was furnished with erotic paintings and explicit sculptures, with plush double seats partitioned from each other so that other members of the audience could not be seen. Receptacles in the armrests contained condoms, phials of amyl nitrate, vibrators, and tissues. The room also had a comprehensive bar. Walt offered them a drink, but no one took up the offer. No one wanted to sit in the double seats, either, so they stood awkwardly by the bar. Walt poured Sylvia a large orange juice, then turned on the screen and switched to a menu of available movies, indexing through them at speed.

"This is Linda's section," he said. "She's one of our best independent directors. Horny as hell, plus unbelievable FX."

Susan looked puzzled.

"Special effects, honey," Sylvia told her.

"Right," Walt said. "We can't figure out how she does it. It's okay for Fox and the big studios. They've got Quantel and other data-imaging equipment. But this is sheer talent, I'm telling you. It'll blow your mind, believe me."

DI Chesterton was looking unhappy, and Illiffe raised his head questioningly.

"Shouldn't we caution him, guv?" Chesterton asked quietly. "If this stuff is bent, we'll have to confiscate it. I'd like to start things off the right way."

"Is there a problem, Officer?" Sylvia asked ingenuously.

"That's what we're here to find out, Mrs. Daniels," Illiffe said. "DI Chesterton asked me if we should caution you before we see any of your products. I'm sure you're familiar with the routine."

Walt nodded happily. "You do what you have to, son," he said to Chesterton. "All I want to do is what you want me to do. You want to see one of Linda's movies, fine. You don't, that's fine, too. Caution me by all means, only my lawyer gets awful upset if anyone does anything out of line, and I think you'll find that a caution would be out of line."

"Not if we end up confiscating your videos, it wouldn't," Chesterton said.

"Okay, Terry," Illiffe said. "Let's not jump to any conclusions here."

"There's nothing on our stuff that isn't on half the major releases these days, plus we do not tolerate bad language. What we sell is ambience," Walt explained amiably.

"That's right," Sylvia agreed. "Ambience on screen and ambience in the audiences. We run a high-class operation, Detective Superintendent."

Walt pointed at one of Linda's titles. "I love this one. *Let's Romp in the Water.* Our little lady sexes up this guy on a boat, then she cuts his cock off. Horniest thing you ever did see, ain't it, honey?"

"I don't mind telling you people, I creamed my pants three times during that particular sequence," Sylvia said. "I just love it when a guy gets chopped like that. Most realistic thing I ever saw. Blood spurting round, all colorful, like."

Illiffe experienced another of those skin-crawling feelings. Unbelievably, Walt and Sylvia were enthusing over what had happened to Alan Peters aboard the *Tiger Shark.*

"What about that one?" Illiffe said, pointing at the list. "*Blowout.* Not a very original title, is it?"

"Linda's latest. Best thing she's given us yet, I'd say. If you don't think the title is original, wait till you see the end product. Fantastic. The way Linda works is, she uses digital cameras for lots of the stuff. They're so damn small you can have one built into the bridge of your spectacles or the strap of your bag. Sure, the quality's not as good as a Betacam, but it's okay where you don't have a lot of moving around. The bit where she takes him out is utterly multiorgasmic, ain't it, hon?"

"You're right there in the room with them," Sylvia said. "Go on, Walt. Play that one."

Illiffe had seen many pornographic videos in his time, and very few had what you might call quality. They were generally produced with a banal story line, stilted script, and a musical accompaniment that had nothing to do with the activity on screen. Some snuff movies had the barest camera skills and no script at all, only the visuals of sadistic rapes, torture, and death. *Blowout* was different. There was a surreal, cinema verité aspect to it, with music that pulsed in sympathy with the images. The dialogue was kept in the background, a murmuring counterpoint to the commentary, a female voice that huskily seduced the audience into taking her side in the harsh world of masculine domination of the female, into the hunt for a partner she could dominate, seduce, and finally destroy. The camera took them on a journey into locations that both Illiffe and Chesterton recognized. The Main Street in Heathside, the White Swan, with the barman Ronnie opening a bottle of champagne, smiling customers bantering in the background, and then a face staring at them. Peter Shackleton's face, eyes widened with that shocked, helpless paralysis that Sicilians call the Thunderbolt.

"There he is," the voice said. "Look at him devouring me. In one split second I have become the center of his universe. Imagine how he feels at this moment, seeing me surrounded by others, wanting me with every cell and every pulse in his body, wondering who I am, how he can meet me, how he can have me. And the wonderful thing is, I need do nothing. He will ask his friends. He will track me down. He will make the overture. He will present the invitation, take the steps that lead him to me. To my body. To my vengeance. . . ."

"What did I tell you folks?" Walt said. "Is that a work of art, or what? We have some of Hollywood's finest FX people working on our products, and none of them can work a latex dummy like she does. It's uncanny."

Sylvia couldn't hide the effect of the film on her emotions. "Ain't that just what we ladies would really like to do to our menfolk, honey?" she asked Susan when she had recovered her breath. "Blow them, blow them out, and blow them up. Gets me every time."

Susan turned red, and looked hard at the notes she'd been taking.

"Show our friends the pictures of the Shackleton job, Terry," Illiffe said quietly.

Chesterton spilled the contents of a large envelope on a table. Walt pushed them around curiously, then became very, very still. Sylvia picked one up. It showed Shackleton's ruptured body in the foreground, with parts of his innards splattered on the walls and furnishings.

"Oh my God," she said.

There was a long silence.

"What I can't understand," Illiffe said to Walt, "is how you expect us to swallow all your crap about latex dummies. We've got enough here to hold you as accessories to murder."

"Hey, come on. We've got heaps of stuff like that in our own studios. I even had a documentary made, showing how it's all done. Even without any digital imaging you can shoot pretty realistic stuff. When you manipulate the image, you can make people believe anything they see. Anything. There's no way anyone could figure this was the real McCoy, believe me."

"I don't believe you," Illiffe said, trying but failing to keep the anger out of his voice. Even if Daniels was telling the truth, he was pandering to warped minds that didn't care if the victims in the films were killed or not. In fact, Illiffe reckoned, they would probably want to believe the deaths were real. Daniels and his wife were in the sadomasochist industry, and that was that.

"Perhaps we should see Linda Marshall's other films and Mr. Daniels's documentary, sir, before we make our conclusions," Susan said.

Two hours later, Illiffe had seen enough to know that Walt and Sylvia Daniels were exactly what Chesterton's research had shown them to be: larger-than-life people with a huge appetite for physical pleasure, who catered for others with the same proclivities without indulging in the extreme behavior often associated with others in the pornographic business. In particular, Sylvia Daniels was genuinely upset that Linda's killings were as real in fact as they seemed in fiction.

He wasn't sure where they stood in the legal scheme of things, but at this stage he was prepared to give them the benefit of the doubt. From the look on DI Chesterton's face, he wasn't feeling so magnanimous, but Illiffe didn't want to have the search for Linda Marshall sidetracked by a witch-hunt into the Daniels duo and their business empire.

"I think you were right, Terry," he said.

Chesterton didn't know what he was talking about, but thought Illiffe was playing a card from a very loaded deck. He had to tread carefully.

"Yes, guv."

Illiffe turned to Walt. "You'll understand that I must confiscate all this material. It's vital evidence in a major investigation."

Walt nodded. "I'll make copies for you."

"Not good enough," Chesterton snapped. "We want the originals."

"We don't have the originals," Walt explained. "Linda keeps her material and sends edited versions to our database in the Philippines. It's done over a satellite link. Gets round local regulatory systems." He paused. "I promise you one thing. We'll be erasing all her stuff off the database, and we won't be taking any more. Ain't that right, hon?"

Sylvia nodded vigorously. "You're damn right, darlin', and I'll be sending that little lady an E-mail telling her what she can do with the next one."

"Next one?" Illiffe said flatly. "What next one?"

"She says she's working on the best movie yet," Sylvia told him. "Here . . ." She leaned over to the control board of the video and tapped several keys. The screen changed to a communications menu with a list of stored inbound E-mail messages. She highlighted one and brought it to the screen.

Dear Walt and Sylvia,

Many thanks for the fat royalty check. I am starting work on a new production for you. Up to now, my story lines have involved Woman as the Trap. But circumstances have changed, and this will no longer be possible. My new approach involves Woman as the Huntress. It'll be irresistible. I know

you'll just love it to bits. My best work yet! I'll keep you
informed of progress.

Love,
Linda

"Can I make a suggestion, sir?" Susan asked Illiffe.

"Sure," he said.

"Shouldn't we let Professor Taylor see all this?"

"Who's Professor Taylor?" Chesterton asked impatiently. The
damn case was getting out of hand. These two porn-peddlers were
in deep shit as far as he was concerned, and he did not like the
direction along which Illiffe was pushing it. Now this Hendon civilian was getting in on the act and bringing someone else to the
party. As far as he was concerned, they should nick Walt and his
oversexed wife and use them to get to Linda Marshall.

"Let's discuss that later," Illiffe told Susan. "In the meantime, Mr.
Daniels, we need to get to Linda Marshall, fast. I'd appreciate any
cooperation you can give."

"Can I have a word, sir?" Chesterton asked, jerking his head
toward the door.

"I know what you're thinking, Terry," Illiffe said smoothly. "But
if we are to believe Mr. and Mrs. Daniels about their system, which
I do, we have nothing here to confiscate. If we had to go through
the formalities, it could take months through international courts,
and we probably wouldn't get a result anyway."

"That's the size of it, son," Daniels said to Chesterton. "My wife
and I are shocked by what you've told us today. You may not think
much of what we do, but we try our darnedest to give pleasure to
our customers without anyone getting hurt. We've managed to
achieve that, until now. Like I said, we ain't accepting any more of
her work."

Susan caught Illiffe's eye and gave him a querying look. He caught
what she was thinking and nodded.

"I think it would be more helpful if you held back on that," Illiffe
said to Walt. "This business is very complex, and we have been taking
some advice from the gentleman Susan mentioned. He's an expert
in serial killings. You and your wife are a lead to a very dangerous
and elusive lady. I'd appreciate it if you left things as they are, and
go along with what she's planning. Can you get any advance details?"

"I don't think we can, honey," Sylvia said. "She just downloads the finished product. We go through it and maybe make a few suggestions. She makes the changes, and that's it."

"And you have no idea how to locate her?"

"Nope," Walt said. "It's all done over the Internet. She could be operating anywhere in the world. There ain't no way of tracking her down."

Chapter 20

AFTER THE DEBACLE AT WINSTANTON, HADDOCK HAD thought long and hard about his future. Defense budgets were shrinking, but there was a new growth industry. Close protection. Increasing threats of kidnapping and random crime were leading wealthy people to look toward the private sector for security. And the private sector would need the same kind of facilities open to the military, so he had used his pension from the Army and his savings from his employment at the school to buy the freehold of the quarry and over fifty acres of surrounding countryside from a local farmer who retained the encircling lands and who kept to himself. An unpaved lane from the main road more than a mile distant provided the only access. That is what made Offa's Quarry so attractive to his clients, and to Haddock. Remote, private, and secure.

The guest lodge in Haddock's quarry was not sumptuous. In fact it was decidedly primitive. A stone barn, whitewashed inside and out, with its original beams supporting an ancient slate roof that had survived over a century of mountain weather, a tribute to the workmanship of the time.

The previous owner had created two stories by installing a beechwood floor and an oak staircase. Haddock took things further by arranging a kitchen, dining room, and bathroom on the ground floor and furnishing the upper floor with several beds and movable partitions. It was primitive, but it worked. His clients were generally

happy to share the accommodation, and if any of them were part-
nered the screens provided a small degree of privacy. Most of them
arrived with a copious supply of alcohol, so by the time they turned
in after a hard day on the ranges there were few scruples about the
sleeping arrangements.

George Weston usually arrived with his latest girlfriend after ensuring no one else would be staying overnight. Haddock enjoyed his
visits. Weston would demand a series of competitions, and Haddock
had yet to win a single contest. Weston had an affinity for weapons
that was unnatural. Shotguns, pistols, submachine guns, sniper rifles,
it was all the same to him. He was world-class. He could have cleaned
up at Bisley. But all he wanted to do was come to the quarry and
pump steel, lead, nickel, and the occasional mercury-tip into bull's-
eyes. The only time he had missed a clay was when Haddock supplied
him with half-charged cartridges. He took one shot, then turned to
Haddock with a cold look on his face.

"I don't pay you good money to be fucked about, Smoky. What
the fuck are you playing at?"

Haddock arranged an annual competition for his best shootists, but
Weston always turned him down. Very, very frustrating, and not just
for Haddock. The day after his father was killed in a site accident,
Weston arrived, out of the blue, face set like one of the quarry work-
faces. An officer and two sergeants from Hereford were proofing a
case of CZ75s, and one of the Czech-made pistols had jammed after
firing six rounds. They didn't have any armorer's tools, so the sergeant who'd been using it placed it on the firing bench to cool down.
Weston sauntered over, picked it up before they could stop him, and
cleared it with a few movements of his hands. Being professionals,
they took note of Haddock's sign to leave off and watched as Weston
reloaded and smacked ten bullets into the bull at twenty-five meters.

"Nice gun," he observed, almost contemptuously, before wan-
dering to the next range to give his Browning a workout.

The word spread, as it does in such circles, and ever since then,
Haddock's visitors invariably asked when the big guy was going to
join the annual competition. But the big guy was adamant. All he
wanted to do was push Haddock to the limit, get pissed, and screw
whichever young lady he'd managed to persuade to accompany him
for a weekend in the country.

Most of Haddock's clients were Army personnel who came to improve their small-arms skills on his shooting ranges and use weapons that were not provided by the Ministry of Defense. Others, like George Weston, were wealthy individuals who stayed in the guest lodge and used the ranges and other facilities to let off steam when the pressure of work needed a release. Occasionally a group of close-lipped, tough young men would arrive in a van and pay him to take a day off while they took over the quarry, no questions asked. Even though they cleaned up after they'd done their business, one of the huts smelled of electricity, burned flesh, and excrement, and there were fresh tracks leading to one of the mine shafts.

Frankly, Haddock couldn't care less. These people were his comrades, and whatever they did to secure the peace of Her Majesty's realm was all right by him.

Chapter 21

BILL TAYLOR SWITCHED OFF THE VIDEO PLAYER AND rubbed his eyes tiredly. Many serial killers took photographs and movies of their work, but this pushed matters into another realm. Professional competence leapt from the screen, creative, persuasive, seductive. It was impossible not to be affected by it. Susan York had brought the videos to his study at the university in Brighton and briefed him on how the police had interviewed Walt and his wife. Now she sat silent and motionless in the chair next to him. There was a spot of color, high on both cheeks.

"Raw stuff," he observed. "No one could accuse her of lacking imagination. I wonder what she has in store for us with her new series."

"It's disgusting," Susan said.

"It's a clue," Taylor corrected. "In fact, it's an encyclopedia of clues."

"Yes, I know, but it's also disgusting."

He shrugged. "Depends where you stand."

Susan looked at him. "You surely don't condone this kind of thing." She sounded disappointed, as if she had expected more of him.

"If we didn't know that the producer had actually killed someone, we might accept all this as a work of art. We might accept it as artistic even now we do know."

"That's a dreadful thing to say."

"Did you ever take the opportunity to wander round the museum where we met?" he asked. She stared and shook her head. "To take just one example, every day hundreds of people marvel at the Assyrian carvings. They marvel despite the fact that the stonemasons worked from human and animal models who were flayed alive so they could get musculature and bone structure exactly right."

"It's not the same."

"Yes, it is. The Assyrian rulers enjoyed inflicting pain. They sat and watched the proceedings. They enjoyed the product. And so do we, three thousand years later. It gives us a secret thrill to see how delicately the executioners slipped their knives under the skin and eased it away from the flesh, even though we're only looking at a lump of stone. I can't see any difference, frankly."

"That's an outrageous thing to say."

"Take Goya's sketches of the Peninsular wars," he continued, unabashed. "He sat there with his charcoal and pad while soldiers hanged prisoners by tying their necks to a shrub and playing tug-of-war with their legs. The sketches sell for hundreds of thousands of dollars."

"If you are deliberately trying to upset me, you certainly know your business."

"What I'm trying to do is get you to see Linda's work in a non-judgmental way. We just sat through an illustration of her mind. Your computer's great for correlating textual factors, but it's no use in this kind of thing. If I'm going to help you and your people, I need computer factors plus reactions from you that are uncolored by prejudice or emotion. It's not easy, but we have to try."

Susan felt relieved. She admired Taylor's work, and for a few moments it seemed that he had let slip a side to his character that was very unattractive. She began to see what he was trying to do.

"I'm not sure what you mean by our reactions."

"Just tell me what you feel about Linda," he suggested. "Don't try anything clever. Give me your top-of-the-head stuff. What you feel about her."

Susan thought for a moment. "It's a pile of things. She's manipulative. Very capable. Determined. Ruthless. Implacable. Amoral . . . And there's something I can't put into words."

Taylor said nothing. Waiting.

"The only thing that comes anywhere near is 'unreal.' "

Susan had summed things up admirably. The woman who had seduced and killed Peter Shackleton was all the things she had said, and more besides. Persistent. Malevolent. Intelligent. "Unreal" was a novel concept, though. Taylor felt instinctively that it was part of a description that was a key to Linda's behavior and her relationship with Lyndsey. And he was certain that there was a relationship. The most powerful he could think of was that they might be lesbian lovers. Quite a few male serial killers in the United States had been homosexual partners. He thought of the thirty-two young men who had been raped, tortured, and killed by Dean Corll and his lover Elmer Wayne Henley around Houston in the 1970s. Henley solicited young men, usually hitchhikers or vagrants, to take part in homosexual sessions for two hundred dollars. When they arrived at Corll's house they were given wine and drugs. Then Corll handcuffed them to his "torture plank" and sodomized them. His tortures included pulling out their pubic hairs, one at a time, and breaking glass rods inside their penises.

By comparison with such outrages, what Linda Marshall had done to Shackleton, and probably to the other cricket team members, was relatively mild. However, Taylor noted the increasingly sadistic nature of the Winstanton deaths. Such a trend was a common factor in serial killings. What he needed now was more information, more corroboration of existing factors, so that he could narrow down the possibilities in the search for Linda and Lyndsey. He picked up his phone and dialed Frank Illiffe.

"Hi, Frank. It's Bill Taylor."

"Good morning, Bill. I was just going to call you. How did you get on with the videos?"

"Very instructive, but I guess Susan could have told me a bit more about how you acquired them."

"In what way?"

"You have a remarkably discreet young lady in Miss York. All she said was that the producers of the videos had released them to you. That implies volumes, Frank. Like you've met the people who know Linda's work. Like you must have asked them a lot of questions and maybe got a lot of answers. Like they let you have the material before you got a warrant, which leads me to think you gave them something in return, like immunity from prosecution. So here I am wondering if you're taking me into your confidence. How am I doing, so far?"

Pretty good, Illiffe thought.

"You're reading too much into this. We didn't get very far with the distributors of the videos, because they're passing the stuff around these damned digital highways. They aren't breaking any UK law that I know of. It would take months to sort it out using due process. They agreed to cooperate with us and keep in touch with Linda over her next offering. That way, we might get a line on her."

Taylor smiled sadly to himself. Maybe Illiffe didn't mean to keep him at arm's length, and maybe he did. But the result was the same, either way. Without realizing it, Illiffe and his colleagues had acquired information of enormous significance to the understanding of Linda Marshall's mind. Taylor had to find out what it meant.

"I'm going back to basics on this, Frank," he said.

"Meaning?"

"First thing, I'd like you to work with Susan, getting all your notes scanned into a text reader for the computer. It might come up with more correlations. Meantime, I'm taking a visit to Lyndsey's school. I want to follow the track she went down when this thing began. I want to get closer to her, you know? On top of that, I need to spend some time with your witness in the Shackleton killing. Deborah . . . ?"

"Deborah Lambert," Illiffe said.

"Right. Meanwhile, I presume you're keeping an eye on George Weston?"

"That's taken care of. What with our chaps and his people, he's more closely guarded than the Monarch."

"I wish I could say that's good to hear," Taylor told him. "But I have a bad feeling."

"*You* have a bad feeling! You should be sitting in my chair."

"You got problems?"

"You could say that. Our mutual friend Julie Adams has been busy. That's to say, her TV company has been busy, which is the same thing. They're now cooperating with one of their group newspapers to cover the story, and the other media have got hold of it. They've been pestering so much that the powers that be have decided to hold a press conference tomorrow. Guess who's chief spokesman."

"That's tough, Frank," Taylor said sympathetically. "What are you going to say?"

"I've no bloody idea."

Taylor left his motorcycle at home and took the train to the station that Lyndsey Barratt had used to get to her drama school. He wanted to meet some of the people who had known her. Get a feel for the places she had been. Let his subconscious take in the unconsidered factors. Work on them. Maybe come up with a new idea or two. He didn't rate telepathy very highly, or the use of mediums in police work, but he did believe that the human mind could assimilate huge amounts of information and sift through it with enormous efficiency, provided you gave it a chance.

Several young people were on the platform when he stepped out of the carriage, waiting for their trains, lounging on backpacks and smoking cigarettes, at least one of which contained substances that Taylor recognized with the unerring skill of a former user. He went to a small group and asked how he could get to the Hershal Academy.

"Turn left out of the station and keep walking," one of the youths told him. "Takes about fifteen minutes. Big gates, on the right. You can't miss it."

"Are you an actor?" an attractive girl asked.

"Hell," he said, "I didn't think I looked that bad."

The youth laughed and coughed smoke. The girl gave Taylor a cool, appraising look.

"You look groovy," she said.

So the old Haight-Ashbury vocabulary was coming back.

"Kind of you to say so. If I was two years younger, I'd ask you out so I could return the compliment in an appropriate manner."

"Very groovy," she repeated, holding his gaze boldly.

Taylor grinned and made his way to the exit. A pretty girl could still make the pulse accelerate. When will we ever learn, he hummed.

The sun was warm on his back as he took the route described by the student. He found himself imagining the young Lyndsey walking toward him on that fateful day, carefree, proud of the new diploma in her briefcase, her future stretching before her in the sunshine. And who could have known how black that future was to be? How short? If only her family had been at the ceremony. If only she had been with a friend. A sudden spasm of rage at the cricket team members hit him, and for a second or so he found himself wishing that Linda or Lyndsey or whoever was responsible for the ten deaths would find a way around George Weston's protection and remove the son of a bitch from the face of the earth. It was people like Weston and all the other perverted bastards that caused normal men to cross the road away from an approaching woman in case she became nervous or frightened by their presence. Goddamn!

He shook the negative thoughts from his head and concentrated on his walk. It took him twelve minutes to reach the entrance to the academy and another three to reach the main building and reception.

Philip Warner received his guest with ill-concealed curiosity. A visiting American professor of psychology from Sussex University who didn't want to discuss anything over the telephone. Very intriguing. He asked Mrs. Bellamy to bring coffee and biscuits and settled down with Taylor in the easy chairs by the window that overlooked the school grounds.

"It's a great view," Taylor said appreciatively. "My own study looks out onto some air-conditioning units."

"Yes, we're very lucky. One of the delights of a country institution. Ah, tea. Milk and sugar, or lemon?"

"A little milk and one spoon of sugar, please," Taylor told the principal's assistant.

Mr. Warner waited until the tea was poured and Mrs. Bellamy had left the room, then asked, "So what brings you to our establishment, Professor?"

"I'm engaged in a research project into a particular kind of criminal activity."

"Good gracious!" Warner exclaimed with genuine astonishment. "How on earth could we assist you in such an enterprise?"

"It involves one of your past students, Lyndsey Barratt."

"Ah," Warner said, and fell silent. Finally he said, "And what particular kind of criminal activity?"

Taylor watched the principal closely. His eyes had clouded with the pain of distant memories. A caring man.

"I could beat around the notorious bush, Mr. Warner, but I'd be wasting your time and mine. I presume you have seen the recent TV program about the Winstanton cricket team."

"Yes. The redoubtable Miss Adams and the successful Mr. Weston. To be quite honest, I didn't know what to make of it. The presumption behind the program was obvious, of course. But no one who knew Lyndsey could believe her capable of such a thing."

"Someone is capable of it," Taylor said flatly, "and it's either Lyndsey or someone very closely involved with her. I've come here to test that hypothesis."

"I'm not sure I understand."

"Ten people have died violently over the past few years. All were members of a group that savagely attacked and violated a talented young actress. She disappeared and has never been found. Lyndsey has reason to kill them, but another person is 'in the frame' as your police put it. Maybe more than one person. One of the things I'm here to ask you is whether Lyndsey formed a particularly serious attachment with any of the other students."

"If you are asking if Lyndsey had a relationship here at school with anyone who might adopt the role of avenger, the answer must be no. She was a truly dedicated young student, and as far as I knew she had no steady boyfriends. In fact I can't recall her ever going out with any of the boys."

"I was thinking more in terms of a girl," Taylor told him.

"Ah," Mr. Warner said again. "I see your drift." He thought for a moment. "I doubt if Lyndsey would seek comfort in the arms of someone of her own sex. I consider her to have been a perfectly normal person. Not that I am being judgmental, you understand. Merely practical. We embrace many faiths and beliefs here. But Lyndsey was more concerned about her family than anyone else. Of course, her experience may well have tipped her into another frame of mind, but she showed no such inclinations during her three years with us. All she talked about in terms of her deeper relationships were her parents and her sister."

"Her sister?"

Taylor was astonished. There was no mention of any sister in Illiffe's files, and neither had Julie Adams mentioned a sister to him. The only explanation was that neither of them knew, and he found this difficult to take in.

"I rather gathered that she was a bit of a black sheep. Lyndsey would mention her occasionally, then stop, as if she were ashamed in some way. I did not inquire, of course."

Taylor had learned the answer to his main question, and added some new information about Lyndsey to his case notes. Not only new, but possibly vital. A sister! There was not much point in taking up any more of the principal's time.

As he prepared to leave, Warner shook his head sadly. "I should have taken heed of Mrs. Bellamy's warning about that fateful day. This year the trustees have agreed to end term on Thursday the twelfth of June."

He smiled at Taylor, expecting him to respond, but Taylor had no idea what he was talking about.

"Thursday the twelfth," Warner prompted. "Friday the thirteenth. That's when it happened."

Chapter 22

Whithout Illiffe walked through the door into his first press conference room, he was disconcerted by the melee of TV cameramen, sound technicians, and presenters, plus photographers and reporters from the print media and half a dozen radio reporters with microphones at the ready. He couldn't see the Action TV camera, but Julie Adams was sitting at the back of the room next to that Glaswegian program editor. But no Arny. No TV crew. Strange! He nodded slightly and received a nod in return. She always looked so damn cool. What was she up to? His colleagues were filing in behind him. Niels Eberhard, senior PR officer in the Met, making sure that name tags were displayed in front of the appropriate chairs. Mike Fisher, assistant commissioner, was in the middle, with Illiffe on his right and Geoff Larson, deputy head of the Serious Crime Squad, on his left. Sound techies were still crawling over the carpet to position their microphones when Eberhard tapped his microphone and started the ball rolling.

"If we could settle down, ladies and gentlemen. Fine. Thanks. I'd like to kick things off by reminding you that this conference is restricted to the subject you can see on your handouts. The deaths of Messrs. Ramshir, Hodgkins, Odonga, Johnson, Nesbit, Elmwood, Peters, Smythe, Squires, and Shackleton, about which there has been recent speculation."

Several in the audience turned to glance at Julie Adams, who sat expressionless at the back.

"Assistant Commissioner Mike Fisher here will make a brief statement, and then we'll take questions, which either he or his colleagues Detective Chief Superintendent Geoff Larson or Detective Superintendent Frank Illiffe will answer. Mike."

Eberhard sat down and Mike Fisher pulled his table microphone closer.

"Thank you, Niels. Good morning, ladies and gentlemen. Your press packs list the names of the deceased together with the circumstances of the deaths and the verdicts recorded by the various coroner's courts. You will see that in all but the case of Mr. Elmwood the coroners recorded open verdicts, there being insufficient evidence to point to any crime having been committed. At the present time, that is the official position. However, our analysis shows that the possibility of ten healthy young men who were all members of the same school cricket team having died violent deaths accidentally within a few years of each other is extremely small. Accordingly we have appointed Detective Superintendent Frank Illiffe from the British Transport Police to head a team that will make further investigation, with the cooperation of regional forces and outside specialists. Thank you."

"If any of you have any questions . . ." Eberhard said.

Illiffe watched as the assembled journalists absorbed the statement. It did not take very long for the reactions to start. A heavy-jowled man with a florid face opened the batting.

"Edmund McInley, *Daily Mirror*. Is that it, Mr. Fisher?"

"That's the official position, Ed, yes."

"So who are these outside specialists who are helping your investigation? Something to do with offender profiling, I suppose."

"That is correct," Fisher said. "We have the assistance of Professor Bill Taylor who is experienced with this kind of work on both sides of the Atlantic."

The journalists scribbled notes, and a young woman said, "Rosie Macdonald. The *Independent*. Is that the same Professor Taylor who is retained by Action TV?"

"That's correct," Fisher said shortly. There was more scribbling.

"And what's your official position on Lyndsey Barratt, who was assaulted by all the men on your list and who disappeared from Hope Green Hospital six years ago?" the *Daily Mirror* journalist asked.

Fisher passed the ball smoothly. "That's one for Frank Illiffe."

"As you should know, Mr. McInley, Lyndsey Barratt made no formal complaint, so no charges of assault were brought in that case," Illiffe said.

McInley bristled. "Oh really? And would I be pushing police intellects too far if I rephrased my question about Lyndsey Barratt, in case you didn't understand me first time round? As I recollect, she was charged with possession, was she not?"

"I am not in a position to discuss individual cases with you."

"Presumably that doesn't apply to Action TV," someone said loudly.

Illiffe craned his head to see who it was and recognized one of the journalists who had been at Hope Green when Lyndsey was in hospital.

"It would be helpful if you gave your name and publication, Greg," Eberhard said.

"Greg Hawkins, *Daily News*."

"Thank you," Eberhard said.

"Well?" Hawkins said, looking at Illiffe.

"Well what?" Illiffe asked as evenly as he could manage.

"I asked if your not being in a position to discuss individual matters applied to Action TV."

Eberhard stepped in before Illiffe could snap out the response that was on the tip of his tongue.

"I don't think we realized that you were asking a question, Greg. What exactly do you want to know?"

"Fair enough," Hawkins said. "My question is, did Detective Superintendent Illiffe's personal relationship with Julie Adams of Action TV influence his decision to meet her in a Soho pub and be interviewed for her program?"

The TV cameras swung to a close-up on Illiffe, and the guys with Nikons began jostling each other as they put the motor drives into top gear.

Illiffe stared at Hawkins, wondering how much the man knew about Julie, if he knew about the room that had been booked for the afternoon all those years ago. He probably did. Illiffe was on the spot, despite the fact that the question was decidedly of the have-you-stopped-beating-your-wife variety. Whatever he said, he was screwed, so the least said . . .

"No."

"That's a negative, is it?" Hawkins smirked.

"Yes," he said.

In the short silence that followed, Eberhard stood up.

"Thank you very much for attending, ladies and gentlemen. Don't forget your press packs as you leave."

No one was leaving. The presenters and reporters surged toward the table with a barrage of questions. Two of the camera crews turned their attention to Julie Adams, who was being shepherded out of the room by Donald Cameron. Eberhard did the same for his police colleagues.

"My office, Frank," Assistant Commissioner Fisher muttered as they pushed their way out of the conference room.

They made their way along the corridors in silence. As they passed through the reception area, the duty civilian looked up from her desk and held out the phone.

"Urgent phone call from a gentleman called Bill Taylor, sir. Can you take it?"

"A moment, sir," he said to Fisher.

"Two minutes," Fisher snapped.

Frank took the phone. "Illiffe."

Taylor had overheard the interchange, wondered what it was about. "Shit hit your fan, Frank, or what?"

"You could say that."

"Well, more's on the way. I've just talked to Lyndsey's school principal. Lyndsey has a sister that no one seems to know anything about."

"Jesus Christ," Illiffe muttered. "When can you get here?"

"Not sure. I'll be as quick as I can."

The press conference was reported on the three o'clock TV and radio news and printed in the early editions of regional evening news-papers. Jean Illiffe turned off her television with the remote control and sat watching the blank screen. She had a strange, empty, pulling feeling in her stomach. Painful. Familiar. She put her hands on the bulge that was Frank's baby and tried to breathe evenly. Frank had looked so angry. So tired. At the end of it there had been a close-up of Julie Adams shaking her head to a fellow reporter, with a slight smile. Jean desperately wanted to know what lay behind that smile.

Satisfaction, that she and her program had got more publicity? Sadness, that a good man had been dragged into the limelight?

The phone rang, and Jean stood up painfully.

"Hello, Alice," she said, knowing that her sister watched the same channel every afternoon.

"Are you all right?"

"I'm not sure."

"Oh Christ. I'll phone an ambulance."

"No. I'll be fine."

But the pain stabbed her again, and she gave a little sob.

"Ring off, lie down, and wait," Alice demanded. "I'm coming over now. Lie down."

Alice disconnected, and Jean walked slowly to the settee and sank to her knees on the carpet. Albert was watering the flower bed by the living room window. He stared in for a few minutes, but as Jean didn't get up he turned off the hose and cautiously made his way inside the house.

"Is anything the matter, Mrs. Illiffe?"

He saw her slowly shake her head. He was well aware of the potential for a miscarriage. That was, after all, why the Illiffes had employed him. The old soldier's training came to the fore. He was more used to dealing with physical injury, but the basic principles of first aid applied in most situations.

"Let's get you more comfortable. Can you lie on these cushions?"

She nodded, so he laid out cushions from the settee and helped Jean to lower herself gently so that she was lying in the fetal position. Then he got her coat from the hall and covered her. Her breathing was fast and shallow. Every few seconds she winced with pain.

"Was that your sister you were talking to?"

"Yes," she whispered.

"A very practical lady. Does she know what's wrong?"

Jean nodded. "She's calling an ambulance."

"Let's make quite sure, shall we?"

He dialed 999 and confirmed that the scheduler had booked an ambulance. It was definitely on its way. No more than five minutes. Jean was crying now, and he held her hand until it arrived.

*   *   *

Linda turned off her TV about the same time as Jean. And like Jean she sat staring at the blank screen for several minutes. Something was happening that she did not understand. She called for Lyndsey, but Lyndsey didn't answer.

"Damn," she said. "Damn, damn, damn."

That detective kept cropping up. And so did the TV reporter, Julie Adams. The news presenter said that a police spokesman had not commented when it was suggested that the police were looking for Lyndsey Barratt in connection with the deaths of ten young men. Then the presenter said that Scotland Yard denied an allegation that an officer had acted improperly with regard to a program recently broadcast by Action TV. Linda remembered the program only too well, with that bastard George Weston blaming Lyndsey for what had happened on the train. Lyndsey had told her that the detective Frank Illiffe was a good man. She said that Julie Adams had helped her. Now they were trying to upset things. Trying to find Lyndsey. Trying to stop what Linda was planning, and there was so much to do before Lyndsey would be completely safe. There was George Weston, for one thing.

Killing Weston was different from the others. With them, no one had known what she was doing. But someone had put it all together, and now they knew that Weston was her next one. No one had said so. But they knew, all right. Georgy Porgy. The one in charge.

"Lyndsey? Where are you?"

Still no reply. Well, that's okay. Linda never, never gave up on a person. That's what it was all about. Never giving up. Loyalty. Keeping a promise. Although Linda was honest enough to admit that it gave her great pleasure and a substantial income to keep this particular promise.

"Lyndsey, where *are* you?"

The door opened, and she felt the gentle breeze and smelled the sweet perfume of the person she loved best in the entire world. Dear, gentle Lyndsey, still bruised and disoriented by the events on that bloody train.

"I'm here," her little sister whispered. "Is something the matter?"

Linda felt the familiar mixture. Tears of sorrow and mad, black rage against the people who had done such horrors.

"I don't know." Things were becoming very complicated, and

she searched for a way to explain it to Lyndsey. "I think some of the people you thought were your friends are not your friends anymore."

Lyndsey was puzzled. "I don't know what you mean."

"Something is turning them against you. It's nothing for you to worry about, little sister. I'll take care of it."

Haddock saw the press conference, too. Didn't know what to make of it. Decided it was none of his business. His business was to establish the best military-style shooting facility outside of Senney Bridge. And his income was good. Very good. If it kept up, he intended to create a driving range and a killing house. Maybe build a pop-up range in the wooded hills overlooking the quarry. Bloody good fun, pop-up ranges, especially with live ammunition. None of this soppy simulated crap. No way.

The following morning, when George Weston arrived at his office he accessed the Internet and opened his electronic mailbox. Most of the messages were from overseas contacts of Weston Construction, but one stood out. It simply said: "Hi, George. Why not access Lyndsey's page on World Wide Web? Get http://lyndsey.per.eur/friday thirteenth/."

He stared at the screen for several minutes, then accessed the Internet and typed in the command to download the WWW page. Nothing happened for a few seconds as the command passed through the gateway and searched for the requested file; then the words REMEMBER FRIDAY 13TH? began growing and vanishing on his screen in a variety of fonts and colors. He tried to exit from the Internet, but nothing responded to his instructions, and the message kept flashing. As a last resort, he turned his terminal off and on again several times. The message kept returning to his screen. He picked up his phone and called the company's information technology manager.

"Clive. Morning."

"Morning, George. I was just about to call you. We've got a virus."

Weston sighed. "I know. How soon can you fix it?"

"No idea. It's not one of the usual bunch. We'll run an analysis on all data brought into the system online, then start checking the physical media."

"Don't bother with that. I brought it in." Weston explained what had happened.

"That's a help. Any idea what it's all about."

"No," Weston lied. He put down the phone and looked at the calendar. Friday the thirteenth. Next Friday.

Chapter 23

THE ILLIFFES HELD A REMEMBRANCE SERVICE FOR THEIR baby's brief experience of life. They weren't religious, but it seemed the natural thing to do. Jean's sister, Alice, made arrangements for the ceremony at the local church. She was there with her husband, Steve, and Jean's mother and father. They sat in silence in the front pews behind Illiffe and Jean, listening to the organ play "Abide with Me." Old Albert was there, lost in his own thoughts. Some close friends and neighbors arrived. And Illiffe's colleagues. Mark Villiers came with Terry Chesterton and Harry Branskill. Susan York and Keith Rogers were there too. Illiffe saw Bill Taylor slip into a pew at the rear of the church, saw Susan glance at him and smile briefly.

Jean leaned her head on her husband's shoulder and took his hand, and he had never felt as close to her as he did at that moment. There was more silence, then a slight disturbance as the church doors opened again and people turned to look at the newcomer. Julie Adams.

When the service had finished, people stood back as Jean made her way to Julie and stared at her.

Julie lowered her eyes. "I'm so sorry," she said.

"Thank you for coming," Jean said quietly to the woman who had loved her husband, who had damaged his career, and who didn't know how to deal with it.

Illiffe was numbed by the loss of their second baby, but the presence of these people sparked a rush of emotions, love for his wife, and for his family and friends, and hate for the surviving member of that benighted cricket team, George Weston. He wanted the man dead, and he was supposed to protect the son of a bitch.

Bill Taylor shook Illiffe's hand, a warm, strong contact.

"Thanks for coming, Bill."

"You okay?"

"I will be. It's Jean I'm worried about."

Taylor had seen the interchange between Illiffe's wife and the Action TV presenter.

"I wouldn't worry too much. You've got a strong lady there, my friend."

People approached Jean and Frank to smile briefly, convey a shared sorrow.

"You'll be taking a few days off, presumably," Taylor said as the last couple left the church.

Illiffe shook his head. "The best thing we can do is carry on. When this Linda Marshall thing is over, that's the time for a break."

"If you're sure, I'd like you to introduce me to this flatmate of Linda's. Both reports I've read suggest she's holding something back. We need her input."

Part IV

HIGH WYCOMBE

Chapter 24

MONDAY THE NINTH. DEBORAH WOKE EARLY. AFTER A cooling shower and quick breakfast she stood at the door of Linda's room and took a deep breath. She hadn't been inside since the plasterers and decorators had finished. It seemed, somehow, to be an intrusion, but she knew she had to face up to it. The absence of Capital Radio blasting from the decorators' battered radio was a gift from heaven, but there was still the lingering smell of building and decorating to deal with. She went into the kitchen and carefully unwrapped the incense sticks and holders she'd bought from the candle shop in the Main Street at the weekend. She'd given a great deal of thought to the matter of aroma, and after sniffing samples of musk, vanilla, cinnamon, rosemary, and strawberry, she opted for opium, having received assurances from the sales clerk that there was, of course, no real opium in the product. But the smell was nice, and the name introduced a certain excitement. It conjured images of a furtive, seductive underworld, peopled by those who refused to conform to rules and regulations, who did their own thing. People like Linda. Light-years away from her world of computer programming and system design.

The clerk said she should light the end of an incense stick with a match and let it burn until the tip was glowing, then blow the flame out. She said that one stick would smolder for about an hour if it wasn't in a draft. The aroma would last much longer. Maybe a whole day. Or a whole night.

She had no matches.

No matches, no problem. She lit the gas burner and held the tip of the incense stick in the hottest part of the flame. The oils in the stick ignited and burned with a bright yellow flame, emitting a disconcerting plume of black smoke. Almost pure carbon. But when the yellow flame was blown out, a reassuring red glow remained, and a thin curl of gray, fragrant smoke rose into the air. She stuck the bamboo end into the little hole in the wooden holder and carried the assembly carefully toward Linda's room. Funny. Linda's room. The day that Linda had left her, alone in the flat with the horror, she had promised herself that she would never, never think of Linda again. But it wasn't so easy. Despite everything that had happened, she missed her landlady, her flatmate, more than she could say. Through Linda, she had seen aspects of life that had been missing from her own routine and rather drab existence. Sicilian cocktails. Exotic French meals. Night visitors. Not so much a landlady. Not a friend, either. Mentor? No, not really. It was difficult to put it into words. Flatmate was, in fact, a good description. It implied closeness, yet allowed for a distance. Joint activities, with the ability to remain independent. Someone who would never take offense if you didn't meet up for days at a time. Weeks or months, even. Someone with whom you could share a trouble or two, without either side taking advantage.

Deborah realized that she was feeling very lonely. Tears prickled her eyes.

She opened Linda's door and went hesitantly inside. Everything was so different. Bare white walls. Polished parquet flooring. An alcove where the bar had nestled against a wall. Another where the bed had been. The walk-in wardrobe and the en-suite bathroom, all new, all stark and impersonal. Deborah blinked back her tears and made a decision. Whatever Linda had or had not done, she, Deborah, would make this room into a place to which Linda could return. A place that would reflect Linda's beauty. Her passion.

That was it! That was what Deborah so much admired, so much missed. Linda's sophisticated passion, her ability to embrace sensuality and sexuality, yet not be controlled by either. Linda was the one who controlled.

"Yes," Deborah whispered. "Yes, yes, yes."

Linda's room would always be Linda's room. She'd make sure of that. Deborah had a few home improvement journals in her room, and for the next hour she scoured them for ideas, but they all seemed so conventional. Pretty, yes. Inventive, yes. But conventional. Above all, Linda was not conventional.

Deborah decided to go to the restaurant and ask Leo and Marge what they thought. They hadn't mentioned Linda to each other since she disappeared, but she was sure they wouldn't mind discussing the room with her. They had both been very kind, very sympathetic. Marge kept asking if she was eating enough. Leo talked about ideas for another book and seemed determined to avoid mentioning the Shackleton business, as if he were embarrassed by it, but Deborah sensed his curiosity, as if his reticence as a gentleman was in conflict with his instinct as a writer.

She listened to *Today* on Radio 4 until nine o'clock, then made her way to l'Étoile to join her friends. They were in the middle of a nondiscussion period, Leo reading the *Guardian,* Marge patting Wilfred as he wolfed down an apple strudel. He looked up briefly at Deborah, growled, and stuck his pampered nose back into the goodies on his plate. She ordered her coffee from Joel and waited for the ten-minute discussion period to begin.

"I'm going to refurnish Linda's room," Deborah announced when Leo looked at his watch and put down his newspaper. "I'm going to redesign it completely."

"I thought you *had* refurnished it," Leo said, sounding surprised.

"Oh no. It had to be sort of cleaned," she said. "Everything taken out. Floor scrubbed and sanded. New plaster. Emulsion paint. That sort of thing."

There was a silence.

"Quite," Leo said.

"The last few weeks must have been a very difficult time for you, my dear," Marge said.

Deborah thought about that. "I suppose so. I mainly got on with things, though. I've had quite a lot of work to do, luckily."

"Often the best way," Leo nodded.

"It's just that I really would like that room to be a bit special, and I'm running out of ideas. In fact, to be honest, I haven't even had any ideas."

"What you need is an interior decorator," Marge said.

"I disagree," Leo told her. "They're crazy, they're irresponsible, and they cost a fortune. I should know. Remember Kenneth?"

"Of course I do! Dear Kenneth."

"Who's Kenneth?" Deborah asked.

"Don't ask," Leo said. "He's outrageous. Wears a kaftan and lipstick. Runs a hugely expensive interior-design consultancy in Belgravia. He wafts in, waves his arms around, and suddenly you have a designer house with a six-figure bill to settle. He's particularly interested in filling every empty space with dried twigs."

"I thought he was sweet," Marge said. "And his rustic arrangements have won international awards."

"Rustic . . . He was outrageous!" Leo spluttered.

"All I want is some ideas," Deborah said.

"You're not the only one, my dear," Marge said, glancing at Leo. "Our novelist friend here has been approached by his agent to write something about this awful Peter Shackleton thing. Apparently a Sunday newspaper wants the serial rights. No prizes for guessing which one."

"Now, Marge," Leo protested. "You promised not to mention it. Especially to Deborah."

"And why not especially to Deborah?" Marge wanted to know. "If you decide to do it, it's perfectly obvious you'll have to ask Deborah for some help. She's the only one who really knew anything about this Linda Marshall person, after all."

Leo looked at his watch and saw that the ten-minute discussion time was up. He smiled and opened his newspaper again. Marge scowled. She didn't like things left hanging in the air.

Deborah sipped her coffee. Talking about Linda made her uncomfortable. She was wondering what to do about it when a car pulled up suddenly in the street outside the restaurant. The nice detective was driving. Detective Superintendent Illiffe. There was another man, sitting in the passenger seat. The policeman raised his arm in greeting and called out of the window.

"Hello, Deborah. We were just going to your place. Mind if we join you?"

She shook her head and moved her bag from the seat next to her as Illiffe parked the car. He noticed the two other people at adjoining tables staring at him with open curiosity.

"This is a colleague of mine, Bill Taylor."

"Nice to meet you, Miss Lambert."

He had an American accent. She was very disturbed by his eyes. Blue and cool. They left her nowhere to hide.

Joel arrived as they sat at Deborah's table.

"Oui, monsieur?"

''*Deux cafés noirs, s'il vous plaît,''* Taylor said, easily slipping into French. He turned to Deborah. "I hope we're not interrupting anything."

"Oh no. These are my friends, Leo Chindwall and Marge Harrison."

"Pleased to meet you," Leo said politely.

"Likewise," Taylor said.

They all leaned over and shook hands.

"How have you been getting along, Deborah?" Illiffe asked.

It was an easy question, based on a genuine concern, but Deborah seemed slightly taken aback by it, as if wondering why it had been necessary.

"Very well, thank you," she said after a pause.

"Professor Taylor is trying to get some insight into what happened here the other week," Illiffe explained. "It's his field of study, and we're hoping he can give us some leads."

"It would be nice to have a chat about it," Taylor said to Deborah. "But I suspect we're interrupting you and your friends."

"Nonsense," Leo said. "Deborah was asking us about interior design, that's all. Maybe you've got some ideas?"

Taylor liked to be surrounded by what he called a comfortable mess of British bric-à-brac, especially Victorian things like desks topped with green leather, and carved walnut pipe racks, and jardinieres, and tiled fireplaces. By no stretch of the imagination could this be elevated to the realm of interior design.

"Depends what you're designing the interior of," he said.

There was a silence.

"One of the rooms in my flat," Deborah said quietly.

"D'you have a theme in mind?" Taylor asked.

No, she thought. Not a theme. A person. A very special person, and this Bill Taylor had come here to talk about her. Deborah was not sure she wanted to discuss Linda with him, but the detective had said she was the only one who might be able to help them understand what Linda had been doing, and why. Deborah did not see how she could help the police any more than she had already, but she supposed that they had to keep asking questions until they eventually pieced things together. That seemed logical, and she believed that people should help the police whenever possible.

"Something that feels safe," she said. She hadn't meant to say "safe." It just came out like that. And it made sense. She had never been really comfortable in Linda's room, with all its erotic devices and pornographic illustrations. It was a dangerous room, and Linda used it for dangerous pursuits. She'd have to find some way of encapsulating the spirit of Linda without the risk.

"Well, I think you should have a chat with Kenneth," Marge said. "I'm sure he'd be willing to give you a few ideas if you mention my name."

"Nonsense," Leo said emphatically. "The man's a nitwit."

"Would you like to see the room?" Deborah asked Taylor suddenly. The question seemed to surprise her as much as it did the others.

He nodded. "Very much indeed, if it's not too much trouble."

"It's just round the corner. It wouldn't take long, and I do need help."

Taylor looked questioningly at Illiffe.

"I'll hang on here," Illiffe said. "It'll give me a chance to read a newspaper for once."

As they left, Wilfred darted out and tried to nip Deborah's ankles. Marge was mortified.

"Wilfred, you naughty little dog. I do apologize, Deborah."

"That's all right, Marge. I'm afraid I don't get on very well with animals, and they seem to sense it. I don't think Wilfred's ever really taken to me, has he?"

"You're having no more apple strudel this week," Marge told Wilfred crossly.

They walked to Deborah's flat in silence, Taylor content to observe and learn. She seemed shy and diffident. He noted that she held her body awkwardly and kept her eyes generally on the sidewalk, as if she had to watch where she was placing each step. Illiffe had briefed him on DI Chesterton's comments and on his own feelings. Taylor's immediate impression was that Deborah was a very controlled and intelligent girl, probably introverted, who dealt with everything in a straight line. Logical. Focused. No room for deviation. Things that fitted in with her occupation in computing.

The silence, by no means uncomfortable, continued until Deborah unlocked the flat and took him into Linda's room.

"There," she said.

Despite its emptiness, Taylor recognized the layout from the video of Shackleton's death. It was one of those very large rooms with alcoves and bays adding space to the main area. The bar had been to his left, and the bed would have been facing him. There was a faint smell of incense, but apart from that there were no subtle vibrations, no "atmosphere," nothing that evoked the violent death of Peter Shackleton. He found the room to be emotionally neutral, and that was also how he felt about Deborah. Everything about her was in neutral.

"It's got great potential," he said. "What's the rest of the place like?"

She gave a fleeting smile. "Would you like to see my room?"

"Absolutely."

It was totally different. Warm, caring, childhood nostalgia. Lots of books and children's paintings. He picked a couple of titles from the shelves, looked closely at the paintings, noted the laptop computer linked to an ink-jet printer on a small desk. A cable ran from the computer into a telecommunications socket.

"I like it. I like it a lot," he said. "You've got very good taste."

She seemed pleased, then became thoughtful. A little shyness again.

"I didn't do all this," she told him after a pause. "Linda did it. She said she wanted to make me feel at home."

Taylor slotted that into the mental files. Linda Marshall was a very complex woman.

"That looks very businesslike." He nodded toward the computer as he placed the books carefully back on their shelves.

"Oh yes," she said, moving toward it. She sat down and caressed the keyboard.

"I suppose you can link up to your clients through that line."

She became more animated. "Yes. But it's not a phone line. I've started dealing in graphics, so I needed a fiber-optic system. You can transfer megabyte files in seconds. It takes hours to do that over a normal phone line."

Taylor understood rather more about computing than Illiffe, and he knew that few business systems such as the one Shackleton Motors required would need graphics. Deborah must be working for other kinds of clients to need such a facility.

"I suppose you design business forms and company logos with it," he said ingenuously.

"Oh no. It's far more complicated than that. One of my clients is developing interactive computer games."

"My chums tell me that lots of games companies in the States are using software writers in Bosnia and other East European countries. Are you undercutting them?"

"I don't know. It's not just the software, it's the concept and the game algorithms too. I can do several jobs at once. It's probably quicker and cheaper in the long run to use someone like me."

Taylor was increasingly impressed. This was a formidable intellect, but he felt that Deborah was too highly focused for her own good. She was certainly in a position to help him to understand more about Linda Marshall, and maybe to help Frank Illiffe to protect George Weston as well. After all, she was the only person who had both seen and lived with a suspected serial killer who specialized in close-up death. If George Weston was on Linda's hit list, the quicker they got Deborah locked into his security, the better. Whether she would agree, or whether she could cope if she did agree, was another matter. He'd have to talk about this with Illiffe. In the meantime, although he made it a rule never to interfere with anyone with whom he was involved in any kind of study, he could not resist the temptation to make a suggestion. She was clearly in need of some advice about the flat, and he couldn't see that it would do any harm.

"I think you should try to make the empty room feel more like this one," he said.

She gazed at him, and her eyes brightened.

"Oh yes," she said. "What a lovely idea. I could never think of something like that, but it's obvious, isn't it?"

"I don't know about obvious, but this room's really homey, so why shouldn't it work with the larger space too? I'd give it a whirl, if I were you."

"Yes, I will," she said excitedly. "I know just what to do, and it won't even cost very much. There's a flea market in the church hall every Sunday. I can get lots of bargains from there."

She rushed back into the room that had been Linda's and started planning how she could make it look like her own room. Taylor shook his head almost ruefully.

"I'll leave you to it, then. Bye."

She didn't hear. He moved politely into her line of vision.

"I'll be off, now," he said. "Bye-bye."

"What? Oh, good-bye."

"I'll give you a call to see how it's going. By the way, we may need to ask your help on a problem we've got."

"Oh yes," she said. "Please do call. And if I can help you I will, really. You've been very kind."

She turned back to the room and promptly forgot all about him. As he let himself out and carefully closed the door, he smiled to himself. That was a truly primitive genius. Quick as a whip in her own field, but haplessly adrift in the real world. He imagined her browsing about the market looking for first editions of *Winnie the Pooh* and *Alice in Wonderland*. Not to mention those Beatrix Potter and E. H. Shepard originals. He had no idea what Deborah thought was a bargain, but she wouldn't see much change from five figures.

Taylor returned to the University of Sussex, filed a report on his meeting with Deborah to Illiffe, and sent a copy to Susan York at Hendon on one of the FBI forms, listing key words and phrases so that the new computer program could scan the form quickly and use data-mining logic to examine the mass of information that she was collecting. Three hours later he took a call from Illiffe. He sounded worried.

"Susan's come up with something, and I've had Weston's solicitor on the phone. We need to get together."

Taylor sighed. "Your place or mine?"

"Weston Construction HQ. Eight A.M. tomorrow. It's just outside High Wycombe. The company chopper will pick you up at the Brighton helipad at six-forty-five. I'll have a car waiting at your flat at six thirty."

Taylor was impressed. Someone was pushing activity buttons at last.

Chapter 25

TUESDAY, THE TENTH. GEORGE WESTON SAT AT HIS DESK looking tense. Charles Ruslin sat beside him, an open notepad on his knee. Taylor lounged in an easy chair next to Susan York, while Frank Illiffe and DI Chesterton had seats at an oval conference table. DC Rogers sat near the door, looking and feeling slightly out of place. Illiffe opened the proceedings.

"We needed to meet, because the threat to Mr. Weston has taken a couple of peculiar turns. Professor Taylor visited Lyndsey Barratt's drama school, where the principal said he thought she had a sister. We checked the Hope Green maternity unit, and their records show that Lyndsey had an older twin sister called Linda. There was a double christening at St. Martin's Church. No one knows what happened to Linda. We're working on school records to see if she went away to school at the same time as Lyndsey went to the academy, but we haven't been able to trace a school for either of the twins. It's the silly season, of course, with summer holidays coming up, and we're still working on it. Whatever the case, there's an obvious implication here. Let's assume that Linda Marshall is this twin sister. She hears what happened to Lyndsey on the train and goes on a vengeance kick. This fits in with what we know about her, what with all these pornographic and snuff videos."

George Weston leaned back in his chair and looked at him.

"What the hell are you talking about—snuff videos?"

"There's evidence that not only did Linda Marshall deliberately kill your teammates, she videoed everything and produced a range of movies that are available over the Internet."

"For fuck's sake!" Weston shouted. "This bitch wipes out my cricket team, makes movies, and no one takes any fucking notice. . . ."

"Now, George," Charles Ruslin admonished. "We need to remain cool if we are to see our way through this."

Weston glared at him, but managed to calm down.

"Thank you, Mr. Ruslin. We're reopening all the cases, of course. There's every chance we will apprehend whoever is responsible before they get anywhere near Mr. Weston. Don't forget that none of the others had any idea they were in danger. Things are completely different now."

Taylor stayed quiet. They were indeed different. Linda had told Walt and Sylvia Daniels that her new video was unlike all the others. She had changed her MO. He needed to absorb as much information as possible before trying to analyze what was happening, and what might be about to happen.

"Smoky Haddock was involved in all that drug shit," Weston said. "Why don't you ask him if he knows anything?"

Of course. Illiffe had always suspected that the cricket team knew about the drugs dumped on Lyndsey. Weston's question proved it.

"As yet, we cannot trace Thomas Haddock," he said. "We're working on it."

"Oh really! And I'm supposed to believe you people know what you're doing, after all this crap?"

"I'm sure everyone is doing the best they can, George," Charles Ruslin assured him.

Weston's phone rang, and he grabbed it. "Yes. On our property? Right. Do it." He slammed it down. "There's a fucking TV crew down there with a power lens aimed at these windows. That bloody friend of yours, I shouldn't wonder."

Illiffe looked at DC Rogers. "Sort it, will you, Keith."

"It's sorted," Weston said angrily before DC Rogers could move. "They're on company property. They're being ejected with what I believe is called appropriate force."

Illiffe went to the window and gazed out. "Like I said, Keith. Go and sort it, or Mr. Weston's employees might find themselves up for GBH." He turned to Taylor. "Grievous bodily harm."

When DC Rogers had left the room, Taylor said to Illiffe, "You mentioned the case had taken two turns."

Illiffe nodded. "You'd better explain, Mr. Ruslin."

The company lawyer adjusted his spectacles. "Last Friday, Mr. Weston received an E-mail message. It invited him to, I believe the phrase is, 'visit' Lyndsey's page on the Internet's World Wide Web. When he did so, a computer virus was imported into the company computer. It blocked everything with the message 'Remember Friday the thirteenth.' "

DI Chesterton looked puzzled. "What's so special about Friday the thirteenth, apart from the fact it's bad luck for everyone?"

Illiffe looked straight at George Weston. "Lyndsey Barratt was assaulted on Friday the thirteenth. That's next Friday. It looks like she's drawn the battle lines."

Weston looked disgusted. "Bit melodramatic."

"We're dealing with a melodramatic person," Taylor said. "Melodramatic and extremely malevolent."

"Well, she's not a fucking magician, is she? My house is secured tighter than a nun's nasty. I fly here most days, and this place is more like a bloody fortress than a company head office." Weston glared around angrily. "As far as I'm concerned, it's business as usual. No homicidal bitch is going to get within a mile of me, Friday the thirteenth or Saturday the fourteenth. All we need now is for Her Majesty's constabulary to do what they're paid to do and arrest the cow, so we can all settle down and get on with our lives."

"I understand your concern," Illiffe said, "and I agree with you. Trouble is, both Lyndsey and Linda have gone to earth, and until one of them emerges there's little we can do. DI Chesterton's team is following leads generated by Susan York's analysis and our previous discussions. She has some more information that could be extremely helpful."

"It's all to do with linkages," Susan said, unraveling a large computer printout. "This is the analysis of all the information gathered up to yesterday afternoon. These clusters—"

"Jesus Christ," Weston snapped. "Talk bloody English, will you?"

Susan waved her hands helplessly over the document. "It is a bit technical, I'm afraid."

"Why not explain it like you did for me over the phone?" Illiffe suggested.

She looked at him gratefully. "Everything points to two people being involved in all the cricket team deaths, but only one is involved in the actual killings. The deaths are hands-on, with a sex angle. Most have been videoed. The MO for the team deaths was changed from time to time. As Frank says, we believe the MO is changing once again, so the threat facing Mr. Weston is not the same as that which faced the other team members. This might mean that someone else will try to carry out the threat. The obvious candidate is Lyndsey rather than Linda."

"You look unhappy at this analysis, Professor Taylor," Charles Ruslin observed.

"It's okay as far as it goes, but we've only run one level of analysis, and there's an awful lot of stuff left out." He turned to Susan. "How long will it take the system to dig another level?"

"We'll have the results early tomorrow morning."

"In that case, I have two suggestions to make," Taylor said. "You might be right about Linda not being the one to make an attempt on Mr. Weston, but we can't know for sure, and there's one way she could already have put a killing plan in place."

"What's that?" Weston asked.

"She could have planted a bomb somewhere she knows you'll be on Friday. Maybe several bombs, covering the usual places. Remote-controlled devices."

"Fine," Weston snapped. "I'll change my appointments."

"That might help you," Taylor said, "but there's a risk that some-one else could be killed. If Frank agrees with my interpretation, we need to search your home and this building."

"What is the implication, in terms of interruption to company business?" Ruslin asked.

"Minimal," Illiffe said. "And I agree with Professor Taylor. We'll get the bomb squad on it right away. What's your other suggestion?"

"There's one person who can recognize Linda if she turns up any-where near you," he said to Weston. "I strongly advise you to em-ploy Deborah Lambert to stay as close as possible until the threat is eliminated."

George Weston's reaction was predictable and very negative.

"Fuck that for a game of soldiers," he said. "I'm not having some prat of a girl acting as my nursemaid."

Chapter 26

WEDNESDAY, THE ELEVENTH. LEO CHINDWALL ARRIVED back at his house in Laburnham Mews in the small hours after an amiable evening in the White Swan having a private drink with Ronnie and a few of the regulars. His agent's letter was still on the small dining table, outlining a publisher's offer for a book about Lyndsey Barratt with the likelihood of a three-part exclusive series in the *Sunday News*, one of Julie Adams's group's newspapers. By exclusive, they meant no other publication must be involved, no television and no radio. They wanted it focused and tied in with the stories that Julie Adams had presented so effectively on TV. They wanted it linked to the Winstanton cricket team and, above all, they wanted personal input from the one person to have known the mysterious Linda Marshall. Deborah Lambert. Leo felt as if he were floating on a sea of success. A book about the Shackleton affair and another about the Barratt case. Wonderful. He was sure Deborah would cooperate, despite her initial reluctance. Why should she not?

He was about to put the kettle on to make his hot chocolate when the phone rang.

"Hello?"

"Mr. Chindwall?" A girl's voice. Hesitant. Subdued.

"Speaking."

"She's on her way. I tried to stop her, but she never listens."

"I'm sorry. Who's that speaking?"

"She just goes on and on. She never takes any notice of me."

"Who takes no notice? No notice about what? Who is this speaking?"

"I know she wants to help me, but what she's doing is wicked, isn't it?"

"Who . . . ?" Leo stopped. Good Christ, he was talking to Lyndsey Barratt. Dear God, where was that bloody tape recorder? Where was his notepad . . . a pen . . . anything . . .

"Yes, yes, I suppose it is."

The recorder, thank God.

"I know she only wants to help."

"Of course she does, my dear. It . . . You . . . you are Lyndsey, aren't you? Lyndsey Barratt?"

"She's looked after me ever since it happened. I couldn't remember, but she told me all about it. She said she'd look after me. She said they'd never be able to hurt me again. Not ever."

"She sounds like . . . like a good friend."

"And then she said that people were starting to interfere, and poor Deborah is involved. She said you and your friend Marge were going to spoil everything if you wrote your book. She wouldn't be able to finish what she was doing, she said, 'cause you were interfering, and I told her that I want her to stop killing people, but she won't listen. She never listens. Not really. She always does what she wants, in the end. She always has. Ever since we were little."

"What do you want me to do?" he asked.

There was a silence.

"You mustn't let her in. I tried to call your friend Marge, but nobody answered. She might have gone there too. She just wouldn't listen."

Ever since they were little? Sisters? Yes, yes. Linda and Lyndsey were sisters. Of course. Incredible. And here he was, getting it all down. Him. Leo Bloody Chindwall. Author extraordinaire!

"It might be best if we had a chat. She could tell her side of the story. Surely that's what she wants."

"No. You mustn't let her in. Please."

"And you and I should meet, Lyndsey. You could tell everything to me, and I'd let you check it through, to get it exactly right. Your story, and Linda's."

"No."

The whispered word faded away, and the phone clicked off. Another click, as the tape ended. Thank God it had lasted all the way through. Thank God.

And then a thought struck him. Caller ID. 1741 . . . 1714 . . . no, no, 1471 . . . Quick, careful . . .

"You were called today at one-forty-three A.M. *The caller withheld their identity."*

Oh well. He still had a verbatim interview with Lyndsey Barratt in his recorder, and the possibility of another interview with Linda, her *sister*! Bloody hell. If only he hadn't drunk so much. If only he had another tape. And he desperately needed that hot chocolate. There was only one way to get himself together, and that was to concentrate on something, like transcribing his conversation with Lyndsey. Had to be done, so why not now, while he was waiting for Linda?

He collected his word processor from his study upstairs and set it up on the kitchen table. More homey down here. More conducive to a relaxed interview.

He was tapping away when the phone rang again. It was Marge.

"Leo, I've just been woken up by—you'll never guess—by that dreadful Linda Marshall person. Can you believe it? First the telephone rings, and I never answer that at night, and then she knocks on my door, bold as brass, asks if she can come in for a chat. A chat!"

"Did you let her in?"

"I most certainly did not. I kept the chain on the door, thank you very much. I had to hold Wilfred to stop him squeezing through and attacking her. He was absolutely furious at being disturbed. Have you any idea what the time is?"

"It's quarter past two."

"The question was rhetorical, Leo. Anyway, she just laughed and said she hoped you would be more hospitable. The cheek of the woman, after all that's happened. Why on earth would she want a chat with us?"

"I think she wants to tell her side of the story to someone sympathetic."

"She's probably on her way this very minute, I shouldn't wonder. I just thought you should know."

"Thanks, Marge. That's very thoughtful."

"Thoughtful? We're talking about the woman who murdered

Peter Shackleton. God knows what she wants with us, but I doubt it has anything to do with telling stories."

"Come on, Marge, the police haven't said Peter was murdered."

"You can make up your own mind about that. I know what I think. Just keep that door of yours firmly shut. I told you to get a security chain like mine."

Leo found himself growing really angry. Marge meant well, but she could be an interfering busybody at times.

"Thanks again for the trouble, but there's no need to worry. It's a wonderful opportunity to get firsthand material for my book."

"Oh, stuff your book. You just keep your door closed. That woman is extremely dangerous. I'm going to call the police."

"Oh, for heaven's sake, Marge. There's no need for that."

"You're . . . you're a bloody old fool, Leo Chindwall, you really are."

The doorbell rang almost as she disconnected. The automatic security light had switched on, and she was caught in the illumination like an actress, center stage. She was wearing one of those modern jumpsuits like workmen's overalls, only they were made of that expensive waterproof material that could breathe, and they had a designer label on the back that added hundreds of pounds to the price. Leo thought they looked common, but he had to admit that Linda looked extremely fetching in it. Her face was meticulously made up, with pale green lipstick and matching eye shadow. Her eyes were green and her hair was green, and she had green bangles hanging from several places in her right ear. The effect was startling, but then, Linda had that quality in abundance.

"Hello, Leo. Can I come in?"

Marge had thrown a monkey wrench into the works. If the police were on their way, maybe he should invite Linda inside and let them turn up. Be a good citizen, and all that.

"Of course, of course."

On the other hand, maybe he should warn Linda, but then he'd lose his chance. What a dilemma! He opened the door wider, and she brushed past him into the living room.

"Sorry to call so late, but I was shopping at the Seven-Eleven round the corner. Bit of a cheek, but I know you and your friends stay at the White Swan until all hours, so I took a chance."

"Not at all, not at all. I'm delighted to see you."

"You are a sport. There's something you can help me with," she said brightly. "Won't take a moment, but I'd love a cup of tea . . . or hot chocolate, if that's what you have in your mug."

"I'll put the kettle on," he said.

"You're an angel." She picked up his agent's letter. "Is this the famous offer for my story?"

"Good Lord, Linda," he said. "Half the police in London are looking for you. What the devil happened?"

Her smile was genuinely warm. "At least it seems you haven't been jumping to conclusions about me, like all the others."

He clicked the kettle on.

"To be quite honest, we've all been jumping to conclusions, but whether they're right or not is another matter."

"That's why I'm here. I'd like to tell someone my side of the story, but I don't really feel like facing up to the police. Not yet. It's all been such a strain. I tried to tell Marge just now, but she didn't understand. Too busy fussing with that dog of hers to bother, snappy little thing."

"Am I to take it that you haven't eaten?" he said, nodding at her shopping bag.

"Oh, I'm fine, thanks. That's just a few things for later."

She smiled again. He couldn't help thinking how incredibly attractive she was. No wonder Peter Shackleton had been so smitten. And here he was, Leo Chindwall, about to get the inside story. His only problem was, would Marge call the police, as she threatened? But why should she? It wasn't as if Linda were on any official wanted list, was it? She was probably back in bed and fast asleep.

"I can make the chocolate while you get ready to take notes," Linda said. "Save a bit of time."

"Good idea. The kettle won't take long."

He sat down at the word processor to create a new document and gave his transcript of Lyndsey's telephone conversation a quick scan before saving it to disk.

"Hello?"

"Mr. Chindwall?"

"Speaking."

"She's on her way. I tried to stop her, but she never listens."

"I'm sorry. Who's that speaking?"

"She just goes on and on. She never takes any notice of me."

"Who takes no notice? No notice about what? Who is this speaking?"

"I know she wants to help me, but what she's doing is wicked, isn't it?"

"Yes, yes, I suppose it is."

"I know she only wants to help."

"Of course she does, my dear. It . . . You . . . you are Lyndsey, aren't you? Lyndsey Barratt?"

"She's looked after me ever since it happened. I couldn't remember, but she told me all about it. She said she'd look after me. She said they'd never be able to hurt me again. Not ever."

"She sounds like . . . like a good friend."

"And then she said that people were starting to interfere, and poor Deborah is involved. She said that you and your friend Marge were going to spoil everything if you wrote your book. She wouldn't be able to finish what she was doing, she said, 'cause you were interfering, and I told her that I want her to stop killing people, but she won't listen. She never listens. Not really. She always does what she wants, in the end. She always has. Ever since we were little."

"What do you want me to do?"

"You mustn't let her in. I tried to call . . ."

As he was reading, Linda reached into the shopping bag and brought out a small bottle filled with a grayish powder, which she emptied into Leo's mug.

"D'you take sweetener or sugar?"

"White sugar's in the cupboard above the cooker. Two spoons for me. Milk's in the fridge."

"I want her to stop killing people, but she won't listen."

Linda poured the water and gave Leo three heaped spoons of sugar. He took a sip.

"Thank you. Very nice. You'll have to go a bit slowly. I'm not the world's fastest typist."

"I want her to stop killing people, but she won't listen."

"I'll be as slow as you want me to, Leo. Just take your time."

"Linda," he said. "My friend Marge called just now. She said you'd been round at her place."

"Yes. I thought you might be round there. Bit of a cheek, calling so late. I think she was quite annoyed. I'll call her tomorrow and apologize."

"I want her to stop killing people."

"The thing is, and I know you'll think this is stupid, but she said she was going to phone the police. I mean, I know they want to interview you, but we have such a good chance for you to tell your story—the way you want to tell it. I was going to ask Deborah for her side of things, but this is so much better. Only, if Marge does call the police, we'll not be able to get on with this. Maybe we should do it some other time. . . ."

When he glanced up at Linda he was astonished to see her expression. No longer the relaxed, attractive smile, but a frozen mask of hate. Or was it fear? For a second, she was unrecognizable; then, with an obvious effort, she turned on the smile.

"Call the police? Well, I'm certainly not ready to talk to *them*. You know what they're like. Everyone's guilty even if they're proved innocent."

She began to back away from him, toward the door.

"It's outrageous, outrageous, to do this to a person after everything I've done to help my sister."

She was fumbling with the door, but Leo was having difficulty seeing her. There was a pain behind his eyes, and his arms and legs were deadweights. The last thing he remembered were her words as she went out into the mews.

"Absolutely outrageous!"

A small, white Rover Metro emblazoned with POLICE insignia rolled down Laburnham Mews, and stopped outside number 17. The driver looked around the mews and called his control.

"Oscar Papa to Charlie Lima. Receiving? Over."

"Charlie Lima. Receiving. Go ahead, Kenny."

"Outside number seventeen Laburnham Mews now. No sign of a disturbance, but the door's open. Am going inside. Over."

"Negative, Oscar Papa. Stay outside. Joe Logan's on his way with a DI Chesterton. They should be with you any minute. Over."

"Roger, Charlie Lima."

The officer got out of his car, and put his hat on. As he did so, an unmarked Vauxhall turned into the mews and pulled up behind his Rover. The sandy-haired man who climbed out first nodded.

"DI Chesterton. How long have you been here?"

"Two minutes, sir."

"Okay. Stay here and keep your eyes peeled.

Chesterton rang Leo's bell. There was no response so he pushed the door further open and went inside with his driver.

Leo was slumped at the word processor, the half-consumed mug of chocolate by his hand. Chesterton quickly took his pulse, then he carefully opened up the shopping bag which Linda had left behind and showed its contents to the driver who thumbed his radio.

"Charlie Delta to Charlie Lima. One IC-two male. Appears to be unconscious. No sign of injury. Possibly an OD. Please send ambulance and backup. Something funny going on. Over."

By ten o'clock on the morning Leo was recovering in the hospital, and the bomb squad experts had cleared Weston's cars, helicopter, and house late the previous evening and were now working on the company headquarters. Frank Illiffe was in his office at Tavistock Place writing yet another report to DCS Villiers, with copies to the other senior officers involved. DI Chesterton was back at his desk at North Central Police Station, continuing his inquiries about sales of Regional Seats of Government. This was taking longer than he anticipated because the agents were not being cooperative. Their contracts with purchasers included confidentiality clauses, and every time he tried to check out an establishment he found himself referred to one lawyer after another.

In Susan York's office at PNC, Hendon, Bill Taylor dumped his motorcycling leathers on top of a metal filing cabinet and stretched. The journey from Brighton on his Harley was a breeze compared with driving a car, but it left him feeling a little stiff. He made yet another mental note to visit a gymnasium for a workout. Susan was staring intently at her computer screen, a pile of used plastic coffee cups in the waste bin.

"Good morning, Susan."

"Oh! Sorry, Bill. Didn't see you come in."

"How about another coffee?"

"Let me get it."

"My treat." He cleared a space at a desk. "You sit down here and take a break. Black or white?"

"Black, no sugar. Machine's by the lift . . . the elevator."

"No need for the translation," Taylor said lightly. "I'm almost a UK citizen."

When he came back with the two coffees, Susan was leaning back in her chair, eyes closed, breathing deeply and evenly. He thought she was asleep, but when he put the cups down she stretched, opened her eyes and looked straight at him. For a moment there was deep eye contact; then the color in her cheeks heightened and she looked away.

"So," he said, "how's it going?"

"I've entered all the new data, including Frank's notes and your report. At the moment we're getting too many obvious factors, like all the deaths involved males between the ages of twenty-five and twenty-six. On the other hand, that's quite encouraging. It means the system is doing its job."

"How long before we get Level Two?"

"Any minute now. It's been running overnight." She pulled off her spectacles and rubbed her eyes.

"Looks like you've been running overnight, too."

"I've been catnapping. I'll be okay."

"I'd better phone Deborah Lambert," he said. "Frank agrees that we need to get her locked into George Weston's security as soon as possible."

When Deborah answered the phone, Taylor asked how her ideas for Linda's old room were coming along. She told him she'd spent most of the previous day browsing in secondhand and antique shops around Camden Passage. Quite tiring, trudging around markets, she said. She had ordered illustrated nursery rugs to cover the parquet flooring and a pastel bedroom suite called Appletime, with matching covers and sheets. But finding books and paintings to match the ones in her rooms was presenting a problem.

"You'll never guess. I took one of the paintings to try and find something similar, and one of the dealers told me it was an original. Worth hundreds of pounds. Can you believe it?"

"It's obvious your ex-flatmate went to a great deal of trouble," Taylor said.

His use of the phrase "ex-flatmate" sounded strange to Deborah. That's what Linda was, of course, ex-flatmate and ex-landlady, and she had to face up to it, but it made her unhappy. It also made her even more determined to get the new room decorated and furnished the way Linda would like it, if she were ever able to return to the flat.

"If a thing's worth doing, it's worth doing well," she quoted seriously.

"I quite agree," he said. "Look, the reason I called so early is to ask for that help I mentioned. It's more of a job, really."

"That sounds interesting."

"It's interesting all right. But you might not want to get involved. I'm hoping you will. The day rate, by the way, is two hundred pounds. The snag is, we really do mean day. Twenty-four hours."

"It doesn't sound as if it has anything to do with computing."

"It doesn't. I have a colleague with me, and we'd like to meet with you and explain."

"Well, I do have some systems work to get on with."

Taylor didn't think looking after George Weston would preclude Deborah from carrying on with her usual work, because she could keep on working at Weston's home or in his office.

"You'll have plenty of time for that. We just need you to keep someone company. If you decide to take it on, we'd need you right away. Why don't you pack enough of your things for a couple of days, plus your laptop, and we'll send a limo to bring you up here to talk about it. If you don't like the setup, we'll drive you home and pay for your time."

"Where's 'up here'?"

"Police National Computer Bureau at Hendon."

"Gosh," she said.

"I take it you'll come." Taylor smiled at Susan. No computer buff could resist such an opportunity.

"I'll be ready in about an hour," Deborah promised.

When he disconnected, Susan York was scanning fanfold paper as it flopped out of the computer printer.

"Do you always manipulate people like that?"

"Manipulate? What's manipulate?"

"And who's going to pay for this limo of yours, not to mention the day rate?"

"Weston's solicitor agreed to cover incidental costs for any improvements in George's security. The way I see it, Deborah's costs are incidental. Is that the Level Two run?"

"It certainly is. I fed in the results of Terry Chesterton's investigations, plus the original statements and reports taken at the time Lyndsey was assaulted and the more recent work. All Frank's information, yours, Keith Rogers. . . . There's a new set of algorithms to examine coincidental factors and assign them a priority rating. It then creates a narrative scenario."

"Hey," he said. "I'm the one who obscures meaning with jargon around here. What's a narrative scenario?"

"It's plain language, not like the earlier output where it just printed out words in boxes and left you to draw your own conclusions. This program draws conclusions for you."

"This should be interesting," Taylor said.

It was. It was also extremely unhelpful.

PNC: FACTORED ANALYSIS OF BARRATT DATABASE

RUN 1—THREAT LEVEL: GEORGE WESTON

Based on the assumption that all but one of the Winstanton School cricket team were murdered by a revenge killer and bearing in mind the modus operandi of the killer the chances of George Weston surviving for more than one month from the date of analysis are approximately four to one against. If the MO changes, the odds of his survival are altered by a positive or negative factor dependent on the new MO which is unknown at this time.

RUN 2—KILLER IDENTITY

Based on the assumption that Linda Marshall is Lyndsey Barratt's twin sister, then the preferred name of the killer is Linda Marshall. If there is no relationship between Lyndsey Barratt and Linda Marshall, then the preferred name of the killer is Lyndsey Barratt. If the killer is not Lyndsey Barratt, then the preferred name of the killer is Deborah Lambert. If the killer is not Deborah Lambert, then the preferred identity of the killer is the witness to the hit-and-run death of Harry Squires or any other witness to any of the other deaths.

RUN 3—KILLER LOCATION

The killer lives at home.

RUN 4—THREAT CONTAINMENT

If the motivation for the killings is revenge, then after George Weston is killed the threat of other killings in this case is reduced to a factor of zero. If the motivation is not revenge, then anyone involved with Lindsey Barratt or Linda Marshall or Deborah Lambert is at risk according to the scale (0–100) as shown in Table 1.

Table 1 listed the names of people involved in every report, including the reports' authors. The names were ranked in the order, highest score first. The first name was George Weston, with a score of 98. Leo Chindwall and Marge Harrison scored 82. Then came Thomas Haddock, with a score of 75. Bill Taylor, Frank Illiffe, Julie Adams, Susan York, and Terry Chesterton were also listed. So was Deborah Lambert.

"It doesn't make sense," Susan said disappointedly. "It's stating the obvious and drawing unacceptable conclusions at the same time. Why does Run Two say that Deborah could be the killer and the table in Run Two say she's at risk?"

"Oh ye of little faith," Taylor intoned. "The system is simply drawing logical conclusions on the information we've given it. If the conclusions seem illogical, it means we haven't given it enough information."

"I still don't see how Deborah comes out as a suspect and as a potential victim."

"I can explain that. If we tell the computer that three people are involved in a murder and the information we give it eliminates the first two, at that point it deduces that the third person must be the killer. Correct logic, wrong decision. Can we add information on a what-if basis and see how that affects the results?"

Susan shook her head. "I've no idea. We haven't had a chance to check that out."

"No time like the present. The first run's fairly straightforward. It just means that no sensible betting man would lay money on George. We're shifting the odds with all the security. Deborah being with George will help, if she takes it on."

"D'you think she will?"

"Sure, if you add your manipulative powers to mine. She'll be itching to see your operation here. In the meantime, I'm puzzled by this relationship stuff. It's stating a logical deduction about Lyndsey and Linda, but I still don't get the reference to Deborah."

"It's another logical deduction, surely. Maybe it's saying that if Lyndsey and Linda are taken out of the equation, we're left with whoever was closest to any of the killings. Deborah was living with Linda when Peter Shackleton was killed. Remove Linda, and Deborah is the killer. Logical, but wrong. Same as including our names on the list."

"Doesn't tell us much, does it? And the second run is pretty obvious. Although it depends what the computer means by 'home.' "

"The computer means what we tell it to mean," Susan said. "All it's done here is aggregate the various meanings of home and produce an average answer."

"Can we ask it what home means for each of the people involved?"

"We can try," Susan said. She sat at her keyboard and tapped in a question: *What is home for Lyndsey?*

There was a few minutes' delay; then the screen displayed: *A place of privacy that cannot be assailed.*

"That's what we figured at the meeting the other day," Taylor said. "Try Linda."

Susan tapped in the same question for Linda, and the same answer was displayed.

"There must be a bug in the program,' she said. "I'll work on it."

Deborah arrived at Hendon in the hired limousine, and Susan gave her the grand tour of the computer suite. She was amazed by the way Deborah picked up details of the hardware configuration and the self-learning software that lay at the heart of the new system. By the time they got back to Susan's office, where Taylor had made coffee, they were chatting away like two old friends.

"Deborah's got an interesting idea on the analysis, Bill. I didn't go into the details, of course. All very confidential, but she was wondering if the self-learning algorithms were capable of extrapolation or interpolation."

Taylor nodded. "The suite we developed at Quantico has both those capabilities. We use them to develop hypotheses about future activity. It's just another way of performing a trend analysis. No one knows how reliable it is, but we've been able to surmise about past murders and link two real crimes to current cases involving serial killers. It doesn't work all the time, of course."

"Is this why you wanted me to come here?" Deborah asked him. "I'd love to work on a project like that."

"No, I'm afraid it's nothing to do with computing. We'd like you to help us to protect George Weston."

Susan and Taylor thought Deborah was going to faint. Her face turned white, and her lips took on a disturbing shade of blue. She seemed to shrink in on herself, but before either of them could do anything she took a deep breath and sat upright.

"He's the captain of that dreadful cricket team, isn't he?"

Taylor nodded. Her reaction was understandable. Most women would freak out at the suggestion, after the publicity the man had received.

"You certainly don't have to. But whatever he might or might not have done, the law says he's entitled to protection. You're the only one who has any real idea what Linda Marshall looks like, or what she might get up to. We thought if you went to his home and looked around his company, generally stayed near to him, you'd provide an extra degree of security."

Deborah was in turmoil. As a citizen, she certainly knew where her duty lay, but how could she do anything that might hurt Linda? On the other hand, Linda told her something like this would happen. *"They'll use you to get to me, and I'll be watching."* What a dreadful situation. If she agreed and then Linda appeared, what would she do? And what would Linda do? Did Linda know how Deborah felt about her? Did she really, really feel the same way about Deborah, the way she told Deborah in her dream? Deborah was totally out of her depth.

And then she realized that the only way to resolve the problem was to test the situation to find the answers, just as she would for one of her clients.

"Yes." She nodded emphatically. "Yes."

"That's great," Susan said. "I'll let Frank Illiffe know, and he'll make arrangements to get you there."

Susan briefed Illiffe and told him that Deborah would cooperate. He decided to take her to Weston's house himself, so he could check the security there. He arrived at Hendon two hours later in the hired limousine. On his way there, he received a phone call on his mobile from Terry Chesterton about Linda's nocturnal visits to Marge and Leo.

"Mrs. Harrison is a bit shaky, but otherwise okay. Chindwall is suffering from the worst hangover in the history of mankind. The lab is still working out what she gave him. Probably some kind of nerve block. She left behind a bag full of surgical instruments. The kind you use for amputations. He's a very lucky man. And before you ask, yes, I've assigned round-the-clock protection."

"And she took off before the first car got there?"

"Yes. No idea why. According to Mrs. Harrison, Leo Chindwall was all set to interview her about the Shackleton killing for a bloody book he's supposed to write. Can you believe it?"

"Like you said, he's a very lucky man."

"He typed something out before she got to him. It looks like he got a phone call from none other than Lyndsey Barratt. There's a fax in the limo, isn't there?"

"Hang on." Illiffe lifted a walnut wood flap and discovered a bar. The next flap revealed the car phone and fax. He gave Chesterton the number, and a few seconds later a page of typescript curled its way into his hand.

"Thanks, Terry."

"You're welcome, guv."

The fax stirred up a number of emotions. After all these years, had Lyndsey really broken cover to phone Leo? Her call was an obvious warning, and Leo clearly took no notice. By the looks of things, Deborah herself might well be in the firing line. *"People are starting to interfere, and poor Deborah is involved. She's such a clever girl, but she hasn't the stomach for all this."* But he was speculating. There was no proof. Even so, when he arrived at Hendon to collect Deborah, he kept quiet about Linda's visit to Leo and Marge in case it might upset her. As for Susan York and Bill Taylor, they didn't have enough reliable information from the computer to report the results, and he didn't understand enough of what they were doing to ask them why not.

Taylor and Susan spent the rest of the day examining computer printouts and feeding in more information. The results were a combination of the obvious, the unacceptable, and the mystifying.

"We've probably taken it as far as it can go, on the information we have at the moment," Taylor said at last. "If Terry Chesterton comes up with anything new, that may help; otherwise we might as well call it a day. I guess I'd better get back to Brighton."

Susan took off her spectacles and stared at the mountain of fanfold paper.

"Would you think it very pushy if I invited you to dinner?" she asked.

Taylor was quiet for a moment. Over the past few months he'd been working so hard that his personal life had been neglected. He had a couple of casual girlfriends in Los Angeles, both of whom held down senior jobs in the media industry, neither of whom was looking for anything permanent. Since he had arrived in England, there had been no one else. He realized with a shock that had been over four months ago, and here was a very attractive young woman inviting him to dinner. She was still staring at the paper, a slight blush on her cheeks.

"I guess we should both be pretty hungry after all this," he said. "Why don't you let me take you out?"

"I do a great carnitas. And if you're working in London tomorrow, you could stay in my spare room."

"That's a very kind offer, but it all depends." He saw the slight blush deepen. "What's carnitas?"

"Marinated pork, Mexican-style."

A few years ago he would have been making the suggestions. Now he found himself making excuses. He was so much older than Susan. He shouldn't get involved with a colleague. Even if he wanted to.

"I don't have any things with me. No toothbrush. You know."

"Yes. I should have thought."

As she turned away, biting her lip, he felt like an absolute shit.

"Listen to me—no toothbrush! There must be a million shops selling the damn things."

"I just thought it would be nice, that's all."

"It will be nice. It'll make a change, it really will."

Chapter 27

THURSDAY THE TWELFTH. GEORGE AND JANET WESTON'S house stood in five acres of grounds overlooking a peaceful, wooded valley between High Wycombe and Oxford. The house and its gardens were surrounded by a security fence topped with three strands of ribbon wire. New cameras were mounted at strategic positions, and Farthingale Security had installed a Portakabin at the main entrance as a temporary guardhouse. A large notice informed visitors that guard dogs were on patrol, and as they approached the entrance a Doberman almost pulled its handler off his feet in an effort to attack the car.

Illiffe nodded to the uniformed policeman and showed the guard his warrant. The man scrutinized it before stepping aside to raise the barrier. Deborah stared ahead, petrified. The dog handler grabbed the beast by the collar, shouting commands at it.

"I hope they've got plenty of third-party insurance with brutes like that about," Illiffe said as he accelerated toward the house. He glanced across at Deborah as she said nothing. "Weston's taking his security pretty seriously, or at least his company is. You'll probably have nothing to do, apart from checking a few faces."

"Yes," she whispered.

Illiffe had taken her to a small restaurant for lunch and told her about Linda's visit to Marge and Leo. He didn't give any details, or mention his fears that she might be a target. She took the news quietly enough, just murmuring, "I wonder why she went *there*?"

*   *   *

Illiffe turned into the Westons' circular graveled drive, and a young auburn-haired woman wearing jodhpurs came out of the front door; an attractive face marred by petulance. Her manner was anything but friendly as they got out of the car.

"Mrs. Weston? Good afternoon. I'm Detective Superintendent Frank Illiffe. This is Deborah Lambert."

"Good God, she looks more like a baby-sitter than a bodyguard."

"Deborah isn't here as a bodyguard, Mrs. Weston. Simply an extra precaution for a few days."

"It's a bloody nuisance, but I suppose we'll have to put up with it. Bring your things and I'll take you to your room. I'm expecting my husband at six-thirty. We eat at seven-thirty."

Illiffe took Deborah's bag out of the trunk, and they followed Janet Weston up the stairs and into a guest room.

"George is at that end of the landing. I'm at the other. I'm a very light sleeper, Miss Lambert. The trouble is, so is George."

"Who else is in the house at the moment, Mrs. Weston?" Illiffe asked.

"I have a cook and a maid, both from the village. There's a gardener. He's in the orchard, least he should be. Lazy old bugger. We have a guest staying in the cottage, but she keeps herself to herself, thank God."

Illiffe blinked. The staff had been cleared by the local police. No one had mentioned a cottage. Or a guest.

"There's no telephone socket here," Deborah said.

Janet Weston was taken aback. "I beg your pardon?"

"Professor Taylor said I'd be able to carry on with my work," Deborah said to Illiffe. "I need a telephone socket."

"Excuse me, Mrs. Weston. What's this about a cottage?"

"More of a cowshed, really. We put a few things in it, of course. It's on the other side of the lake. You can see it if you look out of the window. Well, actually, it's more of a pond than a lake. George lets me rent it out to suitable people. Helps to pay for the fodder."

Illiffe realized that Janet Weston was more than slightly pissed.

"Who's renting it now?"

"Oh, we've known her for years and years. Angela Southgate. Reliable sort of person. Quiet as a mouse. Never even know she's there, not like some of them."

"Exactly how many years?"

She frowned. "Let's see. Two years. Three. Or is it four? No, it's three."

"Mrs. Weston, this could be important. Have you got her home address?"

"Oh yes. She's from London, but then, aren't you all? I've got a letter, somewhere."

Janet Weston went into her bedroom. Illiffe pulled out his mobile phone, but he was out of range of the base station. She came out and handed him an envelope.

"Thank you. Can I use your phone, please?"

"I have my own telephone, in my room. The other telephones are in my husband's study. I never go in there. George's den."

Weston's study contained a computer terminal, two phones, a fax, and other equipment. The walls were covered with photographs of work in progress on building sites dating back many years, some of which had George Weston's father, John, shaking hands with local dignitaries. To the side of a large desk, a glass-fronted cabinet with a security grille contained a selection of handguns. Illiffe saw that it conformed to security regulations as far as locks were concerned, but he couldn't resist giving the handle a squeeze, just in case. In the mood he was in, he'd love to have just one excuse to nick George Bloody Weston. Another cabinet was crammed with sporting trophies, and a banner draped across the top proclaimed: "It is better to have played and won and never to have lost at all."

"That's wonderful." Deborah had followed him down and was gazing at a wall socket. "ISDN-two."

Illiffe decided he was better off not asking what she meant, but assumed she had solved her problem.

"Good," he said as he tapped Terry Chesterton's direct-line number. "So you'll be able to work okay?"

"If Mr. Weston doesn't mind me using his desk. Or I can work over there, on that small table, as long as my cable reaches the socket."

"Right." Illiffe looked around for Janet Weston, but she had left them to it. "You've got your radio?"

"Yes. Susan showed me how to work it."

"If you're worried about anything at all, just press the transmit button. . . . Hello, Terry. Frank. We may have something. Can you check out an Angela Southgate, London post code, W-two, four-NX? I'll hang on."

Deborah was fiddling with the police radio.

"If anything funny happens, just press the green transmit button. It's on the same frequency as the officer at the gate. He'll come straight over, even if you can't talk."

"Do you really think Linda will come here?"

She might be here already, he thought grimly.

"Probably not. But as Bill Taylor told you, we have to take every precaution. She's a very resourceful lady. 'Scuse me. Yes, Terry . . . No one of that name listed. . . . OK. So it could be her. Stand by to get up here, will you? And you'd better inform SO–nineteen, just in case. I'll have a sniff round. . . . Don't worry, I will."

He disconnected.

"Is there a phone in the cottage, Mrs. Weston?" he called.

Janet came out of the kitchen holding a wineglass. "Of course there is. Can I get either of you one of these?"

"Not for me, thanks," he said. Deborah shook her head. "Would you mind putting a call through? If this guest of yours answers, just ask her if the horses disturbed her last night."

"Why would they disturb her?"

"It's an excuse, Mrs. Weston, to check if she's in or not."

"Oh, I see. How exciting." She dialed a number and stood waiting, a determined look on her face. After several minutes she turned to Illiffe. "She's not answering."

"Okay. Would you both mind staying inside while I check things out." He picked up the police radio and thumbed the transmit button. "Sierra Oscar to Bravo Charlie. Receiving? Over."

There was a hiss. "Bravo Charlie. Receiving. Over."

"I'm going down to the cottage. Get the dog handler to join me at the orchard, and stand by. Over."

"Roger, Sierra Oscar. Standing by."

"Have you a spare key, Mrs. Weston? No need to break down any doors if we don't have to."

"Gosh," Janet Weston said. "This is really exciting."

When Illiffe and the Farthingale Security man emerged from the bushes that separated the cottage from the rest of the grounds, they saw a woman lying on a sun lounger in the middle of a small lawn, reading a novel. Illiffe could see that she was attractive, in her late twenties, blond hair, slightly built.

"Good God," she said angrily, as the Doberman started growling. "Keep that bloody animal away from me. I've told you before."

"Miss Southgate?" Illiffe asked.

"It's Ms."

"Sorry for the intrusion. I'm Detective Superintendent Frank Illiffe, and this is—"

"I know who you are," she said to Illiffe. "The copper with the tart of gold."

"I beg your pardon?"

"I was referring to your well-publicized relationship with the do-gooding Julie Adams. Got any ID?"

Illiffe showed her his warrant. Kept his face impassive.

"Perhaps you'd be so kind as to return the favor."

"I'm busy, as you can see."

"Really? You should be aware that there's an offense called 'obstructing the police in their inquiries.' Let's get your ID, shall we?"

She pulled a towel around her shoulders and got up. "Driving license do you?"

"It's a start."

She led them into the cottage and began emptying her bag.

"There you are. Driving license, insurance certificate, blood donor card, Access, Visa, Diners Club . . . that good enough?"

"Not really. Have you a passport?"

"Oh sure. I always carry it when I come to Oxfordshire."

"Birth certificate?"

She glared at him, then smiled. "I get it. You think I'm Linda Marshall, don't you? I should be so lucky."

"Mind if I take a look around?"

"Be my guest."

Illiffe glanced at the dog handler. "Leave Fido outside, and come with us, will you, Pete?"

There was nothing in the cottage except the furniture, Ms. Southgate's clothes, and her personal effects. No cigarettes, no drink, no food. The refrigerator didn't even have a bottle of milk inside. Illiffe held the door open and looked at her questioningly. She stared back.

"I eat out."

"Really?"

Illiffe took out the radio.

"Sierra Oscar to Bravo Charlie. Receiving? Over."

"Bravo Charlie. Receiving. Over."

"Will you collect Miss Lambert from the house and bring her to the cottage, ASAP? Over."

"Wilco, Sierra Oscar."

Deborah's heart beat faster as the young policeman led her through the orchard and down the hill. He hadn't said why Detective Superintendent Illiffe wanted her, but it was obvious. There was someone at the cottage, and it might be Linda. The thought threw her into a panic. She was being paid so she could identify Linda, but she had never believed for one moment that the situation would arise. Linda was too clever for that. Far too clever. But even clever people made mistakes. It might be Linda, and, if it was, what was she to do? How could she identify the one person she loved, despite everything she knew Linda had done?

When she saw the three figures standing in the sunlight on the little lawn, she almost passed out, and the policeman had to turn and give her a hand, thinking she had stumbled. The sun's glare obscured details at this distance, but she could see that the woman was slender and blond, just as she remembered Linda. The last few steps to the lawn were a nightmare.

"Hello, Deborah," the woman said, smiling slightly.

"It's not Linda," Deborah said tightly. "It's not."

Illiffe stared at them both, utterly perplexed, keyed up. Ms. Southgate, or whoever she was, was looking at Deborah as if she'd known her for years, and Deborah looked as if she were about to collapse.

"You know her name," he snapped.

"You said it over the radio."

"Not her first name."

Ms. Southgate smiled at Deborah again. "Deborah Lambert, the flatmate. We girls have been following the case very closely. We wondered if we'd ever be lucky enough to meet you."

"She's not Linda," Deborah repeated desperately.

She wasn't, but she was looking at Deborah with the same kind of expression that Linda had. Half amused, half tender. Loving. Deborah knew then that she would never, ever, be able to tell anyone about Linda. She was too much in love.

"I don't believe you," Illiffe said slowly to Deborah, and she began to cry.

"Jesus Christ, Illiffe, leave the kid alone. My real name's Sharon Rowbotham, and I own a gay club in Kensington. Tinsel Town. I come down here to unwind. My manager'll verify that. Dawn La Boite. Check it out."

"Sharon Rowbotham?"

"Rough, isn't it? You don't get anywhere in show business with a name like that."

Illiffe instructed the young PC and the dog handler to accompany Ms. Southgate, née Rowbotham, to the security cabin to verify her story. The computer had linked Deborah's name with Lyndsey and Linda as a possible suspect, and Illiffe had begun to think, for just a moment, that she might indeed be involved, that Ms. Southgate was indeed Linda Marshall. He was half relieved, but half disappointed, too, when her story checked out. A lesson not to trust computers. After all, it had also listed almost everyone connected with the case as a possible victim. Including Leo and Marge, of course. A coincidence, or was Susan's system doing its job?

"I'd better be off, then," he said to Deborah when everything had been sorted. "You think you'll be all right here?"

"Oh yes," she said. "Mrs. Weston seems very nice."

Very nice? As he drove his way back to the M40 highway, he decided he had never met anyone more naive than Deborah Lambert.

Janet Weston left Deborah to her own devices, so she wandered around the gardens admiring the summer blooms and the ripening fruit trees. Beyond the orchard there was a jumble of waterfalls, fed by a spring, that cascaded down a series of rock pools. Everything was so peaceful that the voice behind her made her jump in fright, fumbling in her bag for the police radio.

"A strange thing this, and no mistake."

She turned to find the gardener standing by a pear tree, painting the trunk with something sticky, an old man wearing a sweaty hat and a worn waistcoat.

"You'll be one of them, I suppose," he continued.

"One of who?"

"Bloody security people. You and your dogs. Never seen such a mess. Dunno what you feed 'em with. Bloody lumps of sawdust, looks like. Turds like tree trunks."

"I'm not really one of them."

He turned to look at her. "You're either one of them, or you ain't."

"Well, I am, and I'm not."

He was puzzling unhappily over this when the dog handler came around the corner of the orchard. The Doberman growled at Deborah, and she stepped back.

"He's okay, miss," the handler said. "Always a bit nervous with a stranger. You just let me know when you want to walk around, and I'll keep him in the cabin."

"Oh no. Please don't bother. I'll go back inside."

Deborah hurried awkwardly to the house.

"She ain't one of you lot, then," the gardener said.

"No way. She's something to do with the lunatic that's been knocking off George Weston's pals. Staying with the Westons for a couple of days, till the fuss has died down."

"A right weird thing. You keep that bloody animal from shitting in my flower beds, that's all."

George Weston's helicopter whirred overhead at precisely half past six, sending clouds of dust spiraling across the well-kept lawns as the pilot set it down on the helipad by the guardhouse. Deborah watched from the reception room window as he strode down the drive, briefcase gripped firmly in one huge hand. He presented a handsome figure. Well set, poised, sun glinting from golden, curly hair. But handsome as he was, his face seemed cast in stone, devoid of expression, only his eyes showing a glint of impatience. A powerful and capable young man, used to getting his own way, pushing the door open. . . .

"Heard the latest," he shouted. "She's only gone and drugged one of her bloody neighbors, for Christ's sake. Turned up at his house with a bag of surgical saws, all ready to kill the bugger. The press say he's lucky to be alive, and that bunch of arseholes think she's got me slated for tomorrow, Friday the bloody thirteenth. . . . Where the devil are you?"

He stomped into the reception room and stopped dead when he saw Deborah. For a moment his confidence drained away.

"Jesus! Who the devil are you?"

"I'm . . ." Deborah managed to say.

"Ah yes. The bloody baby-sitter. Where's my wife?"

"I'm not sure. She might have gone to the cottage, to talk to Ms. Southgate, but she could have gone to see her horses. . . ."

Deborah faltered to a silence.

"Let me get this straight. That jumped-up copper brought you round here to protect me. Right? And I ask you where my wife is, and you're not sure. She might have gone to the cottage, but she might have gone to the stables. How am I doing so far?"

"Well . . ."

Weston pushed his face close to hers. "Just don't say another fucking word, okay? Do whatever it is those stupid bastards have told you to do, but keep out of my way."

"I . . ." She shifted her weight from one foot to the other in an agony of embarrassment.

"Yes?"

Deborah would never have believed that such a little word could be so full of contempt and menace.

"I've set up my laptop in your office. I hope . . ."

Weston glared at her and stomped out of the room. Deborah stared at the door, then walked after him.

"Mr. Weston?"

"What is it now?"

"You said something about someone's neighbor."

"Not someone's neighbor. Linda fucking Marshall's neighbor." He opened his briefcase and shook the contents onto the floor. "It's all there. Help yourself."

Deborah stared down at the headlines. KILLER STALKS NEXT VICTIM. WRITER ESCAPES DEATH. POLICE HUNT LINDA. Detective Superintendent Illiffe hadn't said anything about drugs or surgical saws. Why had Linda gone there? Did she really want to harm Leo? It was all so upsetting and confusing. Tears welled up, and she sobbed helplessly. Poor Linda. What had she done? What would become of her?

The Westons set a place for Deborah at the dinner table, and when she didn't appear at seven-thirty Janet Weston asked the maid to go to her room and tell her dinner was being served. The maid knocked on Deborah's door several times and received no answer, so Janet went upstairs. She banged hard on the door and opened it. Deborah was sitting red-eyed on her bed, rocking backward and forward, the newspapers crushed in her arms.

"Good God, girl, whatever are you doing?"

There was a long sigh. "They think she wants to harm my friends."

"What friends?"

"Leo and Marge. Why would she want to do that?"

Janet eased the papers from her and riffled through them.

"You know these people?"

"They're my neighbors."

"I'd better get you a glass of water," Janet said.

"I'll be all right."

"Nonsense. You look all in." She paused. "How did you get these?"

"Mr. Weston gave them to me. He said Linda wanted to kill Leo. But she couldn't do that, could she?" Tears began to roll down Deborah's cheeks again. "She was so kind to me. I don't see how . . . I don't understand."

Janet nodded slowly. "Wait here."

She went back to the dining room. George had started his pâté, reading a magazine as he pushed the portions into his mouth. She pulled the magazine out of his hand.

"You arsehole. You just dumped those papers on that kid up there. You didn't stop to think how she'd take it."

"What the hell are you talking about?"

"Those people in Heathside are her friends. Didn't you think what her reaction might be when she found out?"

"Jesus Christ, I'm sick and tired of this," he shouted.

"And I'm sick and tired of you!" she shouted back.

"How the hell am I supposed to know who she knows or who she doesn't know?"

"By putting two and two together, stupid. The papers have been full of this stuff for weeks, not to mention the bloody television. Now, I am going to bring her down here, and you will be civil to her. You will not shout or bluster, and I will make sure she has something to eat."

"Oh really?"

"Yes, oh really! And if you misbehave yourself, I'll personally inform Charles Ruslin of some of your more arcane business practices. You know what Charles is like. He'll have you off the board."

"What arcane business practices?" he blustered.

"I'll start with the misappropriation of council archives and go on to the application of water-based lubricants on piling hammers. Then there's the matter of overcharging for the unnecessary use of Weston's mobile soil laboratory. You've played the same trick at three motorway junctions in the last six months."

Weston's brain went into overdrive as he stared at her. Then a nerve in his neck began to throb.

"You cow. You've been shagging Eamonn Grady."

Janet smiled. "He's a wonderful lover, and he's a collector for the IRA, so I'd be careful how you deal with your newfound insight into your lousy marriage. Now, are you going to behave yourself, or what?"

Janet brought Deborah down, and George Weston did behave himself. It was, not surprisingly, a quiet meal, but the food and wine were excellent. By his fifth glass of Chablis, Weston was almost affable.

"What is it that you do, exactly, Miss Lambert, I mean apart from keeping a lookout for serial killers?"

"I work with computers."

"With computers? How interesting. Isn't that interesting, darling?"

"I suppose it is," his wife said. "Not that I know very much about it."

"Well, no, neither do I. I just use them like everyone else. It must be quite difficult."

Deborah looked at her plate. "I find it quite easy, actually. I mean, it's not difficult if you know how to do it."

"Really!"

"Another glass of wine, Miss Lambert?" Janet asked.

"Oh, no, thank you. I've got some work I must do before going to bed, that is, if that's all right, Mr. Weston."

He waved his hand expansively. "Not a problem. You work away, my dear. And if you see the naughty Miss Marshall, just give a holler."

*   *   *

Feeling emotionally bruised and battered, Deborah left the table and went into George Weston's study to turn on her laptop. The familiar clicks and whirr as the hard disk spun into action and the Windows icon appeared were comforting. She might feel out of place with people, but here she was totally at home, clicking on the terminal emulator and selecting high-speed communication links to her client's database. She reveled in the speed with which she could send and receive information. It made her work a joy, a haven into which she could escape the troubles and coarseness of everyday life. Of course, if she had been able to spend the day at her machine as she had planned, this work could have waited until tomorrow; so, tired as she was, she fought off sleep as she constructed machine code and developed the program for her client's interactive video game. She worked as long and as hard as she could, and somewhere down the line she must have dozed off, because the noise of George Weston opening his private bar and pouring himself a brandy wakened her. He had turned the lights off, and the study was only dimly lit by the striplight above the rows of bottles. The shadowy effect made him look huge, a bit frightening, and she kept very quiet, waiting for him to go back out. But he didn't go back out. He turned toward her and smiled, holding the brandy glass high and taking a copious mouthful.

"Little Miss Lambert," he said in a soft, drunken voice. "The quiet little mouse. Did I wake you up, little mouse?"

She tried to speak, but her throat was dry.

"Sorry, very sorry. Just thought I'd pop in. Usually do, this time of night. Give the old guns the once-over. Keep 'em nice and oily. You wanna see them?"

"No, thank you. I don't like guns."

He grinned at her and fumbled with the key of the gun case.

"That's what they all say. All the girls. Don't like guns, don't like motorcycles. What a load of crap. Get you on the back of a Ducati and you'd be having multicolored orgasms all the way to Roma." He unclipped an automatic pistol and started dancing toward her. *"Arreev er durchy Roma . . .* Look at this beauty. Nine-millimeter Browning High Power. Most reliable handgun on the market. You can take your Walthers and your Berettas, and stick 'em up your arse."

She turned her head away as he came closer and pushed the barrel of the pistol against her cheek.

"Y'know, you don't look half bad without the light. You could be quite fanciable if you tried. Let's see." He swayed across the floor and knelt down by her chair. Touched her face. "Bit of lipstick. Eye shadow. Proper bra." The barrel dropped to her body. "Mmm. Nice bit of tit down here, wouldn't you say? Nice, hard little nipples. Mmm."

She didn't move. Couldn't move. Couldn't resist. Couldn't reach out to her bag and press the police radio button. Arms couldn't move. Legs couldn't move as his hand went down there and pressed into her crotch.

"Groin," he muttered. "Groin. Feel my groin, too. Put your fingers down there. Go on, go on . . ."

"Please," she said. "Please don't do this to me."

He was pulling her skirt up now, unzipping his trousers, pulling out his penis and pushing it into her legs, only the chair wasn't the right place so he pulled her off it, onto the floor, feverishly pulling at her panties, panting as he began pushing it into her, and then she screamed, like an animal caught in a wire trap.

"For Christ's sake," he whispered, "shut it, will you!"

But the screaming went on and on, and the lights flooded down, and Janet Weston rushed through the door in her nightgown and began hitting him with her fists, on the back, neck, head, arms, anywhere she could, yelling abuse at him, adding to the infernal noise.

Weston shook his wife off his back and scrambled to his feet, pulling his pants back on.

"I didn't do anything to the bitch," he shouted. "Leave off, will you! I came in for a drink, and she started in on me. I want her out of here. Get the bitch out of my house."

Deborah stopped screaming and lay still.

"If you've done anything to her, you bastard!" Janet bent over Deborah. "It's all right. I won't let him touch you. It's all right."

There was no response. Deborah lay, eyes closed, skin cold to the touch.

"Jesus, George, you've really hurt the poor thing."

"I told you, I never touched her. She's putting it on."

"Help me get her back on the chair, damn you."

They struggled with the dead weight, propping her into a sitting position at the desk.

"Get her a glass of water," Janet said.

"Do it your bloody self," Weston said. "Someone's got to get some sleep around here."

He locked the pistol back in the cabinet, then stumbled out of the study. Janet went to the bar and poured a glass of water. When she turned around she was amazed to see Deborah was tapping on her keyboard and squinting at the laptop screen as if nothing had happened.

"Hello," she said. "I didn't see you come in."

Chapter 28

FRIDAY THE THIRTEENTH. AT HALF PAST SIX JANET WESTON called her husband down for breakfast and looked into Deborah's room. The bed hadn't been slept in, so she went downstairs and into the study. Deborah was fast asleep in her chair, the laptop showing a message passing slowly across the screen: TOUCH ANY KEY TO RETURN TO DISPLAY.

As Janet stared at it, Deborah yawned, stretched, and sat upright. As far as Janet could see, she didn't seem any the worse for the previous night's incident with George. Not that "incident" was the right word. If Janet hadn't come in when she did, little Miss Mouse would have been well and truly rogered. Probably have done her the world of good.

"Good morning," she said. "Sleep well?"

"Yes, thank you. Apart from some funny dreams. Shouldn't really work this way, but I had a deadline for one of my clients. What time is it?"

"Six-thirty-five."

"Gosh. I'd better get ready. What time does Mr. Weston leave for the office?"

"Seven-forty-five. It's a fifteen-minute flight."

"Would it be all right if I had a shower?"

"Of course. It's all en suite. Breakfast is ready when you are. Usual stuff. Cereal. Toast. Bacon. Scrambled eggs. Tea. Coffee. OJ."

"Orange juice and toast would be fine."

Deborah vanished upstairs and a few minutes later George Weston came down carrying the large briefcase he used for overnight stays and talking quietly into his mobile phone.

"Breakfast's ready," Janet told him.

He ignored her. "Yes," he said into the phone. "I'm leaving now."

"It's all ready. Wouldn't take a minute. You should have something to eat."

He went into his study and unlocked the gun cabinet, packed the Browning into the briefcase.

"Another visit to Offa's Quarry, is it? Letting off steam, are we? That's bloody nice, that is. You promised you'd take me out this evening. We never go out these days."

"That silly cow upstairs, is she?"

"She's taking a shower."

"Good. There's no way I'm having her hanging about. Jesus Christ, I've got the combined might of Her Majesty's Constabulary and Farthingale Security on my back. No homicidal bitch is going to get anywhere near me, and if she does I'll tear her fucking head off. Be back on Sunday." As he got to the door he turned round and stared at her, balefully. "You keep your mouth shut about where I'm going. These bloody coppers are doing my head in, all right?"

Deborah heard the helicopter take off and came down to find out what was happening. She found Janet slumped unhappily at the breakfast table, staring at an untouched portion of scrambled eggs and mushrooms.

"He's a bastard. A real true-blue bastard. I get up and make breakfast, and does he give a shit? God, I hate him. He treats me like dirt. You must have noticed. That's the way he is with everybody. The boy bloody wonder. You're better off here, anyway. The sod would probably be groping you all the way to the office. I don't know why I put up with it."

She began to cry, and Deborah stood awkwardly, wondering what to do.

"Has Mr. Weston gone, then?"

"Didn't you hear the bloody helicopter? It's blown half the bloody drive all over the lawn. Bloody show-off. It ruins the blades."

"I'm sorry?" Deborah said.

"Blades. Lawn mower. Gravel. Jesus Christ, don't you Londoners know anything?"

"Well . . ."

"As if I haven't got enough to do without having to find that stupid gardener and stand over him while he rakes it all back. I've got horses to look after, you know. Two donkeys. A bloody flock of puddle ducks. They came with this bloody house."

"I'm supposed to be with Mr. Weston today. The police think it's quite important. I probably should phone them."

Janet looked at her, balefully. "I personally don't think your presence will make the slightest bit of difference. That man's a shit, and if this woman can kick his arse for him, good luck to her is what I say."

Deborah phoned Susan York, who answered with a sleepy voice.

"It's Deborah Lambert, Susan. I'm at Mr. Weston's house, and he's gone to his office without me. I don't know what I should do."

"He's left you behind? Why?"

"I don't know."

"What time is it?"

"Five to seven."

"Hang on a minute."

Deborah heard Susan fumbling with the phone, calling to someone. A pause.

"Hello, Deborah. It's Bill Taylor. What's wrong?"

"I'm supposed to be with Mr. Weston, but he left me behind at his house. I'm not sure what's the best thing to do."

"We'll have to check with Frank Illiffe," Taylor said, "but my guess is he'll want one of us to pick you up and take you over to Weston Construction."

The pilot landed the helicopter precisely in the center of Weston Construction's helipad. Another Farthingale dog handler stood outside the circling rotors and waited until Weston alighted. A uniformed policeman came out of the gatehouse with a cup of tea in his hand, looked toward him, then went back inside.

"Everything's quiet as a grave, sir," the dog handler said. "Some cowboy parked a trailer by the main gate, but we've checked it out. He said another tractor's picking it up this afternoon."

Weston nodded and walked into the building. As far as he was concerned, the whole business was a bloody farce. There was no way some madwoman was going to get to him. No way. The other stupid bastards had played right into her hands. They'd never known what was coming. But he knew, and so did half the country's bloody constabulary. The police were obviously trying to sort out their previous incompetence, and Farthingale's costs were not coming out of his pocket, so what the hell? He stepped with irritation past a cleaner who was buffing the tiled floor, took the express lift to his top-floor office, and went to the bar to pour himself a stiff whiskey. There was a half-empty jar of green olives and a single packet of roasted peanuts. He grabbed a handful of olives and wolfed them down, emptied the pack of peanuts into his mouth, and stood glaring balefully out of the window as his jaws crunched the nuts. Then he picked up the phone and called Thomas Haddock.

Illiffe arrived in his office at seven-forty-five to find a message from Susan York, explaining that Deborah Lambert had been left behind at George Weston's house and was wondering what to do. He called Susan back immediately.

"What happened?"

"I gather the redoubtable Mr. Weston didn't like the idea of having a nursemaid. He took off while she was taking a shower."

"Bloody hell. Can you pick her up and get her over to Weston Construction?" Illiffe asked.

"Well . . . yes."

She was hesitating.

"Is there a problem?"

"Not a problem. Bill stayed round here last night." Susan felt herself flushing. Wondered if Illiffe could sense her embarrassment. Wondered why she even felt that way. After all, nothing had happened between herself and Taylor. Bill had been utterly proper. A gentleman. He'd wanted to, and so had she. They both knew it, but maybe working together put a block on that kind of relationship. Not that it was any of Illiffe's business. "He'd like to collect Deborah."

Illiffe was astonished. It never occurred to him that Susan, that Bill Taylor . . .

"Are you there, Frank?"

"Sure. I'd better have a word with him."

He heard Susan pass over the phone. Some muttering. The chink of a knife being put on a plate. Taylor's voice, munching breakfast.

"Hi, Frank. I guess you want to get Deborah over to Weston's at the double. Susan said I could borrow her car."

"I'll get one of the local coppers to run her over. It'll be less trouble."

"Thing is," Taylor said, "we pulled some interesting stuff from the computer yesterday. I'm convinced that Deborah can help us get a better focus, only we're not asking her the right questions. If I run her over it'll give me a chance to prod around. Anyway, you know how spooky she is. Last thing she needs is to have a stranger turning up. Susan wants to stay at Hendon to tap Terry Chesterton's latest report into the system. Then we'll be in a good position to brief you on possible locations to search for Linda and maybe Lyndsey too."

"How definite can you be on that?"

"We're running the data through some new Canadian software that's having good results. If we get it right now, it'll save a lot of time and manpower later on."

"Okay. But get a move on. If Weston's computer virus is anything to go by, she's threatening to try something today."

"None of the other victims had any security," Taylor reminded him. "He should be fine."

"Absolutely. She'd have to drop a bloody bomb to get through the cordon we've set up. I just want to dot and cross *i*'s and *t*'s."

Taylor did not like cars very much, and Susan's vehicle did nothing to improve his feelings. It was a very basic, garishly yellow VW Golf diesel, manual gearshift, no sunroof and a radio that did everything except tune in to a station. By the time he reached Weston's security hut, he was thoroughly bored. The private guard came out and looked at him questioningly as he struggled to wind down the window. He was used to electrical operation.

"My name's Taylor," he said when he finally managed to lower it a few inches. "I've come to pick up—"

"Absolutely, Professor Taylor. Detective Superintendent Illiffe let us know you were on your way. Miss Lambert's waiting for you at the house."

Deborah was standing in the entrance porch, laptop over her shoulder and luggage at her feet. Taylor thought that was strange—she was supposed to be staying at least for a few nights—but he made no comment. She seemed very quiet and preoccupied as Taylor loaded her cases in the trunk, clutching her laptop as if it were some kind of precious cargo, carefully putting it on the backseat and securing it with the seatbelt. As he was preparing to drive away, the old gardener appeared from behind a hedge and flagged him down.

"You watch my gravel, or Mrs. Weston'll have my guts for garters. You tell him, miss."

"He's worried about his lawn mower," Deborah said absently. "If you drive too fast the gravel gets on the lawn and damages the blades."

"No problem, sir," Taylor told the gardener. "This car is incapable of traveling at such a speed."

"You just watch it, that's all."

"I certainly will."

He inched forward and rolled carefully around the circular lawn toward the drive and back to the main road. As he did so, an attractive auburn-haired woman leading a horse from the nearby paddock stopped to let them go past. She gazed into the car, staring at Deborah, who didn't appear to see her. Neither woman acknowledged the other.

"Mrs. Weston, I presume," Taylor said, as the security guard saluted him.

"Yes."

A whispered response. Why was Deborah so uptight? That business with Weston's wife was strange. Taylor had a feeling that it was central to the problem they had with George Weston. Why would he rush off without Deborah? Did she know? Would she tell Taylor? Maybe some music would help her to relax. He leaned over and fiddled with the radio.

"I can't get anything out of this damn thing."

"It's probably preprogrammed to London stations. You have to let it scan."

She reached out and pressed a button, and after a few minutes the local radio station tuned in. Ads for car dealerships and supermarket bargains. The eight-thirty news bulletin. Latest on the Macedonian crisis. Prime minister rejects peace plan. Education secretary under attack . . . Music . . .

"Did Frank tell you about Leo's late-night visitor?"

She nodded.

"How do you feel about that, Deborah?"

The silence was so long that he thought she hadn't heard him. When he glanced at her, he saw tears streaking her cheeks. Then she said, "She's not a bad person. She told me she's protecting her sister."

"You didn't tell the police, did you?"

She shook her head. "She told me after they took my statement."

"I see. So she's been in touch?"

Another silence. She was twisting her mouth nervously.

"It's okay," he said. "You don't have to tell me."

"I don't know what to do. She . . . Linda came back one night and told me, only I think it was a dream, but it seemed so real. I don't know how she could have got in. She said she had a key for the new locks, but I put the chain on the door. It's one of those with a lock on it too, so I suppose someone with a key could reach round and unlock it."

Taylor was familiar with the effects of stress, and Deborah was showing all the classic symptoms. Maybe near to breakdown.

"You're fond of her, aren't you?"

A sigh. "Yes."

"From what I could see, she took special trouble to make you feel at home. Do you think she's fond of you too?"

"She said we were bound together. She said you knew that and you'd use me to find her. That's what you're doing, isn't it?"

"We have to stop her, Deborah. You know that."

When they arrived at Weston Construction the security guards peered into the VW, gave Taylor a respectful salute and waved him through. The duty officer reported the visitors to his station, noting the car's registration number. The receptionist rang Weston's extension, listened without expression to a voice that could be heard buzzing angrily from her handset. She put down the phone eventually and entered their details into her console and handed them visitors' badges.

"If you take the express lift to the tenth floor, Mr. Weston's personal assistant, Sandy, will meet you."

"Sounds like your employer is not too pleased we're here," Taylor observed.

The lift doors slid open at the top floor, and they found Weston's assistant standing in front of them.

"Good morning, Professor," she said. "Mr. Weston is in conference just now. He asked if you would be kind enough to wait for a few minutes."

"Sure."

"Would either of you like a coffee, or tea?"

"Deborah?"

"Yes, please. Tea would be nice."

"Make that two teas."

The PA smiled. "I'll arrange it in the boardroom. It's more comfortable."

They waited for Weston for over an hour. Deborah was lost in another world, and Taylor had time to go over the complexities of the situation. They had taken every precaution to stop an incident, and while the security was at a high level Weston would be safe. Linda Marshall was resourceful, but she was not a magician. If she made an attempt to kill Weston, she would have to emerge from cover. Then she would be vulnerable. If she stayed undercover, they might track her down. He was sure that Deborah held the clue to Linda's location, but how could he ease his way into the shell? It struck him that he hadn't done the obvious thing. He'd been too busy circling around her. Why not try a direct approach?

"Do you know where Linda is?" he asked suddenly.

She looked startled, but looked at him openly.

"No. She just went away."

"Any idea where?"

Deborah remembered what Linda told her about Lyndsey's visits to the flat in Heathside.

"She's probably with Lyndsey now. All I know is that she said she was keeping Lyndsey somewhere safe."

That was consistent with what the team was calling the RSG theory. Taylor wondered if DI Chesterton was getting anywhere with that approach.

Before he could ask any more questions, Weston came into the boardroom and stared at them coldly.

"I see no need for Miss Lambert to be here. This lunatic's hardly likely to try anything, and I've got a busy schedule."

"It's like Frank Illiffe said, Mr. Weston. Dotting the *i*'s and crossing the *t*'s. Anyway, you're paying for her to be here, so what's the problem?"

Weston looked exasperated. "For Christ's sake, there's nothing for her to do!"

"All I need is a place I can put my laptop, Mr. Weston. I don't want to get in the way."

Weston had a strange expression on his face. A bit on edge. That was understandable, but there was something else. Under the aggression, Taylor thought he looked puzzled.

"You'll have to stay the hell out of my way."

"The idea is, she should be where any visitors will come," Taylor reminded him.

"I'm video-conferencing today. Any clients who arrive will see their project managers. No one else will get past reception."

"Somewhere up here," Taylor persisted.

"Oh, for Christ's sake! All right then. I'll get a desk set up. But just how long is this farce going on?"

A good question, with no good answer. Taylor's private view was that Linda Marshall was hyping them with this Friday the thirteenth stuff. She'd lost the advantage of surprise, but she could lie low for as long as it took. She was wealthy. Enterprising. Provided she didn't try to go abroad or get credit in the name they knew her by, she was untraceable. All they could hope was that the computer would point them in a good direction. If it didn't, he didn't think George Weston stood much of a chance. Sooner or later a determined assassin will always get the target, particularly if the assassin is not particularly concerned about his or her own life. The one thing George had in his favor was that Linda seemed like the ultimate survivor. Taylor did not think she would take suicidal chances. She was too concerned with looking after Lyndsey.

"Let's do this thing one day at a time and revise things as we go, shall we?"

Taylor checked in with Frank Illiffe and unloaded Deborah's luggage from the VW before he left for Hendon to see how Susan was faring. The house services manager arranged for a desk to be placed to one side of the reception lobby on the top floor, and Deborah sat with her laptop, quickly absorbed in formulating machine code and downloading it to clients. Weston's PA took her under her wing and made sure she took a lunch break, and when she came back to her desk, Sandy went for lunch, leaving her alone outside Weston's office. She had been working away for half an hour when the intercom on Sandy's desk buzzed. Deborah looked up, but ignored it. It buzzed again, so she went across and answered it.

"Sandy?"

"Sandy's at lunch, Mr. Weston. It's Deborah."

"It's you I wanted."

"Oh."

"I need to sort something out. Right now."

She heard him disconnect and looked at his door in consternation. The man terrified her. A few moments went by, and he opened the door.

"Come in, for God's sake. I won't bite you."

She went in, and he closed the door and stared at her.

"About last night. I'm under a lot of strain."

She didn't know what to say, but he didn't seem to want her to say anything.

"My problem is, I like women too much. I sometimes get a little carried away. There you were, in my study, and I found myself attracted to you. I mean, you're not a bad looker, but maybe I went a bit far with the Browning. You know, all those bloody films about phallic symbols and how you girls love all that stuff. You can't blame me for that."

Deborah listened in astonishment. The man was describing her bad dream to her, which meant that it hadn't been a dream at all. It flashed back. The drunken voice, the pistol stroking her cheek and moving down . . . him, pulling her off the chair, and the lights going on, and his wife jumping on his back. And the thought came to her that if this dream had been a reality, then so had her dream with Linda. She couldn't understand how, but the shock was enormous. And here was George Weston, trying to explain himself to her.

". . . and that business with Lyndsey Barratt," he was saying. "You have to understand what it was like. We were all hyped up. Just won a big game. We felt great, really great. And she got on the train. A real looker. Sat where we could all see her, those long legs of hers crossing and uncrossing. Bloody hell, she knew we were watching. She seemed like a good sport, so we tried it on a bit. Okay, so she said no at first, but we were only kids. Most of the girls said no at first. You keep on, and they come across. That's all it was. It got out of hand because of the smokes. She was well into that, and we were all out of our skulls. I mean, really out of our skulls. When we piled off that bloody train we had no idea she was in that state. Jesus Christ, we were all in a state. Left our gear in the carriage, our clothes. Jacket, ties . . . I mean, if you go and rape someone, you're hardly likely to go leaving your stuff behind with your bloody name on it, are you? We all had a romp, and it went a bit over the top. That's all it was. You can understand that, can't you?"

No, she couldn't, but she could understand that her own reactions were playing her false. She had always taken great pride in focusing her mind on the job in hand, and here was Weston proving to her that a dream had actually happened. It was extremely disturbing. But then, it proved that those treasured moments with Linda had been real too. The thought gave her a delicious shudder. It somehow made her feel stronger.

"I'm not sure," she said. "It's never right to make someone do something they don't want to."

"That's my point, exactly. Men like me are made to go with women. It's in our nature, but you never know what a woman is really thinking, so you end up doing things she may not like. No one wants to, but what choice have you got? It's not exactly what you'd call fair, is it?"

"It's not fair to force yourself on someone, either."

There was a loud knock on the door, and Sandy came in.

"Sorry to disturb you, Mr. Weston, but I didn't see Deborah, and under the circumstances I thought I'd better check to see if every-thing's all right."

"Everything's fine, Sandy, thank you. We're just having a chat."

When Sandy went back out, Deborah said, "Maybe if you ex-plained all this to someone, maybe to Linda Marshall . . ."

"Christ! D'you think anyone would take any bloody notice? They had us down as rapists from the start, and that's that."

Deborah thought he looked really sorry for himself. She wondered what Linda would think, if she could hear all this.

"What are you going to do?" she asked.

He gave a bitter laugh. "Like the professor said, play it one day at a time. If this friend of yours turns up, she'll have to get past the combined might of the UK security industry. That's where you come in, I suppose."

Once again, Deborah felt very unsure of herself. She knew now that Linda had really come to her room, really spoken her loving words. And made love. How could she possibly do anything to harm her? On the other hand, perhaps she could persuade Linda not to do any more harm, to leave George Weston alone.

"Look," he said. "How long is it since you took a break from work? A real break. Get away from everything for a couple of days?"

She couldn't remember how long. Work had been too important.

"It must have been last summer. I've had a lot of work to get through."

"I've got a great idea. I wasn't going to tell anyone. I was just going to sneak off for a couple of days to a place I know. It's run by a friend of mine. Very isolated, so it's perfectly safe. And if you're there, it would be even safer. Why don't you come with me?"

"Oh no, I couldn't possibly."

"Why not? You'd have a great time. It's a bit primitive, but that adds to the fun. Smoky and I do a bit of shooting, and it's out in the country. What do you say?"

"I don't approve of blood sports," she said quietly but firmly.

"Neither do I. No, no, we use shooting ranges. You know, target practice. And don't forget I'm paying you quite handsomely by the day."

He seemed so animated, so boyish in his enthusiasm. Not a sign of the aggression or the bullying.

"But would they let you? I mean, with all these problems?"

"You leave that to me. I just have to make one phone call, and I can have us out of here in less time than you can boot up that laptop of yours."

Deborah felt herself being swept along by his energy. That nice policeman would be furious, and so would the others. Professor Taylor, and Susan. But George Weston was paying her, after all. And it seemed he would go off whether she came or not. What a quandary!

"I really don't think we'd better."

"You'll have a great time. Good food, open air. Really, a great time."

"When would we get back?"

"Tomorrow evening. We'll bang off some rounds when we get there, have a bloody good dinner, bang some more off tomorrow, then head home. Let me worry about Detective Superintendent Illiffe. What d'you say?"

"Well, as long as we get back tomorrow, I suppose it would be all right."

"That's great. Why don't you go down to reception? I'll get someone to take your luggage to the parking lot, and I'll meet you down there in about ten minutes."

As soon as she had closed the door he grabbed the phone and told his PA to arrange for Deborah's luggage to be taken down to the parking lot and placed by the company Bentley. Then he used his mobile to dial the unlisted number for Offa's Quarry and waited impatiently for Thomas Haddock to answer.

"Smoky? George Weston. It's on . . . Yes. Me too. By the way, I'll need the lodge. . . . Absolutely. Same arrangement as always, but I'm feeling sharp. You won't get a look in with this one. The little bitch is all mine."

The porter placed Deborah's luggage at the side of a Bentley Turbo. It was a beautiful opalescent green, exuding power and luxury, and although Deborah seldom bothered with such things, such a vehicle seemed in keeping with the events of the day. Passion and revelation, she thought. And George Weston was clearly intent on making amends for his previous behavior.

In a few minutes she heard the executive lift stop at the parking lot level, and Weston came out wearing a camouflage vest and jeans. He grabbed her luggage and strode to the back of the lot.

"Not the Bentley," he said as she tried to keep up with his steps. "Too easy to identify. How about this little number?"

He pulled a polystyrene cover from a bulky shape parked in the shadows, to reveal a black Porsche 928. Another Turbo.

"It's registered in a friend's name," he said as he jammed her luggage next to his in the small trunk. "He's in Africa. It's totally untraceable, so no matter how smart your Linda Marshall is, she ain't about to track us down anywhere, and neither will that smart-aleck copper. What d'you think?"

"It's very nice."

"Nice? It's a miracle of modern automotive technology, that's what it is. Antispeed camera, antiradar, antisonics. We'll be there in less than two hours."

He started the engine and eased the Porsche toward the service lift at the back of the car park. Half a minute later a company porter leapt from a packing case and stubbed his cigarette out as the lift doors rumbled apart. As the Porsche eased forward, Weston opened the smoked-glass driver's window and held out a fifty-pound note.

"I didn't see you, if you didn't see me, Alan. Okay?"

"I didn't see who?" the porter said with a grin.

It wasn't the first time the black Porsche had slid out early on Friday afternoon, with a young lady in the passenger seat. He unlocked a chain-mesh gate in the back fence, and watched as his boss negotiated the ruts in the lane that led half a mile to the main road. Weston might be one son of a bitch, but he knew what's what when it came to favors.

Shortly after Weston's departure, a timer clicked shut a relay in the trailer parked on the shoulder of the road opposite the entrance to Weston Construction, and it began to emit a high-pitched buzz. The Alsatian at the gatehouse began whining in response, and the security guard let it lead him along the drive in time to see the sides and the roof of the trailer drop down to reveal an array of massive loudspeakers and lines of tubes linked with white cord. Before he could get close the speakers began to emit a fearsomely loud rendition of a nursery rhyme, sung in a high-pitched, childlike voice.

GEORGY PORGY, PUDDING AND PIE,

KISSED THE GIRLS AND MADE THEM CRY.

WHEN THE BOYS CAME OUT TO PLAY,

GEORGY PORGY RAN AWAY.

After a brief pause, the rhyme was repeated. It was so loud that the dog began screeching and pawing its ears. A passing car slowed down, and the driver wound down his window to see what was going on. So did another. In a few minutes there were several vehicles stopped at the roadside, and the windows of the Weston Construction building were filled with faces, peering out. The policeman at the gatehouse radioed his station, and was patched through to Frank Illiffe, who could hear the cacophony clearly.

"Stop everyone going in or out of the building and get your traffic squad down there immediately," Illiffe told him.

" 'Scuse me, sir," the policeman said as the security guard came running back down the drive.

"Shit!" the guard shouted. "The fucking thing's wired. It could go anytime."

Commander Lionel Tankred of the Oxfordshire Constabulary was one of the unlucky motorists caught in the traffic chaos. He instructed his driver to negotiate a way through to the cause of the problem to find the head of Farthingale Security, Peter Farthingale, talking animatedly to the uniformed inspector in charge of operations. Five minutes later Tankred was talking angrily to Commander Perkins of New Scotland Yard on his car radio. When that conversation finished, Perkins phoned British Transport Police HQ and asked for Detective Chief Superintendent Mark Villiers.

"Frank, there's a suspected bomb outside Weston Construction. Who screwed up?" Villiers was holding back his anger with some difficulty.

Illiffe remembered that Linda Marshall had told Walt and Sylvia Daniels her next video would be different. A bomb was different. Was she videoing the bloody thing? In which case she might still be on the scene. Then again, a bomb was imprecise. According to the police officer at Weston's gatehouse, it was situated on a shoulder of the main road. Hardly a realistic threat to George, he thought, but who could take chances at this stage?

"We screwed up."

"We?" The sarcasm was vitriolic.

"Farthingale Security was helping to protect him. I screwed up and they screwed up."

"Don't play clever buggers with me, Frank."

"Where's Weston?"

"No idea. Find out what went wrong and report to me. You've got an hour."

"It'll take that long to get there in traffic. . . ."

"Do it from here. I want your report in one hour, because the chief constable is going to be all over my scrotum on this."

"With respect, sir, the woman who we believe is responsible for all these killings is probably in the vicinity of the suspect vehicle. She films things. I really should get up there. . . ."

"I don't give a shit about any film. I do give a shit about the chief constable. Get me that report."

Illiffe gathered as many relevant documents as he could into a bundle and wrote an executive summary that included the threat assessment and the steps taken to protect George Weston. Before sending it to Villiers he phoned Susan York for her update on the offender-profiling project. She had heard about the trailer on the radio news.

"There's something else, Frank. Terry Chesterton checked with the Registrar of Birth and Deaths. Lyndsey had a twin sister called Linda all right, but he got nowhere with the local schools, so he checked back with Hope Green Hospital. The medical social worker says she died at home, two months after her birth. Crib death."

In two seconds flat, the vengeful-sister theory had vaporized. So who was Linda Marshall, and why had she targeted the cricket team?

He realized the answer even as the question formed in his mind, and he wondered how he had overlooked it. How they had all over-looked it.

Linda Marshall *was* Lyndsey Barratt.

That's what the computer had been telling them. All those so-called correlations. It was so bloody obvious that everyone had missed it. Even that cocksure expert, Bill Taylor. If her past performances were anything to go on, he had to get to High Wycombe immediately. She'd be there with her video camera, and so would Deborah Lambert. They could get a positive ID.

He took the report to Villiers personally.

"All the evidence we have says that the woman we're looking for is at High Wycombe right now, sir. One of the witnesses who can identify her is there as well. And that's where I should be."

Villiers arranged for a Met helicopter to take Illiffe to Weston Construction. They received clearance to use Horseguards Parade in Whitehall and were airborne in less than fifteen minutes. As they tracked the M40, the pilot relayed the ground situation to Illiffe. By the time they approached the target area, he was aware that the army had taken charge of the operation, and he had talked directly with the unreceptive Commander Tankred, explaining his involvement in a separate investigation. Tankred sounded bloody angry about something. Probably resenting anyone from outside interfering on his turf.

The helicopter began its descent, and Illiffe could see that the area around the front of the building looked like a war zone. The main road was cordoned off, and traffic diversions were operating. The trailer beside the road was being examined by a robot bomb detector, while another remote-controlled machine was piling sandbags around it. The nursery rhyme was still pounding out of the loudspeakers, and the helicopter began to vibrate.

As the aircraft descended slowly to the company helipad, Illiffe could see field broadcast units from the BBC and independent TV companies lined up behind the barriers on the main road, the reporters arguing with the civilian and military police who were keeping them at bay. Some of the TV crews were filming the scene with Telephoto lenses from the tops of their vans, and they all swung around as the chopper dropped the last few dozen feet and touched down. He noted the Action TV emblem and caught a glimpse of Julie Adams staring toward him. He was too far away for her to recognize him through the helicopter window, but he knew that

Army would have zoomed in. He turned away and disembarked from the opposite door, showing his police identification to the soldier who held a carbine at the port position.

"You're expected, Superintendent. The command truck is by the hospital tent. Ask for Major Selby."

The major, clad in a well-pressed battle uniform and sporting a thin bristle of a mustache, was standing next to army technicians operating the two robots and looking closely at the images they were transmitting to the control unit.

"There's no antenna. My guess is the bloody thing's on a timer or a trembler, sir," one of them was saying.

"And you are?" Major Selby asked Illiffe as he entered the cabin.

"Detective Superintendent Frank Illiffe, Major."

"Ah yes. We had a note you might show up. What can I do for you?" Illiffe could sense the man's impatience.

"I'm in charge of an investigation into a series of killings. We believe George Weston is the next target. The woman who is tracking him is almost certainly among the crowd out there, and so is a civilian I need to identify her."

"I've been fully briefed about your investigation, Detective Superintendent. In fact, I caught the recent publicity on television. Frankly, I'm surprised to see you here."

"Might I ask why?" The man's animosity was palpable, and Frank didn't take kindly to it.

"You surely can't believe there's any connection with this incident and the sordid activities of a deranged woman, Superintendent. This is the work of professionals. It took planning, teamwork, money, and expertise to get that trailer on site."

"That's your theory, is it? Got any evidence? Anyone claiming responsibility?"

"I would remind you that the army is in charge of this incident, and you are here on sufferance. The last thing I need is a bunch of civilians stumbling around. Kindly join your colleagues at the perimeter fence until we have contained the incident."

The army technicians were staring into the TV screens, not bothering to hide the grins on their faces.

*   *   *

As he strode through the chaos toward the main road and the crowds gathered there, Illiffe began to react to the day's events, to the whole bloody shebang, by becoming increasingly angry. Unresolved rape cases, police politics, mysterious killings, pornographic videos, disappearing suspects, his family life under strain, failure to keep this threat away from Weston . . . and now this bumptious little fart of an army major giving him his marching orders! He looked over the field that separated the Weston site from the main road, toward Julie Adams and the other TV crews, toward the jumble of Weston employees trying to respond to a security man's attempts at a roll call. He didn't actually make a decision. His feet just started taking him over there. He pushed his way through the crowd and came across the company lawyer, Charles Ruslin, talking to a tall, sunburned man in an expensive suit, and a police officer wearing a Commander's insignia. He was about to turn away, but Ruslin spotted him.

"Mr. Illiffe," he called. "I'd like you to meet Peter Farthingale. I believe Commander Tankred is known to you."

Frank went over, nodding to the commander. "Sir."

"A bad situation, Detective Superintendent," Farthingale observed somberly.

"You could say that. Please excuse me. I have to find someone."

He pushed past the three men, aware that Tankred was watching him angrily, but Charles Ruslin followed, pulling at his sleeve nervously.

"I must talk with you."

"What is it?"

"Mr. George is missing."

Illiffe froze. "What the hell do you mean?"

"He's missing. Gone. He and Miss Lambert. A car has been taken from the garage, a black Porsche, but it's not part of the company fleet, and we have no record of the registration number. The only way he could have left without the security guard seeing him is by using the goods lift at the back of the building, but the duty porter says he didn't see anything. There's a lane, you see . . ."

At that moment Illiffe decided he'd had enough. This case had bedeviled him for years. It had caused sleepless nights. It had brought harm to his family. It had taken a baby away. And he was being dragged over the coals by superior officers who were more concerned about their pension rights than catching villains. On top of that, the arrogant bastard whom he was trying to protect had taken himself off with the only witness whose evidence would be worth a damn.

Julie Adams was talking to camera as Illiffe arrived at her OB van. She didn't even pause as he walked into frame and turned toward Arny. A real professional.

"We are joined by Detective Superintendent Frank Illiffe of the British Transport Police who is in charge of an investigation into the deaths of ten ex-members of the Winstanton School cricket team. Is that why you're here, Frank?"

"That's exactly why I'm here. George Weston was next on the list, and George Weston is missing."

"Missing? So you wouldn't put this down as a terrorist incident, as some authorities are suggesting."

"No. You don't get terrorists broadcasting nursery rhymes. The woman who arranged for that trailer is ruthless and wealthy. It's an effective combination."

"I gather that you have a suspect in mind."

"Lyndsey Barratt."

For a split second, Julie Adams was fazed. She expected a yes or a no, not a name.

"Lyndsey Barratt? The girl who was involved in a serious incident at Hope Green seven years ago?"

"A very serious incident. She was assaulted and raped on a train. According to the medical records, eleven males were involved. Eleven males were traveling in Lyndsey's compartment at the time it happened, and ten of those eleven males are now dead. It doesn't take a genius to work it out. We have been looking for a Miss Linda Marshall in connection with several of these deaths, in the belief that she was Lyndsey Barratt's twin sister. We now have evidence that Lyndsey's elder twin sister, who was indeed named Linda, died shortly after she was born. I now believe that Lyndsey Barratt herself murdered the cricket team members and that Mr. George Weston and other people are in danger."

"Are you referring to Leo Chindwall and his neighbor Marge Harrison?"

"Yes. She's already tried to get at them."

Other TV and radio reporters were trying to push their way toward the Action TV van, but Weston employees and onlookers were crowding around, and the reporters couldn't get through. Their problem wasn't helped by the local police who thought that a public disturbance was about to erupt and were pulling them back.

Julie felt Illiffe's anger as he steadily talked himself out of a career, her own feelings a mixture of excitement and sadness. After all these years, someone was telling it like it should have been told long ago. It was sad that it took a good copper like Frank Illiffe to break ranks. But she had to go for broke on this one.

"If you're right, isn't what you're saying an indictment of how you and your colleagues have handled the case?"

"It's an indictment of the police system and it's also an indictment of a legal system that is so intent on being fair to villains that the innocent suffer. And you and your colleagues in the media aren't exactly blame-free, are you? It was quite obvious to everyone who worked on the Lyndsey Barratt case—or who reported on it—that the Winstanton cricket team had raped and beaten her. To be exact, she was found badly bruised externally and internally, with several fractures, and covered in semen. There was semen in her vagina, her anus, her mouth, and over her ears and breasts. She was not so much unconscious as in a coma. She was incapable of giving permission for an intrusive examination and was unable to make a statement. Without her statement, no charges of rape could be brought, and the Crown Prosecution Service in collaboration with the local chief constable, whose son, incidentally, was a member of the cricket team, decided that any lesser charges involving the use of drugs, or obscene behavior, or sodomy, would be thrown out of court through a lack of conclusive evidence."

"What exactly does that mean?"

"It would have been impossible to prove which boy did what."

"And so they got off scot-free?"

Illiffe looked over to the Weston building. "I wouldn't say that."

"Thank you, Detective Superintendent Frank Illiffe. This is Julie Adams, for Action TV, outside Weston Construction, returning you to the studio."

"That should go some way to repaying your boss for the hundred grand he shelled out to Lyndsey."

"You didn't have to do that, Frank. We would have got the story anyway."

"Oh yes, I bloody well did."

At that moment a timer in the trailer pulsed to zero and a detonator ignited the white fuse cord. Seconds later the onlookers were treated to a dazzling burst of pyrotechnics, with starburst rockets and glaring flares that lit up the late afternoon sky and left huge white clouds drifting slowly away in the light breeze.

Nice one, Linda or Lyndsey or whatever your name is, Illiffe thought as the TV cameras swung up to record the display. Very nice, but now what?

Illiffe was about to step into the helicopter when the pilot stopped his preflight checks and gesticulated, pointing over Illiffe's shoulder. He turned to see Charles Ruslin waving at him from the edge of the helipad.

"Glad I caught you," the Weston lawyer called. "Can you spare a moment?"

Illiffe looked at the pilot, who looked at his watch and nodded. "Ten minutes'll be okay."

Ruslin took him by the arm in a friendly way and began walking into the field, getting away from passers-by.

"You rather put your foot in it with your interview with Ms. Adams. Commander Tankred is livid."

That would be an understatement. Tankred had almost certainly phoned Perkins, who would now be chewing Villiers out, who would be waiting to chew out Illiffe and start the kind of disciplinary procedures that Illiffe had started for several dozen of his erring colleagues over the years. Resignation was the best he could hope for, and he'd be bloody lucky to get that. Illiffe waited to see what Ruslin had to say.

"We'll be looking for a new chief executive, of course. Between you and me, the board already has someone in mind. Good chap. International experience, which George lacks. Or should I say lacked?"

"Bit quick off the mark, aren't you? No body has been discovered, and I doubt whether one extremely powerful person could kidnap him, let alone a slightly built female. If he left with Deborah Lambert, he'll be out of range of any immediate threat to his life."

"Perhaps so, but from the company point of view Mr. Weston is rather—how shall we put it?—headstrong. He gets results, but he's not too scrupulous how he gets them, if you take my meaning."

"Not really."

Ruslin sighed. "Well, it doesn't matter now. As far as the board is concerned, this incident is the last straw. But that's by-the-by. The point is, what will you be doing in a month's time?"

"Probably some much-needed DIY in a neglected home and taking care of my even more neglected wife."

"Yes, you'll need a break. The thing is, Peter Farthingale needs an operations director to head his European business. He apologizes for being unable to put this to you himself, but he had to leave. It's a new appointment. Your remuneration package would be in the region of sixty thousand pounds, plus the usual corporate benefits. Here's his card. He wondered if you could think it over during the weekend and call him on Monday."

Illiffe stared at the card. He didn't need the weekend to think it over, but there was still a job to do.

"Where's the nearest hotel? I'm bringing my team into this. There'll be four of us." He'd need Terry Chesterton to fend off trouble in London.

"There's one at the motorway junction. I'll make arrangements to book you in. Weston will foot the bill."

"Thanks." Illiffe turned to the pilot and shouted, "I'm staying over. Make my apologies."

The pilot nodded and gave the thumbs-up. Illiffe and Ruslin moved away from the helipad and watched the aircraft lift slowly and accelerate back to London.

"What's that porter's name?" Illiffe asked Ruslin.

"Alan Flaxted. You'll find him in the loading bay."

The Army conducted a belated controlled explosion at the trailer, and succeeded in destroying a simple timing mechanism and some expensive PA equipment. The local CID men were furious, because the explosion also ruined possible clues, but as far as Illiffe was concerned, no clues were needed. Lyndsey—Linda—would have arranged it all through third-party suppliers. He made his way back to the Action TV crew, who were packing up to get back to base.

"I presume you want to stick with this thing," he said to Julie.

She nodded. "What do you have in mind?"

"Weston's gone AWOL with Deborah Lambert. I'm getting my team up here, and we're booking into the hotel at Junction 4. There's no law that says you can't book in too. Just you and Arny. I'll keep you briefed. You can record, but absolutely no broadcasting until I say so. Is that a deal?"

"Is Lyndsey here, Frank?"

He looked around the dispersing crowds. "Not now, but my guess is she was filming all this. She's a dab hand at home videos."

"I'll get Arny to check our stuff to see if he can spot anyone with a camera. And thanks, Frank."

Illiffe made his way behind the building and found the porter sitting on a pile of pallets, reading the *Sun,* smoking.

"Sorry, mate. Main entrance is round the front," he told Illiffe, who pushed his warrant card under the man's nose.

"You Alan Flaxted?"

The porter nodded, eyes alert for trouble.

"Okay, Alan, let me guess. Your boss likes a bit on the side. Every now and again he sneaks out, and you turn a blind eye. He probably whacks you a small consideration. How am I doing so far?"

The man sighed. A good thing down the drain. "Not bad."

"Good. Any idea where he goes?"

"Haven't a clue."

"Let me put it another way," Illiffe said reasonably. "You're scared your boss will find out you've told me what's going on. Right now, you should be more scared of me."

"Well, he goes shooting somewhere, I know that. He's a nutter about guns. Loves them. And it must be a fair distance, because he always leaves it to the weekend."

Illiffe remembered Weston's gun cupboard.

"Is that it?"

Another hesitation. The man was weighing consequences.

"For Christ's sake, Alan. This isn't telling tales out of school. Weston's life is in danger."

"There was a waitress he . . . fancied. Annette. Big girl, and I mean big. He took her out in the Porsche one Friday. She didn't turn up to work again. Got a job in Wycombe, and before you ask, I've no idea."

There'd be a reference in the personnel department, Illiffe thought.

"Okay, Alan. If you think of anything else, let Mr. Ruslin know, will you? He knows where to find me."

"Sure thing. Er, this won't go any further, will it?"

Illiffe checked into the hotel and arranged a hire car. Keith Rogers called him from the police car and said he'd picked up Susan York and Professor Taylor. DI Chesterton was staying late at the Yard and would sleep with his phone on the pillow. Illiffe told him he was going into High Wycombe to check a lead. He also mentioned that the Action TV crew were in the hotel, with his blessing.

Annette Francis had a job in a Main Street restaurant, working behind the bar. She was very attractive and self-assured. When Illiffe introduced himself she called a colleague to take over and led him to an unoccupied table.

"You must be the bloke from the telly. Fancy a drink . . . tea, coffee?"

"No thanks. I'm in a bit of a hurry. I need to know where George Weston took you in that Porsche of his."

"I thought that's why you'd come. Who told you?"

"Never mind, but it's very important. He's in considerable danger."

"Good," she said. "I hope that Lyndsey or Linda or whatever her name is cuts the bastard's heart out."

"You may not believe this, Annette, but I'm getting the impression you don't much care for Mr. Weston."

"Care for him? I've only just got rid of the bruises. Have you any idea what it's like trying to hide bruises from a randy husband, Mr. Illiffe?"

He couldn't help smiling. "Okay, so you hate his guts. Unfortunately he took a young lady with him. If he's in danger, so is she."

Annette lit a cigarette. "I'd like to help you, really I would. We went over toward Wales, but I've no idea where. I spent most of the time with my head below window level. He's a very demanding man."

"How long did the drive take?"

"In that car? About half as long as it should have. We were driving for about an hour and a half, maybe more. The last bit was along country lanes. Oh yes, I remember we went through that place with the book festival. Hay something. It was somewhere near there. Maybe another twenty minutes."

"Hay-on-Wye? That's a help. Can you remember anything about the place itself?"

"Only that I never want to go there again. Him and that creepy little mate of his! The guy who lives there, I mean. Soon as we arrived, Georgy Boy pushes me into the kitchen and expects me to rustle up a three-course meal for three, which I did, of course, while they went off and did the macho bit with their guns. We had champagne, too. I was beginning to have quite a good time before the sod decided to use me as a nocturnal punching bag. Likes to rough up his women, does George."

"His friend's name wouldn't be Thomas Haddock, by any chance?" Illiffe asked.

" 'Smoky' is all I know. The creep. He knew exactly what George was up to. I could see it in his face. Tried to get me to shoot one of those bloody things, but I wasn't having any of that, thank you very much."

The others arrived at the hotel before Illiffe returned and were having a drink in the bar. Keith Rogers was chatting with Arny, while Bill Taylor and Susan tried to explain to Julie Adams how offender profiling worked.

"No one's claiming it's foolproof," Taylor said. "In fact, its most valuable aspect is that it can give us ideas we might never have thought of."

"But they could be blind alleys, right?"

"Certainly, but the police go down dozens of blind alleys in any investigation. That doesn't mean they should stop using fingerprinting, DNA comparisons, or whatever. What Susan and I have been trying to do is use the same systematic approach that's paid off for the FBI since the 1970s. That's meant going through reports on all these killings and letting the computer look for similarities. With luck, we can use its results to compare the case with ones we know more about, and so get another lead."

"And have you?" Julie asked.

Susan looked thoughtful. "I think so. We had a run that indicated Leo Chindwall and Marge Harrison were at risk, but the run included our names as well. My guess is the system's telling us that anyone who stands in the way of Linda's plan to eliminate the entire cricket team could become a target."

"Right," Taylor agreed. "It also made very close links between Lyndsey and Linda before we found out that Linda Barratt had died soon after birth. Frank believes that Lyndsey and our Linda Marshall are one and the same."

"Do you think he's right?"

"Why not? Lyndsey simply assumed another identity and went on a vengeance kick."

"Where does Deborah Lambert fit in?"

"That's a puzzle," Taylor admitted. "We know she had some kind of connection with whoever killed Shackleton and Squires. Let's assume it's Lyndsey for the moment. My best guess is that Lyndsey uses people, as and when necessary. Deborah fit the bill for a number of reasons. She was able to get work with the targets and open them up to Lyndsey, for one thing. I doubt if she had any idea what was going on. The computer also listed her as being a possible victim. That makes sense, because she knows a hell of a lot about the killer, and this must put her at risk."

When Illiffe arrived at the bar he took in the seating arrangements and smiled.

"I see you've all got to know each other."

"I'm getting a briefing on offender profiling," Julie told him.

"I think Ms. Adams is finding it less than convincing," Taylor said.

"Not at all," she said. "It's fascinating."

Keith Rogers looked over. "Get you a drink, guv?"

"My shout. What're you all having?" The waiter came across. "Everything again for my friends and a pint of bitter for me, please."

"The thing is," Taylor said with the determination of the evangelist, "it opens the doors of the mind. Let me give you an example. Years ago the guys at Quantico—that's the FBI center for this stuff—well, they found that some sex killers deliberately get involved in the investigation. Two young girls were killed in Michigan and someone gave the name of a possible suspect to one of the local investigators.

It was probably the suspect himself, a local man called Meirhofer. Anyway, Meirhofer offered to take a lie detector test and also wanted to be interrogated after having an injection of sodium pentathol. He passed both tests, so the local cops accepted his story and let him go. Unfortunately for him, the Quantico team figured he might be one of these killers who can't keep away from the investigation. They set some traps, and he fell into them. Bingo."

"There's no sign that Lyndsey has done that, is there?" Illiffe asked.

"We haven't looked," Taylor said mildly. "What do you think?"

"Arny," Julie called. "Did you spot anyone using a video camera on our takes today?"

"Sorry. Nothing. Meant to tell you."

"That's okay."

"I don't see it," Illiffe said. "Not unless she somehow got in place ages ago, and we've not picked it up. We'd better check Weston's personnel department again."

Then he recalled his doubts about the Westons' cottage guest, Angela Southgate. Terry Chesterton had called at the Tinsel Town club, and the manager had confirmed that Angela's real name was Sharon Rowbotham and that, as Sharon, she was listed in the electoral register. On the other hand, Deborah had behaved very strangely during their meeting with Angela. As if she had been shocked for some reason. Why should she be shocked at the sight of Angela Southgate aka Sharon Rowbotham aka who else?

With a growing sense of foreboding, Illiffe called the security guard at George Weston's house. The duty policeman answered.

"No, sir. It's all quiet here. Mrs. Weston hasn't gone out, but the cottage has its own gate to the road."

"Check the cottage, will you? See if Angela Southgate is there or not and get back to me fast. I'll hang on."

The policeman ran from the security cabin to the cottage and hammered on the door for several minutes before puffing his way back to the phone.

"No one there, sir, but Mrs. Weston's car is still in her garage."

"Shit. Keep your eyes open. I'm coming round now." He slammed the phone down. "Keith! Get the car." He saw Julie staring at him. "Hang on here. If we find out where they are, I'll call in, and you can follow with Bill and Susan."

*   *   *

Keith Rogers made it to the house in twenty minutes from the hotel, blue lights flashing from the roof. The duty policeman waved them through, and they broadsided around the drive, scattering gravel everywhere, Illiffe half expecting the old gardener to leap out and chastize him. As Rogers skidded to a halt, he leapt out and banged on the Westons' door, then opened it and rushed inside.

"Look downstairs," he called to Rogers.

Seconds later he flung open the door of the first room on the upstairs landing to find Janet Weston in bed with Angela Southgate.

"Talk about egg on face. My God." Illiffe collapsed into the seat next to Julie and emptied the now-flat pint of bitter. "I was threatened with charges of forcible entry, intrusion of privacy, harassment, you name it . . . but at least I know where the bugger is. The redoubtable Mrs. Weston says he goes shooting at a place in the border country called Offa's Quarry, and guess who's in charge?"

"Thomas Haddock," Julie said promptly.

"Right. It's an unlisted number, and there's no reply. Either they've not arrived yet or they're not near the phone. The quarry's on the map. Pretty rugged country by the looks of things."

"What's the next move?" Julie asked.

"The only thing certain about the next move is that we won't find the place in the dark, and if we can't, she can't. I'll check it out in the morning. All I know for sure is, I'm bushed."

"Bedtime, then," Arny suggested. There was a sudden silence, and he looked curiously at Julie and Illiffe, but Illiffe was too busy looking curiously at Taylor and Susan to notice.

Illiffe was unable to sleep. As he dozed fretfully, images of Lyndsey Barratt's rape swirled in his mind. He realized how deeply the case had affected his life, how dealing with Jenkins had changed his career, how his time with the BTP, working to detect and punish the transgressions of fellow officers, was a barren and thankless task. How it had affected his relationship with Jean. He knew with absolute certainty that the Barratt case was nearing its conclusion. Not that anything truly concludes, of course. It was reaching the end of a phase in its development.

When his bedside phone rang, he knew, also with absolute certainty, that it was Julie Adams.

"Hi."

"So you can't sleep, either."

"'Fraid not."

There was a pause.

"I want to tell you something," she said. "You are the best man I have ever known, and I love you."

She disconnected.

He still couldn't sleep.

Susan continued working with the computer. Professor Taylor said they might not be asking it the right questions, but how would you know which questions were right and which were wrong? Maybe the answer to that riddle was to try to think like a computer. She remembered something called concatenation. If you linked together two or three questions that gave peculiar answers, you sometimes got a different result than when you asked the questions one at a time.

She began tapping instructions on her keyboard, entering program menus, setting up the run. Then she tapped out: "Who is Lyndsey AND who is Linda AND who is Deborah?"

The screen blinked and nothing happened. Susan rubbed her eyes. Maybe the bloody thing had crashed. It was four o'clock in the morning, so she decided to sleep in the office.

Part V

OFFA'S QUARRY

Chapter 29

OFFA'S QUARRY WAS IN AN AREA THAT HAD BEEN MINED in prehistoric times for precious metals, tin, copper, lead, and iron ore, and the cliffs around the quarry were riddled with fissures that might well have been excavated by Iron Age miners to ventilate their shafts running deep into the earth. Approached by a narrow track from the northeast, with the setting sun casting deep shadows, it was a grim place, and Deborah shivered as Weston maneuvered the Porsche skillfully toward the quarry entrance. He had driven like a maniac, and Deborah was not only grateful but also surprised to arrive in one piece. The main building to the left of the entrance had smoke curling out of a granite chimney. The visitors lodge was to the right, among some trees.

"This is the only way in and out," Weston said as they bumped along on the hard suspension. "Safe as houses. No one to disturb anything. Smoky Haddock keeps a bloody good selection of wine, plus venison, Welsh lamb, beef, local pork . . ."

"I'm a vegetarian."

"Are you really?" He wasn't interested. "Oh well, there's plenty of potatoes and carrots and other things. Ah! There he is."

Haddock was standing at the door of the larger of two buildings. He too was dressed in a camouflage jacket, with ammunition pouches slung over his shoulder.

"Good evening. Welcome to Offa's Quarry, miss. Good journey,

Mr. Weston?" Haddock never lapsed into familiarity with his clients when a third party was present.

"As ever, Smoky. Everything fixed up?"

"It certainly is. I've provisioned the lodge, so let's get you settled."

"I'd like to get an hour in, before the light goes," Weston told him.

"Not a problem. I've installed floodlights on Number One Range. You can shoot all night if you want, but I turn in at ten, sharp. By the way, good news about the pop-up range."

Weston opened the trunk, and Haddock helped him carry the luggage to the lodge. Deborah tagged along behind, ignored and out of her depth.

"Got the bank loan?"

"Better than that. Some of the lads are coming in with me on a partnership basis. Solicitors are working on the details, but I won't have to lay out a penny. They'll have exclusive use of the place two days a week, and I retain the majority of shares. I'll show you the plans tomorrow. You'll be impressed."

The lodge was plain, but well equipped with attractive wooden furniture. An ancient coal-burning Aga stood at one end of the open-plan downstairs area that served as kitchen, dining room, and recreation room. The bathroom and lavatory were also downstairs. Wooden steps led up to the first floor. As Weston dumped the cases on the floor, Haddock opened the air vent in the Aga.

"Ever cooked on one of these?" he asked Deborah.

She shook her head.

"You'll soon get used to it. It heats the water, too."

"We'll unpack later," Weston said to her. "Why don't you start getting the meal ready?"

"Everything you need's in the cupboards and fridge. We'll be over at the first range, if you need anything," Haddock said.

"Where is it?" she asked.

"Don't worry, miss. You'll be able to find us, no problem. Just follow the noise."

When they went outside, Deborah examined the kitchen and discovered that Weston had been right. Haddock had stocked the cupboards and refrigerator with a huge choice of food and wine. There was a stone pantry behind a curtain with vegetables stocked in wire containers. She found a carrot, scraped it with a knife, washed it under the cold tap, and began nibbling as she went upstairs. When she turned on the light, her heart almost stopped. The entire upper floor was one large bedroom. Admittedly it was large, and admittedly there were several beds and screens, but there was no way she could stay there with George Weston. It was inconceivable.

Weston and Haddock went to the armory in the basement of Haddock's house. The working parts of the registered weapons were kept in a tempered steel safe set in the concrete floor, while the weapons themselves were stacked in racks, threaded with chains and locked in a caged room. Another safe, hidden behind a cupboard, contained Haddock's unregistered weapons: Uzis, Ingrams, and other specialist guns, complete and ready to use. The ammunition was in another safe in a separate room, apart from a small emergency supply that he kept in a hidden compartment in his desk drawer. All the safes had time locks to avoid unscheduled opening. Everything was logged, new rounds counted out and unused rounds counted in. It was run with military precision, and Haddock had taken the precaution of ensuring that all the local armed police knew they were welcome to call at any time on a Monday to check things out and blast off a few rounds. They kept to this agreement, and never called on any other day. He was justifiably proud of the way it all worked out, and he got his kicks watching his protégés revel in this world of guns, as Weston was reveling now, hefting a brand-new Czech-made CZ75 in his large fist. It came from the batch that had been proofed by Haddock's clients.

"Nice weapon, but it's not a patch on the Browning."

"They've got that action smoother than a baby's arse. You can feel the sear right the way to release, every time. It's a dream. Best I've come across for years."

"Here's fifty that says my Browning's better."

Haddock decided that he had a reasonable chance of winning the fifty. Weston hadn't been at the quarry for weeks, and the Czech pistol was every bit as good as he said it was.

"Best of three?"

Three magazines, eight rounds per magazine. The magazines took more, but it strained the spring. Weston gave him back the weapon. "Best of five, if you like."

"Done. You carry the box."

As range master, Haddock was like the captain of a ship. His word was law. And the range master didn't carry ammo if he didn't want to.

They cleared their weapons, each checking the other's to ensure the breech was empty. They sent the targets zooming down the twenty-five-meter range on their wires, thumbed rounds into magazines and snapped them into the handgrips. Made sure safeties were on and cocked the weapons. Settled their breathing. Snapped safeties off. Brought sights to bear on targets. Focused on being one with the ground, the air, the weapon, and the range. The firing was almost simultaneous. After eight rounds, they cleared their weapons again and brought their targets back to show the other. Each knew exactly where their own shots had gone. Haddock had clustered his in a group about four inches from the bull at two o'clock. Weston's were scattered all over the target. He scored 48 to Haddock's 60. Neither made a comment. Targets were patched and twirled back twenty-five meters. They reloaded their magazines. Another pause. Another burst of firing. Haddock had brought his group nearer the bull, but the shots were more spread out. Weston's were still scattered, but less than before. Fifty-seven to 62. This time, when they were ready to fire, he stood with his arms dangling by his sides staring at his target as Haddock emptied a magazine to score 63. Weston brought the Browning level with his eyes and fired his eight shots down the range. This time they were all within the 8 circle, three of them clipping the black center mark. 71. Twenty-four rounds, and Haddock had scored 185 to Weston's 176. The fourth magazine made it 254 to 248. Haddock cleared his weapon and wiped his hands and his gun butt with a rag. Weston glared down the range. When they were both ready, they brought their guns up together. This time the firing was more measured, and they each scored six bull's eyes and two 9s. Final score: Haddock 332, Weston 326.

"Congratulations, Tom," Weston said coldly.

Haddock said nothing for a moment. It was his turn to revel. A win against Weston was something to set down in the log in large red letters. A new fifty-pound note went into his pocket.

"Early days, George. There's plenty of time to get your fifty back."

Weston nodded. "That's a fact. Right now, I fancy doing a bit of damage."

He wanted to vent his anger, and Haddock had just the thing to help him do it.

"I don't think you've used mercury tips, have you?"

"Only seen them in the movies. Why? You got some?"

Haddock nodded. "Chap who makes 'em coats the drilling with Teflon. Don't ask me how, but it lets the mercury accelerate even faster. It's like a shaped charge. Never seen anything like it. If you want to damage something, you'll find a few pumpkins behind the targets. You set 'em up, and I'll get the rounds."

Weston found five large, ripe pumpkins lying on the ground behind the mound of sand that provided a backing for the targets. He hefted them onto the top of the mound and made his way back to the firing bench. Deborah was there, watching him.

"I can't stay here," she said.

He looked at her, blankly. "What?"

"I can't stay here. I need my own bedroom. There's only one bedroom in there. You'll have to take me back."

Before he could respond, Haddock came back carrying a small box. He took in the scene. Saw Deborah standing, determined. Weston caught between astonishment and anger.

"Something wrong, miss?"

"She says she wants me to take her back because there's only one bedroom," Weston said.

"Ah. Well, I'm sorry about that, miss, but it's a bit like that in these sort of places. Everyone mucks in. There's no harm meant."

"I don't care. When Mr. Weston invited me, I assumed I'd have my own bedroom. He didn't tell me about this, or I wouldn't have come."

Weston took a deep breath, but Haddock forestalled the outburst.

"Tell you what. If that's a problem, Mr. Weston can stay in my guest room. In any case, we all need something to eat before anyone goes anywhere. I'll give you a hand with dinner. How does that sound?"

"As long as I have my own bedroom, that's all."

"That's settled then. I'm sure it makes no difference to Mr. Weston or myself, just so long as you're happy."

Haddock was sure it made a great deal of difference to George

Weston, but anything can happen to a girl's resolve after a few glasses of wine.

"Why don't you stay and watch for a while?" he said. "We'll be finished here in a few minutes. In fact, why don't you try your hand?"

"No thank you. I've never shot a gun. I don't like them."

"Most women say that, but they always change their bloody mind once they've had a go," Weston said, looking exasperated.

"There's absolutely nothing to be frightened of," Haddock said briskly. "Look. I'll take this one apart and you can see how it works."

Deborah watched as his fingers pulled the locking pin of the CZ75. The pistol seemed to fall into pieces.

"Mr. Weston tells me you work with computers."

She nodded.

"You tell them to do something, and they do it for you. A firearm is much the same." He tapped the ammunition magazine. "Here's your removable hard disk. Here's the docking platform, and here's the on-off switch, the safety catch. You've got your communications channel, here, and . . . well, it hasn't got a brain. You have the brain, and you tell it what to do." The fingers moved, and the pieces became a pistol again. "Hold it like this." Haddock pressed the pistol into Deborah's hand and helped her to aim it toward a pumpkin. "Just squeeze the trigger, ever so slowly and . . ."

The pistol clicked, and Deborah jumped.

"Oh!"

"That wasn't so bad, was it?"

She giggled nervously. "It's all right until the bullets go off."

"That's why we wear these ear mufflers." Haddock said enthusiastically. "Once you've got a set of those on your head, firing is no problem. You hold your arm steady, point at your target, and squeeze the trigger."

Weston put his Browning on the bench, pointing down the range with a new magazine of ammunition beside it.

"Breech clear, range master. Have a go with mine, Deborah."

Growing in confidence, Deborah followed Haddock's instructions on how to use the safety catch and managed to load and unload the magazine a few times.

"That's splendid," Haddock told her. "You're a natural. I believe you're ready for your first solo. How about taking a shot at one of those pumpkins? You just point and squeeze the trigger like I showed you."

"Are you sure it'll be all right?"

"Tell you what, Mr. Weston can bring one a bit closer. Okay, Mr. Weston?"

Weston fetched a pumpkin and placed it on the ground about ten meters from the shooting bench.

Haddock helped Deborah to put on the ear mufflers and spoke loudly into her ear. "Remember what I said. Bring the pistol straight up to the target, safety off, and squeeze the trigger. If you're not happy, lower the pistol before you fire and bring it up again. After you fire, safety back on, place the gun on the bench, and step back. Nothing to it."

He joined Weston at the side of the bench, and they watched Deborah go through the routine. She aimed for several seconds and the pistol began to wobble. She lowered it and raised it again.

"Good girl," Haddock muttered.

Weston nudged him. "If you want a good laugh, keep your eye on that bloody pumpkin."

Haddock looked at the box he had brought out. The seal had been broken.

"Hell, George, they're overcharged. It'll frighten the life out of her. . . ."

"Mr. Haddock," Deborah called loudly. "I'm sorry, but I can't seem to pull the trigger."

She had turned around, and the gun was pointing straight at Haddock's chest.

"Sweet Jesus," he whispered, raising his arms. "Turn away!"

The explosion rocked Deborah backward and flung George Weston to the ground. Haddock seemed to puff up, as if a party balloon had been connected to an air compressor. For an infinitesimal part of a second his jacket held everything together; then it ruptured, and Haddock's insides were blasted into a bloody mist of tissue and bone fragments.

"Oh dear," Deborah said.

At six o'clock, while Susan was still asleep at her desk in Hendon, the computer finished its deliberations and flashed its answer down the screen.

Echo: Level 3.

Who is Lyndsey AND who is Linda and AND who is Deborah?

The answer you require is: LYNDSEY
The answer you require is: LYNDSEY
The answer you require is: LYNDSEY
The answer you require is: LYNDSEY
The answer you require is: LYNDSEY
The answer you require is: LYNDSEY
The answer you require is: LYNDSEY
The answer you require is: LYNDSEY
The answer you require is: LYNDSEY
The answer you require is: LYNDSEY
The answer you require is: LYNDSEY
The answer you require is: LYNDSEY
The answer you require is: LYNDSEY
The answer you require is: LYNDSEY
The answer you require is: LYNDSEY
The answer you require is: LYNDSEY
The answer you require is: LYNDSEY
The answer you require is: LYNDSEY
The answer you require is: LYNDSEY
The answer you require is: LYNDSEY
The answer you require is: LYNDSEY
The answer you require is: LYNDSEY
The answer you require is: LYNDSEY
The answer you require is: LYNDSEY
The answer you require is: LYNDSEY
The answer you require is: LYNDSEY

When Susan woke up at eight o'clock, she thought the computer was playing its usual tricks and began working on a new routine.

Weston sat upright, covered in gore, trying to overcome the shock that was stopping his words from coming out. His head was clanging like a fire bell and his ears felt as if someone had stabbed them with an ice pick.

Someone started to laugh.

"You should just see yourself, George. What a sight!"

He tried to focus his eyes, but he was seeing two of everything.

He managed to free his vocal cords. "For Christ's sake, Deborah. Look what you've done!"

"Sorry, Georgy Porgy. Deborah's busy. I'm in charge now."

Weston managed to slide away from Haddock's remains and scramble to his feet, peering at the figure outlined by the floodlights. There was madness here. And the gun was pointing at him now. Who was this woman?

"Deborah?"

"I told you. I'm in charge now. Remember Friday the thirteenth, Georgy Porgy? Can't say I didn't warn you."

"Who the hell are you? Where's Deborah gone?"

"I'm Linda, silly. Deborah's around somewhere, don't you worry. Loud noises make her jumpy. She's been helping me to record all this, you know, for my new video. It's my best one ever."

Weston tried to deal with his confusion. Smoky was giving Deborah basic instructions. She seemed to be doing well, and then Weston slipped a high-charge Teflon bullet into the magazine for a bit of a laugh. Fine! Then she had a problem firing it. Probably had the safety on. Then she turned toward Smoky, and all hell broke loose. There was a hell of a bang, and Weston was thrown backward . . . or maybe he tried to jump out of the way. Anyway, Smoky's down, and this bloody madwoman is standing there waving the Browning at him. Linda. But how did the crazy bitch get here? There was no way she could have kept up with them. No way! Not unless . . . that's it. The cow somehow put a trace on the Porsche. . . .

"Very clever, very clever. What kit did you use? It would have to be omnidirectional, so how did you calibrate it? That car's not been used since I came down here last time."

"Omnidirectional? I like that. Omnidirectional. Has a nice ring to it. Omnidirectional." She laughed delightedly. "What exactly does it mean, in this context?"

"You put a trace on the car. Followed at a distance. Very bloody clever."

The gun was still pointing straight at his belly, and his brain was aching.

"No, I didn't. I've been here all the time."

All the time? Damn. That was one thing he hadn't figured. He'd been too busy making sure no one could follow them. Hell! If she got here before them, she must have known his plans, and only Smoky knew—correction—only Smoky and Janet knew he was coming here. Aha! That bitch Janet had given the game away. Jesus Christ! Weston used his shirt sleeve to wipe Haddock's blood from his eyes.

"We'll have to call the police. I'll say it was an accident."

Her laugh was very pleasant, as if he'd said something clever at a cocktail party.

"I think not. I haven't finished yet."

His head was still ringing with the noise, and nothing made sense. All he could think was that Thomas Haddock had been blasted away, and he was being threatened with the same gun. This woman didn't seem to realize the implications. But then, she wouldn't give a shit, would she—not if she was the one who'd trashed the others. But Deborah had shot Smoky, hadn't she? He was still dazed. He had to play for time.

"It was definitely an accident. I can vouch for that."

"Hardly an accident, Georgy. I've been waiting for a chance like this for years. And you loaded the gun. I don't know what you put in it, but it certainly does the job. I wonder what it would do to your foot."

Weston forced himself to think, willed his heart to slow down, began breathing deeply, concentrated on overcoming the shock, getting ready to make a move. Yes, he had loaded the gun, hadn't he? But Smoky gave it to Deborah, not this bloody idiot.

"I don't get it. What video?"

"I kill people and make videos for Walt and Sylvia. Well, not just any people. Your people, Georgy Porgy. Your cricket team. All those bastards that hurt my little sister."

He nodded. "Lyndsey Barratt, your sister. That makes sense. So where's the camera?"

She tapped the brooch pinned to her jacket, keeping the Browning trained steadily on Weston's stomach.

"Not as good as a Panasonic, but remarkable when you consider how small it is. Deborah fixes up the connections to Walt and Sylvia over the computer. She knows all about that kind of thing."

His body was over the shock, and he needed to make a really accurate assessment of the situation.

"What's the next step? Should I start by calling you Linda, or Miss Marshall? Or would that be Ms. Marshall? No, of course, it's Mrs. Marshall, isn't it? Married, I suppose. Or widowed. That'd be more like it. What happened to the unfortunate Mr. Marshall, then? Is he the star of one of your movies, or what?"

She seemed puzzled by this, puzzled and annoyed.

"I just changed my name, that's all. It doesn't matter what you call me. It's not necessary to call me anything."

"Not necessary for the video? Right. No soundtrack from a camera as small as that. Sorry. Should have realized."

"Sorry? You bastard. You don't have an ounce of sorry in you. Get over there."

She motioned toward the targets, brightly lit by the floodlights. He didn't move. Testing her. She dropped the muzzle toward his feet.

"I'll drag you over there, if I have to."

"Okay, okay. Take it easy with that thing, for Christ's sake."

He moved forward cautiously, and she moved so that he couldn't get close to her.

"At least let me clean myself up. There's a tap just behind you."

Linda thought for a moment. He did look rather disheveled. None too photogenic. She circled around.

"Why not? Just be careful you don't lose your legs."

Weston turned on the tap and sluiced himself with the bitterly cold water, rubbing the half-congealed globules from his hair, his ears, his neck . . .

"That's enough! Get yourself over there, Mr. George bloody Weston."

As he backed down the range she unclipped the brooch and pushed the pin into a wooden upright above her head.

"That's far enough. Need you reasonably close. It's quite a wide-angled lens." He stopped, and they stared at each other. "Lyndsey and I have waited a long time for this."

"I hope it's worth it, you bitch."

"It will be. Take your clothes off."

"Can't we talk about this, Linda? For God's sake, we never meant to hurt your sister. It just kind of happened. We were kids. For pity's sake."

"TAKE . . . YOUR . . . FUCKING . . . CLOTHES . . . OFF!"

Weston fumbled with his zips and buttons, tearing off his jacket, shirt, sitting on the ground, pulling his boots off, standing, taking down his trousers . . .

"Well, well," she said. "What a lovely, lovely target."

She aimed at his erection and squeezed the trigger, just like Haddock had told Deborah to do.

Nothing happened.

She looked at the Browning and tried to squeeze the trigger again, but it wouldn't move.

"Out of ammo, you bitch."

Weston careered into her as she was staring bewilderedly at the pistol. His huge fingers raked into her chemise, and he tore at her clothes until she was naked too. He held her upright by the neck and dragged her so that they were both standing directly in front of the brooch, anger making the veins in his head stand out like cords.

"How about this?" he yelled at the brooch, and began punching her, remorseless blows to her head, her breasts, her stomach . . . "Point my own fucking gun at me! My own fucking gun!"

Linda screamed back at him like a wildcat, blocking his punches, trying to fight back, but he pinned her to the ground, locking her arms in one massive hand. She was weakening now, from the pain of the blows and the rocks that were biting into her back. But she still fought, pushing her head up, trying to bite him as he forced his penis between her legs.

He was so aroused that he did not notice the change that took place as he shouted, "Bitch! Bitch!"

The desperate resistance of Linda was replaced by the pain-racked innocence of Lyndsey, gazing in horror and bewilderment at the furious, contorted face lunging above her. Opening her mouth in a soundless wail, trying to push him away with arms that had lost their strength.

Weston felt the lips of her vagina give and tore his way inside. And then Lyndsey screamed, a cry of pain and terror that echoed and reechoed among the dark rocks.

Chapter 30

THERE WAS A CHANGE IN THE WEATHER OVERNIGHT, WITH a strong southwesterly wind bringing low cloud and driving rain. Illiffe woke from an uneasy sleep at seven o'clock and phoned Haddock's unlisted number again, but there was an "unobtainable" tone. The BT operator told him there was a fault on the line at the subscriber's end, and they would send a field engineer to fix it, and thank you very much for bringing it to our attention. He rang around the other rooms and got everyone out of bed, which didn't increase his popularity rating. During breakfast they discussed the situation. Illiffe was uneasy about the telephone situation and decided that he and DC Rogers would link up with the local police force and visit the quarry to check things out. Susan York and Bill Taylor asked if they could go with him. Taylor had never been farther west than Oxford and wanted to take the opportunity of seeing the Welsh mountains. With Susan. Arny wanted to get back to London, but Julie overruled him with promises of more wonderful footage for their next award-winning documentary and threats of punishments edging toward castration.

They were on the road by eight-fifteen, and Illiffe made contact with the regional force to inform them that he was on his way to the quarry in the course of a BTP investigation. The duty sergeant said they knew Mr. Haddock very well, and said his phone line had probably come down in the overnight winds. It was happening all the time. He suggested a rendezvous at a nearby village so his men could lead the way to their destination, which, he said, was not easy for strangers to find.

They linked up with Sergeant Owen and Constable Jones at a hamlet called Llanveynoe and followed the police car along a rocky lane and into the hills. When they arrived at the quarry, Sergeant Owen went to Haddock's house and banged on the door. There was no reply, so he tried the door of the lodge, which was wide open, and went inside.

"There's a very drunken gentleman in here," he called to the others, who were stretching their legs.

Illiffe followed him, noting the remnants of the laptop by the telephone socket. The case was smashed, and among the rubble of fractured high technology he could see the remains of a radio aerial. Whatever had happened in the quarry had been transmitted to the laptop and passed downline to someone, and Illiffe had no doubt that the phone company records would show an Internet link had been opened. No prizes for guessing where the video images went next.

Upstairs, Weston was lying helplessly, half on and half off one of the beds, mumbling incoherently, naked and reeking of stale brandy fumes. A woman's effects were scattered over another bed, which had not been slept in. While Illiffe was staring around, DC Rogers called from the front door.

"Better come down here, guv."

There are times when instinct takes over the logical processes. As Illiffe approached the brooding rocks of the quarry, he felt as if a primitive, satiated power was enveloping them. Through the drizzle he saw Susan bending over a naked figure, he presumed it was Deborah, covering it with jackets that the policemen had given her. Taylor and the sergeant were staring at a nearby corpse whose remnants were spread over several square yards. The leather name tag stitched to a fragment of camouflage jacket said "Haddock."

No one said very much as they took it all in. Sergeant Owen called for CID backup and an ambulance. Julie and Arny looked subdued as they unloaded the TV gear and started filming. Bill Taylor helped Susan to get Deborah into the lodge and walked slowly over to Illiffe.

"How could we have got it this wrong, Frank? Where the devil is she? How did she get here?"

Illiffe had no answer, just a sick feeling as he looked at what used to be Smoky Haddock.

"We've been getting it wrong ever since it started, years ago."

Sergeant Owen joined them, shaking his head. "You'd better give me an idea of what has happened here, Detective Superintendent. I've not seen anything like this in all my days on the Force. He looks as if he was hit by a missile."

"Would you believe me if I said I've no idea? I won't know until we can question the 'gentleman' upstairs."

The Welshman noted his inflection.

"Fair enough, but I'm not one for TV cameras getting involved in my investigations. I'd appreciate it if you asked your friends to desist until my Scene of Crime Officer has cleared the area."

Illiffe nodded. "My mistake, Sergeant."

He called across to Julie, who tapped Arny on the shoulder.

"Can it, Arny. We're back with the red tape."

An hour later the quarry was cordoned off, and half a dozen policemen began combing the range, picking up shell cases, flagging their location, and putting each one in its own plastic bag. Haddock's corpse was collected together in a similar way by the Scene of Crime Officer's team. The ambulance crew examined Deborah, pronounced that she was in no immediate danger, and advised the sergeant to let her recover a little in the warmth of the lodge before attempting the journey to hospital for a more detailed examination.

Susan was making tea for everyone in the kitchen when an unmarked van arrived. Four men got out of the back, and the driver went straight to the sergeant and showed him a badge of some kind. He turned around to his colleagues and shouted, "Everyone here at the double, please."

Illiffe watched impassively as two of the newcomers went into Haddock's house and the other two trotted into the quarry. After several minutes they returned to the van carrying canvas bags, which they slung inside. The others came out of the house with more bags. When these were in the van the driver went back to the sergeant, who shrugged and turned to Illiffe.

"There seems to be a bit of a problem."

"Really?" Illiffe knew Ministry of Defense goons when he saw them. "Problem" might be a serious understatement.

"It's your friends from the television," he said in his Welsh accent. "These gentlemen are not very happy about it."

Illiffe went to the driver and held his own warrant card a little closer to the man's face than he needed to.

"I don't know what you're doing here, and I don't care, but I know what we're doing here, and I do care about that. Those cameras have been inoperative since the sergeant asked them to stop filming. If I were you, I'd bugger off before someone makes a serious error of judgment."

"Such as?"

"Such as me deciding that you are removing material evidence from a police inquiry."

The man looked at him coolly.

"Very well, Mr. Illiffe, I'll respect your judgment. I just hope you catch the bitch."

As the van bumped its way back along the track, the sergeant looked at Illiffe curiously.

"They seemed to know who you are. Now why would that be?"

"Your guess is as good as mine," Illiffe said, meaning it.

While he was musing on this, Susan came out of the lodge.

"How's Deborah doing?" he asked.

"She's not Deborah, she's Lyndsey, and she wants to make a statement." She paused. Nervous. "Frank."

"What is it?"

"I could have stopped this."

"What on earth do you mean?"

"I asked the computer who they all were . . . Lyndsey, Linda, and Deborah . . . and yesterday it printed out the answer, and I thought it was acting up again, you know, giving those stupid, logical answers because it didn't have enough information."

She was on the verge of tears.

"Susan, we all tried as hard as we could. There is absolutely no way that you or any of us should blame ourselves for what's happened."

Somehow, amazingly, Lyndsey was sitting on a bed, rocking backward and forward and nodding slightly, as if she had solved a troublesome problem. Weston was sitting on another bed, sipping tea, with a police officer standing over him. When Lyndsey saw Illiffe, she tried to smile.

"You want me to give you a statement, don't you, about those boys?"

He looked at the bruises, the cuts on her face, the hurt pain in her eyes, and he knew that Lyndsey was back in Hope Green Hospital.

"Yes," he said. "I do. And there's someone else who wants you to as well. Would you mind if she came up with her camera?"

"Of course not. I've signed an exclusive agreement with her, haven't I?"

Illiffe nodded at Keith Rogers, who went to get Julie and Arny. Sergeant Owen gazed out of a window, content to let Illiffe handle things for the moment. When Arny was ready Illiffe took hold of Lyndsey's hand.

"We need you to tell us everything you can, and when we've written it down you'll have to sign it for us. Can you do that?"

She nodded. She told them what had happened in the carriage, how it had started, how she had tried to stop them, how they hurt her, how she pleaded. And when Illiffe asked if she could see any of the boys among the people in the bedroom, she pointed to George Weston.

Illiffe had to wait until his rage stopped before he went over to Weston.

"George Weston, I am arresting you for the rape of Lyndsey Barratt. You do not have to say anything, but it may harm your defense if you do not mention when questioned something which you later rely on in court. Anything you do say may be given in evidence."

Weston glared at him. "You have to be joking. I don't know what the fuck's going on here, but that little bitch just shot my friend, and Christ knows what else."

"Handcuffs, please, Constable Jones," Illiffe said.

As the policeman reached to his belt, Weston surged off the bed, toward Lyndsey, yelling abuse. The yells stopped abruptly as Keith Rogers smacked him in the side of the head with his extendable baton. Weston fell to the floor and lay there, a trickle of blood seeping from his ear.

"I wondered if those newfangled things were all they were cracked up to be," Sergeant Owen said blandly. "I'll put in a favorable report to my chief constable."

Rogers put his baton away with a feeling of great satisfaction, but he wasn't at all sure of how things had turned out, apart from Weston getting a bloody good clout. The morning's events were completely baffling. How could Lyndsey Barratt *be* Linda Marshall? And what had happened to Deborah Lambert?

"Guv'nor?"

"Don't ask," Illiffe said. "Not me, anyway. Try Professor Taylor. This is his line of country."

Chapter 31

THE MEDICS TOOK LYNDSEY TO THE CASUALTY DEPART-
ment at Hereford General Hospital. They refused to take
Weston in the same vehicle, so Sergeant Owen took the big
man in his car, hands locked uncomfortably behind him. Illiffe
watched the vehicles leave and turned to Julie.

"We started this thing together, and it finishes now. When we're
in the hospital, you take the final shots. You'll wrap up a world
exclusive and your boss can reckon he's got his money's worth. Then
Bill and I are going to make sure that Lyndsey is given a chance to
heal in peace."

The duty policewoman in the hospital looked agitated when she
saw Julie and Arny with the camera.

"Detective Superintendent Frank Illiffe, BTP," Illiffe told her.
"And you are?"

"WPC Hannah Richardson, sir."

"Okay, Hannah, this is my responsibility. Do you know who
you've got in there?"

"Yes, sir. Lyndsey Barratt. She's been assigned to my custody because charges may be brought."

"Does the name mean anything to you, Hannah?"

"It certainly does. She's the train-rape girl."

"It's a long story, but we are all the friends she has in the world,
and we have a job to finish here today. Some people in the force will

want that young girl pilloried. I don't. Do you have a problem with that?"

"Absolutely not. What can I do?"

Illiffe smiled. "Check with the hospital administrator. We need to beef up security. If past experience is anything to go by, you'll have a horde of ravening journalists round here at any time. I don't want them within fifty feet of Lyndsey."

"That's not a problem, and I'll call in some of my off-duty colleagues. My boyfriend's a dog handler."

She went over to the admissions desk and spoke earnestly to the receptionist, then began speaking into her radio.

Bill Taylor and Susan York sat next to each other on the steel-framed chairs.

"Can you make any sense of this, Bill?" Illiffe asked tiredly.

Taylor sighed. There was an explanation of sorts, but it was an area no one knew very much about. Still, he should have suspected something. The signs had been there, but they had all been too busy stuffing the facts into the computer.

"We'll need expert corroboration, but what we've been dealing with all along is a case of multiple personalities. After her trauma, Lyndsey didn't just retreat into a limbo or a coma like some people do; she created other personas who developed their own separate lives, with their own plans, their own reasons for living."

"That makes no sense at all, Bill," Susan said. "Linda and Deborah were living together. Her neighbors would have noticed."

"Noticed what? As far as I remember, no one ever saw the two of them together."

"But they looked so different."

Taylor remembered a paper given by one of his colleagues at a conference on personality disorders. It described how the personalities can differ in temperament, body language, and facial characteristics. Even their handwriting was different. Most remarkable of all, their electroencephalogram readings were different.

"Remember that Lyndsey was an accomplished actress, and she simply invented two utterly different people to help her carry on her life. Maybe she invented others. I guess we'll never know."

"How long will Weston get, Frank?" Susan asked.

"For the rape? Six, maybe eight years. There'll be other charges, but everything will run concurrently. He'll be out in two, with good behavior. On the other hand, there's Lyndsey. She's facing ten charges of murder."

Susan leaned her head on Taylor's shoulder. No one said much. They had to wait for the medical team to finish their examination.

Lyndsey wasn't in the operating theater long, not this time around. Two hours of physical examination, blood tests, X rays, and dealing with her wounds. When he was told who his patient was, the surgeon became another team player. After listening to Bill Taylor he called the hospital welfare officer who immediately contacted a firm of lawyers. The consultant psychiatrist issued a committal order that effectively prohibited the police from taking any further action. In short, the wheels were set in motion that would give Lyndsey all the protection she would need, no arrest, no Crown Prosecution Service, no trial, no imprisonment. But she would have to remain in psychiatric care. For the time being, she would have nothing more to worry about. The thought came to Illiffe that Linda and Deborah would not have to worry about her anymore, either. And then the surgeon asked for a private word.

"Not quite sure how to deal with this, but I thought I'd better let you know. It'll be in my report anyway."

"She's not seriously hurt, is she? I thought—"

"No, no," the surgeon assured him. "It's something else entirely. She's had intercourse, very recently. Within the past twelve hours. Violent penetration."

The red mist came again. Not for the first time, Illiffe found himself wishing George Weston dead. He had to breathe very deeply before he managed to speak.

"You mean the bastard raped her out there?"

The surgeon looked unhappy. "All I know is, she had intercourse which left her torn and bruised. Can't say who the man is without a DNA comparison. And there's something else."

Illiffe wasn't sure he wanted to hear anything else, after everything Lyndsey had been through.

"We managed to have a little chat. She isn't aware of a thing that's happened over the past seven years. She asked me if all the boys are going to be punished with George Weston. As far as she's concerned the Berlin Wall is still standing and Mrs. Thatcher's Britain is still forging ahead."

When the surgeon gave the all-clear, Julie and Arny went cautiously into the private ward and videoed Lyndsey lying still and white as she had once before, Arny not understanding why his hard-nosed colleague turned and buried her face in Frank Illiffe's chest or why a bloody copper could look so lost, just for a moment.

Chapter 32

ILLIFFE TURNED THE KEY IN HIS LATCH, EASED OFF HIS SHOES, and tiptoed down the hall. Everything was quiet, peaceful, and for the first time he realized that his house smelled good, too. It smelled of summer flowers and clean furniture and homely cooking. Most of all it smelled of Jean.

There was a bulky envelope propped up on the hall table. It had the Farthingale Security logo on the back flap, and it contained a contract of employment in the position of operations director with the terms that Charles Ruslin had outlined. There was a handwritten note from Farthingale: *"I like the way you operate, but we do have the odd rule and regulation. Think you can manage?"*

The landing light clicked on, and Jean was standing at the turn of the stairs.

"Hi. Heard you crashing around. Cup of tea?"

He nodded.

They went into the kitchen, and she ran water into the kettle, switched it on, stood watching it. He moved behind her and buried his nose in her hair, breathing her in, deeply.

"It's over, isn't it?"

"Bar the shouting, yes."

"You want to try and make a baby?"

"You want to try and stop me?"

Epilogue

AT GEORGE WESTON'S TRIAL, THE JUDGE RULED THAT LYNDsey was not a competent witness, and the rape charge against Weston was dropped. He stood trial for firearms offenses and three counts of conspiracy to defraud and was sentenced to one year for each of three counts of conspiracy and six months for the firearms offenses, the sentences to run concurrently. He was a model prisoner and was released on parole after serving four months in prison.

Lyndsey was committed to a secure mental hospital. Eight months later, she gave birth to a baby daughter, Kelly. Lyndsey remained incapable of distinguishing between past and present, and her psychiatrists were unable to agree whether or not she was a danger to the public.

When Kelly was three she was adopted by a married couple. Little Kelly settled down happily in her new home, but for the first few months she kept asking her adoptive parents where her mummy was. And her Aunty Linda.

"You haven't got an Aunty Linda, poppet," they told her.